EDUCATING
Young Children
With
Autism Spectrum
DISORDERS

EDUCATING
Young Children
With
Autism Spectrum
DISORDERS

ERIN E. BARTON BETH HARN

A JOINT PUBLICATION

CORWIN
A SAGE Company

NASP

CORWIN
A SAGE Company

FOR INFORMATION

Corwin
A SAGE Company
2455 Teller Road
Thousand Oaks, California 91320
(800) 233-9936
www.corwin.com

SAGE Publications Ltd.
1 Oliver's Yard
55 City Road
London, EC1Y 1SP
United Kingdom

SAGE Publications India Pvt. Ltd.
B 1/I 1 Mohan Cooperative Industrial Area
Mathura Road, New Delhi
India 110 044

SAGE Publications Asia-Pacific Pte. Ltd.
3 Church Street
#10-04 Samsung Hub
Singapore 049483

Acquisitions Editor: Jessica Allan
Associate Editor: Allison Scott
Editorial Assistant: Lisa Whitney
Production Editor: Amy Schroller
Copy Editor: Tina Hardy
Typesetter: Hurix Systems Pvt. Ltd.
Proofreader: Eleni-Maria Georgiou
Indexer: Maria Sosnowski
Cover Designer: Lisa Riley
Graphic Designer: Rose Storey
Permissions Editor: Karen Ehrmann

Printed in the United States of America

A catalog record of this book is available from the Library of Congress.

ISBN 978-1-4129-8728-8

This book is printed on acid-free paper.

SUSTAINABLE FORESTRY INITIATIVE

Certified Chain of Custody
Promoting Sustainable Forestry
www.sfiprogram.org
SFI-01268

SFI label applies to text stock

12 13 14 15 16 10 9 8 7 6 5 4 3 2 1

Contents

Acknowledgments

Corwin gratefully acknowledges the contributions of the following reviewers:

Carol Aymar
Elementary school teacher
Francis W. Parker School
Chicago, IL

Joyce Williams Bergin
Professor of Special Education and
Assistant Dean of the College of Education
Armstrong Atlantic State University
Savannah, GA

Katherine Boone
Case Manager
MHMRA of Harris County
Houston, TX

About the Authors

Erin E. Barton, PhD, BCBA-D, is an assistant professor in the School of Education and Human Development at the University of Colorado Denver. She teaches courses in early childhood special education on evidence-based assessment and intervention practices for young children with special needs and their families. She is a Board Certified Behavior Analyst and has worked with children and families in school, home, and clinic settings. Prior to her current position, she was a special education teacher for the Chicago Public Schools, where she taught young children with autism. Dr. Barton specializes in the education of young children with developmental disabilities in inclusive and naturalistic settings. Her research interests include early intervention and identification of young children with autism, behavioral interventions for young children with developmental disabilities, and professional development of early childhood special education teachers. She has published several papers on evidence-based practices for young children with autism. Also, she regularly provides professional development to programs, school districts, and states on evidence-based, early intervention practices for young children with special needs and their families.

Beth Harn, PhD, is an associate professor within the Department of Special Education and Clinical Sciences at the University of Oregon. She teaches classes in special education and school psychology including instructional design, educational assessment, introduction to learning disabilities, and systems level academic interventions. Expertise areas include early identification, data-based decision making, and designing and delivering effective reading and behavioral interventions. She is currently coprincipal investigator on a number of federally funded initiatives related to reading, attention development, and traumatic brain injury interventions as well as special education teacher preparation. Her research interests focus on early intervention for students with reading and learning difficulties by implementing schoolwide, coordinated instructional and assessment practices and designing intensive interventions. Recently her intervention efforts have included designing computer-delivered supports. She also provides professional development to states, districts, and schools nationally to support the implementation of response to intervention practices. Prior to her current position, she worked as a school psychologist in the Central Valley of California.

1

Classification of Autism in Young Children

Erin E. Barton

University of Colorado Denver

Chapter Objectives:

- Describe the symptomatology of autism spectrum disorders.
- Describe the variability in autism symptomatology across people with autism.
- List and describe the autism spectrum disorders with the DSM-IV-TR.
- Describe two autism classification systems (DSM-IV-TR & ICD-10).
- Describe the current prevalence of autism and the issues associated with measuring the prevalence.

Autism is a neurobiological developmental disorder initially characterized by Leo Kanner (1943) and Hans Asperger (1944). Since their initial descriptions, the identification and classification of autism have undergone many iterative changes. The current approach to autism classification is outlined in the *Diagnostic and Statistical Manual of Mental Disorders–4thEdition–Text Revision* (DSM-IV-TR; American Psychiatric Association, 2000). This manual provides a classification system for diagnosing and differentiating autism under the heading "pervasive developmental disorders." However, the identification of autism typically involves a team of professionals. Chapters 2 and 3 provide descriptions of the autism identification processes. Autism is not a single disease. It is characterized by a spectrum of disorders, which varies across and within children over time. In most cases, autism first appears in early childhood and continues throughout adulthood. Advancements in autism treatment often lead to improved outcomes over time.

Autism symptomatology manifests with much variability. Today there are several different conditions related to autism commonly known as Autism Spectrum Disorders (Volkmar, State, & Klin, 2009). The term *autism* is used throughout this book to refer generally to children with Autism Spectrum Disorders. Although there are many commonalities, there is no single behavioral marker for autism. The hallmark autism symptoms are deficits in social behaviors. The criteria used for classification of autistic disorder mirror the triad of impairments first described by Leo Kanner (1943). Characteristics include qualitative impairments in social interactions, communication, and restricted, repetitive, and stereotyped patterns of behavior. Additionally, delays in social interaction, communication, or symbolic play must be present before the child turns 3 years old (American Psychiatric Association, 2000).

About 60% of children with autism experience significant cognitive delays (Fombonne, 2005), and about 30%–50% will not develop functional speech; however, these numbers are decreasing with early diagnosis and treatment (Chakrabarti & Fombonne, 2005). Although, autism is considered a mental health disorder, it severely impacts development and academic achievement in most children. Thus, the vast majority of children with autism will be eligible for specialized early intervention and education services (see Chapter 3 for more on educational eligibility). Autism is considered a severe disability due to the intense, lasting effects the disorder has on the individual and his or her family.

DIAGNOSTIC CLASSIFICATION

Classification systems are important for helping families understand their child's behaviors, provide access to appropriate treatment, and conduct and replicate research on autism treatments. Two classification systems are widely used to diagnosis autism. The American Psychiatric Association publishes the DSM. The most recent version, the fourth edition with text revisions (IV-TR), was published in 2000. The World Health Organization (WHO) publishes the International Classification of Diseases (ICD).

The ICD-10 is the international standard diagnostic classification system used to record a variety of world health records, including mortality and morbidity statistics. Although these two classification systems define autism along the triad of impairments (atypical social, communication, and patterns of behavior), there are some important distinctions. These are discussed further.

DSM-IV-TR. The DSM-IV-TR includes autism as one of five Pervasive Developmental Disorders (PDDs; American Psychiatric Association, 2000). The five PDDs include the following: Autistic Disorder, Rett's Disorder, Childhood Disintegrative Disorder, Asperger's Disorder, and Pervasive Developmental Disorder-Not Otherwise Specified (PDD-NOS; American Psychiatric Association, 2000). Each of these disorders manifests with pervasive social and behavioral deficits. The most recognized of the PDDs is Autistic Disorder. The criteria for DSM-IV-TR for Autistic Disorder is listed here.

Diagnostic Criteria for 299.00 Autistic Disorder:

A. A total of six (or more) items from (1), (2), and (3), with at least two from (1), and one each from (2) and (3):
1. qualitative impairment in social interaction, as manifested by at least two of the following:
    a. marked impairment in the use of multiple nonverbal behaviors such as eye-to-eye gaze, facial expression, body postures, and gestures to regulate social interaction
    b. failure to develop peer relationships appropriate to developmental level
    c. a lack of spontaneous seeking to share enjoyment, interests, or achievements with other people (e.g., by lack of showing, bringing, or pointing out objects of interest)
    d. lack of social or emotional reciprocity

2. qualitative impairments in communication as manifested by at least one of the following:
    a. delay in, or total lack of, the development of spoken language (not accompanied by an attempt to compensate through alternative modes of communication such as gesture or mime)
    b. in individuals with adequate speech, marked impairment in the ability to initiate or sustain a conversation with others
    c. stereotyped and repetitive use of language or idiosyncratic language
    d. lack of varied, spontaneous make-believe play or social imitative play appropriate to developmental level

(Continued)

(Continued)
3. restricted repetitive and stereotyped patterns of behavior, interests, and activities, as manifested by at least one of the following:
   a. encompassing preoccupation with one or more stereotyped and restricted patterns of interest that is abnormal in intensity or focus
   b. apparently inflexible adherence to specific, nonfunctional routines or rituals
   c. stereotyped and repetitive motor mannerisms (e.g., hand or finger flapping or twisting, or complex whole-body movements)
   d. persistent preoccupation with parts of objects

B. Delays or abnormal functioning in at least one of the following areas, with onset prior to age 3 years: (1) social interaction, (2) language as used in social communication, or (3) symbolic or imaginative play.

C. The disturbance is not better accounted for by Rett's Disorder or Childhood Disintegrative Disorder. (American Psychiatric Association, 2000, p. 75)

Source: Reprinted with permission from the *Diagnostic and Statistical Manual of Mental Disorders, Fourth Edition, Text Revision* (Copyright © 2000). American Psychiatric Association.

International Classification of Diseases. The ICD-10 (WHO, 1992) classification system is widely used in Europe and around the world. The criteria for **childhood autism** are similar to the DSM-IV-TR criteria for Autistic Disorder. They include the following:

- Abnormal or delayed development prior to age 3 in
  o Receptive or expressive language
  o Social interactions
  o Functional or symbolic play
- Qualitative impairments in social interactions
- Qualitative impairments in communication skills
- Restricted, repetitive patterns of behavior

As is evident, the DSM-IV-TR and ICD-10 include similar criteria to diagnose autism.

PREVALENCE

The prevalence (number of cases at a particular time in a particular area) of autism is increasing at a faster rate than any other developmental disability in young children; autism affects approximately 1 in 110 children (Centers for Disease Control and Prevention [CDC], 2007). Recent numbers from the CDC suggest the prevalence might be closer to 1 in 88 children (2012). It affects about 1.5 million Americans and is increasing at a rate of about 10%–17% per year. A new case is diagnosed almost every 20 minutes. These numbers are staggering and call for urgent public health action in the areas of early identification and treatment.

These prevalence statistics are based on a research study conducted by the CDC in 11 states (2007). This study found differences across states in the rates of autism. However, the average prevalence across the 11 states was 1 in 110 children. The differences across states were in part due to the availability of educational and medical records. Individual child records for all 8-year-old children in 2006 across the 11 states were reviewed by trained autism clinicians and coded for meeting autism DSM-IV-TR criteria. The most consistent findings across the 11 states were the higher prevalence of autism in boys than girls. The prevalence also varied by race. Across states the prevalence of autism was higher in white children than black or Hispanic children in all 11 states. The majority of children with autism across all 11 states were receiving special education services in schools. This study also compared prevalence rates over time and found an increase between 2002 and 2006. Although the rate of increased prevalence varied across states, rates increased across all 11 states with notable differences found in the increases in white children. This study also found a notable decrease in the median age of earliest documented autism diagnosis, which is not surprising given the increases in research on early screening and surveillance efforts (see Chapter 2 for more information on early screening efforts). The causes for this increase in autism are unknown. However, the increases are likely due, at least in part, to better diagnostic practices and tools, the expansion of the definition of autism (which includes more behaviors), and an increased awareness of the disorder among medical and educational professionals.

ETIOLOGY OF AUTISM

Autism is a neurobiological developmental disorder, which means it is caused by disorders or impairments in the brain or central nervous system. In general, neurodevelopmental disorders are associated with mental, emotional, and physical impairments. Autism likely results from early brain abnormalities that affect multiple neural systems (Coleman, 2005). Research suggests the brains of children with autism grow at abnormal rates (Courchesne et al., 2001). In fact, Kanner's original description of autism noted an increased head circumference in some of the children with autism (Minchew, Sweeney, Bauman, & Webb, 2005). Autopsy studies have revealed abnormalities in the amygdala, cerebellum, brain stem, and temporal lobes of people with autism (Schultz & Robins, 2005). This research clearly points to neural abnormalities in the mechanics of autism; however, many questions remain.

In recent years, many contentious debates about the nature of autism have emerged. Clinicians debate whether autism is a disorder characterized across a spectrum or a group of related, similar disorders. Likewise, many contentious debates have emerged related to the causes or etiology of autism. To date, the etiology of autism is unknown. Nonetheless, empirically supported research advances in the causes and genetic influences of autism are currently being made. Scientific research is imperative to understand the causes and identify effective treatments for autism.

Since autism was first documented, there have been several ideas about the causes of autism; however, none are substantiated. Several of these ideas have received widespread media attention, and unfortunately, some have had an adverse impact on young children and families. For example, vaccines were inaccurately linked to increases in autism, which led many parents to refuse to vaccinate their children. These claims were based on falsified data that had been published but was recently fully retracted by the medical journal *The Lancet* (Wakefield et al., 1998). This article was retracted because the editors determined that many of the claims made in the original paper were inaccurate. They found that the primary author manipulated patient data and misreported results. Since this study was published, several methodologically sound (i.e., rigorous and accurate) clinical studies have reported no link between vaccines and autism. Unfortunately, many parents continue to refuse to vaccinate their children, which puts the general population at risk for developing previously eradicated diseases (i.e., whooping cough and measles). Both of these diseases are entirely preventable through childhood vaccines, and both can be fatal when contracted by infants who are too young to be vaccinated or people with compromised immune systems. Furthermore, the American Academy of Pediatrics (AAP), the American Medical Association (AMA), the CDC, and the Institute of Medicine (IOM) recently concurred in a joint statement that science does not support a link with autism and vaccines (see Stratton, Gable, & McCormick, 2001). More information is available on the AAP website: http://www.aap.org/healthtopics/Autism.cfm and http://www.cispimmunize.org/. For a list of facts about autism and vaccine safety see the following: http://www.aap.org/advocacy/releases/autismparentfacts.htm.

General consensus among autism researchers is that genetic factors are the most predominant known causes of autism, although the exact genetic links are complex and not well understood. Recent genetic research has demonstrated a greater than 60% concordance rate among identical twins and an increased risk for siblings of children with autism (Baron-Cohen, 2004; Popper, Gammon, West, & Bailey, 2005). Also, research suggests relatives of people with autism have an increased rate of aberrant social, communication, or patterns of behavior (Rutter, 2005). However, no single "autism gene" has been identified. The genetics of the disorder are as complex as the manifestation of the disorder.

CONCLUSIONS AND FUTURE DIRECTIONS

In recent years, more and more children with autism are receiving services in inclusive preschool classrooms alongside typically developing peers. Federal law mandates that children with disabilities receive services within the least restrictive environment, which means inclusive, community settings must be considered and rejected before placement into a segregated classroom can occur. Further, current research supports the inclusion of children with autism into community or public school preschools with typically developing peers based upon four sets of research findings. First, inclusive preschools provide a supportive and responsive context for implementing evidence-based practices. Second, inclusive settings occasion social interactions and communication among children with autism and their typically developing peers, which represent core skill deficits for children with autism. Third, the benefits of inclusive classrooms include generalization of social skills across people, which is an essential component of effective curricula for children with autism. Finally, research has documented more positive attitudes toward children with disabilities by typically developing peers when students with disabilities are included in the preschool environment. Not surprisingly, this shift in the location of services for children with autism has significantly influenced research and professional development for them. Most notably, recent research has shown children with autism benefit from inclusive classrooms when instruction is focused on teaching skills to help them function independently and is delivered in meaningful contexts by contingent, supportive, and responsive adults.

Professional development and implementation of evidence-based practices have emerged as major issues in early childhood autism. The escalating numbers of young children with autism entering schools each year have had a tremendous impact on professional development programs across a range of disciplines (e.g., education, school psychology, speech pathology). The need to train professionals to work with this population of students has required many professional development programs to evaluate their curricula and include educational assessment, programming, and collaboration for young children with autism. To ensure positive outcomes for young children with autism, these programs need high quality materials, which translate the current research base into information that professionals can use (Dunst & Trivette, 2009; Odom, 2009).

Implications for practitioners are threefold. First, currently there is a substantial shortage of practitioners with the assessment skills critical for early identification and intervention. Second, practitioners are often not aware of effective, newer practices. Third, practitioners from multiple disciplines need to collaborate and coordinate their efforts in order to maximize outcomes for children with autism. This text will describe current research on the etiology of autism, a range of effective assessment procedures, approaches for meaningfully integrating family participation and supports in developing goals and interventions, procedures for intervention planning and implementation in natural settings, methods for promoting generalization and maintenance of skills, and strategies to promote collaboration and teaming across multiple disciplines. Thus, the primary focus of this book is to support practitioners working with young children with autism in the use of effective, evidence-based practices. This text will guide practitioners in identifying and implementing effective strategies that address the unique characteristics of children with autism and their families.

2

Early Detection and Medical Classification

Erin E. Barton

University of Colorado Denver

Chapter Objectives:

- Describe the importance of early detection for autism.
- List and describe early markers of autism.
- List and describe autism-specific screening and diagnostic measures.
- Differentiate the medical and educational eligibility determination.
- List the clinical assessment process.

INTRODUCTION

As described in Chapter 1, autism is characterized by a spectrum of disorders, which is classified and differentiated via behavioral characteristics. Although many recent studies have identified a strong genetic link for autism (e.g., Rutter, 2005; Volkmar, Lord, Bailey, Schultz, & Kline, 2004), there is no blood test or single gene that identifies autism. Behavioral measures are the primary means of identification. The purpose of this chapter is to describe early detection and the medical classification of autism. Readers will be able to describe the importance of early detection and screening for autism, red flags for autism, and autism screening tools; differentiate the medical and educational eligibility determination processes; and describe the tools and procedures in the clinical assessment of autism.

THE IMPORTANCE OF EARLY DETECTION

Recent reports from the CDC indicate the prevalence rate for autism is close to 1 in 88 (CDC, 2012). This represents a rapid increase in the number of people affected by and experiencing autism since it was first character- ized by Kanner (1943). These numbers place autism as the fastest growing developmental disorder in the United States (CDC, 2007). This increased prevalence sparked increased research in the diagnosis, treatment, and etiology of autism. For example, intervention research has repeatedly dem- onstrated intensive early intervention is related to improved outcomes for children with autism and their families (Dawson & Osterling, 1997; Harris & Handleman, 2000; Strain & Timm, 2001). The research literature on the treat- ment of autism demonstrates dramatic improvements in social and commu- nication behavior through individualized early intervention. The National Research Council (2001) review of autism interventions concluded there was strong evidence for the efficacy of educational interventions and urged that intervention should occur as soon as autism is suspected. In fact, the Council on Children with Disabilities reports early, intensive intervention is *vital* for children with autism and their families (Myers & Johnson, 2007).

Although many parents report having concerns by age 2, the average age of the autism diagnosis is 4.5 years (Coonrod & Stone, 2004). This points to an almost 3-year lag in treatment during a known critical time. As a result, the AAP (2006) recommended regular use of a general devel- opmental screen and use of a targeted screen for autism, the Modified Checklist for Autism in Toddlers (M-CHAT) at 18 and 24 months of age during well-child checkups (i.e., not when the child is sick; Johnson & Myers, 2007). Also, the American Academy of Neurology, with support by the AAP (2006), called for routine screening of all children for autism dur- ing well-child pediatric checkups. Many pediatricians, however, still rely on clinical judgment and informal checklists and only 8% of pediatricians use an established screening tool (Glascoe, 2000; Hamilton, 2006).

Role of Social and Communication Development

Over the past 10 years, several national projects have been started to increase awareness about early signs of autism and promote early screen- ing (e.g., the First Signs initiative [http://www.firstsigns.org/] or the CDC Act Early campaign [http://www.cdc.gov/actearly]). These projects are based on the increased prevalence of autism, an increase in the availability of early screening tools, increased research on the benefits of early detection and intervention, and current research that points to several "red flags" for autism. The red flags primarily include delays or disordered early social and communication milestones (e.g., lack of babbling, lack of response to name, lack of shared smile in infancy) and should be used to identify children who need further testing. Table 2.1 lists red flags for autism, which were adapted from the CDC Act Early campaign (see http://www.cdc.gov/ncbddd/actearly/index.html). These are not absolute indicators for autism; however, children who demonstrate these red flags should immediately be referred for further testing and early intervention services. A referral should be made to the local early intervention agency or the family's pediatrician if the child is younger than 36 months. The National Early Childhood Technical Assistance Center (NECTAC) provides contact information for early intervention agencies across all 50 states (see http://www.nectac.org). For children older than 36 months, referrals should be made directly to the child's local public school and pediatrician.

Table 2.1 Social and Communication Developmental Milestones in Infants and Toddlers*

Age in Months	Developmental Milestone
12 months	Smiles and imitates simple gestures during play
	Responds to "no"
	Tries to imitate words
	Looks at correct picture or toy when named
	Babbles with changes in tone
18 months	Uses several single words (10 or more)
	Imitates behaviors of adults or older siblings
	Scribbles with crayons or markers on paper
	Turns pages of a book, especially a board book
	Uses a spoon or cup with minimal help
24 months	Engages in pretend play
	Uses simple phrases with two to four words (more juice please, all done, mommy pick up)
	Follows simple instructions
	Understands more than 200 words
	Recognizes several (at least six) body parts by name

* The absence of these behaviors are potential red flags for autism or other developmental delays and indicate the child should be referred for developmental screening and monitored.

Autism is a spectrum of disorders, which means that children will be affected in different ways and demonstrate any combination of the autism symptomatology. Hence, some children may present varying degrees of these early markers of autism. For example, some toddlers may use single words or word approximations (e.g., "Ju" for "Juice") to ask for favorite toys, (e.g., "train"), food (e.g., "cracker") or people (e.g., "momma"), but not display simple pretend play or show an interest in playing with typically developing peers. The absence of any one of these milestones signals the need for follow-up; caregivers should consult with their pediatrician with concerns. For example, infants should be consistently smiling at familiar caregivers by 3 to 4 months. By 12 months, infants should be babbling and imitating sounds (e.g., back and forth babbling) and gestures (e.g., shaking toys, waving bye, pointing).

When screening for autism, it is imperative to identify both the absence of developmental milestones *and* the presence of atypical behaviors (e.g., stereotypic hand or eye movements, repetitive body rocking, unusual aversion to sounds or textures). These atypical behaviors can be particularly difficult to identify because most infants and toddlers will demonstrate repetitive behaviors; thus, it might be difficult for caregivers and pediatricians to identify atypical behaviors in very young children. The lack of developmental milestones often is easier to identify, which can be used to substantiate atypical behaviors (e.g., one might be concerned if an 18-month-old toddler engages in frequent and repetitive behaviors with toys *and* does not use any words regularly). Finally, hearing and vision screenings should always be considered to rule out sensory disorders; infants or toddlers who do not consistently respond to their name or new noises in the environment should be tested for hearing impairments.

Early Red Flags

A lack of joint attention, imitation, pretend play, and interest in and play with peers are four developmental milestones that might be critical early signs of autism or other developmental delays. These are discussed further in the following sections.

Joint attention. Joint attention refers to nonverbal behaviors we use to request, comment, show, or share affect. Joint attention is both communicative and social; we use joint attention to share attention to an object or event with another person. We use joint attention when we point to show interest, follow our friends' eye gaze at something behind us, and gesture to request or ask for something we cannot reach. By 18 months, toddlers should be consistently initiating and responding to prompts for joint attention (e.g., responding to or initiating nonverbal requests). However, many children with autism do not display all forms of joint attention. For example, some children with autism might point to request preferred items or something they cannot reach, but not point to show something to another person or follow someone else's point or shift in eye gaze. In fact, these latter forms of joint attention might be the most salient and important early markers of autism (Charman, 2003; Mundy & Crowson, 1997).

All early autism-specific screening measures include items related to joint attention, due to its strong relation to early signs of autism. Gaze monitoring (i.e., attending to and following where someone else is looking) and protodeclarative pointing (i.e., pointing to show something, such as an airplane flying by or an animal at the zoo) were two of the three most predictive items on the Checklist for Autism in Toddlers (CHAT; Baird et al., 2000). Gaze shifting includes both attending to the gaze of the person you are talking with and following his or her gaze shift across the room. Research shows infants start following their caregiver's gaze by about 4 months (e.g., Bloom, 1974). This is an important early skill and useful for picking up social cues from the environment. However, children with autism often do not attend to these important social cues. Thus, the lack of following another person's gaze shifting is an important early marker of autism, and teaching gaze shifting is an important early intervention goal for children with autism.

Imitation. Vocal and motor imitation are important early social communication skills and mechanisms for learning; research has found a direct link between joint attention skills and imitation in children with autism. Not surprisingly, numerous studies have reported significant delayed imitation in children with autism (Stone, Ousley, Yoder, Hogan, & Hepburn, 1997; Williams, Whiten, & Singh, 2004). In fact, some researchers have suggested that delays in imitation are a primary deficit for children with autism (Ingersoll, 2008). Infants begin imitating their caregivers' vocalizations and eventually their motor actions with objects. This early imitation is important for early language development, social interactions, attachment with the caregiver, play skills, and adaptive skills. Interventions to teach imitation have primarily focused on teaching motor imitation in highly structured adult-directed settings. This approach often resulted in children imitating motor behaviors, which is essential for learning new skills. However, this approach rarely resulted in generalized, spontaneous imitation (Ingersoll, 2008). Recently researchers have focused on teaching generalized, spontaneous imitation within natural social interactions. Using this approach, children with autism increase their imitation behaviors and other social communication behaviors. Thus, a lack in imitation is an important early marker of autism, related to the child's social and language development; imitation is an important goal for young children with autism.

Simple pretend play. During the toddler years, children spend less time manipulating and exploring toys and more time functionally using toys. For example, infants might mouth, shake, look at, or throw toys or objects. Toddlers begin to use objects as they are meant to be used without their intended outcomes. For example, toddlers might put an empty cup up to their mouth making sipping noises or put their mom's cell phone up to their ear and pretend to talk. Eventually, children start using toys or objects as if they were something else (e.g., children often use blocks as cars, or pretend a towel is a cape, or a bowl is a hat). This type of play is referred to as symbolic or pretend play. Many theorists have hypothesized that pretend play develops along with higher cognitive and language skills because of its symbolic nature (Piaget, 1951). Toddlers should begin to demonstrate simple pretend play (e.g., holding a toy phone up to their ear and pretending to talk, rocking a doll back and forth, or using blocks to build houses or train tracks) with toys by 18 months. However, many toddlers with autism will not engage in pretend play. The second highest predictive item on the widely used autism screening tool, the CHAT, is pretend play (Baird et al., 2000). It is important to note that even for children with typical development, play behaviors are dependent on the available toys and child preferences. Ensure toddlers have access to a variety of toys and objects when conducting observations.

Interest in peers. By 24 months, children should be playing near each other with similar toys in similar manners. At this age, children are not expected to be playing together, but should be attending to what their peers are doing. For example, toddlers might be playing with the same train set, rolling trains back and forth, and occasionally looking at each other and switching toys. Conversely, a child with autism might be playing with one train, spinning the wheels back and forth, and rarely glancing at the adults or peers near him. Research shows children with autism are less likely to initiate play with peers, look at peers while playing, and respond to peer initiations to play. In fact, children with autism are likely to prefer playing alone and avoid social interactions. However, as noted earlier, even when children with autism are playing by themselves, their play is likely to be remarkably different from that of their peers. This may further reduce the likelihood of peers initiating play or social interactions, which over time reduces the opportunities for developing friendships with peers and could potentially negatively impact language development. In fact, research indicates children with autism are less likely to develop sustained friendships with peers (Orsmand, Krauss, & Seltzer, 2004). Lack of ability to form or sustain friendships is an item on many autism screening and diagnostic tools (e.g., Lord, 1997).

Communicating Concerns with Caregivers

Childcare providers, early childhood practitioners, or teachers might have concerns about children in their care. This can be a sensitive and difficult topic to breach with caregivers. However, given the importance of early identification and intervention, concerns should always be taken seriously and brought to the attention of parents and caregivers. Table 2.2 lists strategies practitioners or teachers might use when communicating concerns to parents or caregivers. Again, if parents have concerns about delays in social or communication skills or persistent unusual behaviors, they should seek referrals immediately. Table 2.3 provides a list of concerns parents can share with or describe to their local early intervention agency, public school system, or pediatrician. Parents can ask their pediatrician to fill out an Early Intervention (EI) referral form (this form is available for download here: http://www.medicalhomeinfo.org/downloads/docs/EIReferralForm-Final.doc). Figure 2.1 is an example of this form.

Table 2.2   Strategies for Teachers and Practitioners in Talking With Parents About Autism Concerns

Strategy	*Example*
• Ask caregivers if they have any concerns about their child's behaviors.	"How is Ella doing at home?" "Do you have any questions or concerns about Ella's behaviors at home?"
• Set aside 30 or more minutes to talk with caregivers. This might be over the phone or in person. In-person conversations might be advisable to ensure you can best support and respond to caregivers.	Schedule a time with Ella's parents, Marcy and Dante, (ensure it is a time both caregivers can attend) to discuss your concerns about Ella's lack of communication and social interactions. Collect detailed notes and observations about Ella's behavior with specific examples. Have a concrete plan for follow-up including resources for assessment, intervention, and family support. Include a coteacher, social worker, or psychologist if you think it might be useful.
• Be realistic about your concerns, while focusing on the child's strengths	"Ella spent a lot of time today at the water table. She is really good at sharing her toys with the other children there! Does she share with her siblings at home? She does not share as easily when playing with her train. I did notice that she doesn't talk to her peers or respond when they talk to her while she is playing with them."
• Be realistic, keep detailed notes about your concerns, but do not alarm caregivers. Start with the child's strengths and all the positive things about the child.	Keep track of Ella's communication and play behaviors with detailed notes. Record how long she plays by herself, what she does when peers or adults interact with her, and how she communicates wants and needs. Begin by pointing out how much Ella loves to play near her peers at the water table! Also, describe how Ella participates in music time by playing the drum and how she often requests her favorite songs by pointing to the visual schedule.
• In some cases, you will be able to do a screening test (e.g., M-CHAT, Ages and Stages Questionnaire [ASQ]) directly with the parents.	"Based on our concerns, I would like to complete this screening tool. This tool will help us identify Ella's strengths and developmental needs so that we know if we should conduct further testing. Let's walk through this together. Please let me know if you have any questions about the wording or behaviors. As her parents, you spend the most time with her and are the true experts about her. Thus, what you have to say is essential."

(Continued)

Table 2.2   (Continued)

Strategy	Example
• Describe your concerns with specific, concrete examples. Always start with the child's strengths.	"Ella loves playing with the boats and cups at the water table! She shares, looks at the toys other peers have, and often gives her toys to peers. Her favorite songs during music time are 'Wheels on the Bus' and the 'Itsy Bitsy Spider.' She does all the hand movements and plays the drum along to the music all by herself. I am concerned about some of Ella's behaviors. For example, she spent 35 minutes rolling the train back and forth on that carpet. She did not respond when two peers asked her for the train. This is typical for her. She spends most of the 45-minute morning free play engaged in this manner with her red train. She starts to cry and scream when we take her train or attempt to engage her with different toys."
• Have a list of next steps ready. If the caregivers agree with your concerns and want to seek further evaluation, be ready to tell them exactly what will happen next. In most cases, the child should be referred to the local early intervention agency or public school system for further testing. Make sure caregivers know these services are free. Caregivers also will have the option of seeking a referral from a pediatrician.	• Call the local early intervention agency for an evaluation and information about early intervention services. • Contact your pediatrician and give her the results from the screening assessment we did together. • E-mail or call the local developmental clinic for diagnostic testing. • E-mail or call the parent who runs a support group for caregivers with children with special needs. • If interested, look at these websites: Autism Speaks: **http://www.autismspeaks.org/** ○ Parent Resources from the American Academy of Pediatrics: **http://www.aap .org/en-us/aap-store/parent-resources/ Pages/parent-resources.aspx** ○ Centers for Disease Control and Prevention: **http://www.cdc.gov/ncbddd/ autism/index.html**
• Check in with caregivers regularly about the referral process. Again, it is important to note the child's strengths during conversations with the caregivers.	When Marcy comes to pick up Ella, report all the positive things Ella did during the day and ask about the referral process and the checkup with the pediatrician.

Table 2.2   (Continued)

Strategy	Example
• Ask caregivers if they would like to talk to other parents and caregivers who have gone through similar evaluations. Keep a list of parents who are willing to share phone numbers and e-mail addresses.	After Ella was found to be eligible for early intervention services, her parents were given a list of other parents who had recently navigated the early intervention system. The parents have a support group and regularly go on outings together with the families of children with special needs and their siblings.
• Keep a list of local or national resources available for families.	Many states and cities have local chapters of the Autism Society of America.
	Autism Speaks provides an excellent, evidence-based website for families. The site includes links to the 100 day kit, which is a kit for helping families get through the first 100 days after receiving an autism diagnosis (see http://www.autismspeaks.org/family-services/tool-kits/100-day-kit to download the kit).

Table 2.3   Examples of Concerns Caregivers Should Share With Pediatricians

My **12-month-old** child does not respond to his name and does not seem to react or notice when I leave the room.

My **13-month-old** is not babbling. He barely makes any vocalization except when he is upset and crying.

My **16-month-old** doesn't smile back at me. When I laugh and smile or play peek-a-boo with him, he doesn't respond in the same way as his older brother did.

My **17-month-old** does not imitate my gestures or voice, and he only uses one word approximation, "ssss," to request the swing.

My **18-month-old** is not engaging in pretend play with toys. She mostly spends her time staring at and spinning objects.

My **19-month-old** only understands about three words (milk, train, and car) and doesn't use any words.

My **20-month-old** used to use about five words regularly and now he doesn't use any. He stopped using these words about 3 months ago.

My **21-month-old** does not show me things, such as toys or books, like his older sister did at this age.

My **24-month-old** laughs and uses words inappropriately. He sometimes laughs for no reason.

My **26-month-old** doesn't seem interested in other children at all. He plays by himself when we go to the park or visit friends, and his teachers report he plays by himself at day care.

Figure 2.1 Early Intervention Program Referral Form

Parent/Child Contact Information

Child Name: _____

Date of Birth: _____ Child Age: (Months) _____ Gender: F/M

Home Address: _____

Parent/Guardian: _____ Relationship to Child: _____

Home Phone: (_____) _____ – _____

Primary Language: _____

Reason(s) for Referral to Early Intervention

Identified condition or diagnosis (e.g., Down syndrome): _____

Suspected developmental delay or concern (please circle areas of concern):

Motor/Physical   Cognitive   Social/Emotional   Speech/Language   Behavior

Other _____

❏ At Risk (list risk factors): _____

❏ Other (Describe): _____

Person Making Referral: _____ Date of Referral: _____/_____/_____

Address: _____

Office Phone: _____ E-Mail: _____

Early Intervention Program Contact Information

Program Name: _____

Address: _____ City: _____ State: _____ Zip: _____

Office Phone: _____ E-Mail: _____

Feedback Requested by the Referral Source

Date Referral Received: _____/_____/_____

Date of Initial Appointment with Child/Family: _____/_____/_____

Name of Assigned Service Coordinator: _____

Office Phone: _____ E-Mail: _____

After initial appointment, please send the following information:

❑ Status of Initial Family Contact

❑ Changes in Services Being Provided

❑ Developmental Evaluation Results

❑ Periodic Progress Reports/Summaries

❑ Services Being Provided to Child/Family

❑ Other (Describe): _____

_____

Consent for Release of Medical/Developmental Information

I, _____ (print name of parent or guardian), give my permission for my child's health care provider

_____ (print provider's name), to share pertinent information regarding my child,

_____ (print child's name) with _____ (list name of agency

getting information).

Parent/Legal Guardian Signature: _____

Date: _____ / _____ / _____

Source: Council on Children with Disabilities. Role of the medical home in family-centered early intervention services. Published by the American Academy of Pediatrics. Copyright © Pediatrics. 2007, 120(5).

The original version of this form is available on the National Center of Medical Home Initiatives for Children with Special Needs website. Go to http://www.medicalhomeinfo.org/health/EI.html to download this form and learn more about early intervention.

SELECTING A SCREENING MEASURE

The purpose of **screening** is to identify children who need further, more comprehensive assessments. Screenings are intended to be brief, easy to use (by parents and professionals), reoccurring, and inexpensive. Screening tools should identify children who need diagnostic or more comprehensive assessments. They should be capable of telling practitioners and caregivers when there is a concern and the area of concern (e.g., expressive communication, relationship with peers). Screening tools should be brief, family-friendly, **reliable**, and **valid**. Reliable refers to the stability of the assessment score across people, time, materials, and settings. For example, research on the Ages and Stages Questionnaire (ASQ) has high reliability across parents and caregivers. Valid refers to the assessment's ability to provide accurate relevant information. For example, the M-CHAT identifies children who have delays in social or communication skills consistent with the autism symptomatology. Screening tools also should examine functional skills (i.e., skills that are relevant, promote participation and independence in natural settings for all children) and be culturally relevant and sensitive. If the screening indicates a concern, it does not mean the child has autism but that a more comprehensive assessment should be administered. One major difficulty with autism screenings is that children are often missed by earlier screenings. Thus, practitioners should carefully and seriously consider parent or caregiver concerns.

When selecting a screening measure, consider the child's age, areas of concern or question (e.g., Do you have concerns about the child's gross motor skills or social emotional behaviors?), and preferred format (e.g., direct test, semistructured parent interview). Most early intervention agencies and school districts will already have an inventory of preferred screening tools. See Table 2.4 for quality features to look for in screening tools and Tables 2.5 and 2.6 for lists of screening tools. There are a variety of overall developmental and autism-specific screening tools available for use with young children. Screening tools are generally categorized as Level 1 or Level 2. Level 1 screening tools are considered universal or for administration across the general population (e.g., ASQ, regular infant hearing screenings, vision screenings). Level 2 screening tools are for the population of children at risk for a specific disability or disorder. For example, the Screening Tool for Autism in Toddlers and Young Children (STAT; Stone & Ousley, 1997) is a Level 2 screener that was developed to help discriminate between children with autism from children with development delays or others disorders.

Currently evidence-based, autism-specific screening tools are available to identify children as young as 16 months who might be at risk for autism (e.g., M-CHAT; Robins, Fein, & Barton, 2001). However, there are numerous valid and reliable developmental screening tools available for children younger than 16 months (e.g., ASQ; Squires & Bricker, 2009). These can be used to identify children who might be at risk for developing developmental disorders such as autism. Researchers are developing and researching new screening tools, which have the potential to identify children who might be at risk for autism as early as 9 or 12 months (see Figure 2.2 for a description of research on using the overall developmental screening tool, the ASQ, to identify children who might be at risk for developing autism). Effective early autism screening tools increase knowledge of the early markers of autism and enable providers to identify children who need specialized assessment and early intervention (Stone, Coonrod, Turner, & Pozdol, 2004). As with all screening tools, the purpose of autism screening tools is to identify children who are at risk for autism and need further testing, not to make a definitive diagnosis or eligibility determination for special education.

Children develop within the context of their families and cultures; thus, consider cultural variations in developmental expectations when selecting and administering screening assessments. Cultural variations in behavior expectations have been identified across several developmental milestones. For example, expectations about independence during mealtimes, toilet training, play skills, and sleeping behaviors are different across cultures (Carlson & Harwood, 2000). Ask families about cultural expectations around child development. As described in Table 2.4, when selecting a screening tool consider the congruence of the screening tool; this means select a screening tool that has been validated with the population you are screening. Consider the cultural relevance of the items, materials, and format. When appropriate, revise or omit items to ensure cultural relevance. It is essential to develop a cultural awareness when selecting, administering, and communicating screening results.

There are several important characteristics to consider when selecting a screening tool: *specificity, sensitivity,* and *positive predictive value. Specificity* refers to the ability of the screening tool to accurately identify children who are *not* at risk. Conversely, *sensitivity* is the ability of the screening tool to accurately identify children who *are* at risk and do need further testing. The *positive predictive value* is the ability of the screening tool to accurately identify children who are diagnosed with the disability or delays. These psychometric properties of screening tools should be carefully considered prior to use. Additionally, the Division for Early Childhood's (DEC) recommended practices include guidelines for conducting developmentally appropriate, family-centered assessments. See Table 2.4 for descriptions of these eight qualities of assessment. These guidelines should be used for selecting and administering developmentally appropriate screening tools with young children and their families. The following tables and sections describe many of the screening tools used to identify children at risk for developmental delays, including autism.

Figure 2.2   Ages and Stages Questionnaire (ASQ) and Autism

Research based on the results of a clinical sample of children with autism indicates the ASQ might be used to identify children who are at risk for autism. Nickel and Squires (2008) conducted two pilot studies bases on referral samples of children who were referred for an autism evaluation. They compared the results of the ASQ completed by parents at home before the autism evaluation to the clinical diagnosis received by the child in the clinic. In the first study, 45 of 46 children who received a diagnosis of autism failed one or more domains on the ASQ, and all parents noted concerns about their child's behavior. In the second study, 76 of 76 children who received a diagnosis of autism failed one or more domains on the ASQ, and the vast majority of these parents expressed concern about their child's behavior (Nickel & Squires, 2008). In fact, nearly all parents of children who received an autism diagnosis expressed concern about their child's behavior. Nickel and Squires (2008) conducted follow-up studies with a population sample to examine the reliability and validity of the ASQ in identifying children who might be at risk for autism based on scoring patterns. The ASQ is the most widely used screening tool in the country; it is translated into several languages and is used around the world. Furthermore, the ASQ can be administered as early as 1 month after birth. The use of the ASQ as an early screening tool for autism would likely mean earlier identification and intervention for many children at risk for autism. Furthermore, the ASQ meets all eight qualities of assessment outlined by the Division for Early Childhood (Sandall, Hemmeter, Smith, & McLean, 2005; see Table 2.4).

Table 2.4   Eight Essential Qualities of Assessment (Sandall et al., 2005)

Utility	Shows usefulness of the assessment results for informing goals and strategies	The items should include mostly functional and developmentally appropriate items which can be used to identify specific areas of strength and concern for each child. Also, the tools should consider the cultural relevance of items and allow for omission or adaptations.
Acceptability	Has appropriate content and methods for each child and family	The tool should be easily and quickly completed.
Authenticity	Provides information about functional skills in natural settings	The tool should include items related to skills typical children have and provide opportunities for them to demonstrate and master those skills in natural settings.

(Continued)

Table 2.4   (Continued)

Collaboration	Allows for practitioners to gather information from multiple people, including caregivers, settings, and routines	The tool should encourage gathering and synthesize information from parents, teachers, and therapists across settings and materials.
Convergence	Gathers functional, reliable, and valid information across people and settings	Information is synthesized and summarized across settings and people and differences are highlighted and directly linked to programming.
Equity	Allows for acceptable accommodations and modifications for children and families	Materials include opportunities for several different response methods and are accessible by children with a variety of abilities.
Sensitivity	Shows results that are sensitive enough to show meaningful change over time for all children	The tool measures progress for children of all abilities including small increments of behavioral change.
Congruence	Is evidence-based for the population it is used to assess	The materials must be designed and tested with children who will be assessed.

M-CHAT (Modified Checklist for Autism in Toddlers)

The M-CHAT (Robins, Fein, Barton, & Green, 1999; see Figure 2.3) is available for free download for clinical, research, or educational purposes (see http://www.mchatscreen.com). The M-CHAT is a modified version of the CHAT. The M-CHAT was developed to address the low sensitivity rate of CHAT in the general population (Robins, Fein, & Barton, 2001). The M-CHAT was developed to be completed by parents and caregivers for children between 16–30 months of age. The M-CHAT is available in more than 20 translations for use around the world. The M-CHAT is a relatively brief and easy screening test with 23 yes or no questions. The developers encourage users to administer The M-CHAT Follow-up Interview (FUI; Robins, Fein, Barton, & Green, 1999), a structured, follow-up interview for children who screen positive on the M-CHAT. Recent research indicates the FUI reduces the false positive rate, which reduces unnecessary referrals and alarm for parents. Children who screen positive on the M-CHAT and the FUI should be referred for further testing and early intervention services. Children who fail the M-CHAT and not the FUI should be monitored with a developmental screening test (e.g., ASQ).

Figure 2.3   M-CHAT

M-CHAT

Please fill out the following about your child's usual behavior, and try to answer every question. If the behavior is rare (you've only seen it once or twice), please answer as if your child does *not* do it.

1.	Does your child enjoy being swung, bounced on your knee, etc.?	Yes No
2.	Does your child take an interest in other children?	Yes No
3.	Does your child like climbing on things, such as up stairs?	Yes No
4.	Does your child enjoy playing peek-a-boo/hide-and-seek?	Yes No
5.	Does your child ever pretend, for example, to talk on the phone or take care of a doll or pretend other things?	Yes No
6.	Does your child ever use his or her index finger to point, to ask for something?	Yes No
7.	Does your child ever use his or her index finger to point, to indicate interest in something?	Yes No
8.	Can your child play properly with small toys (e.g., cars or blocks) without just mouthing, fiddling, or dropping them?	Yes No
9.	Does your child ever bring objects over to you (parent) to show you something?	Yes No
10.	Does your child look you in the eye for more than a second or two?	Yes No
11.	Does your child ever seem oversensitive to noise? (e.g., plugging ears)	Yes No
12.	Does your child smile in response to your face or your smile?	Yes No
13.	Does your child imitate you? (e.g., you make a face—will your child imitate it?)	Yes No
14.	Does your child respond to his or her name when you call?	Yes No
15.	If you point at a toy across the room, does your child look at it?	Yes No
16.	Does your child walk?	Yes No
17.	Does your child look at things you are looking at?	Yes No
18.	Does your child make unusual finger movements near his or her face?	Yes No
19.	Does your child try to attract your attention to his or her own activity?	Yes No
20.	Have you ever wondered if your child is deaf?	Yes No
21.	Does your child understand what people say?	Yes No
22.	Does your child sometimes stare at nothing or wander with no purpose?	Yes No
23.	Does your child look at your face to check your reaction when faced with something unfamiliar?	Yes No

© 1999 Diana Robins, Deborah Fein, and Marianne Barton

Table 2.5 Autism-Specific Screening Tools for Children

Tools	Format	Age range	Cost	Publisher
Modified Checklist for Autism in Toddlers (M-CHAT)	Parent/caregiver interview	16–48 months	Free, online	m-chat.org (Robins, Fein, Barton, & Green, 1999)
Screening Tool for Autism in Toddlers and Young Children (STAT)	Interactive direct test	24–35 months	$500.00	Vanderbilt University (VU e-innovations)
Social Communication Questionnaire (SCQ)	Parent/caregiver questionnaire	Over 4 years	$110.00	Western Psychological Services
Checklist for Autism in Toddlers (CHAT)	Parent/caregiver questionnaire	18–24 months	Free, online	Autismresearchcenter.com (Baron-Cohen et al., 2000)
Autism Spectrum Screening Questionnaire (ASSQ)	Parent/caregiver questionnaire	7–16 years		(Ehlers, Gilberg, & Wing, 1999)
Quantitative Checklist for Autism in Toddlers (QCHAT)	Parent/caregiver questionnaire	18–24 months	Free, online	Autismresearchcenter.org (Allison et al., 2008)
Systematic Observation of Red Flags (SORF)	Parent/caregiver questionnaire	18–24 months	Free, online	http://firstwords.fsu.edu/

Table 2.6 Developmental Screening Tools for Young Children

Tools	Format	Age range	Cost	Publisher
Ages and Stages Questionnaire (ASQ)	Parent/caregiver interview	1–66 months	$250.00	Brookes
Ages and Stages Questionnaire: Social Emotional (ASQ:SE)	Parent/caregiver interview	3–66 months	$200.00	Brookes
Parents Evaluation of Developmental Status (PEDS)	Parent/caregiver interview	0–8 years	$300.00 (approximately)	PEDStest.com, LLC
Developmental Indicators for the Assessment of Learning (3rd edition; DIAL-3)	Direct test	3–7 years	$600.00	Pearson Assessments
Denver Developmental Screening Test	Direct test	0–6 years	$150.00	Denver Developmental Materials, Inc.
Temperament and Atypical Behavior Scale (TABS)	Parent/caregiver interview	11–71 months	$75.00	Brookes
Brief Infant Toddler Social Emotional Assessment (BITSEA)	Parent/caregiver interview	12–36 months	$99.00	Pearson Assessments

STAT (Screening Tool for Autism in Toddlers and Young Children)

The STAT (http://stat.vueinnovations.com/) is an evidence-based screening tool for use with children between 24 and 36 months (Stone, Coonrod, & Ousley, 2000). The STAT was designed to be administered by practitioners working with children with autism in classroom or clinical settings. The STAT is an interactive assessment with 12 behavioral test items that are administered within interactive, play-based activities. The items examine important social and communication behaviors (e.g., pretend play, imitation, joint attention).

SCQ (Social Communication Questionnaire)

The SCQ (Rutter, Bailey, & Lord, 2003) was developed to identify children who need specialized assessment for children at risk for autism spectrum disorders such as Asperger's syndrome. The SCQ is a parent or caregiver questionnaire and typically takes less than 10 minutes to complete. Research supports the use of the SCQ for identifying children older than 4 who are at risk for autism and should be referred for specialized assessment (Chandler et al., 2007). The SCQ is brief, inexpensive, and can be routinely administered to screen children for autism.

SORF (Systematic Observation of Red Flags)

The SORF (Wetherby, Woods, Allen, Cleary, Dickinson, & Lord, 2004) is an interactive evaluation conducted by the clinician with the caregiver and child. The SORF contains 20 items, which include both behavioral markers (e.g., excessive focus or interest in specific toys) and absence of milestones (e.g., does not point to show me things).The SORF demonstrates high sensitivity, specificity, and positive predictive value in discriminating children with autism from children with other developmental delays and typical development.

QCHAT (Quantitative Checklist for Autism in Toddlers)

The QCHAT (Allison et al., 2008) is a modified version of the CHAT developed to identify toddlers at risk for autism from the general population. The QCHAT includes two important differences from the CHAT. First, authors created the QCHAT to be completed by parents or caregivers, rather than by parents and clinicians. Second, the 25 QCHAT items are scored on a 5-point Likert-type rating scale (ranging from 0–4) rather than a dichotomous yes or no system. This allows parents to indicate the relative frequency or intensity of the behaviors. There are many QCHAT items that are similar to the M-CHAT and CHAT, such as items about joint attention, speech, pretend play, repetitive or unusual behaviors, and communication. The QCHAT was recently developed; thus, research is limited. However, preliminary research indicates the QCHAT adequately discriminates toddlers at risk for autism from the general population (Allison et al., 2008). Researchers are conducting a large-scale investigation of the QCHAT to determine if there is evidence for use as a universal screening tool. The QCHAT is available for download at http://www .autismresearchcentre.com/tests/qchat.asp. Parents, clinicians, and educators can download the QCHAT and initial research on the QCHAT from this website.

ADMINISTERING AND COMMUNICATING SCREENING RESULTS

Screening tools should be administered in comfortable, quiet settings. Oftentimes, screening tools can be administered over the phone. In this case, ensure you schedule an appropriate time with the caregiver (i.e., a block of time where distractions will be minimal). When possible, administer the tool in the family's home to ensure the parents feel most comfortable and gather information about the home environment (e.g., amount of toys available, other family in the home, etc.). While administering, frequently check for understanding by asking parents if they have any questions or additional concerns. Oftentimes, these tools might bring up new concerns or evoke strong emotions by caregivers. Be prepared to provide emotional support and resources to families. Prior to starting any screening tool, have a clear plan for follow-up and referral if necessary. When introducing the screening tools to caregivers, clearly explain the purpose of the tool. For example, tell parents, "The tool asks questions about your child's social and communication behaviors" or "We will use this tool to talk about your concerns about your child and identify her strengths." As much as possible, ask caregivers to provide specific examples of behaviors and concerns. Also, elicit information about the family's routines and priorities. Make notes about parent concerns, child behaviors, and family routines to provide clear, relevant, follow-up or recommendations in the screening report.

When communicating screening results always start with the child's and family's strengths and address the parents' initial concerns. Avoid negative phrases or words such as fail, test, or did not pass. Discuss observed behaviors and have clear examples of the child's behaviors. Know and be prepared to utilize community resources. As mentioned earlier, have a clear plan for follow-up and recommendations for the family regardless of the child's score. If the child "passes" the screening test, you might provide the family with a list of community resources or activities to promote the child's continued typical development. If the child scores in the monitoring range or close to the clinically significant range, provide the family with specific, clear guidelines for monitoring and when and how to follow up. Check in with the family in a month or two to rescreen the child. If the child scores in the referral range or "fails" the screening tool, discuss the family's options. Clearly explain to the family that this score indicates the child might benefit from a more comprehensive assessment; the scores do not indicate the child has a disability. Make the appropriate referral (e.g., for children younger than 3 years you might refer the family to a developmental pediatrician and local early intervention agency; for a child older than 3 years you might refer the family to their public school district and a developmental pediatrician or psychologist) and provide the family with information about relevant community and appropriate Internet resources. Finally, given the idiosyncratic and gradual emergence of autism symptomology, professionals should refer children and families for intervention as soon as there is a concern about autism and not wait for a conclusive diagnosis (Zwaigenbaum et al., 2009).

DIAGNOSTIC PROCEDURES

After the screening indicates a concern, or if a pediatrician or parent is concerned, a comprehensive evaluation should be administered. The eight qualities of assessment described earlier for screening tests also should be applied to the diagnostic evaluation procedures. Table 2.7 describes the medical diagnostic procedures. Both the medical evaluation and educational eligibility (see Chapter 3 for a more detailed discussion of the educational eligibility determination) assessment processes should consider all areas of functioning (e.g., social development, intelligence, adaptive behavior, language, etc.), across multiple settings (e.g., home, school/day care, social situations), and identify the child's strengths and areas of need (Sparrow, 1997). The following sections describe four evidence-based assessment tools commonly used in the formal identification of autism.

Table 2.7   Autism Diagnostic Procedures

Procedures	Who	Example
1. Referral	Physician, early interventionist, parent	Identify children at risk for autism who need further evaluation.
2. Description of concerns or current behaviors by caregivers	Caregivers	Caregivers indicate concerns about language or social behaviors.
3. Developmental and health history	Psychologist, physician	Pediatrician summarizes any previous health issues.
4. Medical evaluation	Physician	Pediatrician conducts a physical evaluation to rule out medical conditions.

Table 2.7   (Continued)

Procedures	Who	Example
5. Autism specific diagnostic tool (e.g., Autism Diagnostic Observation Schedule [ADOS], Childhood Autism Rating Scale [CARS])	Trained clinician	Psychologist administers the ADOS.
6. Gathering of information from both direct observation and interviews	All team members	Psychologist and speech-language pathologist (SLP) conduct observations of parent child interactions and child play skills.
7. Psychological assessment	Psychologist, developmental specialist	Psychologist administers the Bayley.
8. Communication assessment	SLP	SLP administers a language assessment.
9. Assessment of adaptive skills	Psychologist, occupational therapist (OT), SLP	OT administers the Vineland (a structured interview) with parents.
10. Team Evaluation Summary	Parents, psychologist, SLP, OT	The team meets and discusses parents' concerns, child strengths, evaluation results, and next steps.

DIAGNOSTIC TOOLS

ADOS (Autism Diagnostic Observation Schedule)

The ADOS (Lord, Rutter, DiLavore, & Risi, 2002) is a semistructured assessment tool to identify and diagnose autism. The ADOS is widely used for clinical and research purposes and considered the "gold standard" for autism assessment (Lord et al., 2002). The ADOS contains four different modules. Assessors select the module based on the child's age and expressive communication level. For example, Module 1 is for children (at least 30 months old) who use little or no expressive communication. Module 2 is for children with some expressive communication but no fluent speech. Each module contains activities designed to elicit language skills, social-communication, or restricted, repetitive behaviors relevant to the autism diagnosis (e.g., joint attention, communication, pretend play, sharing affect, and friendship; see Chapter 1 for a comprehensive description of autism behavioral characteristics). The ADOS typically takes about 40 minutes to administer. The administrator takes notes during the administration and uses all child behaviors during the assessment process in scoring. The ADOS involves extensive training to administer. The developers recommend attendance at a 2-day workshop for use in clinical settings. Research administration and scoring involves a 5-day workshop with at least a year of follow-up coaching. The ADOS is currently being revised and the ADOS-2 will be available in the summer of 2012. This second edition includes a new toddler module (i.e., a total of 5 modules), additional and revised components, and updated protocols for more explicit administration and scoring instructions. The toddler module (ADOS-T; Luyster et al., 2009) was developed to expand the use of the ADOS with infants and toddlers from 12 to 30 months old who do not consistently use speech. The ADOS-2 scoring for modules 1 – 4 yields the same classifications as the ADOS: *Autism, Autism Spectrum,* and *Nonspectrum.* Whereas the toddler module scoring yields *ranges of concerns.*

ADI-R (Autism Diagnostic Interview–Revised)

The ADI-R; Rutter, Le Couteur, & Lord, 2003) is a caregiver interview that takes about 2 hours to complete. The ADI-R includes items related to social interactions, communication, and restricted, repetitive behaviors. The interview includes 93 items, which are high standardized and designed to elicit information about the family history and the child's current functional repertoire, developmental history, communication, social, and play behaviors, interests, and atypical behaviors. The ADI-R provides categorical results (rather than a rating scale or comparisons to norms); thus, the results can be used to corroborate an autism diagnosis.

CARS2 (Childhood Autism Rating Scale [2nd edition])

The CARS2 (Schopler, van Bourgondien, Wellman, & Love, 2010) is a behavior rating scale used as part of the autism diagnosis based on observations of the child over time. There are 15 items and several unscored parent/caregiver questions on the CARS2 relating to social communication skills, activity level, object and body use, and relationships. A trained clinician scores the 15 items based on information gathered from the parent/caregiver questions. The scale for each item ranges from 1 (typical for the child's age) to 4 (severely abnormal for a child's age). The CARS2 is an expanded and updated version of the first edition CARS. The CARS2 includes a separate set of items for children with high-functioning autism (i.e., children older than 6 who have fluent verbal language and an IQ higher than 80). The CARS2 should be considered one part of a comprehensive autism diagnosis, and it should be considered with information gathered from other relevant sources for the diagnosis of autism.

GARS-2 (Gilliam Autism Rating Scale [2nd edition])

The GARS-2 (Gilliam, 2006) is a norm-reference assessment that can be used to diagnose and assess the severity of autism in children and adults

3–22 years of age. The GARS uses a semistructured interview format for gathering information from parents, caregivers, and teachers. The tool consists of 42 items related to communication, social, and stereotypic behaviors and is typically completed in 10–20 minutes. The GARS provides a percentile score, which is used to determine the likelihood of autism and severity of autism symptoms. The GARS was designed as a supplementary tool and meant to be used along with information gathered from other relevant sources for the diagnosis of autism (see Table 2.8).

Table 2.8 Autism Diagnostic Tools

Tools	Format	Age range	Cost
Autism Diagnostic Observation Schedule (ADOS)	Interactive direct test	2 years +	$1,480.00
Autism Diagnostic Interview-Revised (ADI-R)	Parent/caregiver structured interview	Mental age 2 years +	$199.00
Childhood Autism Rating Scale (2nd edition; CARS2)	Clinician rating scale and parent/caregiver questionnaire	2 years +	$150.00
Gilliam Autism Rating Scale (GARS-2)	Parent/caregiver questionnaire, rating scale	3–22 years	$148.00

DIAGNOSIS VERSUS ELIGIBILITY

There are two different autism identification processes in the United States: medical and educational. While the goals of both are accurate identification, they have slightly different purposes, which is often confusing for families and practitioners. There are three major differences between the two processes. First, they use different criteria in making a diagnosis. The medical profession uses the autism criteria based on the DSM-IV-TR or ICD-10 for consistency across professionals and to assist in health insurance billing. The educational field uses federal and state eligibility criteria that is often more vague, but its intent is to determine if the child needs to receive specialized services (special education) to be successful in early childhood or school settings. Second, the medical identification is determined by licensed physicians, psychologists, and so forth, in medical and psychological settings, whereas the educational eligibility is determined by the educational professionals working as a team and evaluating skills in consideration of the educational context. Third, the purpose of the medical process is to provide a diagnosis and to possibly develop an intervention or treatment plan. The purpose of the educational process is to determine eligibility and access to specialized services in school. In many states, the medical and educational processes are completely independent of one another. In fact, under Individuals with Disabilities Education Act (IDEA), the child does not need a medical diagnosis to be found eligible for special education services under the autism category. However, a medical diagnosis is the first step in determining educational eligibility in many states. It is imperative for teachers, practitioners, and other school personnel to understand these differences between educational eligibility and medical diagnosis and communicate these distinctions with families as they navigate these different systems.

Many of the tools and procedures used in the medical and educational autism identification are the same. For example, both systems should use a diagnostic or eligibility team to administer both autism diagnostic tools (e.g., ADOS, CARS) and domain specific tools to assess the child's developmental level across domains (e.g., language, motor skills, social skills). However, the educational eligibility should include curricular-based assessment to determine the child's strengths and needs with the school curriculum (for more information about educational eligibility, see Chapter 3). Information from all sources (i.e., including both assessment and parents) should be gathered and used to determine placement, goals, and intervention strategies. Strategies for linking assessment results to goals and intervention are discussed in Chapters 3 and 4.

CONCLUSIONS AND FUTURE DIRECTIONS

Autism is a neurobiological developmental disorder, which manifests itself differently across children. There is no single marker of autism and no single exclusionary behaviors. There *are* strong and consistent behavioral indicators, particularly related to social behaviors. Genetic research continues to point to a strong heritable link with autism. Likewise, research continues to identify early markers and red flags that are likely to predict who will develop autism. Future research should continue to identify early biological markers or genes that may predict who will develop autism before symptoms emerge, given the importance of early identification and intervention. Also, research should continue to examine early individual differences across children with autism. Likewise, policies and practices have to be developed and implemented to create sustainable systems of early identification and intervention to ensure children with or at risk for autism have access to evidence-based treatments. This will improve outcomes for children with autism and their families.

LEARNING ACTIVITIES

1. Describe the assessment process (i.e., from screening to diagnosis) for young children suspected of having autism.

2. What are the red flags for autism in young children? What behaviors might you look for in infants, toddlers, or preschoolers?

3. Why is it important to consider the family's culture when conducting screening and diagnostic assessments?

4. List and describe three autism diagnostic tools.

5. Who are the members of a diagnostic/evaluation team? Why is it important to use a team-based approach to autism diagnoses?

RESOURCES

ASQ (http://www.agesandstages.com/): This website provides information about the ASQ and the ASQ:SE, which are low cost, developmental and social emotional screening tools, respectively.

ASQ Oregon (http://pages.uoregon.edu/asqstudy/): The ASQ Oregon project is an online research project. Parents and caregivers of young children can complete a series of questionnaires to obtain information about their child's development.

American Academy of Pediatrics (http://www.aap.org/healthtopics/autism.cfm): The American Academy of Pediatrics website includes information about screening, diagnosis, and treatment of autism for both caregivers and professionals.

Autism Speaks (http://www.autismspeaks.org/about_us.php): The Autism Speaks website provides information on early signs, diagnosis, and treatment for children with autism and their families. The website includes a video glossary of developmental milestones, information for families, a resource library, and opportunities for researchers.

Autism Speaks 100 Day Kit (http://www.autismspeaks.org/comm unity/family_services/100_day_kit.php): The Autism Speaks 100 Day Kit is available for free download from this website. The 100 Day Kit provides useful information and resources for families of children recently diagnosed with autism.

CDC Learn the Signs. Act Early. (http://www.cdc.gov/ncbddd/actearly/index.html): The Centers for Disease Control and Prevention

Act Early campaign disseminates information for parents, caregivers, and professionals working with young children about the early signs of developmental disorders, including autism.

First Signs (http://www.firstsigns.org/): First Signs is a nonprofit agency focused on disseminating information to parents and practitioners about the early signs of autism and developmental disorders.

3

Educational Eligibility

Erin E. Barton

University of Colorado Denver

Beth Harn

University of Oregon

Chapter Objectives:

- Describe the difference between medical and educational identification of autism.
- Describe the components of free and appropriate public education (FAPE).
- Describe the components of and differences between an Individual Family Service Plan (IFSP) and an Individual Education Program (IEP).
- Describe different educational service delivery models.

ELIGIBILITY VERSUS DIAGNOSIS

In general, when people think of identification of autism, they probably think of a medical diagnosis. However, there are two types of identification for autism in the United States: (1) medical diagnosis and (2) educational eligibility. Both types function to identify children with autism to procure appropriate services and supports. However, the procedures, guidelines, and location of services are different across the two types of identification. A **medical diagnosis** is made to develop a medical treatment strategy to address development and independent functioning, determine prognosis (what will happen in the future), involve insurance payers, and emphasize diagnostic accuracy. As described in Chapter 2, a comprehensive medical diagnosis involves several assessments administered by a variety of medical professionals. The DSM-IV-TR, which is written by medical and mental health professionals, is the standard used for medical diagnosis. The medical diagnosis also will identify any comorbid disorders (e.g., obsessive-compulsive disorder, anxiety disorder). The medical diagnosis is not designed to address the child's educational or academic needs. However, the information from a comprehensive medical diagnosis often is helpful in the educational eligibility.

Conversely, the purpose of the educational evaluation is to establish eligibility and determine if the child's disability/disorder is significantly and negatively impacting his or her academic development and if the child needs specialized services (see Table 3.1 for a list of differences between medical and educational identification). Eligibility criteria are established under federal law as specified in the IDEA with 13 eligibility categories, including autism (e.g., deaf-blindness, intellectual disability, orthopedic impairment, traumatic brain injury, speech or language impairment). Each state develops eligibility criteria for these special education categories. Unlike the medical diagnosis, where the DSM-IV-TR is ubiquitous, there is not a uniform eligibility procedure or criteria for educational eligibility. The standards cannot be more restrictive than what is specified in IDEA, but they can be more permissive. The implication of this individual state control is that there is huge variability across states for how students are identified and a range of services that may be delivered.

IDEA does not require that a medical diagnosis is necessary as part of determining educational eligibility; however, some states do require this as part of the process for determining eligibility. Within the educational evaluation process, schools/districts are required to gather a range of information from a variety of sources (i.e., formal assessments, record review including medical diagnosis, interviews, observations, etc.) to assist in the process of determining if the student's disability requires special education services so that the child receives appropriate services. As such, if the state/district requires a medical diagnosis as part of the eligibility process, the diagnosis must be provided at public expense and *not* paid for by the parents/guardians of the child. Additionally, the medical diagnosis *cannot* be used as the sole criterion in determining educational eligibility (i.e., additional assessment and evaluation by educational personnel is

Table 3.1   Differentiating the Identification Process Between the Medical and Education Professions (Brock, Jimerson, & Hansen, 2006; DSM-IV-TR, 2004; National Research Council, 2001)

Medical Diagnosis	*Educational Eligibility*
• Based on DSM-IV-TR criteria	• Based on IDEA
• Identifies a specific Autism Spectrum Disorder (e.g., autistic disorder, PDD-NOS)	• Refers to the broad disability category: autism
• Used in private, medical, and clinical settings	• Used in public schools
• Requires symptoms to be present prior to age 3	• Eligibility can occur at any age, given all criteria are met
• Does not examine academic performance	• Determines extent to which behaviors affect academic performance and access to general education curriculum
• May be determined by an individual or a team of medical professionals	• Must involve the educational team, including the child's parents/guardians
• Describes prognosis	• No prognosis provided; reevaluation every 3 years to determine need for services
• Links services to insurance providers	• Determines need for necessary services and supports at no cost to parents
• Paid for by parents or insurance providers	• Free for parents; paid for by school system
• Used nationally	• Criteria determined by states based on IDEA guidelines

necessary to determine the full range of skills and potential needs for the child; see additional questions and answers on this topic available at the following IDEA website: http://idea.ed.gov/explore/view/p/%2Croot%2Cdynamic%2CQaCorner%2C3%2C). Again, the point of this educational evaluation process is to ensure that children receive a FAPE (see Figure 3.1). FAPE is an educational right for all children identified as having a disability to receive services that are educationally beneficial. It also does not allow public schools to deny services to children with disabilities. See Figure 3.1 for more information related to FAPE.

Figure 3.1 Information About FAPE

What is FAPE?

- It is a legal mandate that requires schools to provide access to general education and specialized educational services.
- It requires children with disabilities to receive free supports as is provided to children without disabilities.
- It provides access to general education services for children with disabilities in their general education settings with peers without disabilities, to the extent possible.

What does FAPE provide?

- Special education and related services are provided free of charge under public supervision and direction.
- Eligible children receive necessary supports and services, modification, and accommodations to address academic needs and ensure access to the general education curriculum.
- Services and supports are provided to eligible children so that ALL children benefit from instruction in general education and access the general education curriculum, to the extent possible.

Who is entitled to FAPE?

- All children with disabilities as defined by IDEA (eligibility criteria) are entitled to FAPE.

What is an appropriate education?

- Educational services are designed to meet the individual, educational needs of students with disabilities as adequately as the needs of students without disabilities.
- Education and services of students with disabilities are provided along with their nondisabled peers, to the maximum extent possible.
- Regular and periodic evaluation procedures are provided to ensure appropriate services and placement are selected.
- Due process procedures are established to ensure parents and guardians receive notice of meetings, record reviews, identification and placement decisions.

IDEA Guidelines

Autism eligibility. The autism eligibility category was added to IDEA in 1997. Prior to 1997, children with autism were likely receiving special education services under the developmental or cognitive delay categories. The general IDEA definition for children with autism include the following characteristics:

- Delays in nonverbal and verbal communication skills that adversely affect the child's educational performance
- Delays in social interaction skills that affect the child's educational performance
- May present with engagement in restrictive or repetitive behaviors, demonstrate a resistance to changes in routines or the environment, and display atypical responses to sensory experiences

In 2004, the Individuals with Disabilities Education Improvement Act (IDEA) further classified children with autism. The exact wording is as follows:

IDEIA 2004 Autism Classification

P.L. 108–446, Individuals with Disabilities Education Improvement Act (IDEIA), 2004

U.S. Department of Education Regulations for IDEA 2004 [§ 300.8(c)(1)]

Autism means a developmental disability significantly affecting verbal and nonverbal communication and social interaction, generally evident before age three, that adversely affects a child's education performance. Other characteristics often associated with autism are engagement in repetitive activities and stereotypical movements, resistance to environmental change or change in daily routines, and unusual responses to sensory experiences. (i) Autism does not apply if a child's educational performance is adversely affected primarily because the child has an emotional disturbance, as defined in paragraph (c)(4) of this section. (ii) A child who manifest[sic] the characteristics of autism after age three could be identified as having autism if the criteria in paragraph(c)(1)(i) of this section are satisfied.

The autism eligibility determination alone is not sufficient for determining the child's educational needs or the provision of services. This assessment should help the IEP team determine the primary eligibility category impacting educational performance, determine present levels of functioning and areas of need (goals), select appropriate strategies, supports, and services to meet the child's needs, and identify an appropriate placement. Specialized education eligibility provides access to a range of specialized services and personnel that may work either directly or indirectly with a child with autism. Special education includes decisions about the type of services a student may need (e.g., speech and language, behavioral supports, etc.) as well as determining the best location (e.g., typical setting, part-time, pull-out, self-contained, etc.) for the service to be provided. These decisions are made by the child's IEP team, which includes a range of educational specialists (e.g., school psychologist, SLP, special education teacher, parent advocate, etc.) and the parent/guardian who meet to discuss the unique and individualized needs of the child and determine the appropriate goals and supports (see Chapter 4 for more information about writing goals and developing IEPs). The following sections provide additional detail on eligibility, decision making in developing the IEP, as well as different approaches in providing specialized services.

Differences across states in eligibility. IDEA lists and provides general definitions and descriptions of the eligible disability categories. However, states choose how they want to assign disability categories, as long as they cover all of the federal disability terms and definitions.

Individual states set their own eligibility assessment standards and procedures within the limits of IDEA. Many states use the DSM-IV-TR criteria to guide assessment procedures. However, not all states do. In fact, other states have created their own assessment guidelines, which are different from the DSM-IV-TR. Thus, in many states, children who are eligible for services under autism do not meet the DSM-IV-TR criteria. Remember that states cannot be more restrictive than the IDEA standards, but they can be more permissive.

Evolving nature of the eligibility. A main difference between the educational eligibility and a medical diagnosis is the evolving nature of the educational eligibility. As described earlier, eligibility is determined based on the extent to which the child's behaviors affect his or her ability to access the general education curriculum and academic performance, and it can be determined at any time for students younger than 22 years. Conversely, the medical diagnosis of autism must include documentation that the characteristics were evident prior to age 3. Although IEPs are reviewed at least every year, eligibility determination is reviewed every 3 years for children older than 3 and every year for children younger than 3. Thus, depending on the child's progress and treatment, eligibility might change over time. Some children with a medical diagnosis of mild or high-functioning autism might not be eligible for specialized services because their disability does not negatively impact their academic performance. Additionally, some children may have received services in preschool and early elementary school and were determined to not need specialized services in later elementary because the disability is not negatively impacting their academic performance.

Individual Education Program (IEP). Once a child is determined as eligible and needing services within the autism category, the child's team develops an IEP. All students age 3 and older who are eligible for specialized services (in any of the eligibility categories) are required to have an IEP. Children younger than 3 years old are required to have an Individual Family Service Plan (IFSP). The IEP is a legal document describing the child's services and supports. The IEP serves as the framework for the child's individualized education plan and is collaboratively developed with all members of the child's educational team (e.g., the parents, special education teachers, general education teachers, speech-language therapist, occupational therapist, social worker, etc.). The team determines the child's placement, necessary services, service providers, goals, accommodations or modifications, and so forth. The IEP is reviewed annually to monitor the child's progress and determine if the supports and services are appropriate (Bateman & Herr, 2006; Ruble, McGrew, Dalrymple, & Jung, 2010). Table 3.2 provides a list of specific terminology and descriptions used in developing an IEP. A complex aspect in developing the IEP is determining the least restrictive environment (LRE) for services to be provided, which is discussed next.

Least restrictive environment (LRE). IDEA specifies that services must be provided in the LRE for all children with special needs. The LRE delineates that children with autism should be educated with typical peers, to the maximum extent possible. The LRE is one that appropriately educates children with special needs with their typical peers, to the greatest extent possible, in the same school the child with special needs would attend if he or she did not have a disability. This means that these children should have access to the general education curriculum and all school activities with their typically developing peers.

Placement decisions can range from highly restrictive to full inclusion. For each of the examples provided here, there are a myriad of reasons why one approach may work best for a specific child. The following

The basic principles of LRE include the following:

- Placement should be based on the child's *individual* needs.
- Placement should include the general education curriculum, regardless of location.
- Placement should be with same-age, typically developing peers.
- The team should consider the continuum of placement options and services available to all children with disabilities.
- Placement in the general education classroom with supports and services should be considered first.
- Placement in a segregated classroom or school should only occur when the severity of the disability prevents or impedes education in general education classrooms with supports and services.
- The team should consider the academic and nonacademic (social interactions with same-age peers) benefits of the general education classroom.

are examples and considerations for placement decisionmaking. Critical factors involved in determining placement are (a) the age of the child and (b) the intensity or severity of skill or behavior deficits. For children under 6, most research indicates that placements with same-age, typically developing peers are ideal for promoting overall development and generalization of skills (e.g., Schreibman, Stahmer, & Suhrheinrich, 2009; Strain, McGee, & Kohler, 2001). As children age, the gap in skills (e.g., language, academic, social skills) might become more pronounced, thus making it more challenging for the child to succeed in the general classroom. IDEA promotes placement in the general classroom for all children when appropriate. However, setting does not dictate how specialized services can be delivered (see discussion on continuum of services that follows).

The most restrictive placement setting is for children to attend a specialized school that includes only children with disabilities. In such settings, students may receive highly intensive specialized interventions; however, the children are not exposed to typically developing peers or the broad academic content provided in public schools. Research has been inconsistent in demonstrating that this setting is necessary or ideal for children regardless of disability category. The more common placement is a public school/early childhood setting, but even with this setting, there are variations in how services are delivered. When children are fully included in the general education classroom, special education service providers (special education teacher, speech-language teacher, etc.) might consult with the general education teacher to best meet the needs of the child with autism. In addition, service providers may work directly with children within the classroom setting or occasionally in a classroom nearby. As previously mentioned, because children with autism vary widely in the range of skills and needs they present, decisions about placement and services need to be made individually by the IEP team and reviewed regularly to maximize child outcomes.

Once placement decisions are made, the team needs to determine the range or continuum of services that the child may need. These services are individually determined by examining the skills of the child and the expectations of the parents/guardians and school personnel. This includes identifying the service providers (e.g., autism specialist, SLP, OT), service delivery methods (e.g., consult, 1:1, small group), and specific frequency and duration of services (e.g., once per week for 60 minutes; 45 minutes of consultation per week). A continuum of services for children with autism might include the following:

- Instruction is provided using the typical age/grade-level general education curriculum with accommodations and modifications provided by the general education teacher with consultation by the special education teacher.

- Instruction is provided using the typical age/grade-level general education curriculum with accommodations and modifications provided by the special education teacher in an alternative location.
- Instruction is provided using the typical age/grade-level general education curriculum with accommodations and modifications provided by the special education teacher in the general education classroom.

Table 3.2   Components of an IEP

Component	Description
Eligibility	The eligibility category is identified.
Team	The members of the child's educational team are identified. This always will include the child's parents/guardians, administrator/principal, special education teacher, and a general education teacher.
Present level of development	The child's strengths, needs, and relevant assessment information are documented.
Goals	Annual goals and short-term objectives are included.
Services/supports	The services and supports needed to achieve goals are listed. This includes the service providers, service delivery methods, and specific frequency and duration of services.
Accommodations and modifications	Accommodations or modifications necessary to ensure the child can access the curriculum and benefit from instruction are documented.
Placement	The location where the range of services will be provided is identified. The LRE must be considered first and the percentage of participation in general education must be documented.
Evaluation plan	The timeline for evaluating the child's progress and IEP is described.
Transition plan	Beginning at age 14, IEPs must plan for how the child will be transitioned to adult services and support by age 22.

504 plans. In some cases, children with high-functioning autism or a medical diagnosis may not be found eligible or need special education services but may receive supports within Section 504. Section 504 is part of the Americans with Disabilities Act, which ensures that all persons with disabilities cannot be discriminated against because of their disability. Children with autism who are ineligible for special education services may have a 504 plan developed to ensure they have equal access to the general education curriculum. A 504 plan is written documentation of any "reasonable accommodations" the child needs to access the general education curriculum as a function of his or her disability. Reasonable accommodations might include a special seat assignment, extended time for taking tests, a different location for taking tests, extra bathroom breaks, permission to eat extra snacks during the day, highlighted textbooks, visual aids, enlarged print, and frequent feedback. As with IEPs, 504 plans are reviewed at least annually with the parent/guardian and involved school personnel. In some cases, children may transition from an IEP to a 504 plan when the IEP team determines that the student no longer needs special education supports. Occasionally, children will move from a 504 to an IEP.

Early intervention eligibility. As described earlier, IDEA is the federal law that requires all children have access to FAPE. Part C of IDEA, established in 1986, provides services to infants and toddlers (children younger than 3) with special needs. As with children older than 3, eligibility for Part C services are outlined by IDEA, and assessment procedures and standards are specified by each state, based on the state's definition of delay. Part C services are not mandated by IDEA, but all states currently provide Part C services, although the eligibility procedures and criteria and services vary widely across states. Part C eligibility requires establishing that the child's disability affects his or her development; the disability does not have to impact the child's academic performance. Part C emphasizes providing services in natural environments and focuses on strengthening the family's capacity to enhance the child's development. The IFSP documents and guides the early intervention process for children with disabilities and their families, and it is developed and implemented by the child's team (see Table 3.3 for a list of the primary differences between an IFSP and an IEP). The team is comprised of the child's family and service providers. A service coordinator is identified to manage the services and supports provided to the family. At least 3 months prior to the child's third birthday, the IFSP team starts preparing for the transition to an IEP and specialized education services. However, not all children receiving early intervention services will be eligible for specialized services. The transition process will include an educational eligibility evaluation.

Early intervention (EI). Perhaps the most significant finding of autism intervention research is the impact of early and intensive behavioral

Table 3.3   Differences Between an IFSP and an IEP

IFSP	IEP
✓ Reviewed every 6 months	✓ Reviewed annually
✓ Eligibility based on disability impact on development	✓ Eligibility based on disability impact on academic performance
✓ Focused on enhancing family's capacity to promote the child's development	✓ Focused on providing supports and services to increase academic performance
✓ Includes child and family outcomes	✓ Includes child goals
✓ Includes services provided by other providers with payment information	✓ Includes free services provided in public schools
✓ Focuses on providing services in a natural environment	✓ Focuses on providing services in the LRE with typical peers, to the maximum extent possible

intervention. Numerous treatment studies have highlighted the benefits of early intervention (i.e., starting treatment during the first three years of life) for young children with or at risk for autism (Dawson & Osterling, 1997; National Research Council, 2001). The research literature on the treatment of autism demonstrates dramatic improvements in social and communication behavior through individualized EI. In fact, the Council on Children with Disabilities reports early, intensive intervention is vital for children with autism and their families (Myers & Johnson, 2007). Although many parents report having concerns by age 2, the average age of autism identification and eligibility is 4.5 years (Coonrod & Stone, 2004). In fact, research indicates signs of autism are apparent in some infants by 16 months and possibly as early as 9 months (Vismara & Rogers, 2008). This documents a potential 3-year lag in treatment during this critical window. Early and appropriate identification is essential to avoid inappropriate or lags in treatment (Mandell, Ittenbach, Levy, & Pinto-Martin, 2007). Given the idiosyncratic and gradual emergence of autism symptomology, professionals should refer children and families for intervention as soon as a concern about autism is noted (Zwaigenbaum et al., 2009). Referrals can be made to the child's pediatrician or local early intervention provider (see Chapter 2 for more information about early intervention referrals). Child Find (http://www.childfindidea.org/) is a component of IDEA that requires states to have policies and procedures for identifying children with disabilities (age birth to 21) who are in need of early intervention or special education services at no charge to families. State EI providers can be found on The National Early Childhood Technical Assistance Center website (http://www.nectac.org/contact/ptccoord.asp).

Specialized Services

There are a variety of specialists working with children with autism within early intervention and school districts. For the most part, the types of specialists working across both systems are similar. However, there are minor differences. These are delineated here.

Early intervention services. Part C of IDEA emphasizes providing services in natural settings for infants and toddlers with disabilities. This means services and supports are provided in the home, child care center, or community setting where the child and family spends most of their time. Part C services also emphasize providing supports and services to the family, rather than directly to the child, to enhance the family's capacity to promote the child's development. The EI specialist teaches the family to provide learning opportunities across daily routines and activities rather than providing direct services to the child. This might involve modeling, role-play, and practice related to language or social skills instruction to address the family's primary concerns about the child's development. In this manner, the actual intervention occurs between home visits (McWilliam, 2010a) and maximizes learning opportunities for the child (Jung, 2003). Families of infants and toddlers receiving EI services will be assigned a service coordinator. The service coordinator manages supports and service providers for the family. The family also might receive support from a speech therapist, autism specialist, developmental specialist, occupational therapist, and/or behavior specialist. The service coordinator ensures the family receives the necessary supports and manages the services provided by the therapists for the family. This model of service delivery is referred to as *interdisciplinary model* (see Figure 3.2). In this model, different professionals provide their own services and address specific developmental areas based on their specialty area. For example, the speech therapist delivers services related to the child's communication and language skills, and the physical therapist provides services related to motor development. The therapists mostly work independently but might occasionally meet to discuss the IFSP. Conversely, other early intervention agencies use a *transdisciplinary model* of service delivery (see Figure 3.2). In the transdisciplinary model, one therapist is identified as the primary service provider for the family. The primary service provider collaborates and consults with the other therapists to provide needed, evidence-based supports to the family. Thus, the family regularly works with one therapist and addresses all areas of need for the child and family. For example, the speech therapist might be the primary service provider, and she will coach the family in addressing the child's speech and language skills across daily routines. She also will consult the other service providers on the IFSP (e.g., occupational therapist and developmental specialist) to coach the family in addressing the child's adaptive and developmental skills. In this model, the family develops a strong relationship with one primary therapist who provides comprehensive supports to address all developmental domains. This model requires consistent collaboration among therapists to ensure the family receives appropriate supports (see Chapter 12 for more information about coaching with families). The primary service provider works directly with the family, coaching and helping family members provide natural learning opportunities for their child throughout their daily routines and activities. The transdisciplinary model ensures the family receives consistent, comprehensive supports to promote the child's development.

Specialized services in schools. Specialized educational services for children ages 3 years and older are provided in public schools. IDEA supports educating children with special needs (including autism) in settings with their typical peers, to the maximum extent possible and in the LRE. As a child's needs are identified, the team will carefully consider the nature of the services (both placement and types of service) necessary to appropriately meet the child's goals. Regardless of the placement, many children with autism will receive services and supports from a variety of professionals (e.g., speech therapists, occupational therapists, autism specialists, social workers, school psychologists, etc.). Services and supports are provided directly to the student by the specialist or through consultations with the child's teacher. For example, if a child with autism is included in the general education classroom, the autism specialist might provide consultation to help the teacher arrange the environment, make accommodations, and implement evidence-based practices to ensure the child makes progress on IEP goals. A speech therapist might consult with the teacher or work directly with the child in the general education classroom to help the child communicate wants and needs and increase social interactions with peers. Similarly, an occupational therapist might consult with the teacher or work directly with the student to help the student complete tasks, follow the daily routines, and work on writing and other fine motor skills. If the child has a behavior plan, the behavior specialist will work with the general education teacher to ensure the behavior plan is implemented. In some cases, children with autism will be placed in special education classrooms. In a similar manner, the special education teacher might provide direct services to the child and consult with the speech and occupational therapists. All members of the child's IEP team, regardless of placement, ensure the child receives effective instruction and makes progress toward IEP goals. In sum, collaboration among the child's parents/guardians and all professionals is essential to achieve maximum results. The next chapter provides strategies and evidence-based practices for developing effective instructional goals, including IEP goals.

Figure 3.2   (a) Interdisciplinary Model of Service Delivery
(b) Transdisciplinary Model of Service Delivery

(a)

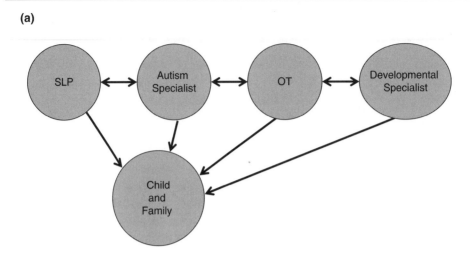

(b)

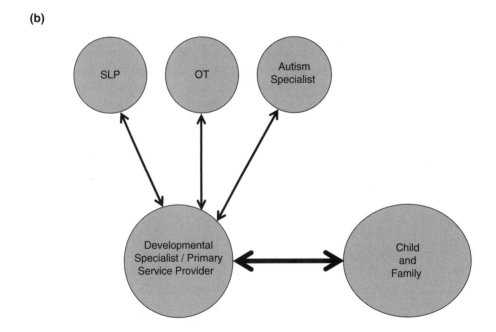

The following vignettes introduce four children with autism including information on their family contexts and identification process. Each child has been identified with autism at different times and presents the myriad of strengths and challenges children with the disorder present to their families and schools. We will be using these children as examples for how to implement the specific evidenced-based practices discussed in the remaining chapters of this book.

DJ.

DJ is currently 3 years and 2 months, and he is the youngest of three children (sisters Ani, age 7, and Patty, age 5). He lives with his biological parents and his paternal grandmother, who is actively involved in supporting the family. His parents had been concerned about his ability to speak and understand what they were saying since he was about 18 months old. At age 2, they mentioned their concerns with his pediatrician. The pediatrician referred them to the local early intervention (EI) agency and a developmental pediatrician. The EI team evaluated him and identified him with significant developmental delays. DJ's EI team (including his parents) determined DJ and his family would benefit from developmental, speech, and occupational therapy. About 2 months later, the developmental pediatrician evaluated and diagnosed him with autism.

DJ's EI team wrote several IFSP goals based on his strengths and needs and his parents' needs, strengths, and concerns. His IFSP goals are as follows: increased communication to get needs met, playing with toys appropriately, and increased parallel play with peers both in home, day care, and social settings. His receptive language skills are approximately 6 months delayed, but he follows many simple directions at home and interacts with the family and siblings during preferred activities and meal times. He uses one-word utterances (which are about 50% intelligible) to request preferred items and activities. His parents have begun to use sign language, with limited success. He often (about 3–4 times per day) gets frustrated when he can't have a preferred item or activity or there is a change in the daily routine, which escalates to tantrums (e.g., screaming, throwing objects, or flopping on the floor) about half of the time and take more than 5 minutes to subside. He rarely interacts with people outside his immediate family and almost all interactions are prompted. He feeds himself (spoon only and sippy cup) with ease (has a small but healthy range of food preferences) and has a predictable daily schedule, which he expects to follow and becomes upset with any modifications.

He currently attends child care four days a week for about 25–30 hours per week. DJ receives speech and occupational therapy at home twice per month and consultation with a developmental specialist. Recently, the day care staff has expressed concerns about his tantrums, which tend to be more frequent and intense at day care. DJ's developmental specialist has been working with the day care staff to ensure DJ's needs are met.

Jim.

Jim is 10 years old and is the eldest son of two children. His brother Bob is 3 years old and is receiving speech and language services due to communication delays. They live with their biological parents. Jim was diagnosed with autism at age 3 1/2 at a local medical clinic. His mother became concerned after meeting and talking with her neighbor, who also has a son about Jim's age with autism. Jim's language skills are significantly delayed. He uses complete sentences when prompted and when related to a topic of his interest or need. He does have frequent (multiple times a day) echolalic behaviors and will only face the person he is talking to when verbally prompted. His eye gaze during instruction and social interactions is infrequent; however, it is clear he is still attending even when his gaze is not focused (i.e., he correctly answers questions). He independently follows his daily schedule and uses a clipboard with each day's routines and activities. He expects this to be followed to the minute. Changes in routine significantly upset him (e.g., he will rip papers, break pencils, or write on walls, books, or desks). As described in Chapter 11, this eventually escalates to destroying materials, throwing objects, and cursing. He has a behavior plan in place to help him self-regulate and calm down when he is frustrated. His current IEP includes the following: special education services for 1 1/2 hours a day to address academic skills in math and social skill development; reading and writing instruction in the general education classroom with consultation from his special education teacher; speech and language therapy three times a week, focused on improving expressive and receptive language skills; occupational therapy once a week to improve fine motor skills; inclusion with peers during cross-grade reading buddies (twice a week) and literacy circle sharing (three times a week) for 60 minutes a day. He also participates with same-age peers during physical education class (30 minutes daily), recess, and lunch. He has a few high interest areas (i.e., dinosaurs, football, bees) and the school maximizes this interest to support interaction during the structured general education activities (i.e., reads books to kindergartners on one of the topics, shares his knowledge of facts about NFL players and rules of the game). His team identified the following IEP goals for him: increase basic reading, writing, and math skills (currently at the second-grade level across each area); increase the quality and frequency of positive social interactions with peers during preferred activities; decrease the frequency and intensity of tantrums when variations in schedule are necessary (i.e., increase use of self-regulation strategies when upset); and improve and increase unprompted expressive language during classroom instruction.

Leroy.

Leroy is currently 4 years old and the only child of his adoptive parents. He has a large, adopted, extended family with both sets of grandparents and an aunt that live in the local area. Leroy was adopted at age 6 months. His birth history indicated that he was 4 weeks premature and was exposed to alcohol, marijuana, and nicotine in utero. At about age 3, his maternal grandmother expressed concerns about the lack of verbal interactions and behavioral issues and brought him to the local public school for an evaluation. The evaluation team identified him with autism and significant developmental delays and determined he was eligible for specialized education services. His IEP team (including his adoptive parents and grandparents) enrolled him in a Head Start classroom located at the community elementary school. He receives speech and occupational therapy in the Head Start classroom. Both the speech and occupational therapist work closely with the classroom teacher to ensure Leroy has opportunities to practice IEP goals across daily activities and routines. Also, an early childhood special educator consults with the classroom teachers about twice per month to ensure Leroy's needs and IEP goals are being met.

Leroy has delayed receptive skills and no verbal communication. He has been successfully using a visual schedule to follow the daily routines. He visually recognizes his printed name, identifies basic colors, letters, and numbers, and feeds himself (has a limited range of food, has aversion to hard and crunchy textures). His parents are significantly concerned with his physical aggression toward adults and peers and with tantrums, which are most likely to occur when he is denied access to a preferred activity, object, or toy. He has become physically aggressive (hits, bites) toward adults and children both at home and in the preschool setting. Additionally, he engages in self-injurious behavior (biting his hand, occasionally drawing blood) again when he becomes frustrated. His IEP includes full-day preschool support in an inclusive setting with an adult-student ratio of 1:4 to ensure quality experiences, including two special education teachers and one general education teacher and an additional educational assistant. Within the preschool time he also receives 30 minutes of speech-language services daily, embedded social skills development, and weekly behavioral specialist consultation and support. Home support includes recently implemented behavioral specialist consultation and coaching weekly, along with an occupational therapist to consult with the family on diet and expanding his eating repertoire.

Fatima.

Fatima is 8 years old and one of two children (she has a 4-year-old brother) that lives with her biological parents. According to her parents and pediatrician, Fatima met all developmental milestones until age 2 1/2, when her language and social interaction skills seemed to regress. She was diagnosed with Pervasive Developmental Disorder-Not Otherwise Specified (PDD-NOS) just before her 3rd birthday at an autism clinic at the local university. Her parents paid for her to receive in-home speech and language services. The local school district also identified her as having significant expressive language delays and offered speech services once per month at the local elementary school. Her parents declined these services. Once she was ready to attend kindergarten, the education team reevaluated her and identified her with significant social and expressive communication delays, but average to above average receptive language and overall intelligence scores. She has been in a general education classroom since kindergarten. Her current IEP has her receiving the following support: all primary instruction provided within the general education classroom (student has been fully included since kindergarten and without an assistant since last year); social skills training with the school psychologist 2 times a week to improve quality of social interactions with peers and self-advocacy skills; occupational therapy monthly to gauge fine motor skills and quality of technology

(Continued)

(Continued)

support and training; and speech and language therapy 2 times a week to increase verbal communication. Her team identified the following IEP goals: increase the quality and frequency of positive social interactions with peers during classroom activities, increase the use of self-advocacy skills (i.e., moving when someone is too close, asking for assistance when necessary), and increase verbal expression usage during classroom instruction.

She uses one- and some two-word utterances to request preferred items and functional needs (yes, no, want ___, leave, etc.). However, her preferred mode of communication is through the use of an AlphaSmart computer. Her parents bought her an AlphaSmart at age 4 and she quickly learned to use it effectively and efficiently to communicate with adults. Her writing skills (spelling, grammar, syntax) are above average and she spends a considerable amount of time on the computer reading about mystical themes (e.g., unicorns, fairies, etc.), which are her primary interests. She rarely initiates interactions with peers, but she will join a group when prompted; however, she sits with her body not directly facing the group. She displays similar, nondirect social interactions (e.g., no eye contact, no overt acknowledgement of listening) toward adults. If asked to look at her speaker, she will comply and look for about a minute. She does not like sitting close to peers or adults and becomes agitated (e.g., makes verbal noises, flaps her hands, cries) when people get too close to her.

LEARNING ACTIVITIES

1. What are the major differences between a medical diagnosis of autism and autism educational eligibility? Who is involved in each process?

2. What are the major difference between an IFSP and IEP? Why are these differences important for children with autism?

3. Review the vignette about DJ. Describe the components of a transdisciplinary service delivery model and delineate how this model would be used to support DJ and his family.

4

Writing Effective Educational Goals

Dylan S. Carelli and Erin E. Barton

University of Colorado Denver

Chapter Objectives:

- Describe the goal setting team.
- Describe how to gather data to inform goal development.
- Identify the family's concerns and resources.
- Describe the components of goals.
- Describe strategies to identify and ensure that necessary supports are present in the environment.

Setting appropriate and meaningful goals is a critical component of successful intervention. In fact, having functional, well-written goals are an essential component of intervention plans. The success of an intervention plan starts with an individualized, well-written goal. Effective goals are developed by a team including parents and providers. In this chapter, we describe the goal setting team and strategies for gathering information to then create meaningful goals based on the child's strengths and needs. The family is the primary care-giving system for most young children, so goals should be family-centered and increase the ability of the child to participate in the family's routines and activities. We discuss several ways to gather information and then ensure that goals are meaningful in the child's everyday life, including the use of routines-based interviews (RBI; McWilliam 2010a, 2010b). In addition to identifying concerns of the family, we also discuss ways to prioritize those areas of concern and to determine the resources available to the family and the team.

Once concerns, resources, and priorities have been identified, the team will then establish goals for the child. We discuss the importance of developing goals that are functional and relevant. Goals will often, but not always, address the core deficits of autism (see Chapters 1 and 5). Goals will be recorded and progress monitored through the IEP or the IFSP, depending upon the age of the child in question. An IEP is a written educational plan developed by a team that lists the specific services a student with a disability will be provided to receive a free appropriate public education. An IFSP is a written plan to deliver early intervention services to an infant or toddler with a disability. Finally, we briefly discuss tools to address academic and pre-academic skills and to identify academic settings and activities in which social, emotional, communication, or other nonacademic skills might be addressed.

WHO IS ON THE TEAM?

Randy Chapman (2005) references IDEA mandates when describing the members of the IEP team:

1. The student's *parents or caregivers;*

2. Not less than one of the student's *regular education teachers,* if the student currently is, or may be, participating in regular education;

3. Not less than one of the student's *special education teachers* or, where appropriate, someone else who provides special education services to the student;

4. A representative of the school district who is qualified to provide, or supervise providing, specially designed instruction to meet the unique needs of students with disabilities and who is knowledgeable about both the general curriculum and the availability of the district's resources;

5. An individual who can interpret how the information from evaluations can impact the child's instruction;

6. At the parents' or school district's discretion, *other individuals who have knowledge or special expertise regarding the child, including related services personnel;*

7. The student with a disability whenever appropriate;

8. The Part C service coordinator or other representatives of the part C system if the student has received part C early childhood services and if the parents request their presence to help with the "smooth transition of services" from Part C to Part B. (p. 30, emphasis added)

Connect (2009) listed IFSP team members:"The regulations implementing Part C require that the IFSP team must consist of: *the parents; other family members* as requested by the parents and if feasible; an advocate or person outside the family if the family requests the presence of such a person; *the service coordinator; a person who was directly involving [sic] in conducting the evaluations and assessments;* [and] *a person who will be providing service(s) to the child or family"*(p. 3, emphasis added). Regardless of the legal requirements as to team makeup, "[t]eams should feel comfortable including any individual who will be able to add a unique perspective or offer support that other members cannot" (Kluth, 2003, p. 243, emphasis added).

Oftentimes one person may fill multiple roles on an IEP or IFSP team. For instance, a special education teacher may fill roles numbered 3, 4, and 5 as outlined earlier by Chapman. Regulations for both EI (Part C) and school-age (Part B) services make particular mention of the need for parents to be members on IEP and IFSP teams. Including families as members of goal setting teams is mandated by law, and best practice, as families are the true experts on their children.

Parents act as the child's first teachers, and the family system provides many, if not most, of the child's guiding experiences across all developmental domains: social, communication, physical, motor, and cognitive. Family members have the longest history of interacting with the child and therefore have invaluable knowledge about the child's interests and strengths within their natural home environment. They are integral to developing functional goals that will enable the child to successfully participate as a member of his or her family.

Parents may not realize that they are allowed to bring other individuals who know their child, and it is important for IEP/IFSP team leaders (e.g., school case manager) to make this known to parents. Other care providers, including extended family and child-care providers, may have valuable information regarding how a child interacts with peers and the environment in a setting with different routines and expectations than those of the home environment. If their insight is not sought out, there may be significant gaps in the information used to develop goals. Additionally, parent advocates can be very useful in supporting parents to feel more comfortable in working with the school team by ensuring they understand their legal rights and the entire process. Parent advocates can either be school district employees or from outside the school district. Many states have developed an advocacy agency within the state-level departments of education and there are national services provided by the Council of Parent Attorneys and Advocates at the following website: http://www.copaa.org/.

Professionals, including educators, speech-language pathologists, occupational therapists, physical therapists, and psychologists, will also participate in goal setting teams. These professionals may have interacted with the child infrequently, during evaluations and assessments, or more often, as more active members of the child's intervention and/or educational team. Each professional brings a unique perspective based on his or her area of expertise and so can provide insight about the different areas of need a child may have and how best to make progress in those areas.

Another provider who can, and should, be an important member of educational teams is the paraprofessional. This is often a person who works directly with the child in both the special education setting of resource rooms as well as assisting the teacher in the general classroom to carry out individualized curriculum and behavior plans designed by the special education teacher.

Gathering information from the team. Special education and intervention services are usually planned and delivered not by one individual but by members of an interdisciplinary or transdisciplinary team. An interdisciplinary team is a group that consists of specialists from several fields combining skills and resources to present guidance and information to families. A transdisciplinary team is a group that consists of specialists from several fields working across disciplinary boundaries, together with family members, to plan and implement intervention.

Vignette: DJ

DJ was identified by a ChildFind team as having developmental delays at 2 years old. Subsequently, his IFSP team, which consisted of DJ's mother, father, and paternal grandmother, the service coordinator, and developmental specialist, completed an IFSP. The IFSP included goals for increased communication to get needs met, playing with toys appropriately, and increased parallel play with peers at daycare. Early intervention services were provided in the home setting.

Several months later, after DJ had received an official diagnosis of autism, the daycare provider told the parents, "No wonder he has such a hard time even being near the other children. I didn't want to worry you, but I usually put him in a playpen so that none of the others accidentally touch him and set him to screaming." She asked that they find childcare at another location, since she didn't know how to work with "autistic kids."

How might the goals developed in the IFSP meeting have been different if the daycare provider's input had been actively sought? How might this additional information have affected the ways in which services and supports were provided?

McLean and Crais (2004) further defined these different types of teams as follows:

> [I]n the *interdisciplinary team*, a premium is placed on communication among team members so that the outcome of assessment and program planning is more unified . . . . The *transdisciplinary team* model is an attempt to maximize communication and collaboration among team members by crossing disciplinary boundaries . . . . Families are involved to whatever extent they choose in assessment and program planning, and family choices predominate. All team members share responsibility for assessment and development of the intervention plan. (p. 58)

The main difference between these models is that in a transdisciplinary model, it is generally the role of one or two primary care providers working along with the families to provide the intervention based on collaboration and consultation with other team members, while in an interdisciplinary model, many providers provide the intervention based on their areas of expertise. In general, a transdisciplinary model may be more frequently used in delivering EI services, where the family is the recipient of services rather than just the child; an interdisciplinary model may be used more often in school settings based on the availability and specific roles and responsibilities of different team members.

Both of these team-functioning models place an emphasis on family participation, communication, and collaboration between all team members during both the assessment and planning stages of service provision. In a transdisciplinary team, an early childhood special educator (ECSE) may work closely with a SLP to assess multiple developmental domains and will consult with OTs, physical therapists, and other team members during assessments and while developing appropriate goals and teaching strategies based on the assessments; the ECSE and SLP will have primary responsibility for developing the goals and especially, for intervention provision. In an interdisciplinary team, each team member usually does a specific assessment and develops goals related to the developmental domain, which is his or her specialty; all team members communicate with each other regarding what they have observed during assessments and which goals they want to include in the plan. Each team member then has opportunities to work directly with the child to make progress toward those goals.

Each professional will likely have assessment instruments developed to evaluate the child's functioning in his or her area of expertise. Many of these are standardized assessments, assessment tools that have specified content, procedures for administration and scoring, and normative data for interpreting scores; these require administration in a precise fashion without room for individualization. These standardized assessments are often used to establish initial diagnoses, and for children with autism, they may have been administered in a clinical setting, assessing "the strange behaviours of children in strange situations with strange adults for the briefest possible periods of time" (Bronfenbrenner, 1979, p. 19). Although these assessments may be necessary for diagnostic purposes, they are not designed to showcase the strengths of students, and in many cases, they are not culturally sensitive to the many differences evidenced by children being evaluated.

Although it may be of some value to know how the child with autism differs from the general population of children, it is often more valuable to use a form of criterion-referenced assessment, which is an assessment tool designed to provide information on specific knowledge or skills possessed by a student. The tool measures specific skills or instructional objectives and allows for individualization in materials, settings, and assessors. When assessments are carried out in primary childcare or educational environments, this helps to ensure that the goals developed reflect behaviors actually seen in (or not seen but important within) that environment. In general, the best method of discovering how a child measures up to any predefined set of criteria is to do observations in natural settings. Of the eight essential qualities of developmentally appropriate assessment explained by Sandall et al. (2005), the qualities of *authenticity* and *equity* are best met through direct observation of children interacting with their natural environment in situations with which they are familiar. Direct observations are, of necessity, authentic; that is, the child is showing what he or she can do in a typical setting, with familiar people and without contrived activities. Individual differences are accommodated by attending to what the child is currently doing in those typical situations; direct observation would be considered equitable because the child is not being required to perform tasks that may not be familiar in a standard way. It may be helpful to intentionally prepare the environment to increase opportunities for the child to show his or her strengths and challenges in the areas of concern. Greenspan and Meisels (1996) then recommend "using a developmental model as a framework for integrating all the data obtained from parents' reports, direct observation, and other sources, and conveying and discussing assessment findings in the context of an alliance with the child's primary caregivers, with the potential for starting an intervention process if needed" (pp. 18–19).

WRITING FAMILY-GUIDED GOALS

To build an alliance with the child's primary caregivers, it is essential to learn their concerns and priorities for their child's learning and development, as well as to identify what resources and supports family members can draw upon to help the team help their child. Although educational and intervention teams have many demands on their time and resources, gathering this information is essential to ensure success outcomes; "[g]iven that the children's life outcomes are affected by the services they receive across the school years, it is critical that educational services are meaningful for the children and their families and incorporate learning opportunities beyond the school environment" (Chambers & Childre, 2005, p. 20).

Concerns. When parents are asked simply to identify their concerns, it may be difficult for them to do so on any particular day, or they may not wish to talk about their child in negative terms because they feel it reflects badly on them as parents. Some families may not have specific concerns about their children that a team is expecting to be identified; for instance, for a family that values parental nurturance over independence of young children, a parent may not identify a lack of the child's independence at mealtime to be a concern. For these reasons, it can be extremely helpful to do some form of routines-based interview (e.g., RBI; McWilliam, 2010a) with families, because allowing them an opportunity to describe daily routines will usually result in a clearer overall picture of the child's functioning across the family's settings and activities. An RBI is an assessment strategy designed to obtain information about the daily routines in which a child participates and the successes or challenges he or she faces in each routine. This also provides information about the interaction between the child and the family members during these routines. It may give the team, including the parents, ideas about times of day, particular skills and activities, settings, and communication partners that are either identified with challenges or as supportive of the child's successful functioning. As McWilliam (2001, 2010a) described, the RBI process (discussed later), an ideal method of gathering information related to concerns and for helping parents to prioritize those concerns and the outcomes which they would like to see arise from intervention.

McWilliam, Casey, and Sims (2009) further identified 10 quality indicators for the interviewer to practice while conducting RBIs: "1. Active listening; 2. In-depth follow-up questions; 3. Continuing the conversation; 4. Proactive questioning about child development; 5. 'Smart questions'; 6. Nonverbal behaviors; 7. Social milieu of routines; 8. Seeking evaluative and interpretive opinions; 9. Managing the conversation; 10. Empathizing" (p. 229). They emphasized that the interviewer's ability to empathize with the family members and demonstrate acceptance of their viewpoint, both through nonverbal cues and through asking questions that indicate understanding of what the family member has already said, will lead to information that is relevant to the goal setting process, while simultaneously building the relationship upon which future teaming is based. Many instruments have already been developed for guiding RBIs, and some of these are noted at the end of this chapter; providers can also check with their agency or school district to see if there are forms which are recommended.

Steps in the Routines-Based Interviews (RBIs) McWilliam, 2010a

1. The first step of the RBI asks family members to identify their daily routines and activities. This often starts with the interviewer asking, "How does your day begin?" and "What happens next?"

2. As family members identify their routines, the interviewer asks questions to determine the following for each routine:
   a. What does each person, including the child, do during this routine activity?
   b. Does the child participate independently?
   c. How does the child interact or communicate with others?
   d. Is the caregiver satisfied with the routine?

3. Throughout this process, the interviewer makes notes about strengths and concerns of the family and child. The interviewer then reviews these with the family.

4. After reviewing all routines, the interviewer asks the family to identify goals or areas to work on. These become the "outcomes." These should be worded as closely to how the parent stated them as possible. Typically, this should result in 6–10 outcomes. The interview does not push certain goals but does remind the family about areas of strength and concern when necessary.

5. The interviewer shows family members their list of outcomes and asks them to prioritize these outcomes. The structure and goals for subsequent home visits will be based on the priority order of these outcomes.

Source: McWilliam, 2010a

Another type of interview-based format which may be useful, and is similar to the RBI, is one that is structured by developmental domains and important daily routines. In this type of interview, the provider would ask caregivers to identify what the child is currently doing and what the parents would like to see the child doing, across different developmental domains. For older children, it may also be helpful to ask the children themselves what they are good at and what they would like to learn, as well as getting input from family members and other caregivers.

Priorities. As noted previously, once concerns have been identified, it is then important to prioritize those concerns. One way teams can assist families to set priorities is to consider what goals will strengthen family functioning and facilitate participation in the community. Having a child with autism can be especially difficult for family members because it is a "hidden disability"—the child may not be immediately identifiable as having a disability apart from displaying challenging behavior. Parents

About Our Young Child (ages 1–6 years)

Type of Skill or Routine	Some things our child already does well in this area:	Next steps for our child in this area:
Play (playing with materials appropriately, sharing, taking turns, playing alone, playing with others, putting items away)		
Using Language (using words, phrases, sentences, or alternative methods to communicate wants and needs, showing objects to others, describing what they experience)		
Understanding Language (following one- and two-step directions in familiar and in novel routines, understanding concepts such as *in, on, up, down*)		
Pre-academic (matching or sorting objects, identifying numbers, colors, shapes, letters, using scissors, looking at books)		
General Adaptive (Daily Living) Skills (undressing, dressing, brushing teeth/tolerating having teeth brushed, brushing hair/tolerating hair being brushed, toileting [indicating need to be changed or to go to the bathroom, successfully using toilet, wiping self, washing hands])		
Adaptive—Meal Time (staying at the table, eating with utensils, drinking from cup, eating a variety of foods)		
Adaptive—Bath Time (sitting and staying in the tub, washing self, tolerating being washed/shampooed)		
Adaptive—Community Activities (shopping, eating in restaurants, riding in the car, going to playgrounds, library, etc.)		

Behaviors that interfere with learning or other activities

	With peers:	*With adults:*
During Transitions:		

Note: Adapted from Laus, Cordisco, Hanna, and Rapp (1991).

63

About Our Elementary-Aged Child (ages 7–12 years)

Type of Skill or Routine	Some things our child already does well in this area:	Next steps for our child in this area:
Play (trying new activities, continuing and building upon peers' play ideas, tolerating "losing" in win/lose games, showing flexibility within games and activities)		
Using Language (using words, phrases, sentences, or alternative methods to communicate wants and needs, using language to interact appropriately with adults and peers in a variety of settings)		
Understanding Language (developing understanding of idioms and other nonconcrete language, understanding nonverbal social cues of communication partners)		
Academic (decoding and understanding reading materials, using numbers for a variety of purposes, using writing and other materials appropriately)		
General Adaptive (Daily Living) Skills (increasing independence getting self ready, including bathing/showering, toileting, dressing, brushing teeth)		
Adaptive—Meal Time (sitting at the table, eating appropriate amounts of food, eating a variety of foods)		
Adaptive—School (following daily school routines, staying on-task during lessons, attending to teacher, attending to peers when appropriate, persistence in tasks)		
Adaptive—Community Activities (participating in activities like shopping, traveling by car or bus, and leisure activities—library, movies, sports)		

Behaviors that interfere with learning or other activities

During Transitions:	*With peers:*	*With adults:*

Source: Adapted from Laus, Cordisco, Hanna, and Rapp (1991).

may be discouraged from bringing the child to extended family events or into the community. They may have their parenting abilities questioned or challenged, either by others or by themselves.

Team members can use ethnographic interviewing techniques to identify family values, which can then guide goal setting that positively impacts those skills that the family values. Providers can ask open-ended questions, such as the following:

- Are there activities that you or your family would like to participate in, which are difficult right now? Which of the identified concerns, if addressed, could lead to more opportunities for your family to participate? (e.g., For a child with safety concerns, would the family be more likely to go to the park if the goal targeted complying with safety directions, such as "stop" or "come here"?)
- Are there activities which your child has shown an interest in, which would lead to more increased independence in leisure time? What adaptations or supports would help your child to be successful in this activity? (e.g., If your child likes to swim, would he be successful in a swim club or swim team if some visual supports were provided to show him how many laps he needed to do before a break? Would it be helpful to provide a peer-buddy to help him learn the routines, and could that buddy then lead to a friendship at other times?)
- If any of the identified concerns were addressed, would it lead to a less stressful routine at a time of day that is especially difficult? (e.g., If the child had less tantrums during transitions, would it make getting him to school less stressful for the parents?)
- Are there any goals identified that would lead to increased interaction between the child and other family members? (e.g., For a father who doesn't feel he can connect with a child who doesn't show an interest in sports, would a goal of playing simple ball games strengthen the relationship between the child and his father? For an older child who has a special interest in bees, can this be used to have him read books about insects with a younger sibling?)
- Are there any instances where one concern is mentioned across different routines or times of day, and would this be a good goal to target for generalization? (e.g., If the child can participate in toileting routines by pulling up his own pants, will he also be able to participate in dressing himself in the morning and after bathing? If an older child is routinely hugging peers inappropriately because she doesn't have a variety of ways to interact with others, how can the peers help to model and reinforce appropriate ways to initiate interactions by saying "hi," giving high-fives, or waving to peers? Will this then generalize to appropriate initiations in various settings?)

You may notice that while many of the questions and examples listed here are targeting skills that will be useful in the home, they also help to identify goals that can be practiced in school or other community settings. Following directions, and especially safety-oriented directions, would be important across all environments. Transitions are traditionally challenging for many children on the autism spectrum, and facilitating smooth transitions will promote success across activities and settings. Any simple play routines, whether they involve balls or blocks, trains or dolls, will not only strengthen relationships within the family but also promote interactions with peers; this is also true for all social interaction skills as children get older and interactions involve less play and more activity around common interests. Any adaptive skills that are targeted, whether they focus on eating, toileting, dressing, or other self-help skills, will increase independence in all settings and also may facilitate the child's involvement in more integrated and typical surroundings.

Resources. Identifying resources entails much more than simply listing who is available to provide services. Each team has a large pool of resources to draw on, including the specialized knowledge of each of the team members, experiences of families, special interests of the child and of other team members, and support of others in the community.

One way to identify resources is to look at the capabilities, interests, and strengths of each of the team members, including the child with autism. Whenever possible, educators should be building on the strengths of their students. By identifying what the child can do and what the next steps are, the team can work to build on the child's current functional repertoire; it can also be an opportunity to identify those skills the child already demonstrates and which he or she can model for others, to increase the child's status as capable within the classroom or other environment.

There are multiple versions of "reinforcement (or reinforcer) inventories" that teams can use to list the interests and preferences of the child with autism. A reinforcer inventory is a list of items or topics that the child enjoys. Typical categories on reinforcement inventories include social, tangible, and activity. Special interests, including favorite books, toys, characters, movies, and other favorite topics, are also important to identify. Remember that some children may not initially be comfortable with social reinforcement, and it may be helpful to pair social reinforcement with other types until the child responds more positively to social types of reinforcement. This is important, since many children with autism have special interests that are outside of the realm of interests displayed by the majority of children. Special interests can be utilized to increase the child's engagement in learning activities or as motivation for completing less-preferred activities. One example of a reinforcer inventory is displayed in Figure 4.1.

Figure 4.1   Example of a Reinforcer Checklist

Reinforcer Checklist

Name: _____   Date: _____

Check items/activities that the child enjoys. Review this form periodically, as reinforcers can change frequently.

Social:

❏ Attention from adults/peers
❏ Hugs
❏ High fives
❏ Verbal praise (list):_____
❏ Thumbs up sign
❏ Big cheers
❏ Applause
❏ Tickles
❏ Hand Shakes

Activity:

❏ Toys (list):_____
❏ Outside play (list): _____
❏ Puzzles
❏ Go for Walk
❏ Draw/Paint/Cut/Art
❏ Dressing up
❏ Computer
❏ Books

Sensory:

❏ Roll in blanket
❏ Bubbles
❏ Swinging
❏ Squeezes
❏ Shoes off
❏ Spinning
❏ Jumping
❏ Visual toys
❏ Special smells (list):_____
❏ Music/Singing (list):_____
❏ Water play
❏ Sand play

Special Interests:

❏ Animals (list)_____
❏ Dinosaurs
❏ Trucks/Cars
❏ Numbers
❏ Alphabet
❏ Tools
❏ Sports
❏ Trains
❏ Shapes

Favorite TV shows/Movies: _____

_____
_____

Tangibles:

❏ Chips   ❏ Crackers
❏ Fruit   ❏ Goldfish
❏ Cereal   ❏ Cookies

Favorite TV/Cartoon/Movie characters:

_____
_____

Identifying special interests, knowledge, and abilities of other team members can be important to determine who can best help target specific goals. Once target goals have been established, the team can then work to determine which team members will participate in routines where these skills can be taught, practiced, and reinforced.

Beyond simply identifying the current members of the educational or intervention team, it may also be beneficial for the family to make a record of the persons and organizations already present in their lives and who may bring additional talents to the table. One way to make a visual record of this "people resource" is to draw a Family Circles of Support map, a visual tool designed to represent the people and groups that support a child, including family, friends, acquaintances based on mutual interests, and persons paid to interact, such as service providers, teachers, or employers, so that the team can get an idea of levels of support which the family already has access to, as well as levels that may benefit from intentionally seeking out and strengthening those types of relationships:

- A diagram with four concentric circles is used to record the names of individuals who are supportive of the student and family.
- Inside the inner circle is the student's name.
- The people closest and most important to the student are written around the inner circle.
- The names of individuals who are close to the student, but not quite as close as those in the inner circle, are written on the diagram around the second circle.
- The student and family are asked to name the groups of people in the student's life, such as those associated with church, sports teams, or clubs. These names are written around the third circle from the center.
- Finally, the student and family are asked to name the people who are paid to be in the student's life, for example, teachers, bus drivers, doctors, and so forth. These names are written around the outer circle.
- The facilitator summarizes this activity by pointing out that the focus in planning must shift from preparation of individuals to the identification of needed supports for community participation. (National Secondary Transition Technical Assistance Center, 2008)

Occasionally, a child will have a particular challenge that can best be addressed by outside consultants; for instance, a child who shows food selectivity may benefit from a nutritionist or other consultant with specialized knowledge in this area. In these instances, it is helpful for the team to have access to specialists within the community and the ability to work collaboratively with new members of the child's team.

Vignette: Jim

Jim is a 10-year-old boy with autism. The figure represents the people with whom his family interacts. His younger brother is 3 and also receives specialized services for a speech and motor delay. Having family members identify the people already in their life was helpful as they thought about who might be supportive of the goals they are developing for Jim's current IEP. It was also helpful as a means of identifying persons not currently "in the picture" who the family would like to bring into their circles, as another goal for the team.

Jim Family Circles

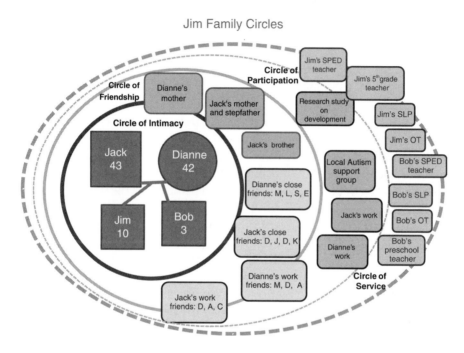

Who would you want to see included in this family's circles? How might "support circles" look different for a typically developing fifth-grade student?

RBIs provide information about the places and activities already accessed by the family in the community or by the child within the school environment. This information can be used to identify the settings in which new skills will be taught and generalized. Often, knowing the activities and environments in which the child and family participate has the added benefit of having persons in those environments who may have specialized knowledge which the team can utilize. For instance, if a family already takes its child to a local library to pick out books, the team may be able to work with the librarians to access story-time activities in a manner that more fully engages the child with autism. Another tool for identifying current family resources and needs is an eco-map. An eco-map is a graphic representation of a person's connections to other people and/or systems in their life, a visual representation of the people and places with which the child and his family interact. It should express the strength and effect, or directionality, of each relationship.

When creating an eco-map, the following domains should be included: family, neighborhood, service providers (past and present), neighbors, social groups, employment, education, religious/spiritual aids, and other significant people. When drawing an eco-map, the strength of each relationship must be included. Each relationship should be judged as strong, tenuous, or weak. This should be considered when identifying resources that are going to be put on the map. The strength and impact of relationships is subjective. With the name of the person whom the map is about in a circle at the center of the map, begin to make circles representing the people and resources identified at varying distances from the center. The closeness of the relationship to the featured person and the closeness of proximity to the center circle should be represented as such. People close to the featured person should have their circle close to the person's. Subsequently, people whose relationship is more distant should be drawn farther away from the featured person's circle. Once all of the circles are drawn on the page, you should connect all of the surrounding circles to the center circle. The lines to make these connections should correspond with the strength of the relationship between the two people. A bold or double line depicts a strong relationship, a dotted line represents a tenuous relationship, and a thin or single line represents a weak relationship. If there is not a current relationship there should not be a line. Once all of the lines are drawn, each line needs to be revisited. You must add an arrow head to each line. The arrow should be pointing in the direction of the flow of resources. If the featured person at the center is helping or offering assistance to the person in the orbiting circle, the arrow should point out toward that person. If the person in the orbiting circle is helping the featured person, then the arrow should point in toward the person at the center. If any of these relationships is particularly stressful, this should be depicted by a superimposed zigzag line over the initial line (Supervisory Training to Enhance Permanency Solutions, n.d.).

Another method of identifying concerns, priorities, and resources, especially strengths and capacities of the child and the family, is to facilitate a *person-centered planning process,* which is a unique planning process based on the belief that people are best understood in terms of their contributions, personal interests, and gifts. Person-centered planning facilitates a shift in thinking from relying on systems for guiding a person's life to focusing on personal control, belonging, and choices. Person-centered planning facilitates the development of personal support circles and positive, proactive life plans to assist young people with disabilities and their families in realizing their goals for the future (PEAK Parent Center, n.d.). The following components typically are included:

(1) the individual is placed at the center of the planning process;
(2) all team members, including the student and the family,

Here is a first draft of an eco-map for Fatima.

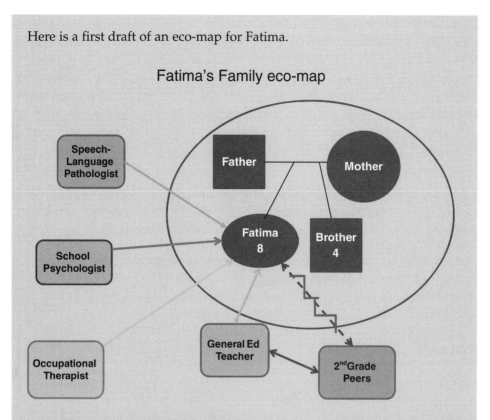

Fatima's Family eco-map

At this time, we have some information about the providers interacting with Fatima, but not much information about the relationships between the members of Fatima's family, their interaction with her school team, or other outside supports or community settings or activities in which they may participate.

What other information would you want, to help you identify settings in which Fatima can generalize the IEP goals already identified (to increase the quality and frequency of positive social interactions with peers, to increase the use of self-advocacy skills, and increase verbal expression)? Is there any cultural information which may be helpful as you consider the information you know about her non-verbal communication during social interactions, i.e., sitting with her body not directly facing the group and no eye contact towards adults?

are involved as contributors in the planning process; (3) all members take a positive and proactive view of the student by focusing on strengths and abilities rather than the disability; (4) consideration of the student's strengths, interests, and dreams are central to the process and form the basis for understanding the student and determining educational needs; and (5) current plans and goals developed are viewed as a stepping stone for reaching dreams and plans for the future. (Chambers & Childre, 2005, p. 22)

Student Form

Who I Am:

My friends are _____.

I like to _____
with my friends. I (do/do not) want more friends.

For fun away from school (or at school) I like to _____.
To help at home (or at school) I get to _____.

I really want to do _____
at home (or at school), but I do not get to.

At school I am learning to _____.

I would like to learn to _____.

When I grow up, I want to _____.

Preferences:

I like to spend time with _____.

Things I like (do not like) to do are _____

_____

_____

_____

_____

_____.

I get happy (mad, sad, or frustrated) when _____

_____.

I am afraid of _____.

My favorite thing about myself is _____.

I am good at _____.

All on my own I get to do (or decide) _____

_____

_____

_____

_____

_____.

Source: Adapted from Chambers and Childre (2005, p. 24).

Family Form

Family Members Interviewed: _____

Interviewed by:_____Date: _____

Life Connections:
Identify people involved with your child and the role they play in your child's life. Include family, individuals in the community, service providers, and others. What are the most important relationships for your child? Are there relationships that your child does not have that you would like to develop?

_____

_____

_____

_____

_____

_____

_____

_____

_____

Dreams:
What dreams do you or your child have for your child this year, next year, or for far in the future? Share dreams about any area from friendships to academic skills or anything you want your child to be able to do.

_____

_____

_____

_____

_____

_____

_____

_____

_____

Goals:
We need to set goals to help your child achieve the dreams your family has identified. What skills will help us reach those dreams? What needs does your child have now? Identify what is important for your child to learn now. Consider skill areas such as social/behavioral, self-help, academics, communication, motor, or other.

_____

_____

_____

_____

_____

_____

_____

_____

_____

Source: Adapted from Chambers and Childre (2005, p. 23).

Team Form

Team members present (include primary contact information):

_____

_____

_____

_____

_____

_____

_____Date:_____

Life Connections *(Include information from Family form)*:
Consider relationships the family identifies. Share any additional relationships not identified by the family. Who/what are important persons, services, or organizations that currently support the child? Are there relationships to expand or to minimize?

_____

_____

_____

_____

_____

Community Survey:
Identify skills that need to be targeted in natural or community environments. Determine places in the community that the family frequents that may be potential teaching environments (e.g., restaurants, parks).

_____

_____

_____

_____

_____

Now:
Generate an ability-focused present level of functioning. What are the child's strengths, abilities, and preferences? What are the child's accomplishments? Do not focus on problems or weaknesses but do problem-solve how to address any issues that do exist._____

_____

_____

_____

_____

_____

What Works:
Prompt team members to share information from their experiences about what supports child learning and creates a positive educational experience. Consider areas specific to the child's need (e.g., instruction, communication, adaptive equipment, behavior)._____

_____
_____
_____
_____
_____

Dreams *(include information from Family form)*:
Team form: What are the family's and child's dreams? Create a picture of the future. If a dream seems unrealistic, discuss to discover the motivation behind the dream. This step can be used to identify attainable goals._____

_____
_____
_____
_____
_____

Goals *(include information from Family form)*:
Utilizing information from the prior forms, determine goals to target. Consider: (1) What knowledge does the child need to acquire? (2) What skills does the child need to develop? and (3) What relationships does the child need to maintain or build? _____

_____
_____
_____
_____
_____

Where, Who, & When:
Determine: Where will services take place? Who are the individuals involved in the child's educational program and what are their responsibilities? What is the child's role? When will each team member accomplish and report on identified responsibilities?_____

_____
_____
_____
_____
_____

Source: Adapted from Chambers and Childre (2005, p. 25).

In their "True Directions" model, Chambers and Childre (2005) recommended first meeting with the family to fill out several family-oriented forms, "Life Connections," "Dreams," and "Goals," and to work with the child and their family to fill out several student forms, "Who I Am" and "Preferences."

When the planning team comes together, they would use the information already gathered, as well as several additional forms, "Community Survey," "Now," "What Works," and "Where, Who, & When" to identify not only the goals that will best help the child to participate in natural and inclusive settings over the coming year but also will bring that child closer to a lifetime of meaningful participation (Chambers & Childre, 2005).

FOCUSING ON FUNCTIONAL SKILLS

Once the team has identified family-guided priorities for intervention that will strengthen family functioning and promote lifelong participation within inclusive settings, the team can work together to develop the specific goals and objectives that will lead to longer-term success for the student. Using "keystone behaviors (skills that serve as prerequisites to other skills or skills on which other important skills depend)" (Wolery, 2004, p. 532) as the foundational skills that will foster competence in other skills is one way to ensure that the goals will be useful. Well-written goals are an essential component of good teaching.

Writing generative, functional, measurable goals   Goals and objectives for all children should be observable, measurable, positive, and attainable. If you can't describe what you want to see and how you'll know when you see it, it will be nearly impossible to know when you've attained success!

* *OBSERVABLE*—Writing a goal as an observable behavior, or one that can be observed and recognized by multiple team members, is difficult, but it is critical to developing goals that can be tracked for progress monitoring. Coming to agreement among team members is important, since different providers could be talking about different behaviors and *think* that they're talking about the same behavior, which would lead to inaccurate data.

Consider the following scenario: A **team wants to see appropriate behavior increase during circle time. What does "appropriate behavior" look like? Is simply sitting in the circle appropriate? Should the child be responding to teacher questions? Should the child be looking at the teacher or book? Do we expect the child to be silent or to verbally (or otherwise) participate in songs and activities with repetitive phrases? Do we expect hands to be in laps,** or is it appropriate for a child to use a fidget toy? Can the child be participating in circle time if he or she is not sitting but standing or pacing near the circle? You can see how different team members could easily be looking for different behaviors, and so their data on the child's observable behavior would look very different, based on what they are looking for. Coming to a team agreement about what behaviors comprise "appropriate behavior" will allow the team to be consistent in its data collection, but more importantly, in its expectations and the behaviors which team members teach and reinforce in the child.

• MEASURABLE—Once a skill or behavior has been defined so that all team members agree upon the definition and will all know it when they see it (observable), discussion will turn to measurement. How do we measure a skill? It is easy to use descriptive words and phrases like "increase," "decrease," "better," "well," "more quickly," "with less assistance," and "independently," but these words have little meaning when we are doing progress monitoring. A team might subjectively believe that a child is increasing time spent close to peers, but without having some way to objectively measure that behavior, it will be just that, subjective—which is not enough in the current climate of accountability and record-keeping. There are various ways to measure skills; the team should consider which standard of measurement will give the best information relative to development of the particular goal in question. Length of time doing a behavior or length of time between a prompt and the start of the behavior, number of instances of a behavior during a certain amount of time, number of instances of successful behavior within a number of opportunities to display the behavior, amount of assistance or prompting required (agree beforehand exactly what the different levels of assistance would look like), number of steps within a specific routine which a child can complete: All these are various ways to measure progress toward identified goals.

Consider the same scenario: **How do we measure the child's appropriate behavior? Do we time how long the child spends sitting, standing, or pacing, in or close to the circle (how close does the child need to be to "get credit" for the behavior)? Do we count the number of times the child responds to a teacher's questions, and does he or she get credit for echolalic responses? Do we count the number of minutes that the child appears to be looking toward the teacher or book, and does the child get credit for only whole minutes when he or she looked for the entire minute, or does it count if the child glanced and then looked away? Does the child get credit for independence when he or she follows a teacher-given direction that was given to the entire group, or will that count as a "verbal prompt" if** no additional assistance is needed? (Remember that in classroom settings, children are often given group directions. Many typically developing children may need a gesture to remember where they are supposed to go next. Are we holding our student with autism to a higher standard than what we would expect for the typically developing peers in a classroom?) Again, you can see that different measuring and data collection systems could be helpful in monitoring progress in this scenario, but unless team members know what they are tracking and how they are measuring it, ultimately, it will be difficult to objectively show that progress.

• *POSITIVE*—Although it may be relatively easy for team members to identify what they would like to see a child do fewer, especially when the child is currently engaging in challenging behavior or is not maintaining attention to tasks, it is more helpful for team members to identify and define goals in terms of the positive behaviors which they would like to see the child display. Using positive language to define what a child is working to achieve is much more useful than writing what the child will stop doing or decrease. Not only does this give us something to strive for, but it significantly changes the tone of the team, the intervention, and the documentation.

Consider again the circle time scenario: **How does your impression of the child change based on the following goal statements?**

"A will respond to peer greeting and will remain seated next to peers during adult-led story time." "A will not leave the group when a peer greets him, and he will decrease the number of times he leaves group during adult-led story time."

Which of these children would you rather work with? What is your perception of them as capable of participating in group activities with peers? Words are powerful; they shape ideas and beliefs, and it is crucial that we use our words in a positive way to create a belief that our children with autism are competent and capable.

• *ATTAINABLE*—When making New Years' resolutions, we often doom ourselves to failure by making the goals unattainable, or less often, by making them too simple to achieve! Saying that we want to lose 100 pounds may be setting the bar too high, while if we say we want to lose 2 pounds, it may be such a slight improvement that it does not bring us closer to our overall ambition. Because goals are usually written in IEPs and IFSPs as longer-term benchmarks to be monitored every 6 to 12 months, it is reasonable to set the bar high, keeping in mind what we think the child is capable of doing, given his or her strengths, if we can adequately motivate the child and engage him or her in learning. Objectives are the stepping-stones that are the means of reaching those longer-term goals. Consider what the child can currently do with assistance and what you would like for that child to do longer, better, or more independently. Starting with what the child can do is the easiest way to keep our goals attainable.

Consider the behavior scenario once again: The goals that we write for appropriate behavior will vary greatly depending on the current abilities of the child. For a child who often wanders around the class-room and is not currently attending to any one activity for longer than a few seconds, has no functional means of communication and often engages in challenging behavior, would it be appropriate to have a goal for him to independently remain in the group area with peers and actively engage in group activities for the entire 20-minute circle time period? Conversely, for a child who currently shows an interest in peers, is communicating using a combination of picture icons and two- to three-word phrases, can remain engaged in activities from 5 to 10 minutes, depending upon his preferences, and demonstrates challenging behavior when adult interaction decreases, would it be appropriate to have a goal for him to sit near the other children for 5 minutes (without including goals for interacting with the other chil-dren and actively participating in group activities with the teacher)? The one may be setting the child and the team up for failure, and the other may be too low—reachable within a week or two and not helping the child to substantially make progress based on his current interests and abilities. For goals that seem unreachable in the monitoring time available, look at how to break that goal down. Is there some part of it that is reasonable to work toward? If the team and the child feel that they are failing, it is difficult to keep momentum going to continue working toward a goal. By setting attainable goals that will take some time to reach, the child will have many opportunities to be successful.

As you may be coming to realize, developing appropriate and mean-ingful goals for children with autism is no easy task, but considering the large amount of time and resources that are spent on intervention, it is crucial that teams spend the time to proactively develop goals that will be observable, measurable, positive, and attainable. Ideally, goals devel-oped for young children with autism will, in addition, be generative and functional.

Generative goals are often set to increase foundational, or keystone, behaviors of children. Again, keystone behaviors "represent relatively narrow targets for change that have the possibility of widespread benefits to clients" (Barnett, 2005, p. 279). For instance, increasing the length of time that a child will sit down at a table can then lead to benefits across multiple activities and settings: lengthening time spent in proximity to peers at a table, enabling family members to spend mealtimes sitting down together which may in turn lead to better motor skills associated with eating and increased opportunities for social interaction among family members, and increasing the length of time when the child will be physically located in proximity to specific learning activities. Some other keystone behaviors to consider as targets for intervention include making requests, asking for help, following simple directions, imitating motor actions, imitating verbalizations, or using a visual schedule. Making requests and asking for help can be done verbally, but if any child is not consistently using vocalizations and/or verbalizations, the team's first and most important goal is to find or develop a communication system that enables the child to have a voice, and therefore, choices, within his or her world. For a child who is using sounds, words, and phrases, but not in a way that is meaningful for others, encouraging imitation of verbalizations (with or without supplemental forms of communication) can teach the child to use language as a useful tool. Each of these skills can be taught, practiced, and generalized across settings, materials, activities, and communication partners. They are also prerequisite skills for many, if not most, other skills which we may want to teach across a child's day; motor imitation is one example of an early skill upon which other skills are founded. If a child can imitate what a teacher or peer does, he or she is able to learn through peer and adult modeling.

Goals are functional when they serve a purpose. As mentioned previously, having team members identify their dreams for the child gives the team a destination to head toward, and functional goals will act as road signs directing the child and the team to continue down the correct path to reach that destination. For example, goals related to interactions and relationships with peers are usually functional, because they serve the purpose of increasing the child's comfort and acceptance within inclusive environments, which would generally be one of the dreams for parents and other team members.

Another way to ensure that goals are written in such a way that they lead to desired outcomes is to use the S.M.A.R.T. goal acronym as a reference to remember to make goals Specific, Measurable, Attainable/Achievable, Relevant/Realistic, and Timely. S.M.A.R.T. goals are increasingly used in business settings, and they are equally useful in educational and intervention settings. The website S.M.A.R.T. goals (2010) describes the following aspects:

- Specific—The goal should identify a specific action or event that will take place. It answers the questions "who?" and "what?"
- Measurable—Include in the specific goal statement the measurements to be used to determine that the results or outcomes expected have been achieved. It answers the question "how?"
- Attainable—Goals should challenge people to do their best, but they need also be achievable.

Leroy's team met with his parents and completed an RBI to ascertain what goals might be helpful at home. His mother has identified that he currently "grazes" throughout the day and does not sit down to eat during mealtimes. Teachers from Leroy's preschool class note that he routinely sits down to eat a snack at the appropriate time when he is at school. The team decides to include a goal which supports Leroy, to generalize his ability to sit down to eat, in the home setting. Baseline data is gathered by the parents and a home provider as to Leroy's current mealtime behavior at home and by his teachers as to his behavior at snack time. A 6-month goal is written: "Leroy will sit at the table and remain seated for 10 minutes during mealtimes, five of seven opportunities over two weeks." The team identifies environmental supports that are present in the school setting and work with the parents to implement the following: visual supports (a placemat with Leroy's name, in the same color as his placemat at school and a simple First/Then schedule that shows eating and then a somewhat less-preferred activity, so that he is less likely to rush away from the table to get to a favorite TV show), physical support (a footstool for him to rest his feet on, so that he has appropriate postural support and is more able to concentrate on eating), a timer so that he knows when time is up, and an increase in the parents' verbal reinforcement of his appropriate sitting and eating behavior.

After 5 months, Leroy is consistently sitting at the table for 8 minutes during mealtimes and his mother tells his teacher that for the first time in several years, she invited Leroy's grandmother to their home for a meal. Leroy's grandmother commented on how much better Leroy was doing and on "what a good job" she was doing as a mother. By the next IEP meeting, not only had Leroy met this goal of sitting during mealtimes, but Leroy's mother reported that she felt more supported by the members of their extended family.

Was the goal observable (can you see whether or not Leroy is sitting at the table during mealtimes)? Can a team member take data and measure how long he sits and how many times he is successful based on the number of opportunities (times when the family sat at the table for a meal)? Was the goal phrased in positive language? What other settings (materials, activities, and people) might this goal generalize to? Will this goal make it possible for Leroy and his family to participate more fully within their extended family and community? Does it increase others' perception of Leroy as competent?

- **R**elevant—Goals need to pertain directly to the performance challenge being managed.
- Timely—There should be enough time to achieve the goal but not too much time, which can affect performance. It answers the question "when?"

Addressing core deficits related to autism. To obtain a diagnosis of autism, an individual must exhibit characteristics to meet the criteria identified by the American Psychiatric Association. Essentially, a person with autism exhibits challenges related to social interaction, communication, and restricted interests and/or repetitive patterns of behavior. For most children with autism, goals should address those areas that are identified as the core deficits. Goal areas that will support the child in independently participating in home, school, and community settings include the following: increased and more flexible social interaction, increased and more complex language and communication, and more flexible and complex play patterns in a larger number of interest areas (see Chapters 1 & 5).

USING AUTISM-SPECIFIC CURRICULA

There are several curricula currently available that target the skills which are often more challenging for our students with autism. Once the family and team have identified goals which will positively affect the child's ability to interact within his or her current environments and which will promote the child's ability to function more independently, these autism-specific curricula can further guide intervention, both by breaking down goals into smaller objectives and often, by giving specific teaching strategies for those skills and goals. The team can use the curricula for initial assessment across the core symptomatology of autism, for setting specific goals and objectives and having a planned and structured strategy for teaching the skills to reach those goals, and then for periodic progress monitoring to ensure that the child is reaching the goals set. These curricula also can be used to identify and address gaps in skills and knowledge. It is not uncommon for children with autism to display strengths in some skills, such as reading or visual-spatial activities, without demonstrating mastery of prerequisite skills.

Using the STAR (Strategies for Teaching Based on Autism Research) program. This curricula combines principles of applied behavior analysis (ABA), using discrete trial training (DTT) and pivotal response treatment (PRT) strategies, and embeds instruction into functional routines (Arick, Loos, Falco, & Krug, 2005). The STAR program includes detailed lesson plans, teaching materials, data systems, and a curriculum-based assessment. The STAR program addresses the following six curricular areas: receptive language, expressive language, spontaneous language, functional routines, academics, and play and social skills. Arick and colleagues (2005) developed this curriculum based on over 30 years of research into best-practices teaching strategies for students with autism; it was designed to be used in classrooms. The efficacy of this program has been reviewed in several journal articles: "The data show that many of the students have made significant progress in the areas of social interaction, expressive speech, and adaptive language concepts" (Arick et al., 2003, p. 83). Odom, Boyd, Hall, and Hume (2010) evaluated a number of comprehensive treatment models across several dimensions, and the STAR model received the highest rating of 5 for operationalization and replication and a high rating of 4 for outcome data (p. 431).

ABLLS-R (Assessment of Basic Language and Learning Skills-Revised)

[T]he ABLLS-R is an assessment, curriculum guide and skills tracking system for children with language delays. The assessment enables you to identify a young learner's skills and deficits in order to establish a baseline and structure an IEP. It contains a task analysis of the many skills crucial to successful communication and to learning from everyday experiences. The first book in this two-book package is The ABLLS-R Guide that contains scoring instructions and information on how to complete the skills tracking information contained in the assessment. The Guide also presents strategies that enable parents, educators and professionals to use the information obtained from the completed assessment to develop an effective Individualized Education Program that is tailored to each student's unique needs. The Protocol provides criterion-referenced information regarding a child's current skills, along with a curriculum that can serve as the basis for the selection of educational objectives. A set of grids is also included to provide a skills tracking system that allows parents and professionals to document a child's progress and their acquisition of critical skills. (Different Roads to Learning, 2008, n.p.)

The ABLLS-R (Partington, 2006) assesses the child's language and learning skills to use in the development of an instructional program. The ABLLS-R is a complete curriculum for children with autism because it includes assessment, curriculum guides (i.e., content to teach), and progress monitoring systems. The curriculum guide includes task analyses for many communication and adaptive skills. The content and structure of the ABLLS-R is based on the verbal behavior approach (Skinner, 1957) and is consistent with the principles of behavior analysis. As with other curricula, the ABLLS-R is not a norm-referenced assessment; it does not compare across children. Furthermore, the ABLLS-R is not a diagnostic tool; it does not diagnose autism. It does provide content across 25 categories of behavior, which are consistent with the core symptomatology of autism (e.g., imitation, communication, social skills, play). Assessment information is primarily gathered from direct observation in natural settings. The assessment results will be used to identify goals and instructional strategies for the child. The ABLLS-R allows for goals to be set in increments that are meaningful for the child and directly result in learning new skills. For example, Section E focuses on vocal imitation. The skills progress in meaningful increments: imitating base sounds, imitating sound combinations, imitating words, matching the model, imitating phrases, and so forth. The skill tracking system allows parents and professionals to monitor the child's progress, acquisition, and fluency of skills. The ABLLS-R is appropriate for children ages 3–9 with autism; however, it can easily work with children with other developmental disabilities. The ABLLS-R can be completed by parents or professionals who have a basic understanding of behavioral principles. Preliminary psychometric data on the ABLLS-R indicate that typically developing children demonstrate most of the basic skills by the time they are 3 years old; however, there is considerable individual variation across typically developing children. The authors emphasize caution in interpretations of this initial data due to a small sample size (n=81). Research is currently underway examining the sequence of skill acquisition, which will be important for developing goals with young children with autism. Finally, the ABLLS-R is available in English and Spanish and in paper and online versions (all versions are available at http://www.behavioranalysts.com/).

VB-MAPP (Verbal Behavior Milestones Assessment and Placement Program)

The VB-MAPP represents a major improvement over existing materials as its assessment items represent milestones achieved in typical development and it is linked conceptually and procedurally to a "verbal behavior" analysis of the function of language. A verbal behavior approach to language represents a full application of behavioral principles to language and is something that has been lacking in previous EIBI [Early Intensive Behavior Intervention] curricula (Sundberg & Michael, 2001). While the main focus of the VB-MAPP is on assessing language abilities, it also assesses aspects of motor, play, social, and academic skills. (Dixon, Tarbox, Najdowski, Wilke, & Granpeesheh, 2011, p. 507)

The VB-MAPP was developed by Dr. Mark Sundberg in 2008 and consists of a protocol booklet which can be used to assess and track attainment of milestones by individual students, as well as a guide which gives more detailed information on each of those milestones and how to use this assessment tool. In addition to milestones across multiple domains, including functional communication, play, social interaction, and early academics, this system also includes an assessment of what type of barriers to learning are currently displayed, such as challenging behaviors used to avoid challenging tasks, a "Transition Scoring Form," which looks at multiple skills that may be helpful in determining placements that will provide the best level of support for the student, and finally, sections to develop functional and meaningful goals and objectives based on the information gained through this assessment tool. It is a criterion-referenced assessment tool that is meant to be used over time to track progress over different domains. The VB-MAPP may be especially helpful when working with individuals with autism whose primary needs are in the areas of social interaction, communication, play, or adaptive skills. Currently, psychometric characteristics of the VB-MAPP are not reported.

There are many gradations of skill levels, which allow for good sensitivity. Also, it gives information relative to a student's strengths, which then guides intervention strategies to work toward goals and objectives. For instance, a child who shows strong echoic skills but weaker imitation skills may be a good candidate for using verbal models when teaching requesting, whereas a child with weak echoic and vocal skills but stronger imitation skills may benefit more from an intervention approach that uses a Picture Exchange Communication System (PECS; Frost & Bondy, 2002) or sign language. Likewise, for a child who shows strong beginning reading skills and demonstrates an interest in printed material during assessment observations, a teacher might want to gear interventions in adaptive skills to using stories with favorite characters and reinforcement systems that use letters and books. The barriers assessment portion of the VB-MAPP helps teachers and interventionists to prioritize goals, since teaching functional replacement behaviors as a way to remove those barriers will then facilitate learning in other areas, making these important, generative goals.

The VB-MAPP can be used with individuals of any age to ascertain whether they have met milestones primarily related to functional use of communication as well as foundational play, social interaction, and cognitive skills. Because the milestones assessed are directly linked to domains which are, by definition, challenging for people on the autism spectrum, it is a particularly helpful tool for assessing individuals with autism spectrum disorders. Since the VB-MAPP also breaks down these milestones into supportive skills, this program can be used as an intervention curriculum with shorter-term objectives as well as long-term goals. This assessment is useful in identifying areas in which an individual will benefit from more intensive and direct teaching of skills. The visual scoring form also makes it easy to see clearly where an individual has strengths; this can help to guide how we present new material.

ADDRESSING ACADEMIC SKILLS

The beliefs of team members provide an important foundation to the success of the child with autism. As the team drafts goals to be addressed in the school environment, it is important that individual team members share some core beliefs that "seem to be critical to the success of all students:

- All students can think and learn.
- All students have value and unique gifts to offer their school.
- Diversity within a school community should be embraced and celebrated.
- All students differ in the ways they most effectively learn and express their understandings.

- All students learn best when they are actively and collaboratively building knowledge with their classmates and their teacher.
- All students learn best when studying interesting and challenging topics that they find personally meaningful.
- Effective teaching for students with disabilities is substantively the same as effective teaching for all students." (Jorgensen, 2003, p. 15)

Consider school readiness. As mentioned earlier, the VB-MAPP provides a Transition Scoring Form which is designed to assess the student's ability to access information and learn in different types of instructional settings; this information is certainly valuable to understand what types of settings are optimal and which ones may present challenges for the goal setting team to proactively plan to overcome. To that end, educators can consider the "goodness-of-fit" of the student to the available educational settings and how they can promote inclusion of all students by planning for environmental changes and levels of support that will benefit the student with autism, as well as his or her peers.

There is a large body of research-based evidence that all children benefit from education in inclusive settings; it is also clear that students with autism benefit from multiple types of support. As team members consider the unique strengths and challenges of the student, they will also want to consider what types of classroom and intervention settings are available and also what levels of support will be most appropriate for the student across the school day. Castagnera et al. (2003) described the different types of support that can be provided within an inclusive classroom; support provided by staff other than the teacher can range from full-time support, to scheduled support, to intermittent support. In all cases, it is helpful to utilize different support staff, to assist the student to interact with various adults. When support personnel are in a general classroom with a student fulltime, they should intentionally provide support to other students, so that the student with autism has an opportunity to learn directly from the teacher and also so that the paraprofessional does not become a barrier to peers' interactions with the student with autism. During scheduled support, an additional staff member would be in the general education setting during periods that are known, or suspected, to be challenging for the child; they could also be providing individual or small-group intervention for specific goals. Intermittent support is provided when a student suddenly needs additional assistance, whether this is for redirection to address a behavioral challenge or for some sort of educational support, such as scribing for a student during a spelling test. The takeaway message is that a single student will often benefit from different levels of support throughout the school day, and it is the team's responsibility to not only address those times when more support will be needed but also to identify those periods of time when the student can experience success with less intense supports in place.

Jim's general-education classroom teacher, Ms. Mayes, enjoys having him in her class, but she isn't sure how he can work toward some of his IEP goals when she has so much academic content that she needs to teach before the yearly state assessments take place.

Using the "Infused Skills Grid," she decides that she can plan for him to participate in the morning check-in period in a way that encourages growth in two of his IEP goals: to greet peers and to verbally participate in group activities. Using the student profile, she knew that Jim showed strengths in typing and reading aloud and that he appeared to show an interest in one of his classroom peers, Maggie.

Each morning, Ms. Mayes gave the entire class a general question to answer (e.g., "What did you have for dinner last night?"), and initially, Jim was not answering when she asked him the question. Ms. Mayes changed the structure of the check-in so that students needed to pair and share and then report back to the class their partner's answer. Jim was paired with Maggie, and he was prompted to ask Maggie the question of the day, which Ms. Mayes had written out for him. He was then directed to type out her answer, and he reported her answer when the class came back together. Maggie got to ask Ms. Mayes the question of the day. After several weeks of teaching Jim the new routine and reinforcing his participation, the pairs were changed, and Jim got to practice the new routine with another peer. Several peers indicated an interest in being paired with Jim, because they liked to watch him type their answer, and they enjoyed getting to ask their teacher the question of the day. After several more weeks, Jim was given a choice of which peer to ask the question; next he was instructed to find out what two peers' answers were; by the end of the school year, Jim was asking the question of five peers each morning, and he was beginning to answer the question when it related to a concrete/tangible item. Jim now had a way to actively and successfully participate in the group activity, and he was routinely getting multiple opportunities to practice greeting his peers, asking them questions and listening to their answers.

On the following pages, you will find several forms that can be used to plan for how and when a student will work on his or her goals throughout the school day. Using the Infused Skills Grid enables the team to identify the different routines, activities, centers, or classes in which a child participates and which goals can be targeted and practiced in each. Across the top of the form, the IEP or IFSP identified goals are listed, and the different activities are listed down the left side of the page; it is primarily used to identify when a goal can be addressed, without specifying strategies. This form can be helpful to hand to staff members who say that "my class is academic; I don't have time to work on IEP goals." The bottom of the form includes a student profile; it outlines strengths and interests, successful learning strategies, communication and positive behavior supports, accommodations and modifications that will be helpful to each teacher.

Infused Goals Grid and Student Profile

Student Name:

Age:

Grade:

Parent/Guardian:

Sponsor Teacher:

Educational Team Members:

Schedule or Activities	Goals or Objectives								
	Goal:	Goal:	Goal:	Goal:	Goal:	Goal:	Goal:	Goal:	Goal:
1									
2									
3									
4									
5									
6									
7									
8									
9									
10									

Student's Strengths (social, academic, communication, etc.):

Student's Special Interests (topics, subjects, pop culture, etc.):

Successful Learning Strategies, Modifications/Adaptations/Accommodations Needed:

Communication Strategies (expressive and receptive):

Positive Behavior Support Strategies and Specific Reinforcers:

Grading and Assessment Accommodations:

Student Academic Unit Planning Form

Student Name:

Age:

Grade:

Parent/Guardian:

Sponsor Teacher:

Educational Team Members:

Class:	Unit:

State or class standards or learning objectives:

Materials (books, worksheets, software, videos, etc.):	Accommodations/Modifications to materials:
Instructional methods (large and small group, learning centers, individual learning, team or pair work):	Accommodations/Modifications to teaching methods:
Projects, activities, homework:	Accommodations/Modifications:
Interim assessments (i.e., quizzes) and final products/assessments:	Alternative ways for student to demonstrate mastery of objectives:

Aligning with state grade level standards

To Preschool To Preschool Song

Phonological/Phonemic Awareness Lesson Plan

Colorado Academic Standard Addressed:

Reading, Writing, and Communicating (Oral Expression and Listening): Early knowledge of phonemic awareness is the building block of understanding language.

Learning Objectives:

According to their ability level, children will:

- Sing/recite the repetitive lyrics of the two versions of the song
- Use the visual cue to identify the first word in the rhyming pair
- Use the repeated pattern in the song to predict second (nonsense) word in rhyming pair

   Setting: "To Market To Market" nursery song will first be taught in large group (facilitated by 2 coteachers) of 15 children; in teacher-facilitated small group of 7–8 children, new version will be introduced.

Activity Procedure:

In Large Group:

1. Teacher will indicate that it is time to learn a new song.
2. Teacher will point to the song lyrics as she models singing the first verse, pointing to the picture of the pig while emphasizing the word "pig."
3. Teacher also emphasizes the rhyming word "jig" and then asks the children how the words "pig" and "jig" are alike; teacher facilitates discussion of rhyming sounds.

4. Teacher asks children what sound "jig" starts with, models sound if needed, and tells children we're going to make more rhyming words in the song using the /j/ sound.

5. Continue with other verses, using visual cues and emphasizing the /j/ sound to facilitate rhyming nonsense words.

Activity Procedure, continued:

In Small Group:

1. As children come to the table, teacher leads several verses of "To Market To Market" nursery song.

2. Once all children are seated and have had the opportunity to join in at least one verse of the song, teacher tells them that we are going to make our own song book using our names to rhyme.

3. Teacher demonstrates gluing her photo onto construction paper above the preprinted words, printing her name on the first line and sings the song using her name:

"To preschool, to preschool to see _____,

Home again, Home again, jiggety J_____"

4. Teacher asks each child to find their picture and glue it on a piece of construction paper and then asks each child to sing the song using their own name (teacher and other children can join in on repeated words and encourage others to let child sing own name and rhyme on their own).

5. Each child has time to write their name on the construction paper, while friends are singing or afterward.

6. After class, teachers will bring together all of the pages and laminate them to create a class song book for the library (if any children were absent during small group, a teacher will work with them during centers time later in the week to ensure that all children are represented in the class book).

Adaptations:

The child will be encouraged to join in song by clapping hands and vocalizing/verbalizing (adults to socially reinforce any attempt to vocalize during any version of the song)—after watching and listening to peers sing their names and rhymes, when it is his turn, give extra wait time to see if he tries to vocalize his name, if not, sing it slowly and with emphasis. In small group, the child will also be encouraged/reinforced for participating in the song. He will be given one direction at a time to a) get picture of himself , b) put glue on back, c) turn it over and press on, and d) write his name (any written representation will be accepted).

Assessment:

Teacher will note next to child's name if they participated in singing, if they were noted to identify first word using visual cue, and if they attempted to rhyme any of the words (there will also be an opportunity to note this in small group); in small group, their participation with new version of the song and ability to rhyme their name will also be noted. Following is a sample checklist which will be filled out for all children in class.

Name	Participated in nursery song (L = Listen, + = Listen and sing/clap)	Uses visual cue to sing first word	Attempts to rhyme word (+ = rhyming word; P = part of word or same word)	Participated in new version of song	Attempts to rhyme own name (+ = rhyming word; P = part of word or same word)
XXX					

Source: Adapted from Castagnera, Fisher, Rodifer, Sax, and Frey (2003, p. 47).

Notice that information is stated in the positive, to increase all staff members' perceptions of the student as competent and able to learn.

The Academic Unit Lesson Plan is most helpful as students enter elementary grades where they become involved with more specific academic classes. The teacher can use the form to plan ahead for accommodations and modifications that may be needed for different aspects of the unit, including materials, learning settings, activities, and assessments. As we note in the next section, it is imperative that teachers be mindful of the state academic standards to which all students are held accountable. By using an Academic Unit Lesson Planning form, the teachers and interventionists on the team plan for instruction of the appropriate academic curricula.

The Academic Unit Lesson Plan also has a section to identify the major standards to be addressed in the unit. Because all educational systems are currently involved with a high level of assessment to meet No Child Left Behind guidelines, most teaching staff are expected to ensure that their students attain some level of familiarity with specific academic curricula. This is equally important for students with autism. If a particular topic has been deemed to be important knowledge for a student to have by the time he or she leaves school, then certainly it would be equally important for a person with autism to have that knowledge as well. For this reason, it is critical for teams working with students with autism to keep informed of standards required for general education students, so that they can identify ways in which the student with autism can interact with materials and gain knowledge in a given area.

Teachers and other service providers will need to be intentional in planning while preparing learning objectives that align with state standards and also in creating adaptations and/or modifications to the activities so that the child with autism can participate in meaningful curricula. The previous example of an academic unit lesson plan shows how a teacher might organize a learning activity for all children while thoughtfully planning for the inclusion of a child with autism.

FUTURE DIRECTIONS

It is our firm belief that functional, generative, family-guided goals are an essential component of an instructional plan. In this chapter, we provided examples of tools that can be used to work with families and children with autism, to provide goals and objectives to support their independent participation at home, school, and in communities. It may be hard to visualize the young child with whom you are working as a high school student or young adult, but the goals you set for the child today will largely affect that child's future. Effective goals are an essential, critical component of education programs for children with autism. The next two chapters describe strategies for developing and evaluating instructional plans for children with autism. Chapter 5 provides an overview of additional essential components of education programs for children with autism. Chapter 6 provides an overview of designing and evaluating instructional programs for individual children.

This chapter has discussed the need for goal setting to be a team effort and the importance of including families in all phases of goal setting, including information gathering, prioritizing, and developing functional goals that will be relevant across different settings in which the child with autism participates. The authors recognize that, for most intervention teams, policies and budgets in place at the systems level of their organizations may dictate the amount of time that can be spent on team meetings and goal setting. Practitioners may therefore need to be creative in developing procedures and strategies to include families and to spend adequate time on setting goals that will truly move the student toward a future with a higher quality of life. As change agents, practitioners will need to work together with their administrators to create systems change to accommodate for time and resources to be applied to this critical element of the intervention process.

LEARNING ACTIVITIES

1. Conduct a semistructured interview focused on the child and family's daily routines with a classmate or friend who has a young child. Consider times of day, general daily routines (mealtimes, school or daycare, chores, self-care, frequent outings, etc.) as you use open-ended questions to develop an understanding of "a day in the life."(You can use the "About Our Young Child" or "About Our Elementary-Aged Child" questionnaires to structure the interview.) Based on the information you gain, are there routines that could be developed or improved upon?

2. Using one of the case studies in this book, or a child with whom you work, fill out a Reinforcement Inventory. How can you use this information to plan for teaching opportunities?

3. Consider yourself or your own family; draw a "Circle of Support" and an eco-map to visually represent the connections and supports. Are you surprised at the number of connections you have? Can you identify any persons or groups who you would like to bring into a closer circle or with whom you would like to strengthen the connection? Identify strategies to make that happen.

4. Using one of the case studies in this book, outline three goals that would address the core issues related to the child's autism spectrum disorder. Go back and review each goal to see if it meets the S.M.A.R.T. goal criteria. Are there any areas that you want to practice, to improve upon?

RESOURCES

The following forms can be downloaded from the Siskin Children's Institute at http://www.siskin.org:

Scale for the Assessment of Teachers' Impressions of Routines and Engagement (SATIRE) by Beth T. Clingenpeel and R. A. McWilliam (2003): an eight-page form to work with childcare and preschool staff to determine "goodness of fit" between target child and center-based routines and expectations. http://www.siskin.org/downloads/SATIRE.pdf

Vanderbilt Ecological Congruence of Teaching Opportunities in Routines (VECTOR) classroom version by Amy M. Casey, Peggy J. Freund, and R. A. McWilliam (2004): a four-page form to assess the opportunities for children to be engaged across a number of daily routines and how often the child is taking advantage of those opportunities. http://www.siskin.org/downloads/VECTOR.pdf

RBI Report Form by R.A. McWilliam (2003, revised 2006): a 12-page form to conduct Routines-Based Interviews with families and/or school staff. http://www.siskin.org/downloads/RBI_Report_Form.pdf

The Foundation for Autism Training and Education: http://www.thefate.org.

Example of a **Reinforcer Inventory**:http://www.thefate.org/library/public_document/1%20Pairing%20with%20Reinforcement/3%20Reinforcer%20Inventory.pdf

5

Essential Components of Educational Programs

Erin E. Barton

University of Colorado Denver

Chapter Objectives

- Identify the strengths and needs of children with autism.
- Describe the characteristics of highly supportive teaching environments for children with autism.
- Describe strategies for selecting evidence-based practices.
- Identify characteristics of evidence-based practices.
- Describe strategies for conducting ongoing program evaluation.
- Describe the role of the family in educational programs for young children with autism.

The purpose of this chapter is to describe characteristics of effective curricula for children with autism and essential components of educational programs. Chapter 4 provided an overview of writing effective goals, which are a primary component of educational programs. A curriculum consists of three general components: assessment (e.g., eligibility, diagnostic, programming, progress monitoring, program evaluation), content (i.e., individual and classroom goals and objectives), and intervention strategies (i.e., evidence-based practices). Most curricula also include a scope (e.g., social emotional content, developmental skills, or teaching bilingual learners) and sequence (e.g., hierarchy of goals and objectives). Specific features of effective curricula for students with autism have been identified and include the following: (a) a focus on core content skills, (b) delivering highly structured learning environments with multiple and varied learning opportunities, (c) instruction employing evidence-based practices, (d) a functional approach to addressing challenging behaviors, (e) active family engagement, and (f) methods for ongoing, systematic progress monitoring (e.g., Dawson & Osterling, 1997; Harris & Handleman, 2000; National Research Council, 2001). Each of these is described in this chapter, which focuses on curricula for young children (ages 0–8 years); however, many of the components are relevant for children throughout elementary school. Curricula for elementary students with autism should be linked to the state grade-level standards and the student's individual needs.

CORE CURRICULAR CONTENT

Curricula for children with autism should address the core skills consistent with autism symptomology. Core content includes skills related to learning, development, and independent functioning. There are specific core skills that are considered essential content for curricula for young children with autism. Dawson and Osterling (1997) included the following as core skills for young children with autism: the ability to discriminate and attend to important information in the environment, imitation, communication, object play, and social interactions. The National Research Council (2001) included the following as core skills for children with autism: social skills, communication, engagement and participation in the environment (e.g., including classroom activities and routines), play, fine and gross motor skills, cognitive skills (e.g., symbolic play), replacement behaviors, and organizational skills. We synthesized these into six core content areas: (1) the ability to attend to relevant environmental stimuli, (2) imitation, (3) joint attention, (4) communication (using receptive and expressive language), (5) the ability to participate in daily routines and classroom activities (e.g., including play with toys), and (6) social skills.

The ability to attend to relevant stimuli. As discussed in Chapters 1 and 2, a core characteristic associated with autism is the inability to attend to and interpret environmental and social cues. This is problematic because traditional school experiences are provided in multidimensional, social interactions with various stimuli displayed simultaneously. For example, in preschool classrooms teachers instruct students to sing, participate in hand movements, and look at the calendar in front of the room. If the students are not visually attending to the teacher and calendar, they are missing many learning opportunities. These types of activities are particularly challenging for children with autism because they have attention difficulties in three main areas: (a) attending to relevant stimuli, (b) shifting attention, and (c) attention to more than one stimuli at a time. First, a variety of studies have examined eye gaze and attention in young children with autism. This research has used eye-tracking devices to examine where children attend and follow their gaze patterns when looking at still photos and faces. This research demonstrates that children with autism attend to different stimuli than children with typical development or other developmental disabilities. Children with autism or children at risk for developing autism (i.e., siblings of children with autism) spend less time looking at the eyes of faces in static pictures than children with typical development (e.g., Dalton, Nacewicz, Alexander, & Davidson, 2006; Klin, Jones, Schultz, Volkmer, & Cohen, 2002; Merin, Young, Ozonoff, & Rogers, 2006; Pelphrey, Sasson, Reznick, Paul, Goldman, & Piven, 2002). In fact, some studies have suggested a lack of eye fixation in infancy might be an early marker of autism (Merin et al., 2006). Nonetheless, this difference in focus provides one example of how children with autism attend to different social stimuli than children with typical development. This has major implications for teachers and practitioners working with children with autism. Whereas, children with typical development may follow social cues and attend to the teacher in the front of the room, or another person's facial expressions, or writing on the blackboard, or the names on the desks, or the worksheets on the table, and so forth, children with autism may have to be explicitly taught to direct their attention to relevant stimuli.

Second, children with autism also show difficulty shifting attention from one stimuli to another (Courchesne et al., 1994; Wainwright-Sharp & Bryson, 1993). This means if a child is playing with a train set in a preschool classroom, he might have difficulty attending to a verbal direction to clean up by the teacher. Additional prompts for gaining attention (e.g., proximity, physical prompt, etc.) might be necessary at first and then faded once the child is able to attend to the typical verbal prompt. This ability to shift attention is an early social milestone and typically observed in older infants (around 12–15 months).

Finally, children with autism often demonstrate a lack of attention to multiple cues or stimuli (e.g., Pierce, Glad, & Schreibman, 1997). There are a variety of ways to teach this core skill, yet, like all core skills, intervention should begin as soon as autism is suspected. Children have been taught to attend to relevant stimuli through discrete trials, incidental teaching, the use of visual schedules, and shaping.

Imitation. The ability to imitate others is an essential method for learning and generalizing new skills. Imitation is particularly important for learning social and communication skills and is a prerequisite skill for many evidence-based practices (e.g., Pivotal Response Treatments, modeling). Imitation also is important for demonstrating empathy (e.g., responding appropriately to the emotions in others) and self-regulation (e.g., regulating behavior, activity level, and emotional responses to match the environment and context). Finally, imitation skills increase the likelihood that children will learn from naturally occurring opportunities in the environment. In fact, observational learning, or teaching children to attend to and imitate the behaviors of others, is a highly effective strategy for learning new behaviors, particularly for children in inclusive classrooms (Bandura, 1977). Effective interventions for teaching imitation include discrete trials, play-based instruction, or embedded instruction (Ledford & Wolery, 2011). Effective instruction for teaching imitation should be individualized, taught within naturally occurring contexts and activities, and focused on generalization and maintenance (Wolery, 2005).

Joint attention. Joint attention also should be considered a core skill and essential content for autism curricula. As discussed in Chapter 2, a lack of joint attention in older infants and toddlers is a red flag for developmental disabilities, particularly autism. Joint attention (i.e., pointing or looking to share information; Schertz & Odom, 2004) is an early social and communication milestone for infants and toddlers. Joint attention is an early form of communication and social competence (Vaughan et al., 2003). Many infants will develop joint attention skills before the end of their first year (by 12 months). Young children with autism demonstrate delays in overall joint attention skills, and, many children with autism do not use joint attention to comment or show something of interest (Charman, Swettenham, Baron-Cohen, Cox, Baird, & Drew, 1997). Joint attention should be taught as soon as autism is suspected using shaping, prelinguistic milieu teaching (Yoder & Warren, 2002), antecedent-based interventions (modeling and prompting), and incidental teaching. Joint attention is a core skill, essential for communication and positive social interactions with peers and caregivers, and it should be included in autism curricula.

Communication. Teaching children spontaneous, functional communication in the preferred modalities (e.g., verbal, sign language or pictures) is essential for all children with autism. Communication skills are an important predictor of a range of outcomes including language, IQ, adaptive skills, and academic achievement for children with autism (Venter, Lord, & Schopler, 1992). Also, impairments in communication are likely to lead to challenging behaviors and increased family stress (Bristol, 1984). Effective instruction for teaching children to communicate begins by responding to the child's slightest communicative behavior (e.g., a look toward the juice, reaching for the cookie, moving toward the toy). In this manner, instruction is focused on teaching the child to understand communicative intent and reinforcing spontaneous language. For example, incidental teaching strategies are effective with young children with autism. When implementing incidental teaching, the adult arranges the environment (e.g., puts a preferred toy on a high shelf or a cookie in a tightly sealed plastic container) to elicit a child communicative behavior (e.g., pointing to the toy, reaching for the cookie). Once the child initiates any communicative behavior, the adult models a more sophisticated response (e.g., "help me" or "cookie, please"). Over time the child learns to initiate communication and the appropriate response. Curricula also need to focus on teaching children with autism to communicate to share events, information, or experiences. Many children with autism will not be motivated to communicate to share information or comment on things or events in the environment (Stone et al., 1997). One effective teaching strategy to promote commenting is to link the activity to the child's natural preferences and interests to maximize student motivation to use communication skills. Likewise, curricula need to focus on teaching young children with autism to understand various modalities of language (e.g., visual symbols, spoken language, written language, gestures). Chapter 9 describes evidence-based strategies for teaching communication skills.

Ability to participate in daily routines and classroom activities. The ability to participate in daily routines and classroom activities is an essential skill for children with autism. Children with autism should be taught to independently participate in the same routines and activities as their typically developing peers to maximize the potential for learning essential communication, social, and academic skills. Oftentimes this will involve making accommodations to the environment, activity, or materials to ensure the child independently participates (e.g., using a visual picture schedule to support a child in following the hand washing routine, using a timer to help a child transition inside after recess). Focusing on independent participation is the first step to independence in their communities and environments. Many children can be taught self-care skills, participation, or task completion skills using self-management strategies. For example, children with autism can be taught to use structured work systems, which increases independent task completion (Carnahan, Harte, Dyke, Hume, & Borders, 2011). Work systems are visually structured activities with clear expectations, sequence of activities, and a beginning and end. With very young children, work systems might include two or three brief activities with large visual supports. As children get older and more advanced, work systems can be modified to include more tasks, more complex skills, and less visual supports. Over time, structured work systems might be faded to resemble a written daily schedule and be socially appropriate for a school-age student with autism.

For young children, independent participation includes teaching them to play with the materials in the environment. An extensive body of research demonstrates that young children with autism exhibit less frequent and varied pretend play behaviors (e.g., Charman & Baron-Cohen, 1997; Jarrold, Boucher, & Smith, 1996; Kasari, Freeman, & Parapella, 2006). Play is an important skill for several reasons. First, play promotes inclusion in less restrictive environments. Research has shown that children who play with toys in functional, meaningful ways are more likely to be included in general education preschools and environments. In general, inclusive environments are higher quality and provide higher quality experiences with more opportunities for learning, engagement, and positive interactions with peers. Second, play occasions social and communicative interactions with peers. Young children with typical development or other disabilities spend the majority of their day engaged in play with the toys and materials in the environment. Thus, teaching children with autism to engage with the same materials in the same way increases opportunities for social interactions and learning from more advanced peers. Finally, play has practical value because it ensures children are engaged in the environment in meaningful ways and is incompatible with restricted and repetitive behavior. When children with autism engage in restricted, repetitive behaviors, it decreases their time and attention to the natural environment, minimizing social, language, and academic learning opportunities. Also, play has predictive value. Research has found that play skills in toddlers with autism predict later social and communication skills (Charman, Baron-Cohen, Swettenham, Baird, Drew, & Cox, 2003). Teaching children functional play skills decreases the likelihood that children with autism are engaging in nonfunctional, repetitive behaviors. Research indicates children with autism learn to play with systematic adult modeling. The system of least prompts is an evidence-based practice for teaching young children to increase generalized play skills (e.g., Barton & Wolery, 2008, 2010; Kasari et al., 2006; Lifter, Ellis, Cannon, & Anderson, 2005). With the system of least prompts, the adult delivers prompts from the least to most intrusive (naturally occurring prompt to hand over hand prompting) such that over time the child learns to play with the naturally occurring prompt. When teaching play, the adult delivers prompts based on what the child is doing; thus, prompts are related to the child's behaviors. The system of least prompts might be particularly suited for teaching play because the adult can deliver prompts without interrupting the play interaction. Chapter 7 describes the system of least prompts in more detail.

Social interactions. Impairments in social skills are the core symptomology of young children with autism and they influence skills across other domains (e.g., play near peers, communication). Children with delays in social skills are more likely to be placed in restrictive, segregated classrooms or environments. Furthermore, delays in social skills will have lifelong implications for independent living, job retention, and participation in families and communities. Children with autism demonstrate delays in initiating social interactions with peers and adults, interactive play with peers, turn-taking, and responding to social interactions (e.g., Freeden & Koegel, 2006). Effective programs for young children with autism focus on initiating, turn-taking, and sharing within highly structured, supportive adult interactions and gradually generalize to interacting with peers (e.g., Strain & Odom, 1986). Evidence-based practices include peer-mediated intervention (e.g., Laushey & Heflin, 2000), scripts (McClannahan & Krantz, 2005), and video modeling (e.g., Wert & Neisworth, 2003). Also, the most effective programs for young children with autism focus on developing and sustaining nurturing, positive relationships among children, practitioners, and families, rather than just discrete social skills. This includes promoting friendships between peers and teaching parents and caregivers to be responsive, sensitive, and nurturing (Fox, n.d.). See Chapter 9 for a description of evidence-based strategies for teaching social skills.

HIGHLY STRUCTURED TEACHING ENVIRONMENTS

Highly structured organized teaching environments are important for teaching new skills for many learners, in particular children with autism. Due to difficulties with attention and negotiating complex language, children with autism benefit from environments that include predictable routines, a focus on repetition, minimal distractions, and the highlighting of relevant cues and learning opportunities. As mentioned earlier, effective curricula for young children with autism include intentional strategies teaching children to attend to relevant environmental stimuli. High structured environments help children with autism attend to important features in the environment to promote learning and independence and minimize the likelihood of time to engage in nonfunctional stereotypical behavior. For example, when teaching social initiations (i.e., teaching a child with autism to request a toy from a peer or ask a peer to play), an adult might physically and verbally prompt the child to ask a peer to play in a one-on-one setting in a separate area of a classroom. As the child learns the skills, the teacher might start prompting the child to initiate with peers during free play, or outside on the playground, during a less structured activity. Dawson and Osterling (1997) found effective programs for young children with autism include providing instruction or experiences with a low student-teacher ratio such as 1:1 of 2:1. These arrangements allow adults to systematically individualize the environment to ensure children with autism learn to attend to relevant stimuli while learning "core" skills (e.g., imitation, joint attention, play, social interactions). In this manner, children with autism receive repeated, meaningful teaching opportunities to learn and practice new skills. In essence, implementing highly structured environments help children with autism "learn to learn."

Research indicates children with autism demonstrate large differences in performance levels between highly structured and complex environments (Dawson & Osterling, 1997). Thus, effective instruction for young children with autism also must focus on systematically generalizing and maintaining skills. Strategies to promote generalization include slightly adapting the materials, using new materials that serve the same function, teaching across adults or peers, teaching new activities or in a new setting, and using different cues or prompts. Generalization strategies should be individualized based on the child's learning history and the skill. Strategies to promote maintenance (e.g., continuing to perform the skill over time without prompts) include embedding instruction into naturally occurring routines and activities and systematically fading prompts or cues. See Chapter 8 for more specific strategies for generalizing and maintaining new skills. In sum, instruction for children with autism should be systematically planned and implemented to ensure that children can independently demonstrate any of the core skills across settings, activities, routines, materials, and people. To increase the likelihood of independent use of these core skills, initial teaching should occur in highly structured environments and systematically plan for generalization.

PREDICTABILITY AND ROUTINES

Predictability and routines are essential components of highly structured environments and important components of classrooms for young children with autism. Children with autism are likely to insist on strictly following routines and resist environmental changes. This is a core symptom of autism, yet true for many young children. Children benefit from predictability and routines as they learn new skills and navigate new contexts. Children with autism, however, are particularly sensitive to changes in schedules, routines, and environments (Dawson & Osterling, 1997). This insistence on sameness is likely to negatively impact opportunities for learning and can elicit negative or challenging behaviors. Thus, effective curricula for young children with autism include predictable schedules, routines, and activities, and minimal environmental changes. However, effective curricula also embed instructional opportunities that teach children with autism strategies for coping with changes and unpredictable events that are common in natural settings. For example, many children with autism struggle with the inevitable transitions between activities, which are a typical, regular part of every school day. Effective programs for young children with autism include strategies to minimize the disruption and help the child independently transition between activities. Effective strategies include using visual schedules, verbal and visual transition warnings, First/Then visual cues, or transitional objects. Oftentimes, these strategies can be paired with other goals or embedded into the routine or activity. For example, to help preschoolers with autism transition from naptime to toileting, the teacher might have a peer hand the child a visual First/Then cue (i.e., First: a picture of a toilet/Then: a picture of the computer) once the child wakes up, which helps the child understand that he will get to use the computer after he finishes in the bathroom. Involving the peer is important because it provides an opportunity for a positive social interaction with a peer, while teaching the child to independently comply with transitions and routines.

COMMITMENT TO EVIDENCE-BASED PRACTICES

Effective curricula for young children with disabilities must include a system for identifying, selecting, and implementing evidence-based practices. Although new, innovative interventions are constantly emerging, the field of autism has a large body of evidence-based practices from which practitioners can select and implement (see National Autism Center, 2009b). In fact, in recent years, researchers have published several articles, literature analyses, books, special issues of journals, practice manuals, and technical reports compiling and synthesizing the research on children with autism. However, the gap between research and practice remains large for children with autism (Dunst & Trivette, 2009; Stahmer, 2007). Evidence-based practices are informed by science and have research documenting their effectiveness (Strain & Dunlap, n.d.). Evidence-based practices integrate research, family values and priorities, professional judgment, and data-based decisions (see Figure 5.1 for examples of questions to ask of interventions). Thus, evidence-based practices are individually selected and adapted to meet the needs of the child with autism. Effective curricula allow for individual adaptations to interventions and include strategies for selecting appropriate interventions given the child and families needs, priorities, and concerns. Furthermore, evidence-based practices also have robust social validity. Social validity refers to the extent to which the goals, procedures, and outcomes are socially relevant and meaningful (Strain, Barton, & Dunlap, in press). Thus, evidence-based practices address socially important goals for the child and his or her family, involve intervention procedures that can be implemented by teachers and practitioners in natural, complex settings, and result in meaningful change for the child and family. Evidence-based practices, however, only are effective when implemented as planned. Effective curricula include procedures that are practical and reasonable and able to be implemented in natural settings (e.g., inclusive classrooms, homes, and schools). See Chapter 12 for specific strategies to maximize implementation.

Figure 5.1   Questions to Guide the Selection of Evidence-Based Practices

- Have several studies documented the practice or has the intervention been reported in peer-reviewed journals?
- Does the research support using this intervention to teach this child's goal?
- Has the research been conducted in settings similar to this child's setting?
- Does the research support generalization and maintenance of the target behaviors?
- Are there other interventions that might be more effective or efficient for this child?
- Does this intervention address the child's primary needs and utilize the child's strengths?
- Can the child's teachers or primary caregivers implement this intervention in natural settings across daily routines and activities?
- Does this intervention address the family's priorities for the child?
- Are the materials needed for this intervention readily available in the child's environment or home?
- Can the intervention be systematically faded over time to ensure the child spontaneously performs and generalizes the new skill?

FUNCTIONAL APPROACH TO PROBLEM BEHAVIORS

Young children with autism are particularly prone to challenging behaviors due to delays in communication and social skills. Effective programs for children with autism include universal preventative strategies (e.g., focus on nurturing relationships between children and adults, regular screening, and supportive environments); targeted strategies to prevent and teach social and communication skills; and intensive interventions based on functional assessments for children demonstrating persistent, challenging behaviors (Fox, Dunlap, Hemmeter, Joseph, & Strain, 2003). Functional assessments involve collecting observational data, interviewing parents and teachers, and analyzing information to determine the function(s) of the challenging behavior(s) (i.e., to obtain or avoid something). A school-based team creates a behavior support plan based on the information gathered and the function of the behavior. Effective behavior support plans are function based and include strategies for preventing challenging behaviors, teaching new skills (i.e., to replace the challenging behavior), and responding to the challenging behavior. Successful behavior support plans make the challenging behavior *ineffective, inefficient,* and *irrelevant* (Wolery, 2005). For more information about evidence-based strategies to prevent and alleviate challenging behaviors in children with autism, see Chapter 11.

TRANSITIONS

Effective programs for children with autism spend a good deal of time planning for transitions. This includes planning for the transition from early intervention to early childhood services at age 3, from preschool to kindergarten, from elementary school to middle or high school, and to adult or postsecondary programs for students with autism. The law requires timely planning for many of these transitions (i.e., planning for the transition to preschool must be included on IFSPs for children 6 months and before they turn 3, and planning for postsecondary life must be included on IEPs once children turn 14). These transitions might be particularly difficult for children with autism, because they often have difficulty generalizing skills across settings. Successful transitions involve extensive planning, individualized strategies, collaboration among the child's education team, significant input from the family and student when appropriate, effective communication across settings and team members, and a system of evaluation. Successful transitions begin with collaborative relationships among children, families, and practitioners. Also, written policies, procedures, and timelines are important for guiding families and practitioners.

FAMILY INVOLVEMENT

Effective programs for children with disabilities, including children with autism, include a family or parent training component (e.g., Dunlap & Fox, 1999; Moes & Frea, 2000; Strain & Timm, 2001; Strain, Young, & Horowitz, 1981). Family involvement and training increases the frequency of learning opportunities because caregivers can implement interventions at home. Also, family involvement is essential to ensure children generalize new skills across settings, people, and materials, and maintain skills over time in settings without prompts. Also, parents are likely to spend more time with their children than teachers or practitioners, and they have the most insight into their needs, unique learning styles, and interests. Thus, parents are essential members of the educational planning team and enhance the child's overall learning experiences by increasing the individualization of goals and planning for behavior and social supports. Parents should have significant input on the child's intervention plan. Furthermore, parents should be encouraged and empowered to advocate for their children. Parent involvement might include parent trainings at school or home, frequent parent conferences, parent support groups, parent members of the program's committees, or regular events for families at school or in the community. Effective programs encourage and sustain collaboration and communication between practitioners and family members to ensure child and program success. Chapter 4 provides more information on involving parents and families in the child's educational program.

MECHANISM FOR ONGOING PROGRAM EVALUATION

Monitoring progress on individual child goals and overall program evaluation is essential to ensure students with autism achieve their goals and move toward becoming independent members of their schools and communities. Program evaluations should assess child short- and long-term outcomes, family outcomes, the implementation of evidence-based practices, the physical environment and resources, and professional development opportunities. Effective curricula for children with autism include strategies and procedures for monitoring progress in individual children and aggregating outcomes across students and families to make decisions about program improvements. Child progress should be ongoing and directly related to the child's goals. The process for monitoring progress should be outlined on the child's IEP. This should include the procedures, the responsible person(s), and mastery criteria. Chapter 6 provides more detailed information for monitoring individual child progress and differentiating instruction.

Program evaluation is the systematic analysis of the success and merit of a program. This includes individual child progress, as well as overall program goals. Administrators and program directors are primarily responsible for program evaluation, and occasionally programs will bring in outside consultants to help with program evaluation. Program evaluation procedures should include both formative (i.e., gather ongoing information about the process and outcomes over time) and summative (i.e., gather information about the effectiveness and major outcomes of the program) evaluation. In this manner, program evaluation occurs throughout the school year and is summarized at the end of the school year. Program evaluation should examine the following: child progress, parent satisfaction, provider satisfaction, and stakeholder and community partner satisfaction. Mechanisms for overall program evaluation should be ongoing, sustainable, linked directly to the program philosophy, goals, and curricula, and include input by consumers (i.e., families, students) and practitioners. This type of evaluation provides information to guide decisions about the program (e.g., needs, progress process to meet state or federal standards or child outcomes, impact on consumers, and cost effectiveness). For example, program evaluation might result in minor adjustments for an individual child (e.g., making accommodations to an intervention to teach a child to communicate), minor changes to a curriculum unit or activity (e.g., changing the materials or assessment methods within a classroom activity), changes to the environment (e.g., changing the classroom's physical structure or the number of assistant teachers in a classroom), or major program changes (e.g., starting a program-wide implementation of positive behavior support). Also, many early childhood programs (e.g., Head Start and many preschool programs) and elementary schools are required to participate in standards reporting (e.g., Head Start Performance Standards and Measures) and standardized testing, respectively. These types of summative evaluation are used to provide accountability and ensure children meet local, state, and national standards. However, all programmatic changes must be informed by multiple types of data (i.e., formative and summative) and continually monitored to ensure children and families are successful and programs are meeting their needs.

FUTURE DIRECTIONS

Future directions for effective programs for children with autism should focus on the gap between research and community practice. There is a significant gap between research and the methods employed in most school systems, despite the plethora of research demonstrating the relation between interventions and positive outcomes for children with autism. Future research and practices should focus on systematic implementation of evidence-based practices for children with autism in natural settings.

There is currently no cure for autism. However, educational experiences that include a focus on teaching the core content skills, with explicit and evidenced-based approaches and an emphasis on family involvement, have increased independence and improved functioning in many children with autism. The next steps include ensuring effective interventions are implemented within natural settings and that **all** children with autism have access to evidence-based interventions. Furthermore, preservice and in-service professional development efforts need to focus on training a cadre of professionals to support and sustain the implementation of evidence-based practices. The next chapter, 6, provides an overview of designing and evaluating instructional programs for individual children.

LEARNING ACTIVITIES

1. What are the essential characteristics of curricula for children with autism?

2. Refer to the vignette in Chapter 3 on Leroy. How would you adapt an inclusive preschool classroom for Leroy?

3. Refer to the vignette in Chapter 3 on Jim. How would you adapt the general education, fourth-grade curricula for Jim?

4. Describe how to identify and evaluate evidence-based practices for young children with autism.

RESOURCES

National Autism Center: **http://www.nationalautismcenter.org/**

The National Professional Development Center on Autism Spectrum Disorders: **http://autismpdc.fpg.unc.edu/**

The National Professional Development Center on Inclusion: **http://community.fpg.unc.edu/npdci**

6

Designing and Evaluating Instruction Based on Student Skills and Responses

Beth Harn

University of Oregon

Shanna Dee Davis

Chicago School of Professional Psychology

Erin E. Barton

University of Colorado Denver

Chapter Objectives:

- Recognize the importance of current skill performance of the child when selecting and implementing instruction.
- Understand how to determine the need for using specific strategies.
- Determine when and how to modify instructional support.

When planning instruction for students with special needs, including autism, the main considerations are the student's current skill levels across domains; the student's strengths, preferences and interests; preferences of the family; and resources available within the community or school setting (Schwartz & Davis, 2008). This information is critical in implementing a support plan that maximizes student engagement and learning and assists in determining the following: (a) what will be taught (e.g., language, social skills, etc.) and (b) how it will be delivered (e.g., where to deliver, who is the best instructor, what grouping arrangement). This chapter describes how to use different types of assessments to plan for meaningful engagement of students in classroom settings and experiences. Specific strategies for differentiating instruction for children with autism within typical classroom settings are described. The final section reviews methods for evaluating child response to intervention as well as considerations and methods in modifying instruction to ensure children receive responsive instruction to maximize development.

CONSIDERATIONS IN ASSESSMENT TO LEAD TO IMPROVED OUTCOMES

The first consideration in the assessment process is the child's present level of development. For children with autism, the present levels of development should be assessed across "core skills" or essential behaviors that will impact a wide range of other social or academic behaviors and future learning (e.g., communication, attending to multiple stimuli, initiations; Koegel & Koegel, 2006; see Chapter 5 for more information about "core skills" for children with autism). The assessment process also should target skills linked to goals and objectives from the IFSP/IEP and focus on positive changes in behavior (e.g., "increasing positive interactions with peers" vs. "decreasing negative interactions with peers"; Hojnoski, Gischlar, & Missall, 2009a). Thus, curriculum-based or curriculum-linked assessments should be used to the extent possible. For example, the assessment should be directly linked to the intervention strategies and child's goals. Curricular-based assessments (i.e., either direct tests or observations in the natural environment) are more likely to reflect how the behavior will be performed and used in natural settings. By examining the frequency or quality of how the child performs the skill (e.g., number of words spoken per minute, quality of completion, independence of completion of tasks), educators and parents can monitor skill growth over time. This growth aspect informs instructional planning more effectively than simply monitoring whether the child can or cannot perform a skill (e.g., yes or no recording). However, if standardized tests are used, the assessor should understand the underlying skills targeted in test and move beyond the specific item to the broader skill for instructional planning. For example, a standardized assessment may have students stacking blocks in a pre-scribed order and time how long it takes them to complete it accurately. Performance on this test provides useful information in planning instruc-tion related to the broader skill of the child's skills to independently pick up and release items in a purposeful manner, rather than planning to develop block-stacking skills. The frequency of assessment or observa-tions should reflect the specific skills. For example, you might observe the child's expressive communication skills across several activities across several days, whereas you might observe independent hand washing one or two times per day. Finally, the data or information gathered should be organized to examine performance over time. For example, observational data can be graphed to show increases or decreases over time (Browder, Demchak, Heller, & King, 1989; Fuchs & Fuchs, 1986). Anecdotal data might be organized by response (e.g., verbal versus gestural requests) or level of prompt (e.g., full hand over hand prompt, model prompt, independent).

Matching the Intensity of Instruction to the Child's Needs

The second concept to consider in assessment is matching the intensity of the instruction to the child's needs. This might include enhanced sup-ports in the general education classroom. Examining the graphed data over time can provide a meaningful opportunity to determine the magnitude of intervention support needed to obtain the goal (Barnett et al., 2006). The main consideration in determining the intensity of the instructional support needed is to compare the child's skill performance in relation to typically developing peers. If the child with autism is significantly differ-ent than his peers, then the instructional support needs to be significantly higher if the goal is to catch him up with his typically developing peers. For example, in Fatima's second-grade class they have social skills instruc-tion for all children a few times a week to promote positive peer interac-tions. The teacher has determined that the typical second grader has about 20 positive peer interactions each school day. However, Fatima has about 2 positive peer interactions each day, and they are usually prompted by school staff. This difference indicates that she will need more support (i.e., more prompting, practice, reinforcement) than if she were already display-ing 15 positive interactions each day. This type of objectively derived data could assist the intervention team to make better decisions about support (Howell & Nolet, 2001).

Creating an Inclusive Classroom
Environment for Children With Autism

Once a child's present levels of performance are understood and considered, the team should create an instructional environment that promotes the meaningful inclusion of the child with autism. This section provides examples of specific strategies and approaches that might be useful for working with children with autism. With each strategy, we discuss how it is implemented for individual students and at the classroom level.

Visual Supports

Many children with autism have visual strengths and receptive language delays. Thus, visual supports (e.g., picture schedules, pictures of expectations, written scripts) are often effective when used to provide "cues" for desired behaviors (Gresham, Beebe-Frankenberger, & MacMillan, 1999; Mesibov, Shea, & Schopler, 2005).Visual prompts such as pictures, shapes, or words provide structure and routine in a classroom environment. These might include graphic activity schedules or organizers or visual pictures of desired behaviors such as initiating social interactions.

How to implement. Visual supports can be used to identify behavioral expectations, work tasks, routines, or activities. Examples of visual supports for identifying work tasks include written or picture schedules. Using a picture schedule system, the classroom staff describes the instructional sequence (e.g., activities, tasks) through a series of pictures, shapes, or words to represent individual steps or activities. Classroom staff identifies difficult, new, or routine times such as transitions, settings, or activities and describes a short sequence using pictures or symbols. Pictures can be line-drawn or photographic images and represent nouns or objects (e.g., books for reading time) or verbs or actions (e.g., jumping for gym time). Teachers might have to teach the students the correspondence between the symbols or pictures and expected behaviors (e.g., the picture of the table represents small group time; the picture of the +/- sign represents math time). Also, teachers identify and implement a reinforcement schedule following the completion of individual behaviors or sequences. Picture schedules can be used for whole-class sequences or designed for individual students or activities.

Visual supports also can be used to prompt individual behaviors such as verbalizations or social interactions. Teachers might use individual pictures or symbols that represent these behaviors (e.g., using a picture of two students playing to prompt asking to join an activity) to prompt the behavior, reinforce the target behavior, and systematically fade the use of the picture to promote the maintenance of the behavior.

An added advantage to using visual supports or schedules in a classroom or home setting is the ability to use the schedule or sequence as a task-analysis and teaching tool. When the sequences are not followed or are unsuccessful, having the specific order or sequence from the schedule provides valuable data to classroom staff about where students may need additional practice, instruction, or prompting to be successful. See Figure 6.1 with an example related to DJ.

Embedding across the day. Visual supports can and should be embedded across the day in early childhood settings. Because visual supports are prompting and providing ongoing instruction, the early childhood setting is a prime opportunity for embedding visual supports that will benefit all of the students in a classroom.

To embed supports for individual students, classroom teams need to identify the specific activities and settings where students need support or prompting to be successful. Some students may only need this level of support during specific parts of a school day (e.g., circle time and center time or lunch time and recess). Classroom teams should identify tasks or situations where students have already shown difficulty in successfully or independently completing specific expectations and new skills. School teams will determine the individual level of support a child will need to complete the task or behavior successfully. Examples of different levels of support include verbal prompting, visual prompts only, or hand over hand prompting. Greater detail and examples (e.g., least to most, most to least, and simultaneous prompting) are provided in Chapters 7 and 8.

To embed supports for the whole classroom, classroom teams need to identify the different activities and settings where students may benefit from increased support to (a) remediate difficulties or (b) to support students to a higher level of independence in the classroom. In structured, effective classrooms, visual supports are used to identify important areas of the classroom (e.g., eating, play, bathroom, math, quiet reading, science), number of tasks/minutes allowed in that area, and number of students allowed. Additionally, if there are particular activities where students are not using materials appropriately, a visual support may be helpful to prompt appropriate use of the materials. Visual supports are commonly used to provide a sequential or time schedule of the daily activities. These adaptations teach independence and can be used to embed instructional opportunities throughout the day. For example, visual supports could be used to assist DJ during frustrating times. The team might teach him to communicate frustration by giving a card saying "I need help" to a teacher. A picture schedule might be useful for providing DJ with information about upcoming schedule changes. Since DJ becomes upset at any modifications to his schedule, a daily schedule could be created for DJ and reviewed at the start of each day or activity and reviewed again at the end. This would provide DJ with predictability and allow his daily schedule to change, thus promoting generalization. A picture schedule will prepare DJ for activities ahead of time, which might be particularly important for nonpreferred or less-frequently occurring activities. The team also might identify the situations where DJ is unable to independently engage. His teachers might embed choices into his individual picture schedule and teach him to make choices between an activity or materials (e.g., the center time card might have a water table or art; the math time card might have counting or sorting). His teachers might teach him to make choices using modeling and reinforcement for each time he made and followed through with a choice.

Figure 6.1 Sample Picture Schedule

DJ's Morning Schedule		
Puzzle/Activity	Play/Language	Art/Fine Motor

For example, to address DJ's goal of developing language and play skills and address his natural avoidance to socializing and preference for art activities, the team developed a picture schedule (see Figure 6.1) that has the less preferred activity between two preferred activities. This provides the visual cue and structure DJ needs and has the overt schedule the classroom staff needs to ensure DJ's school experience is directed toward his goals. The team puts DJ's "I need help" card in his pants pocket each morning and he has been taught to use the card when he gets frustrated, which often occurs during play time.

Structured Work Systems

An area many children with autism have difficulty with is independent functioning within a classroom setting (e.g., knowing the daily routine, completing meal time independently, gathering necessary materials for tasks, beginning and completing a task). An effective approach to developing these skills is through structured work systems (Carnahan et al., 2011; Dawson & Osterling, 1997; Hume & Odom, 2007). Structured work systems arrange the physical environment and individual academic tasks into smaller, manageable tasks by incorporating a structured physical environment and visual supports. They are individually developed based on the skills the child has and designed to direct his attention to the important aspects of the tasks rather than being needlessly distracted by irrelevant environmental stimuli or information. They are designed to promote independence and reduce dependence on adult prompting (Carnahan et al., 2011; Mesibov et al., 2005). When designing a structured work system, it should help the child answer the following questions: (a) What do I need to do? (b) How do I do it? (c) What will it look like when done? and (d) What do I do when finished? When providing the initial teaching, the level of support from the teacher is very high and the support is systematically faded to build independent child performance over time (see Chapter 8 for more information about fading prompts). The goal of an independent work system is to teach the child independent task completion and persistence. Thus, the individual tasks should include skills that the child has mastered and can do easily. Independent work systems provide opportunities for the child to generalize or maintain skills, but they are not appropriate for teaching new or developing skills.

How to implement. To design and implement a structured work system, the team collaborates to identify individual learning tasks that a child has mastered. Structured work systems are usually used in designated areas of the classroom where children can work individually, free from distraction. The work system specifies where a child will complete work and uses visual cues to identify how much work will be completed, when each individual task and the session is completed, and the reinforcement. For example, a teacher may use a set of numbers on a Velcro board that corresponds to a series of tasks that are also numbered. The child matches each number on the Velcro board to the specified task and completes the task so he or she sees the progress and it prompts the child to complete the next step. When each task is completed, the child moves on to the next task. When the all of the numbers are removed from the Velcro board, the child is finished with the task. The final row might be a picture of the reinforcement (e.g., a picture of a preferred activity or toy) or it might be a picture of two or more reinforcements, which prompts the child to make an independent choice. A card also might be used to prompt the child to move to the next activity or routine.

Embedding across the day. The structured work systems can be used during individual work times and during free or "play" times. For children who have difficulty organizing play or independent activities, structured work systems provide academic practice, content, and organizational skills needed to function more independently in a classroom. For example, a structured work session could consist of puzzles, worksheets, simple dump and fill activities, sorting games, or preferred activities. Again, the outcomes of structured work systems are independent task completion, task persistence, and organizational skills. For example, a structured work system could be implemented with DJ to teach him independent task completion and generalization of toy play. The team identifies the tasks or toys that require pieces or a sequence to complete such as puzzles, Legos®, or blocks that DJ knows how to play with. The team identified a visual sequence or steps, and a visual/picture of the finished product. The team designed the sequence, provided DJ the time to finish the activity, and delivered reinforcement based on the finished task or completion of a predetermined set of tasks. Also, because DJ has trouble initiating, sharing, and cleaning up during free playtime, the team created a 4-step sequence that DJ checks off as he completes tasks during free play to increase the likelihood of success (see Figure 6.2). The team monitored progress by collecting the number of steps DJ completed each day as well as noted the level of support the teacher provided to obtain that performance (see Figure 6.3). These data are used to evaluate DJ's independent performance over time and identify steps needing further instruction or adaptations (e.g., a visual script or pictures for sharing toys).

Figure 6.2   DJ's Structured Work System in Using Toys Appropriately

Playing With Toys	
Steps	

Figure 6.3   Sample Progress Monitoring Chart for DJ's Toy Play

Step	Monday	Tuesday	Wednesday	Thursday	Friday
Take Out					
Play					
Share					
Clean Up					
Steps Complete	/4	/4	/4	/4	/4
Level of Prompting Needed					

Identifying and Utilizing the Child's Specific Interests

Another effective teaching strategy for children with autism is building skill development within highly preferred tasks. Many children with autism have a persistent preoccupation with a specific topic or interest area (e.g., dinosaurs, football, bugs, music, etc.) and are highly motivated to engage in activities or discussions on certain topics. Creating learning activities that incorporate preferred topics might increase motivation and learning. Another way to keep motivation high is by giving children choices about activities (Carter, 2001). Due to the nature of the disorder, providing choices or features of preferred activities within tasks may help children with autism attend to relevant stimuli and remain engaged (Baker, 2000; Ducharme, Lucas, & Pontes, 1994).

How to identify. Teams can identify preferences using family, classroom, and child information from interviews, observations, and task demands made on the child (see Chapter 4 for more information on reinforcement assessments). Preferences can include activities such as music, computer time, reading, or blocks. Preferences may also include tangible items such as objects or toys. Children may also prefer the presence or absence of others and specific settings in which to complete tasks or activities.

Embedding instruction within the child's special interests. Teams can identify the activities that children either have difficulties or resistance to initiate or complete and identify simple or logical adaptations to include their personal preferences. A prime opportunity to embed the use of preferences is with language and social skills. The interests or preferences of the child with autism can be incorporated into play or social skill interactions with children with typical development. These types of minor alterations to instruction have been shown to be highly effective in getting children with autism to increase the frequency and the quality of social and language interactions (e.g., Koegel & Koegel, 2006). With support, students with typical language and social skills can be used as models and facilitators of social interactions using the preferences or specific interests of children with autism. In addition to social interactions, embedding features of preferences or interests can be used during challenging learning tasks. For example, Fatima's teacher embedded mystical themes into her literacy instruction. They created stories about fairies and princesses and taught her to write stories using mystical themes. Jim's team used a high-interest area (i.e., knowledge of football) to increase his participation with other students. His teachers taught other peers strategies for initiating and maintaining social interactions with Jim using his interest area. In addition to talking about football, they taught the peers to discuss similar features of other sports to increase the length, frequency, and quality of their interactions.

EVALUATING PROGRESS
AND RESPONSE TO INTERVENTION

Collecting and reviewing progress monitoring data is a central feature of responsive instructional practices, and it has become particularly relevant in early childhood (Hojnoski et al., 2009a, 2009b). Instruction that incorporates the regular and systematic use of collecting and reviewing data has been found related to improved child and student outcomes and more individualized instructional plans (Gischlar, Hojnoski, & Missall, 2009; Hojnoski et al., 2009a, 2009b). Additionally, having timely and efficient ways of showing student progress might promote more consistent and engaged parent and family participation in educational programming. This section reviews some commonly used measures designed to effectively and efficiently monitor skill development in areas that many children and students with autism have as individual goals. The next section describes strategies for evaluating progress and gives suggestions for modifying intervention practices when data warrant a change.

For example, the work completed by the researchers at the University of Minnesota in developing the Individual Growth and Development Indicators (IGDIs; http://igdis.umn.edu/) has been particularly helpful in improving the outcomes of students with a range of disabilities. They have developed very targeted and efficient measures that are designed to monitor changes in skill development on a weekly or bimonthly basis in the following essential skill areas: language development (picture naming) and phonological awareness (rhyming and alliteration). While the measures were not designed to comprehensively measure all important skill areas, they are purposely designed to measure essential skill areas in an efficient way (e.g., each measure takes less than 3 minutes to administer) and allow for performance to be collected over time and evaluated to determine if instruction should be modified to improve child development (knowing when a change is necessary is discussed later).

Once children have moved into elementary school, there are similar measures available to monitor development in early literacy and reading development called the Dynamic Indicators of Early Literacy Skills (DIBELS; Good & Kaminski, 2003; https://dibels.uoregon.edu). They are developed in a similar way as the IGDIs, to be efficient, targeted, and easy to administer, to assist schools and teachers in identifying students needing additional instructional support (screening) and for monitoring the response to the interventions in place. Measures are available to measure the following skill areas: phonemic awareness (initial sounds and segmentation), letter knowledge, alphabetic principle (knowledge of letter sounds and initial recoding), and fluency in reading connected text. The accompanying website is designed to help teachers monitor student responses. Teachers can enter their student performance data and have graphs be automatically created for them.

Figure 6.4   Leroy's Daily Compliance Behavior Across Daily Activities

Activity	Monday	Tuesday	Wednesday	Thursday	Friday	Total
Circle Time	x	x	xx	x	xx	7
Art/Activity	xxx	xxxx	xxx	xxx	xxx	16
Puzzles	xxx	xxxx	xxxx	xx	xxxx	17
Snack	xxx	xx	xx	xx	xx	11
Language	xxxx	xx	xxx	xxx	xxxx	16
Total	14	13	14	11	15	

Monitoring functional repertoires (e.g., choice making, self-management, initiating interactions) is typically done using observational approaches and simply counting the number of instances of a particular behavior (e.g., rate of communication, number of self-injurious behaviors) or by recording the duration of certain behaviors (e.g., time on task, time engaged in play/talking, time in independent work). While there are other types of recording procedures available (e.g., interval or momentary time sampling), these are typically done by an outside observer (i.e., not classroom staff) and not the focus of this chapter. For an excellent review of a range of other observational approaches, the reader is referred to the National Autism Center's report entitled, "Evidence-Based Practice and Autism in the School," which is freely available at http://www.national autismcenter.org/. For preschoolers and early elementary-aged students, most agree that the essential social skills they need to engage successfully with typical-aged peers include the following: listening to others, following classroom rules, complying with directives, asking for help, cooperating with peers, and controlling temper in conflict situations (Elliot, Roach, & Beddow, 2008). For example, Leroy frequently becomes frustrated, which escalates to aggression when denied his way. The team decides to count and reinforce Leroy each time he follows a direction to decrease the likelihood of him becoming frustrated. Team members use the chart (see Figure 6.4) to keep track of compliance across daily activities to monitor performance and see where he has the most trouble. At the end of the week, the team examined the data and noticed that he is more compliant in the more structured activities (language group) and independent activities (puzzles) and has more difficulties during less structured (circle time and snack) activities.

Knowing When a Change Is Needed

Graphing performance over time enables an easy and objective way to assist in determining when interventions need to be modified. See Chapter 12 for more suggestions on how to readily and regularly gather data to

Figure 6.5   Graph of Jim's Performance

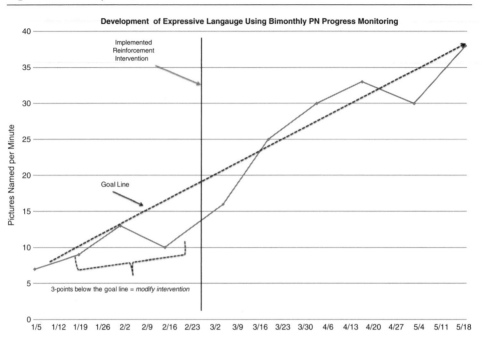

assist in both collaboration and evaluating intervention effectiveness. See Chapter 4 for more information about developing goals. If performance is on track or above the goal line, then the team might conclude that instruction is working and no modifications are necessary. However, if the performance is consistently below the goal line, the instructional practices should be adapted or modified to ensure student success.

Because of the instability of a single brief assessment such as the DIBELS or IGDIs, teachers should examine multiple forms of assessment, including observational measures (discussed later), looking for a trend in child performance in relation to an established goal line. A valuable approach is to examine child performance using the *Three-Point Rule*. To employ the Three-Point Rule, look at the most recent three data points collected. If the last three points are above the goal line, the teacher should (a) continue the intervention or (b) increase the goal (if performance is consistently well above goal line). If the last three points are below the goal line, the teacher should modify the intervention so that it matches the child's needs (see the next section for specific suggestions for modifying intervention). If the last three points are around the goal line (i.e., points may be on, one below, one above), the teacher should continue the intervention while closely monitoring student response over time. For example, in Figure 6.5, Jim was receiving a language development program to improve his overall language skills monitored with a Picture Naming (PN) measure, but his progress monitoring data indicated a need to modify his instructional experience because performance was consistently below his goal line. In discussing his performance during his small group, the team decided to

Figure 6.6   DJ's Frequency of Initiating Play

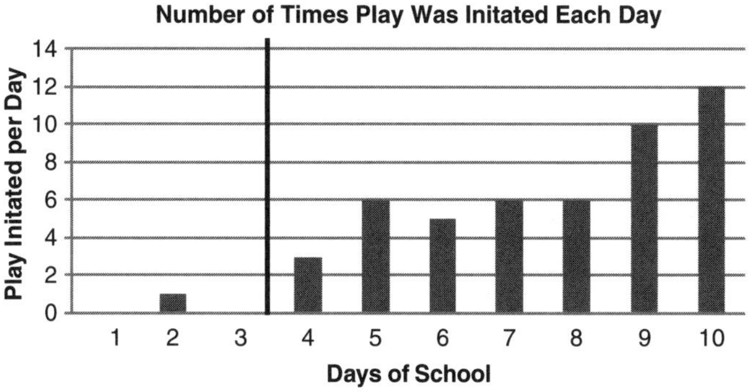

Number of Times Play Was Initated Each Day

increase how often he was reinforced during small group but linked it to his overall point system and his reinforcement system for time on task that was already in place. The program continued with the enhanced behavior management system and his progress dramatically improved.

Observational measures are also helpful in monitoring responses to individualized interventions. For example, because much of DJ's instructional time is spent developing language and play behavior, the team is recording the number of times he initiates play behavior across the day by putting a tally mark on the dry erase board in front of the room (see the discussion in Chapter 12 for more ideas about easily gathering data). At the end of each day, the lead teacher records the total number, graphs it, and examines performance in relation to the goal. The team noticed the limited initiations after 3 days and decided to provide verbal praise and access to a preferred toy after initiating and his initiations increased across days, with a bit of variability (see Figure 6.6). This variability is sometimes due to a change in the class schedule and sometimes due to DJ's behavior, so noting schedule changes anecdotally would be necessary to determine overall performance across time.

CONSIDERATIONS IN INTERVENTION MODIFICATION

Areas to consider when the intervention is not effective relate back to the two major factors of instruction: Are we teaching the right content? Are we delivering it in the best way? A critical area to consider is to ensure that instruction matches the child's current skill level. If the content being taught is well beyond or too difficult for the child, he or she won't progress as expected and can elicit frustration from the student in the form of problem behaviors. Conversely, if the skill level of the instruction is too low, it may not be intellectually stimulating or engaging for the student and can lead to minimal development as well as elicit problem behaviors. Reexamining child performance data can be very helpful in addressing this aspect. Additionally, some established curriculum programs have developed placement tests for students to directly aid in determining the right level of instructional support. Once you have ensured the proper match of instructional support to child level of performance, we need to consider whether aspects of the content or delivery are minimizing development.

Are We Teaching the Right Content?

Extensive reviews have been done by established research groups and are freely available on websites (e.g., National Autism Center http:// www.nationalautismcenter.org/) and discussions on autism-specific programs in Chapter 4, communication programs in Chapter 9, and social skills programs in chapter 10. The real challenge comes in selecting the program that has a good "contextual fit," meaning, does the focus of the intervention match the following: (a) the child's needs and preferences, (b) the skill level of the interventionist/teacher, and (c) the classroom setting (e.g., number of students, time schedule, routine)?

Matching child's needs and preferences. Ensuring that the program is teaching the skills that the student needs is readily determined in typical assessment practices. An additional consideration when working with children with autism is thinking about how that content and general approach to the teaching skills map on to the child's temperament and preferences. For example, many children with autism have a difficult time interpreting subtle social cues. So when teaching social skills, programs that do not provide explicit teaching and practice of social skill development may not be as successful as programs that provide explicit teaching and regular, contextually relevant practice of the skill. Additionally, some academic programs have built-in, regular opportunities to respond verbally (i.e., choral responding in response to a teacher's question). For some children, this may create an overstimulating environment for the child with autism and impact his or her performance and behavior during such lessons. In both of these examples, there are a couple of options to consider. One option is to select a different program to use to better match the child with autism. A different option is to consider how to modify the intervention delivery in such a way to better match the child with autism (Roach & Elliott, 2008). In making this decision, educators need to consider whether the program is being used with the entire class. If so, then changing a program for the whole class based on the needs of one child is quite a challenge and major expense. A better approach might be to think about how to modify the delivery that may make it more conducive to the child. For example, if the available social skills program that is effective with all the preschoolers is not explicit enough for the child with autism, the teacher could simply modify the instructional specificity (explicit wording, increase the number of practice opportunities, provide specific feedback) when that child is to practice the skill. For the academic example, if the math program used in kindergarten is effective for all the students but the high level of choral responding is distressing for the child with autism, the teacher can teach all the students to use the "in-class work voices" (i.e., whisper) when answering questions as well as consider the placement of the child in a quieter area of the classroom rather than in the front of the class or right next to the teacher (i.e., students will be looking at and talking to the teacher, so sitting next to teacher will be the most stimulating location). As both of these examples show, educators need to think creatively about how they can adapt instruction that will meaningfully increase the engagement of the child with autism.

If the program selected is being used in a small group or one-one setting, the same considerations in modifying general delivery aspects that do not change the intent and focus of the program might be effective. However, children needing a more intensive instructional arrangement might need more intensive modifications or different programs. Select established, evidence-based practices that match the student's needs and can be implemented within the classroom, which leads to another dimension of contextual fit: skills of the teacher.

Matching the skill level of the teacher. Many programs in use in preschool and traditional school settings are systematically designed and have many different components. In today's economic situations, educators frequently purchase evidence-based programs and then do not receive training on the program or curriculum, either by choice or lack of monetary support to get trained. This is particularly a problem when teachers move from one school to another; even if the district had provided the necessary training when the program was first purchased, follow-up trainings are rare (see Chapter 12 for more information on implementation and professional development). This frequently leads to inaccurate implementation, in which case children do not benefit as expected (Strain & Bovey, 2011). In some situations, educators will incorrectly think the program does not work or is "ineffective" when actually it was the delivery that was "ineffective." A common approach seen in settings these days is to evaluate the "fidelity of implementation" of a program before considering modifying an instructional plan by changing a child's placement. Assessing fidelity of implementation is done in a variety of ways and the field does not have consensus on the best way to do it. But in general, the instructional group is observed by someone with expert knowledge of the program (e.g., trainer, behavior specialist, etc.) and the observer evaluates whether the program was delivered as it was intended. If the observation indicates that the program was not delivered as expected (i.e., with low fidelity), then the teacher should receive training and support of how to improve delivery and then evaluate how children respond to a higher quality of delivery. If the observation indicated that the program was delivered as expected (i.e., with high fidelity) and child response is low, then the team should consider potentially changing the program or modifying the delivery, which is discussed in the next section. First though, considerations in selecting programs that match the classroom setting are discussed.

Matching the classroom setting. As mentioned before, evidence-based programs are designed in a specific manner, and if they are not delivered as they were initially designed, then we should not expect impressive improvements (Chard & Harn, 2008). For example, if a research-based first-grade reading program was initially demonstrated as being effective when it is delivered five days a week, in a 45-minute session, and in groups of four to six children, but the school only has 30 minutes a day and has nine students in the group, the growth of the students will most likely be less than if it was implemented as it was intended. This is an example of poor contextual fit; the results for all those children will not meet expectations because they are receiving two-thirds of the intervention and not receiving as much individualized attention as intended. The school has a choice to make if it wants children to benefit from the instructional time: (a) rearrange the school schedule to allocate 45 minutes to instruction, (b) add additional instructional groups to deliver within the expected group size, or (c) find a program that matches the available instructional context (e.g., schedule, time, grouping). Continuing to deliver a program with low fidelity wastes instructional time.

Are We Delivering It in the Best Way?

Research has found inconsistent effectiveness of instructional grouping. Many have considered 1-1 instruction the "gold standard"; however, this isn't necessarily the case (Vaughn & Bos, 2011). The "best" instructional setting depends on the skills being taught and the strengths and needs of the student. Children with autism should be included with their typically developing peers to the greatest extent possible and in as many activities as feasible (Strain, McGee & Kohler, 2001). Furthermore, evidence-based practices for adapting, modifying, and embedding instruction into inclusive settings for young children with autism exist (e.g., McConnell, 2002; National Autism Center, 2009b; Odom, 2009; Strain et al., 2001). This is particularly the case when the content includes social and play skills (Sandall et al., 2005; Schwartz & Davis, 2008).

FUTURE DIRECTIONS

An essential, often underappreciated, aspect of education is the role of assessing child skill performance for initial planning and regular progress monitoring to maximize child development (Gischlar et al., 2009; Hojnoski et al., 2009a). This chapter provided information and rationale of using different types of assessments and how they can be used to plan and evaluate specific types of instructional supports for children with autism in the typical classroom setting (e.g., visual supports, work systems, picture schedules, and individual child interests). The final section provided suggestions on how to modify instruction when children are not benefiting as expected by specifically considering the match of what is being taught to the student, teacher skills, and classroom setting. The next two chapters (i.e., Chapters 7 and 8) describe evidence-based instructional practices for teaching new skills and generalizing and maintaining skills over time. In this day and age, where evidence-based practices are widely available, the importance of regular performance monitoring is even more important. We now have more effective tools at our disposal, but we must ensure that they are used as intended and not assume all will work well for all children. Thus, regular evaluation is essential for maximizing instruction and promoting child success.

LEARNING ACTIVITIES

1. Describe how you would use a visual schedule to support and increase Leroy's compliance during circle or snack time.

2. How would you monitor DJ's structured work system plan to ensure it was effectively supporting him to use toys appropriately?

3. When selecting a new evidence-based program for use in a kindergarten classroom that includes a child with autism, what should a school and teacher consider?

4. If the student performance data indicate that a student isn't progressing as expected, what are some issues that the school, teacher, and specialists consider before changing the intervention?

RESOURCES

For more detailed information on visual supports, structured work systems, and using preferences, see the following:

TEACCH Autism Program: http://teacch.com

Autism Internet Modules: http://www.autisminternetmodules.org/

7

Evidence-Based Strategies for Teaching Children With Autism Spectrum Disorders

Skill Acquisition and Fluency

Brian Reichow

Yale University

Terrell Reichow

Area Cooperative Educational Services

Chapter Objectives:

- Distinguish between a prompt and a cue, and be able to differentiate the intrusiveness of two different prompt types.
- Plan (and execute) appropriate intervention using response prompting strategies to teach new behaviors.
- Identify ways to increase the efficiency of learning.

Although there are many treatment options for young children with autism, no single option has been shown to be superior to others and for all children (National Research Council, 2001; Warren, McPheeters, Sathe, Foss-Feig, Glasser, & Veenstra-VanderWeele, 2011). Recently, an increasing number of children with autism are being educated in school settings (Palmer, Blanchard, Jean, & Mandell, 2005; Shattuck, 2006), which means that education professionals will need to become increasingly competent in instructing these students. Unfortunately, many of the ways in which autism manifests (e.g., limited communication skills, impaired social reciprocity, insistence on sameness, restricted and repetitive behaviors) create barriers to teaching and learning, creating a situation in which students with autism can be some of the most challenging students to educate.

Fortunately, there are many evidence-based methods for helping students with autism learn. Chapter 6 provided practices for using different types of assessment for program planning and suggestions for modifying instruction. In this chapter, we introduce and demonstrate evidence-based strategies to teach students with autism new skills and behaviors, provide examples of how you can use these strategies so your students achieve acquisition and fluency, and suggest modifications that maximize the efficiency of learning for your students.

TEACHING NEW SKILLS AND BEHAVIORS

Learning New Skills and Behaviors: Acquisition

Learning is "a relatively permanent change in performance as a result of experience" (Wolery, Ault, & Doyle, 1992, p. 2) and occurs in four phases: acquisition, fluency, maintenance, and generalization. In this chapter, we cover the first two stages, acquisition and fluency (maintenance and generalization are covered in Chapter 8). *Acquisition* is the first stage of learning and involves learning the basic requirements of a behavior and how to perform that behavior (Wolery et al., 1992). Because this is when the child is learning how to perform a new behavior, it is a very important period and usually involves a great amount of time and effort. It is also a critical stage for children with autism because they often have difficulty attending to the salient aspects of instruction. For example, if you are teaching a student to identify coins, you might expect students to attend to the color of the coins, the different sizes of the coins, or the different faces on the coins. A student with autism might only attend to whether or not each coin has ridges on the side of the coin without reference to color, size, or face. Therefore, you will need to highlight the most salient aspects of the target stimulus (i.e., a penny is brown and has a picture of Abraham Lincoln; a dime is silver and is the smallest coin) and provide explicit and detailed instruction on how to do the behavior (i.e., name coins) you are teaching. Prompts can be used to provide explicit instruction on how to do a behavior.

Prompting. You can help a child perform new behaviors using prompts. A prompt is something you do to help a child perform a behavior (MacDuff, Krantz, & McClannahan, 2001; Wolery et al., 1992). The purpose of a prompt is "to cause students to perform the target behavior so that it can be reinforced when the target stimulus is present" (Wolery et al., 1992, pp. 42–43).Prompts give the child clues about how to perform the behavior and varying levels of assistance on how to perform it (e.g., providing a motor model of waving good-bye, placing your hand behind a child's hand and assisting him or her in performing the actions of waving good-bye). Prompts are not cues or task directions; cues or task directions inform the child that it is time to perform a behavior, whereas a prompt provides assistance to the child that helps him or her do the behavior (Wolery et al., 1992).

There are many different types of prompts; prompts can be classified in multiple ways. One way to describe and classify prompts is with respect to the delivery methods and how they look. A second way we can classify prompts is along a continuum of how much assistance they provide to a child. Table 7.1 uses these two classification schemes to provide descriptions, advantages, disadvantages, and examples of common prompting techniques.

A third way we classify prompts is with respect to the child's behavior (i.e., whether or not the child performs the correct behavior after being prompted). A controlling prompt ensures the child performs the behavior you are prompting and receives reinforcement. Full physical prompts, such as placing your hands over a child's hands to complete a task, are always controlling prompts. For example, Fatima's teachers taught her to request using her AlphaSmart keyboard by hand over hand prompting (controlling prompt) to type "j-u-i-c-e" and immediately gave her the juice. Less intrusive controlling prompts include guiding a child down the hall by providing a light touch on his or her shoulder. A verbal model can also be a controlling prompt; for example, Jim's teachers taught him to read by showing him a flash card with the word "cat" written on it, asked him, "What does this say?", and immediately provided a verbal model by saying "cat." This was a controlling prompt for Jim because he always imitated the verbal model. Additional information on prompts and prompting can be found in the Autism Internet Module website (http://www.autisminternetmodules.org/) on prompting (Neitzel & Wolery, 2010).

Reinforcement. One reason we provide prompts is to help children perform the behavior we are teaching so that we can reinforce them for performing it. Reinforcement is the process of adding or removing a stimulus after a behavior occurs that results in an increase in the frequency the child performs the behavior in the future (Cooper, Heron, & Heward, 2007). For example, DJ's teachers immediately give him access to the computer every time he uses the bathroom, which increases his use of the bathroom. There are two types of reinforcement: positive reinforcement, which is the presentation of a desired stimulus (e.g., descriptive praise, giving child a chip), and negative reinforcement, which is the removal of an aversive

Table 7.1   Types of Prompts (adapted from Wolery et al., 1992)

Type of Prompt	Description	Amount of Assistance
Gestural	Nonverbal behaviors that inform the child about how to do a behavior	LEAST
Verbal	Statements that help a student perform the correct behavior	
Visual	Pictures or written words that inform a student how to do a behavior	
Models (verbal, motor, video)	Demonstrations of the correct behavior; students are expected to imitate behavior	
Partial physical	Teacher behaviors that involve physical touch but not controlling student's behavior	
Full physical	Teacher behaviors that involve full control of the student's behaviors; teacher often places hands over student's hands and completes target behavior	MOST

Source: Wolery, et al., 1992.

Advantages	Disadvantages	Examples:
Not intrusive; easy to give; can give to groups; can do from a distance	Child must see prompt; can be more difficult for child to understand	• Teacher points to the sink • Teacher points to a block and signals for the child to place block in the bucket
Not intrusive, easy to give; can give to groups; can be given from a distance	Child must hear prompt; child must be able to understand verbal language	• Saying, "Walk to the sink, turn on water, wet hands, get soap . . ." • Saying, "Pick up the block and put it in the bucket"
Not intrusive; easy to provide and can be provided when teacher not present; can be permanent	Child must understand pictures or written message; some behaviors difficult to illustrate	• Providing a picture activity schedule for washing hands over the sink • Showing the child a photograph or line drawing of a hand placing a block in the bucket
Not intrusive; easy to give; can provide to groups; can be given from a distance; provides a lot of information on how to do behavior	Some behaviors difficult to model; child must be imitative	• Demonstrating how to wash your hands • Picking up a block and putting it in the bucket
Provides some, but not total, control; easy to give; provides a lot of information	Very intrusive; involves touching the child; cannot be used from a distance; can be difficult to use with groups	• Nudging child's hands toward the water; helping child pump soap • Moving child's hand from desk to on top of the block; gently lifting child's hand toward bucket
Provides full control of child's behavior	Very intrusive; involves a lot of touching the child; cannot be used from a distance; cannot be done with groups	• Placing your hands around or over a child's hands and completing all steps of hand washing while holding child's hands • Placing your hands on top of a child's hands and manipulating the child's hands to pick up block and place in bucket

stimulus (e.g., buckling your seatbelt to terminate the buzzing noise). Positive reinforcement is the main type of reinforcement we use to teach new behaviors and is the type of reinforcement to which we refer for the remainder of this chapter. A more detailed discussion of reinforcement is beyond the scope of this chapter and can be found in Cooper et al. (2007) and the Autism Internet Module on reinforcement (Neitzel, 2010b).

The additional stimulus that you present to the child is called a reinforcer. The reinforcers that you use should be related to the skills or behaviors you are teaching, and whenever possible, it is advantageous to use naturally occurring reinforcers. For example, if you are teaching a child how to use a fork, providing a preferred food that the child can pierce with the fork and eat would be a reinforcer. When you are teaching a child how to request an item using a picture exchange, giving the child the item after he hands you the picture can serve as a reinforcer. It also is important to conduct a preference assessment to determine what stimuli are reinforcing to the child. Reinforcers can be idiosyncratic, especially for children with autism; a stimulus that serves as a reinforcer for one child might not be reinforcing to another. For example, anything related to dinosaurs is consistently reinforcing for Jim. However, sometimes he prefers dinosaur stickers to dinosaur figures. Finally, when using reinforcement, it is important to use a variety (rotation) of reinforcers to avoid saturation. For example, Fatima's teachers know that access to her favorite books are reinforcing at the beginning of the day. However, by the end of the school day, books are not reinforcing and she prefers the computer. Figure 7.1 provides examples (but by no means an exhaustive list) of positive reinforcers.

Figure 7.1   Examples of Possible Positive Reinforcers

Specific Verbal Praise

- Mary, I like the way you washed your hands before lunch.
- Great job keeping your hands to yourself!

Gestures

- Thumbs up
- High-five
- Clapping and cheering (e.g., pumping fists in air)

Edibles

- Candy and chips
- Spray candy

Tangibles

- Stickers
- Blowing bubbles
- Access to preferred activity

Although closely related natural reinforcers are the best reinforcers to use, it might be difficult to identify these reinforcers for children with autism. Many individuals without autism find social approval (e.g., smiles) and social praise (e.g., teacher saying, "I am so proud of you") reinforcing. These types of reinforcers are common in classrooms. However, social deficits are a defining feature of autism (American Psychiatric Association, 1994; Kanner, 1943) and therefore socially based praise might not serve as a reinforcer. We are not suggesting that you abstain from using social reinforcers, as they are naturally occurring reinforcers in inclusive classrooms that should be used; but for students with autism, you will likely need to pair social reinforcers with other stimuli to maximize the effectiveness of the reinforcement you are providing.

When you deliver reinforcement to a child, you deliver it on a specific schedule of reinforcement. (Figure 7.2 provides brief descriptions and examples of the common reinforcement schedules used to teach children new behaviors. Table 8.2 in Chapter 8 provides additional descriptions of schedules of reinforcement.)

When you start teaching a child a new behavior, you should begin by providing reinforcement on a heavy schedule (e.g., reinforcing every approximation or successful performance of the target behavior; CRF schedule). This will increase the likelihood of having the child continue to perform and later increase the frequency of performing the behavior you are teaching. However, we do not want to continue reinforcing every behavior once the child becomes proficient with the new behavior. Once the child achieves proficiency, thin the reinforcement (i.e., deliver reinforcement less often) using one of the ratio schedules described in Figure 7.2. Because a

Figure 7.2   Common Schedules of Reinforcement

Continuous (CRF)

　Providing reinforcement after every correct response.

　Example: Teacher provides reinforcement every time a child asks a peer to play.

Fixed ratio (FR)

　Providing reinforcement after the last of a specified number of correct responses.

　Example: Teacher provides reinforcement after every third time a child asks a peer to play.

Variable ratio (VR)

　Providing reinforcement after the last of a variable number of correct responses.

　Example: Teacher provides reinforcement to the child on average every third time a child asks to play (sometimes after every second, sometimes after every third, and sometimes after every fourth response).

fixed ratio (FR) schedule often results in a low response rate immediately following the delivery of the reinforcer, we recommend thinning reinforcement using a variable ratio (VR) schedule (e.g., after the child is consistently performing a behavior on a CRF schedule, thin the reinforcement to a VR-3 schedule, which would reinforce the child on average every third time he or she performs the behavior). For example, when teaching Leroy to independently follow his visual schedule, his teacher gave him a sticker and specific praise every time he used the schedule appropriately. As he learned to use the visual schedule, the teacher thinned the reinforcement to give him a sticker and praise about every other, then every third or fourth time he used his schedule appropriately.

Stimulus control and differential reinforcement. Once you identify a controlling prompt, the controlling prompt becomes a discriminative stimulus and the behavior is under stimulus control. For example, if you are teaching a student to name colors, you might show the child a red crayon and ask, "What color is this?" and wait 5 seconds for the child to respond. If the child does not respond, you would provide a controlling prompt (e.g., a verbal model; saying "Red"). The controlling prompt will elicit the child to say, "Red," and you would then reinforce her for correctly identifying the color. After the child has been reinforced numerous times for saying "Red" when the red crayon is shown, the red crayon has become a discriminative stimulus and the desired behavior (naming the color red) is under stimulus control. *Stimulus control* is the reliable or predictable performance of a behavior when a stimulus is present and the absence of that behavior when the stimulus is not present (Cooper et al., 2007; Wolery et al., 1992). You can gain stimulus control by using differential reinforcement. *Differential reinforcement* is reinforcing a child when he or she performs the target behavior in the presence of the target stimulus and not reinforcing the child if he or she does not perform the desired behavior. When using differential reinforcement, you only reinforce the child when he or she performs (or approximates) the target behavior. For example, if you were teaching a child to read the word "bubble," you would reinforce the child when he or she said "bubble" or made a "b" sound, but you would not reinforce the child for saying "banana." Because the child is only receiving reinforcement for performing the behavior you are teaching, differential reinforcement should *increase* the frequency the child performs the behavior, thus providing you more opportunities to reinforce the child for performing the behavior. Likewise, since reinforcement is not provided when the child does not perform the behavior or skill or performs a different behavior in the presence of the target stimulus, differential reinforcement decreases the frequency with which behaviors not similar to the target behavior occur in the presence of the target stimulus. The pairing of reinforcement with the desired behavior in the presence of the target stimulus and lack thereof in the absence of the target behavior helps the child learn when to produce the behavior. This can be a powerful tool that you can use to help a child learn new behaviors and to help move the child into the next stage of learning.

Practicing New Skills and Behaviors: Fluency

Once a child has mastered the mechanics of a new behavior (i.e., once the child can readily perform the behavior), he or she moves into the second stage of learning, which is fluency. This stage of learning occurs when the child learns how to perform the behavior accurately, consistently, and independently at a natural level (Wolery et al., 1992). An example of a fluent behavior would be a child greeting his or her teacher one time at the beginning of each school day within 1 minute of entering the classroom (not having the child greet his or her teacher five times in one day every fifth day). Children increase fluency through practice. When practicing a behavior, it is important to provide the child with multiple opportunities to practice it (several times a day, if possible). It also is important that you keep the practice sessions motivating and fun; this will help the child want to continue to practice, which will help increase fluency. Once a child is performing the target behavior fluently, it is important to then systematically fade and remove the prompts to more naturally occurring stimuli to ensure the skill will continue to be performed.

As shown in the vignettes introduced in Chapter 2, DJ, Jim, and Fatima are often dependent on adult prompts to perform skills they have learned. Prompt dependency is common for children with autism, as they frequently only perform skills and behaviors they have acquired when asked to do so by an adult, regardless of whether natural prompts are present. For example, you might have a child that can walk to the sink to wash her hands, but she will not start washing her hands until an adult turns on the water for her and provides assistance for each step. Another example would be a child who is learning how to say "hi" to his friends but only does so when the teacher says, "Say hi" (and many children with autism then echo, "Say hi"). Prompt dependency is undesirable; we want children to be independent, and therefore, it is essential to systematically fade prompts and thin reinforcement schedules to ensure that stimulus control is transferred from artificially delivered reinforcement (e.g., giving a student a chip) to more naturally occurring stimuli and reinforcers (e.g., having a peer respond to a social bid and ask to play a preferred game with the child).

USING RESPONSE PROMPTING STRATEGIES TO TEACH NEW SKILLS AND BEHAVIORS

Response prompting strategies (Wolery et al., 1992) are instructional techniques that can be used to teach many different discrete and chained behaviors. Response prompting strategies use different forms of prompts to elicit the desired behaviors from the child. Once the behaviors occur, differential reinforcement is provided and the prompts are systematically faded. The method by which the prompts are faded differs by strategy and will be outlined with each description. Advantages of response prompting strategies include (a) minimal student errors, (b) efficient use of resources (e.g., teacher time), and (c) the programmed introduction and removal of prompts (Wolery et al., 1992).

Although there are multiple types of response prompting strategies, all share five procedural characteristics. First, the target stimulus is originally presented in its final form; that is, the target stimulus is not modified in later trials or sessions. It remains the same throughout instruction. Second, response prompting strategies deliver prompts systematically to ensure the target behavior occurs in the presence of the target stimulus. When using response prompting strategies, it is essential to identify a controlling prompt. Third, learners can respond to the target stimulus with or without prompts across trials in most instructional sessions. Fourth, differential reinforcement is used to transfer stimulus control from the prompt to the target stimulus. Thus, one procedural requirement is the identification of a deliverable reinforcer. Finally, the prompts are systematically faded and removed. When using response prompting strategies, it is important to find a controlling prompt (i.e., a prompt that ensures the student will perform the target behavior and receive the reinforcement).

Although there are many similarities across the response prompting strategies, they do vary with respect to the type of prompt or the timing of the prompt delivery. We describe three response prompting strategies in this chapter: simultaneous prompting, time delay, and the system of least prompts. Each strategy also has specific procedural prerequisites and necessary child prerequisites, which are shown in Table 7.2. Although we hope the information in this chapter provides the detail necessary to implement these strategies, more detail on response prompting strategies can be found in Wolery et al. (1992), the Wikipedia entry on "response prompting strategies," and the Autism Internet Modules on prompting (Neitzel & Wolery, 2010) and time delay (Neitzel, 2010d).

Simultaneous Prompting

Simultaneous prompting involves providing a controlling prompt immediately after presenting the target stimulus. Simultaneous prompting only uses one prompt, and since there is only one prompt, it must be a controlling prompt. Because the controlling prompt is always provided immediately after the presentation of the target stimulus, prompts are not faded in this strategy and two types of sessions are needed: instructional sessions, which are used to teach the student the new behavior, and probe sessions, which are used to assess the child's acquisition of the new behavior.

Instructional sessions are sessions in which learners are prompted with a controlling prompt on each trial. An example of an instructional

Table 7.2 Procedural and Child Prerequisites for Response Prompting Strategies

	Prerequisites	
Strategy	*Procedural*	*Child*
Simultaneous Prompting	• Two types of sessions	• Identify controlling prompt
	• One prompt (must be controlling)	• Identify deliverable reinforcer
Constant Time Delay	• One type of session	• Identify controlling prompt
	• One prompt (must be controlling)	• Identify deliverable reinforcer
	• Constant response interval	• Child must be able to wait for help
	• Two types of trials (0-second trials and delay trials)	
Progressive Time Delay	• One type of session	• Identify controlling prompt
	• One prompt (must be controlling)	• Identify deliverable reinforcer
	• Specify response interval schedule	
	• Two types of trials (0-second trials and delay trials)	
System of Least Prompts	• One type of session	• Identify controlling prompt
	• One type of trial	• Identify deliverable reinforcer
	• Prompt hierarchy with at least three levels ordered by degree of assistance	• Child must be able to wait for help

trial is provided in Table 7.3. As shown in the table, to conduct a trial during an instructional session trial you would present the target stimulus, immediately deliver the controlling prompt, provide a short learner response interval (e.g., wait 3 to 5 seconds, giving the child an opportunity to respond), and provide response contingency (see Step 7 in Table 7.3 for examples of the consequences used for the time delay strategies). Because the student does not have the opportunity to perform the target behavior without (before) a prompt during instructional trials, you must use a probe session to assess his or her performance. Probe sessions are sessions in which no prompts are provided and are necessary to monitor learning. The only difference between instructional trials and probe trials is the presence of the controlling prompt—probe sessions do not have the controlling prompt.

Although you must use two different types of sessions for simultaneous prompting (i.e., instructional sessions and probe sessions), these sessions can occur back-to-back (i.e., conduct the probe session immediately before the instructional session). This back-to-back arrangement of probe and instructional sessions for simultaneous prompting adds some, but not a significant amount of time compared to the time delay strategies. Moreover, it might not be necessary to conduct daily probe sessions (Reichow & Wolery, 2009a), although further study of alternative session arrangements is needed before broad generalizations can be made. Although adding the probe sessions might not add much more teacher time, it does add complexity, thought, and preparation, which you should consider when choosing to use this strategy. Simultaneous prompting has been studied nearly exclusively in preschool-aged children with disabilities in one-to-one teaching formats, and it has been shown to be a highly effective treatment option for teaching mainly discrete behaviors (a single behavior). Additional information on simultaneous prompting can be found in the Autism Internet Module for prompting (Neitzel & Wolery, 2010).

Time Delay

Time delay strategies (sometimes referred to as prompt delay strategies) have been used for many years to teach new behaviors. We cover two time delay strategies in this chapter: constant time delay (CTD) and progressive time delay (PTD). The time delay strategies have many similarities with simultaneous prompting (Table 7.3 shows the similarities and differences among simultaneous prompting, CTD, and PTD). Like simultaneous prompting, CTD and PTD use only one prompt, which must be a controlling prompt. Unlike simultaneous prompting, only one type of session is used, which is similar to the instructional session used in simultaneous prompting. Although there is only one type of session, the time delay procedures use two types of trials: 0-second trials, which are identical to instructional session trials of simultaneous prompting, and delay trials. When you conduct a 0-second delay instructional session trial, you would present the target stimulus, immediately deliver the controlling prompt, provide a short learner response interval (e.g., 3 to 5 seconds), and provide differential consequences. After the child responds correctly to the controlling prompt, you cease using the 0-second delay interval and begin delaying the delivery of the controlling prompt after the presentation of the target stimulus. For example, if you were conducting an instructional session trial with a 4-second delay interval, you would present the target stimulus, wait 4 seconds (i.e., provide the delay interval), deliver the controlling prompt, provide a short learner response interval (e.g., 3 to 5 s), and provide differential consequences (see Step 7 in Table 7.3). With the time delay strategies, the prompts are faded temporally; that is, after the 0-second trials, the delay interval is inserted, allowing the child to perform the behavior without assistance. A more detailed description of the trial sequences for CTD and PTD are shown in Table 7.3, and more information on CTD and PTD can be located in Wolery et al. (1992) and in the Autism Internet Module on time delay (Neitzel, 2010d).

The procedures for CTD and PTD are exactly the same except for the delay interval. Each procedure begins with 0-second delay trials. After the 0-second delay trials, the delay interval increases. In CTD, the delay interval begins and remains at the maximum value (e.g., 5 seconds). To use CTD, the child must be able to wait for assistance (see box at left for a description of teaching a child how to wait). With PTD, the delay interval is gradually increased until the maximum value is reached. For example, if you had a maximum delay of 4 seconds, you might increase the delay by 1 second every third trial; thus the delay sequence would be a 0-second delay until correct responding to controlling prompt, three sessions of 1-second delay, three sessions of 2-second delay, three sessions of 3-second delay, and a 4-second delay until the child achieves fluency.

Because many children with autism have difficulty waiting and CTD has not been shown to be superior to PTD for children with autism, we recommend using PTD to teach new behaviors to your students. Overall, CTD and PTD have both been shown to be very successful for teaching a variety of behaviors to young children with autism (see Walker, 2008, for a review of using CTD and PTD to teach children with autism).

Teaching a Child to Wait for Assistance (i.e., Wait Training)

Constant time delay and the system of least prompts require the child to wait for assistance. Not all children come to school with this skill, so it will be necessary to teach some of your students how to wait. For some students, teaching them to wait can be as simple as telling them to wait for help if they don't know the answer (this can also be paired with a gestural cue; i.e., showing the child a flat palm as a cue to stop). Other children might need more explicit instruction. For these children, you will want to create a situation in which they are presented tasks they cannot complete without help (i.e., something that is too hard for them to do). When using this procedure, at first you will immediately provide the correct response (i.e., 0-second interval trials) and then gradually increase the interval after the child responds correctly until the desired interval is obtained. The child should be reinforced for providing the correct response after waiting. If the child responds before the end of the delay interval, you would say, "No, wait for me to tell you," and proceed to the next trial. See Wolery et al. (1992) for additional descriptions and examples of wait training procedures.

Table 7.3   Procedural Comparison of Instructional Trials for Simultaneous Prompting, Constant Time Delay, and Progressive Time Delay (the skill being taught follows the procedure's name in parentheses)

Step	Simultaneous Prompting with error correction (reading sight word—"dog")	Constant Time Delay (requesting preferred item [e.g., bubbles] using a line drawing)	Progressive Time Delay (clapping hands)
1	Deliver attending cue (e.g., say, "Look at me")	Deliver attending cue (e.g., state child's name)	Deliver attending cue (e.g., say, "Are you ready?")
2	Secure attending response (e.g., child looks at you)	Secure attending response (e.g., child looks at you)	Secure attending response (e.g., child says, "okay")
3	Present target stimulus and provide task direction (e.g., show the child a flash card with the word "dog" written on it and ask the child, "What is this?")	Present target stimulus and provide task directions (e.g., show the child a line drawing of a can of bubbles and ask the child, "What do you want?")	Present target stimulus (and task direction; e.g., say, "Clap hands")
4	No delay interval (i.e., 0-second delay interval)—child should not have time to respond before you provide the controlling prompt, but if the child does respond (and even if he or she is correct), go to Step 5	Provide constant delay interval (i.e., always 3 seconds)—if child hands you the line drawing of bubbles before the controlling prompt, go to Step 7—if child makes an error (e.g., says, "Juice") or does not respond, go to Step 5	Provide programmed delay intervals (e.g., 0seconds, 1second, 2seconds, 3seconds)—if child claps hands before controlling prompt, go to Step 7—if child makes error or does not respond, go to Step 5
5	Deliver controlling prompt (verbal model; e.g., say, "Dog")	Deliver controlling prompt (full physical prompt; e.g., place child's hand on line drawing of bubbles and assist the child in picking up the line drawing and handing it to the teacher)	Deliver controlling prompt (e.g., full physical prompt; place your hands over child's hands and clap child's hands)
6	Provide response interval (e.g., wait 3–5 seconds)	Provide response interval (e.g., wait 3–5 seconds)	Provide response interval (e.g., wait 3–5 seconds)

Table 7.3   (Continued)

Step	Simultaneous Prompting with error correction (reading sight word—"dog")	Constant Time Delay (requesting preferred item [e.g., bubbles] using a line drawing)	Progressive Time Delay (clapping hands)
7	Deliver response contingency: • Correct—reinforce (e.g., say, "That's right, this spells dog," and give child a chip) • Wrong—error correction (e.g., say, "No, this spells dog") • No response—ignore	Deliver response contingency: • Correct—reinforce (e.g., say, "You want bubbles," and blow bubbles for child) • Wrong—ignore • No response—ignore	Deliver response contingency: • Correct—reinforce (say, "Good clapping hands," and give child highfive) • Wrong—ignore • No response—ignore
8	Provide 2- to 5-second-intertrial interval and proceed to next trial (i.e., wait 2–5 seconds and move on)	Provide 2- to 5-second-intertrial interval and proceed to next trial (i.e., wait 2–5 seconds and move on)	Provide 2- to 5-second-intertrial interval and proceed to next trial (i.e., wait 2–5 seconds and move on)

Vignette 1: Teaching Colors Using Progressive Time Delay (PTD)

PTD is an excellent strategy for teaching discrete identification skills to children with autism. For example, a teacher might use PTD to teach DJ to identify colors using PTD in a 1:1 massed trial format during his afternoon work session. During the work session, the teacher would work on having DJ expressively name three different sightwords (e.g., "dog," "cat," "rat") and would present them for four trials each session (total of 12 trials for the entire session). The teacher might then ask DJ to name the sightwords when they are presented during an inclusive circle-time each morning. By priming the student in an individual session, the teacher not only increases the likelihood that he will generalize the skill (it is being taught in a different location by a new person) but also provides a means of increasing his participation in activities with his peers, which is often difficult for students with autism.

System of Least Prompts

Simultaneous prompting and the time delay strategies can only accommodate one prompt, which has to be a controlling prompt. However, sometimes it is desirable to have multiple prompts. One procedure that accommodates multiple types of prompts is the *system of least prompts.* The system of least prompts uses a prompt hierarchy that orders prompts with respect to the amount of assistance that they provide to the child and is the third and final response prompting procedure we cover in this chapter. When using the system of least prompts, you provide the student an opportunity to perform the behavior independently. If the child does not perform the behavior, you then offer increasing assistance until he or she performs the behavior. Typically, a hierarchy of three, four, or five levels is used with this procedure.

When you use the system of least prompts, the first prompt you present is the one that provides the least amount of assistance to the child (typically presenting the target stimulus to the child). After you present the prompt, you then provide the child with an opportunity to respond. If your first prompt is solely the presentation of the target stimulus, the child has the opportunity to perform the behavior without assistance and therefore this level is often referred to as the independent level. If the child performs the behavior you are teaching, you reinforce the child for performing the behavior. If the child does not perform the behavior you are teaching, you will re-present the target stimulus and then provide an intermediate prompt. An intermediate prompt is a prompt that provides greater assistance to the child. Whenever the child performs the behavior, he or she is reinforced. If the child does not perform the behavior, you move to the next level of the hierarchy (i.e., moving to the next level is the consequence for not performing the desired behavior). You can use up to three levels of intermediate prompts when using the system of least prompts. To ensure the skill or behavior that you are teaching is performed, the final prompt of the prompt hierarchy will always be the controlling prompt. For example, you might use the system of least prompts with four levels in which the first level is presenting the target stimulus (e.g., teacher says, "It is time to wash hands"), the second level is a verbal prompt (e.g., teacher says, "Monique, wash hands"), the third level is a partial physical prompt (e.g., you place your hand on Monique's shoulder and gently directing her toward the sink"), and the fourth level is the controlling prompt (e.g., full physical prompt in which you assist Monique to the sink).

As with simultaneous prompting and the time delay strategies, reinforcement is delivered for all correct responses (regardless of where in the hierarchy the behavior is performed). However, unlike the time delay strategies and simultaneous prompting, which might not use an error correction procedure, the system of least prompts has programmed consequences; no responses or errant responses trigger the next level of prompt (i.e., a more intrusive prompt). In the system of least prompts, the prompts are faded temporally; as the child becomes more fluent performing a behavior, he or she will begin performing the behavior earlier in the response interval, which will not trigger moving to the next level of the prompt hierarchy.

The system of least prompts is often used to teach chained behaviors and has been shown to be an effective method for teaching many behaviors to children with autism. However, this procedure requires many more teacher decisions than the time delay strategies and can be more difficult to implement. It has also been shown to be less efficient than the time delay strategies. However, the procedure allows the child to "choose" the level of support needed, which can help the child learn to learn (Doyle, Wolery, Gast, Ault, & Wiley, 1990). Moreover, it has recently shown promise for teaching pretend play behavior (Barton & Wolery, 2008, 2010), which is a difficult skill to teach children with autism. Collectively, the strategy can be used very effectively and should be considered when designing systematic instruction for children with autism.

TEACHING CHAINED BEHAVIORS

To save space, most of the examples of the response prompting strategies provided in this chapter have focused on discrete tasks, that is, behaviors that can be completed in one behavior. This is not to say that these strategies are not appropriate for chained tasks, which are tasks that take multiple steps to complete. All of these strategies can be used and have been shown to be an effective method for teaching chained tasks. The first step in teaching a chained behavior is to complete a task analysis of the skill you are trying to teach. A task analysis involves breaking the chained task into smaller teachable steps (Cooper et al., 2007). For example, if you task analyzed washing hands, the discrete steps might be as follows: (1) go to the sink, (2) turn on the water, (3) put soap on hands, (4) rub hands, (5) place hands under water and rub for 30 seconds, (6) turn off water, and (7) dry hands. When using response prompting strategies to teach chained tasks, you would use the strategy for each step of the task; that is, you would provide prompts for all steps. Additional information on using response prompting strategies to teach chained tasks can be located in Wolery et al. (1992), and additional information on task analysis can be found on the Autism Internet Module website (Szidon & Franzone, 2010) and in Cooper et al. (2007).

Vignette 2: Teaching a Child to Put on a Shirt

Putting on a shirt is a skill that has many different components, which is sometimes referred to as a chained task. To teach a chained task, one must complete a task analysis to identify each step in the task. A task analysis of putting on a T-shirt might include the following behaviors:

- *Pick up the shirt*
- *Ensure front of shirt is facing away from you*
- *Put both hands through bottom of shirt*
- *Place right hand through small hole on right*
- *Place left hand through small hole on left*
- *Place head through large hole on top of shirt*
- *Pull down shirt*

Sometimes there are multiple ways to do a skill; in this example, one might teach the child to put his head into the shirt before his arms, and a shirt that has buttons would require a whole new analysis. This is fine; it is important to develop a systematic way to teach children new behaviors. The system of least prompts is one strategy that could effectively be used to teach this behavior and would help ensure that the least intrusive prompt is being provided at each step.

MODIFYING INSTRUCTIONAL ARRANGEMENTS TO INCREASE THE EFFICIENCY OF LEARNING

Educating children who have autism takes much preparation and skill and is often very costly. Therefore, we should strive to use effective methods (i.e., evidence-based practices), and we should aim to use the methods with the greatest efficiency. To be an evidence-based practice, a strategy must have been repeatedly shown to be effective; that is, the strategy must be shown to work for many children. All of the procedures described earlier are evidence-based treatments for teaching new behaviors to young children with autism.

Although a goal of evidence-based practice is to identify which treatments are most effective for teaching specific children specific behaviors under specific conditions, our knowledge of treating children with autism has not reached this level and you must rely on your clinical and practical expertise when choosing intervention strategies. This is important to consider when teaching children with autism, because although no single technique is likely to work for every child who has autism, it is likely that multiple techniques will work with individual children.

Different teaching strategies have varying degrees of efficiency; that is, two different strategies can be equally effective but one strategy can be more efficient. Wolery et al. (1992) defined efficiency as, "an instructional procedure that results in learning (i.e., is effective) *and* is better than some other instructional procedure" (p. 220). Wolery and colleagues suggested five types of efficiency: (1) more rapid learning, (2) greater generalization, (3) emergence of unintentional relations, (4) broader learning, and (5) promotion of future learning. While all of the teaching strategies covered in this chapter are effective (e.g., evidence-based), there are differences with respect to their efficiency. When faced with choosing between two equally effective teaching strategies, we recommend examining the efficiency of the strategies and choosing the strategy that is most efficient or choosing a strategy that can be modified to increase learning efficiency. If two methods have equal effectiveness and efficiency, we recommend using the law of parsimony and choosing the easiest method to implement. In this section of the chapter, we provide additional recommendations on how to maximize learning efficiency by modifying instructional arrangements.

Instructive Feedback

Instructive feedback is an instructional modification in which you add extra, nontarget stimuli to the consequent events of direct instructional trials. For example, a teacher may show a child a picture of a dog and say, "What's this?" When the child answers "dog," the teacher might say, "That's right, this is a dog, and a dog is a mammal." The teacher's statement, "a dog is a mammal," is the instructive feedback. Students are not asked or required to respond to these extra stimuli (although many do respond), and you do not provide the child with a reinforcer if he or she does respond (Werts, Wolery, Holcombe, & Gast, 1995). Research has shown that children frequently learn the instructive feedback without additional instruction when instructive feedback is presented (Werts et al., 1995).

There are three variations of instructive feedback: expansion, novel, and parallel. The types of instructive feedback are defined in terms of their relation to the new skills or behaviors that are being taught directly to the child. For expansion instructive feedback, the new skill or behavior you are teaching and instructive feedback that you are teaching are different from one another, but they are related conceptually. For example, if you are teaching a child to name shapes (e.g., triangle, square), you could present instructive feedback telling the child how many sides each shape has (e.g., "a triangle has three sides"; "a square has four sides"). A variation of expansion instructive feedback can be presenting instructive feedback that is different and not conceptually related but comes from a similar curricular domain. For example, if you are teaching a child to verbally name different fruits (e.g., apple, grapes, and orange), you might show and name different fruits for instructive feedback (e.g., pear, cherry, plum; Reichow & Wolery, 2011). Novel instructive feedback is different from the new skill or behavior you are teaching, has different responses from the new skill or behavior, is not conceptually related to the new skill or behavior, and it is not from the similar curricular domain. For example, if you are teaching a child to request bubbles, you could tell the child addition facts (e.g., say, "one plus one is two") for instructive feedback. The last type of instructive feedback is parallel instructive feedback. With parallel instructive feedback, the stimulus for the new skill or behavior you are teaching and the instructive feedback stimulus are different from one another, but the responses are the same. For example, if you are teaching a child to name Arabic numerals (e.g., 3 and 4), you might show the child the Roman numerals for instructive feedback (e.g., III and IV; Holcombe, Wolery, Werts, & Hrenkevich, 1993).

Reichow and Wolery (2011) recently examined instructive feedback with four young children with autism using the PTD procedure. Their findings showed when the PTD was paired with instructive feedback, the students learned twice as many skills in a similar amount of time. Reichow and Wolery extrapolated their data two ways to show how instructive feedback increased efficiency. First, 10 sessions (one session a day for 2 school weeks) might be needed to teach *two* skills using PTD without instructive feedback, but *four* skills could be taught if PTD was paired with instructive feedback in the same number of sessions. Second, if a teacher wanted to teach *four* new skills, approximately 145 minutes would be needed if the teacher used PTD without instructive feedback, while only 74 minutes would be necessary if the student was taught using PTD with instructive feedback. Although there is not extensive research on using instructive feedback with children who have autism, emerging research (e.g., Ledford, Gast, Luscre, & Ayres, 2008; Reichow & Wolery, 2011) suggests it can be a very effective method for increasing the efficiency of instruction and should be integrated into instructional practice whenever possible.

Capitalizing on Preference for Predictability and Routines

Although not a modification per se, a strategy that might increase efficiency is using predictable and familiar instructional arrangements. As described in Chapter 3, children with autism often prefer consistency and routines in their lives and benefit from having predictability and routines throughout the day. Although such insistence on sameness can cause problems (e.g., a student might have a tantrum if it is raining outside and she is not able to walk through the courtyard on the way to lunch), it might be something that you can use to your advantage. You might capitalize on this preference of predictability and routines by using a consistent teaching format or method (e.g., 1:1 discrete trial training in which the teacher and child are seated across from one another at a table [Lovaas, 2003] or visually structured tasks [e.g., Mesibov et al., 2005]). Reichow and Wolery (2011) recently showed that once students learned an instructional format, they could acquire additional information more rapidly when the same format was used.

One method that capitalizes on predictability and routine is the structured teaching format described by Mesibov and colleagues (Mesibov et al., 2005, http://www.teacch.org), which is comprised of six elements: (1) organization of the physical environment to suit the specific needs of the child, (2) a predictable sequence of activities so the child knows what is coming next and when the activity will end, (3) visual schedules to increase predictability and communicate what to do, (4) routines with flexibility, (5) work and activity systems for providing materials allowing independent performance, and (6) visually structured activities serving to clarify expectations. Structured teaching has been used to teach individuals with autism a variety of skills, and it might be a strategy that can be modified for use in regular education settings. For example, Bennett, Reichow, and Wolery (2011) recently incorporated interlocking puzzles into a structured work system (the puzzles were visually structured and placed in a work system paired with a visual activity schedule) in an inclusive preschool classroom for a 5-year-old girl with autism (Bennett et al., 2011). Another example would be providing seatwork (e.g., worksheets) in a double pocket folder in which the left side was labeled "To Do" and the right side was labeled "Finished."

Small Group Instructional Arrangements

Research has shown direct instruction in one-to-one arrangements is an effective method for educating young children with autism (e.g., Reichow, in press; Reichow & Wolery, 2009b). Although parents of children with autism often request one-to-one instruction for their child, it is not always feasible in many education settings. An alternative instructional arrangement that is often used is small group instruction, which has been shown to be an effective teaching arrangement for students with autism and has many potential advantages (Lewis, Ledford, Elam, Wolery, & Gast, 2010). First, small group instruction can increase teaching and learning efficiency when students have the opportunity to learn each other's target behaviors through observational learning (e.g., Ledford et al., 2008). For example, you might create a small group with two students (Jeremy and Max). During the small group instruction, you can teach Jeremy two target behaviors and two instructive feedback targets and teach Max two target behaviors and two instructive feedback targets. In this arrangement, you will only be teaching each student two target behaviors, but each student will have the opportunity to learn eight behaviors (their two target behaviors, their two instructive feedback behaviors, their peer's two target behaviors, and their peer's two instructive feedback behaviors), which is a 300% increase in efficiency! Second, small group instruction creates an arrangement in which children with autism have increased social contact with peers. This social arrangement affords you the opportunity to embed social learning opportunities (e.g., turn taking, waiting, responding to peer, exchanging objects with peer), which can also increase the efficiency of your teaching since you are covering more targets during instruction. Finally, teaching in small groups helps a child acquire behaviors needed for learning in other formats (e.g., waiting for turn, attending to instruction when not given directly to the child), thereby increasing their ability to participate in other instructional settings, such as whole class formats that are common in many general education settings.

FUTURE DIRECTIONS

There are now many treatments and interventions for young children with autism that are classified as evidence-based practices (National Autism Center, 2009a, 2009b; Reichow, Doehring, Cicchetti, & Volkmar, 2011; Rogers & Vismara, 2008; Scottish Intercollegiate Guidelines Network, 2007). Recent outcome analyses also suggest that the overall outcome for individuals who have autism is improving (Howlin, 2005; Levy & Perry, in press). Although the increasing number of evidence-based practices is encouraging, little is known and few guidelines exist that recommend which treatment will be effective for learners with specific characteristics (cf. Yoder & Stone, 2006; Schreibman, Stahmer, Barlett, & Dufek, 2009; Scherer & Schreibman, 2005). Although this chapter provides some guidance, we must continue to refine our knowledge about which instructional techniques work best (i.e., are most efficient) for which skills and behaviors.

Finally, no single instructional strategy or modality is effective for all individuals with autism. Although our knowledge of the effectiveness of treatments for individuals with autism has increased greatly over the last few decades (e.g., Reichow & Volkmar, 2011; Volkmar, Reichow, & Doehring, 2011), there are still children receiving good treatment programs that make little to no progress. When you introduce a new technique to a class of children, it is not uncommon for some children to respond well and learn quickly and others to make slow or no progress. It is therefore essential to continuously monitor progress and evaluate the data to make treatment decisions (see Chapter 6; Gischlar, Hojnoski, & Missall, 2009; Hojnoski et al., 2009a, 2009b, for a description of the data-based decision making process and the National Autism Center [2009b] resource for practicing evidence-based practices in schools). Chapter 8 provides an overview of the next component of instruction—programming for generalization and maintenance. Work also must be done on how to identify individuals who are not responding to treatment. We must continue to develop more sensitive measures to track progress and develop guidelines that practitioners can follow, informing them when to cease one treatment and begin a new treatment.

LEARNING ACTIVITIES

1. Describe how you would use PTD to teach DJ to identify letters and numbers. When and how would you teach?

2. Describe how to use the system of least prompts to teach DJ to play with toys and peers at school.

3. How would you teach Leroy to independently complete self-help skills (e.g., getting dressed, washing hands)?

4. Describe how you would use PTD with instructive feedback to teach Jim reading comprehension.

RESOURCES

Suggested Texts and Resources

Applied Behavior Analysis (2nd ed.). Cooper, Heron, and Heward (2007).

Applied Behavior Analysis for Teachers (8th ed.). Alberto and Troutman (2008).

Teaching Students With Moderate to Severe Disabilities: Use of Response Prompting Strategies. Wolery, Ault, and Doyle (1992).

Evidence-Based Practice and Autism in the Schools: A Guide to Providing Appropriate Interventions to Students With Autism Spectrum Disorders. National Autism Center (2009b).

Suggested Websites

Autism Internet Modules—Modules on prompting, reinforcement, task analysis, and time delay: **http://www.autisminternetmodules.org**

The National Professional Development Center on Autism Spectrum Disorders—Evidence-based practice briefs on prompting, reinforcement, task analysis, and time delay: **http:// autismpdc.fpg.unc.edu/**

National Autism Center (National Standards Project):**http://www .nationalautismcenter.org/**

Wikipedia entry on response prompting procedures: **http://en.wikipedia .org/wiki/Response_Prompting_Procedures**

Wikipedia entry on reinforcement: **http://en.wikipedia.org/wiki/ Reinforcement**

8

Evidence-Based Strategies for Maintenance, Generalization, and Self-Management

Sarah E. Pinkelman

University of Oregon

Erin E. Barton

University of Colorado Denver

Chapter Objectives:
- Define and describe strategies for promoting maintenance.
- Define and describe strategies for programming generalization.
- Define and describe strategies for teaching self-management.

Children learn new skills through a variety of methods (e.g., obser-vation, adult prompting, environmental cues). Once a student has learned a new skill, it is imperative to ensure the student has generalized (i.e., performed in different settings, activities, or routines; with different peers or adults; and with different stimuli [materials, cues]) and main-tained the skill over time (i.e., performs the skill for consecutive days, weeks, or months with naturally occurring antecedent cues and without the adult or environmental prompts). This may be particularly impor-tant for young children with autism, given their propensity for repetitive behaviors and adherence to sameness (http://www.cdc.gov/ncbddd/autism/signs.html). Students with autism often have difficulty general-izing new skills to new contexts (National Autism Center, 2009b). Also, many children with autism will need to be explicitly taught to monitor their own behavior to promote independence and fluency of new skills (Koegel, Koegel, Harrower, & Carter, 1999). Thus, strategies to promote generalization, maintenance, and self-management are essential aspects of effective curricula for children with autism (Dawson & Osterling, 1997; National Research Council, 2001). This chapter further describes these important issues, provides recommendations based on the current litera-ture, and describes specific examples.

MAINTENANCE OF NEW SKILLS

Many new skills are initially taught in highly supported, adult-directed contexts; this is an effective practice for many young children with autism. Once the child has learned a new skill in a highly structured context, it is important to ensure they maintain the skill in natural, less controlled contexts. This means that the child can perform the skill over time, even after systematic prompting is withdrawn (Alberto & Troutman, 2008). Maintenance of skills cannot be assumed. Just because a child can perform a behavior in one setting today does not mean he or she will be able to do so a month from now. In fact, children with autism often display deficits in maintaining previously acquired skills and might become prompt depen-dent. As such, instruction should include components for intentionally teaching maintenance. The subsequent section describes evidence-based strategies for promoting maintenance of new skills.

Fading Prompts to Promote Maintenance

Adult prompting is an effective method for teaching new skills (see Chapter 7). However, prompts must be systematically faded as effi-ciently as possible to ensure the child learns to perform the skill indepen-dently. Prompts should be viewed as a temporary teaching tool or support system and meant to enhance the student's capacity to perform the skill independently under natural conditions. This is particularly important for children with autism, because many children with autism are likely to become prompt dependent (Maurice, Green, & Luce, 1996). *Prompt dependency* is when a child has difficulty performing the behavior without a prompt or becomes *dependent* on the prompt for correct responding (Maurice, Green, & Luce, 1996). Stated more technically, prompt dependency occurs when stimulus control does not transfer from the prompt to the naturally occurring cue, for example, if the teacher is instructing DJ to greet a friend by vocalizing "Hi Miguel" using a script (in the form of an index card with "Hi Miguel" written on it). After several days of correct responding, the teacher should start fading the prompt (e.g., not showing the card at all). If DJ does not greet Miguel at all after the teacher faded the prompt, transfer of stimulus control from the prompt (script) to the naturally occurring cue (presence of Miguel) did not occur. The teacher should review the fading or teaching plan and begin systematically fading over time (e.g., showing a smaller index card, showing an index card that only says, "Hi," or showing the index card every other opportunity). Figure 8.1 illustrates this prompt fading procedure. A child's instructional program must include intentional strategies for ensuring the child performs the behavior independently under the appropriate, naturally occurring conditions—without a prompt. For example, when teaching a child with autism in a preschool classroom to start putting away toys when the teacher plays the cleanup song, you might give the child a verbal warning, show the child a visual cue or picture of the cleanup routine, use a First/Then visual reminder (e.g., **First** clean up, **Then** get snack), and physically help the child clean up toys. Eventually you want to fade all prompts (visuals, First/Then, physical help) so that the child independently starts putting away toys after hearing the cleanup song.

Table 7.1 in Chapter 7 outlines types of adult prompts. There are three prompt delivery methods: physical, visual, and verbal. Physical prompts include physical contact with the student (i.e., full and partial physical). Visual prompts require that the student attend to some form of visual stimuli (e.g., pictorial cues, gestural prompts, motor skills modeled by the teacher, etc.). Verbal prompts include a vocal prompt made by the teacher (e.g., verbal models, verbal prompt). Prompts also are provided along a continuum support. For example, gestural prompts provide the least amount of support, whereas full physical prompts provide the most. Fading from a more supportive (or intrusive) prompt to a less supportive prompt is commonly referred to as most-to-least prompting. For example, a teacher might write a teaching plan that "begins with a full physical prompt for the desired response, then fades to a gesture or model, and ends with the verbal instruction" (Maurice et al., 1996, p. 189). In this manner, the teacher systematically fades prompts over time, based on the child's performance. On the contrary, fading from a less supportive prompt to a more supportive prompt is referred to as least-to-most

Figure 8.1   Instructional Plan for Teaching Miguel to Use Greetings

Child: Miguel
Goal: Greeting friends
Instructional procedure: Most to least prompting
Materials: Visual cue card of greeting: "Hi [peer's name]," with picture of peer
Data collection procedure: Frequency count of prompted and unprompted greetings

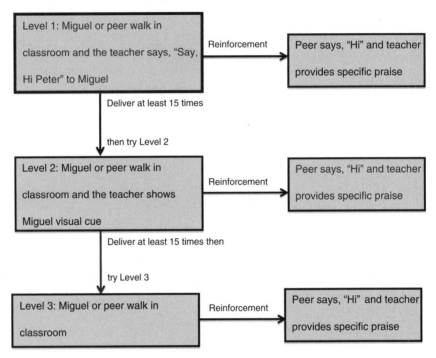

prompting. Here, "the task is presented in its terminal form at the start of a trial, and successive prompts within a trial provide increasingly more assistance to the individual" as needed (Fisher, Kodak, & Moore, 2007, p. 490). For example, when teaching a child to make a verbal request, the teacher might place a preferred object in front of the child and wait for a response. If the child does not respond, the teacher might point to the object, give a choice between two objects, or model the request, "I want the doll." If the child responds, he or she gets the object; if the child does not respond, the adult might use a full verbal or physical prompt: "Say, I want doll." In this manner, the teacher also fades prompts over time based on the child's performance within the instructional session.

Both prompt delivery methods and the amount of support provided to the student are essential considerations when fading prompts. It is typically (but not always) appropriate to fade within the prompt delivery method. For example, if a child is learning hand washing utilizing a full physical prompt, the next step would be to fade to a partial physical prompt at the child's wrist, then at the child's elbow, and so forth.

According to this hierarchy, the next step in the fading process would be a model prompt. However, depending upon the needs of the child, it may be inappropriate to model hand washing. Rather, it might be best to continue with a physical prompt, by fading to a light touch on the student's back to prompt hand washing. Table 8.1 outlines common fading procedures for most-to-least and least-to-most prompting.

Considerations should also be made regarding a within-stimulus prompt as opposed to an extrastimulus prompt. Early research in the area of stimulus control has been applied to working with children with autism and is relevant here. Schreibman (1975) compared the effectiveness of extrastimulus prompting and within-stimulus prompting to teach visual and auditory discriminations to children with autism. The researchers taught the children to identify differences between two simple stick figures. Other discriminations that might be taught in the classroom are identifying colors, letters, shapes, or sight words. Extrastimulus prompting is similar to the prompting methods described earlier, where an additional cue is presented (e.g., a gestural prompt is provided by pointing to the correct answer). Here, the child must attend to two stimuli: the prompt and the training stimulus. On the contrary, within-stimulus prompting is when an "exaggeration of the relevant component of the training stimulus" (Schreibman, 1975, p. 91) is provided. Here, the child only needs to attend to one stimulus: the training stimulus. The within-stimulus method is more effective than the extrastimulus method for teaching some skills to children with autism (Schreibman, 1975). For instance, when teaching a child to identify a triangle from an array of several shapes, a within-stimulus prompt would be to increase the size or change the color of the triangle so that it differs from the other shapes and figures.

Within-stimulus prompts should be systematically faded in a manner similar to any other prompt. Stimulus features that were manipulated to be more salient (e.g., size or color) should be gradually faded as the child is successful, until the stimulus is in its original form. In the previous example, say the teacher manipulated the color and made the triangle green, while keeping the other shapes black. Fading would include gradually darkening the green color over a period of several days or weeks (depending on the child's success with each step in the fading process) until it is the same color as the other shapes (black).

Regardless of the prompt used, intentional, systematic fading is essential. This means that teachers monitor the child's progress over time to ensure instructional and fading procedures are effective. If a child is performing at a low rate of success, it is inappropriate to fade to a less supportive prompt. Rather, it is more effective to remain at the current prompt level or even provide a more supportive prompt so the child's rate of success increases. Fading is more effective when commenced after a high rate of success has been maintained for a period of time (i.e., the amount of time depends on the child's learning history and the specific skill).

Table 8.1 Examples of Prompt Fading Procedures

Fading Procedure	Level	Skill 1: Communication (requesting an activity)	Skill 2: Following directions (line up to walk outside)	Skill 3: Social interactions
Most to Least*	1	"Say, Computer" or physically hand over/hand prompt the child to point to the computer card. Deliver 10 to 15 times and try Level 2. Move back to Level 1 if the child is not successful with Level 2 or adapt the Level 2 prompt.	Physically guide the child outside (hold the child's hand or teach a peer to hold the child's hand). Deliver 10 to 15 times and try Level 2. Move back to Level 1 if the child is not successful with Level 2 or adapt the Level 2 prompt.	Hand over/hand prompt the child to catch the ball, then throw the ball. Deliver 10 to 15 times and try Level 2. Move back to Level 1 if the child is not successful with Level 2 or adapt the Level 2 prompt.
	2	Verbal model: "Computer" or "I want computer" and point to computer card. Deliver 10 to 15 times and try Level 3 or 4.**	Use a First/Then verbal and visual cue. First line up with friends, then go outside. Deliver 10 to 15 times and try Level 3 or 4.**	Use a First/Then verbal and visual cue: First Lucy's turn to throw, then your turn to throw. Deliver 10 to 15 times and try Level 3 or 4.**
	3	Give two verbal choices: "Computer or books?" or "Computer or books" while showing a picture of each. Deliver 10 to 15 times and try Level 4.	Give verbal directions with visual cues (pictures of lining up and going outside) or verbal directions and peer modeling (point to peer models in line). Deliver 10 to 15 times and try Level 4.	Give verbal choices: "Do you want to throw or catch?" or "Do you want to ask Lucy or Molly to play ball?" (use visuals if necessary). Deliver 10 to 15 times and try Level 4.
	4	Present the items.	Give the verbal directions.	Present an activity, materials, toys to two or more children (playing with a large ball).

Least to Most*			
1	Present the items. If the child does not make request, go to Level 2.	Give the verbal directions. If the child does not follow directions, go to Level 2.	Present an activity, materials, toys to two or more children (playing with a large ball). If the child does not interact with the peer, go to Level 2.
2	Give verbal choices: "Computer or books?" or "Computer or books?" while showing a picture of each. If the child does not make request, go to Level 3 or 4.**	Give verbal directions with visual cues (pictures of lining up and going outside) or verbal directions and peer modeling (point to peer models lining up). If the child does not follow directions, go to Level 3 or 4.**	Give verbal choices: "Do you want to throw or catch?" or "Do you want to ask Lucy or Molly to play ball?" (use visuals if necessary). If the child does not interact with the peer, go to Level 3 or 4.**
3	Verbal model: "Computer" or "I want computer" and point to computer card. If the child does not make request, go to Level 4.	Use a First/Then verbal and visual cue. First line up with friends, then go outside. If the child does not follow directions, go to Level 4.	Use a First/Then verbal and visual cue: First Lucy's turn to throw, then your turn to throw. If the child does not interact with the peer, go to Level 4.
4	Controlling prompt: "Say, Computer" or physically hand over/hand prompt the child to point to the computer card.	Controlling prompt: Physically guide the child outside (hold the child's hand or teach a peer to hold the child's hand).	Controlling prompt: Hand over/hand prompt the child to catch the ball, then throw the ball.

*If the child demonstrates the correct response or target behavior at any point during instruction, deliver the reinforcer.

**Least to most prompting and most to least prompting hierarchies can have three or four levels based on the child's learning history or progress.

Figure 8.2   Within Stimulus Prompting

Child: Jenny

Goal: Identifying her name

Instructional procedure: Within stimulus prompt fading with visual cue

Materials: Visual cue cards with names in an array with Jenny decreasing in size and alternating positions

Data collection procedure: Frequency count of correct identification of her name

Level 1:

Jenny Timmy Molly

Level 2:

Mark **Jenny** Carly

Level 3:

Johnny Molly **Jenny**

Level 4:

Casey Jenny Lucy

The child's instructional program should include a specific plan for fading prompts over time. The program should include which prompts will be faded and criteria for when they will be faded. For example, suppose DJ's teacher is teaching him to sign for "more" during snack. She begins by modeling the sign and vocalizing "more." Once DJ signs "more" after a model and verbal prompt for three consecutive attempts, she stops modeling and only provides the verbal prompt. Once DJ signs "more" on three consecutive opportunities after only the verbal prompt, she fades to using only a gestural prompt (i.e., pointing to the object). If at any point he stops using the sign after the gesture, she returns to using the verbal prompt. Figure 8.2 illustrates how you might use within-stimulus prompting to teach a child to identify her name.

Thinning Reinforcement to Promote Maintenance

When teaching a child a new skill, it is often necessary to initially reinforce the behavior more frequently and with more intensity than is present in the natural environment. For example, a child might receive verbal praise and the delivery of a preferred toy every time he or she correctly vocalizes the question, "Can I play with that?" However, when the child performs the same behavior in the natural environment (e.g., at home while playing with a sibling), it is unlikely that the response will be followed by verbal praise, and the child may or may not be given the toy. When teaching new skills, the reinforcement schedule might be quite different than the reinforcement schedule in the natural environment. In the teaching situation, a *continuous rate of reinforcement* (CRF) might be used, where every occurrence of the behavior is reinforced. In the natural environment, a *variable ratio* (VR) schedule of reinforcement is usually in place, where the behavior is reinforced after a variable number of occurrences (e.g., approximately every third occurrence; Catania, 2007). Table 8.2 provides descriptions of reinforcement schedules.

For behaviors to maintain and generalize from teaching situations to the natural environment, the reinforcement schedule must be gradually and systematically thinned. Otherwise, it is likely the child will stop performing the behavior (i.e., extinction will occur) in the natural environment (Alberto & Troutman, 2008). For example, the behavior "Can I play with that?" was suddenly changed from a CRF to a VR schedule. In the natural environment, this behavior might be reinforced on a VR10 schedule (where the child is given the toy approximately every tenth time they ask, "Can I play with that?"). Because the delivery of the reinforcer maintaining the behavior decreased, the child might use "Can I play with that?" fewer times and eventually stop using it all together (i.e., extinction). To avoid extinction, a gradual and systematic thinning of the reinforcement schedule should be programmed. In this example, it might be appropriate to first put the behavior on a VR 2 schedule (where the behavior is reinforced approximately every other time it occurs), then a VR 4 (where the behavior is reinforced approximately every fourth occurrence), and so on. Data should be collected to determine when it is appropriate to change the schedule of reinforcement. If the child is not performing the skill at a desirable level with CRF, it is inappropriate to thin the schedule. Rather, teaching should continue on a CRF until the data indicate the behavior is occurring at a desirable level.

In addition to thinning the reinforcement schedule to achieve maintenance of skills over time, it is also important to select reinforcers to promote maintenance in the natural environment. When initially teaching a skill, it is sometimes necessary to use reinforcers that would not occur in the natural environment. However, once the child acquires the skill, it is essential that reinforcers be introduced that will maintain the behavior in the natural environment. For instance, when initially teaching a child to tie his or her shoe, it may be necessary to deliver reinforcers such as preferred toys, verbal praise, edible items, and so forth, to motivate the child and ensure he or she performs the skill. However, once the child learns the skill, naturally occurring reinforcers should be systematically introduced.

Table 8.2 Schedules of Reinforcement

Schedule	Description	Examples	
Continuous rate of reinforcement (CRF)	Reinforcement is delivered after every occurrence of the target behavior.	A child is reinforced for every social interaction on the playground.	A child is reinforced for every verbal request during snack time.
Variable Ratio (VR)	Reinforcement is delivered on a variable schedule based on the child's behavior without regard to the amount of time that has passed. This schedule is often identified as the average number of responses per reinforcer. These schedules generally produce fast, steady rates of responding.	VR 3: Reinforcement is delivered every third behavior on average. A child is reinforced for every third social interaction on average on the playground.	VR 5: reinforcement is delivered every fifth behavior on average. A child is reinforced for every fifth verbal request on average during snack time.
Variable Interval (VI)	Reinforcement is delivered for a behavior after a specified amount of time has elapsed. The amount of time between reinforcers varies. The number of responses does not influence reinforcement.	VI 3-min: Reinforcement is delivered for a single response after an average of every 3 minutes A child is reinforced for the first social interaction after every 3 minutes on average on the playground.	VI 5-min: reinforcement is delivered for a single response after an average of every 5 minutes. A child is reinforced for the first verbal request after every 5 minutes on average during snack time.
Fixed Ratio (FR)	Reinforcement is delivered on a fixed rate. FR schedules require a predetermined number of behaviors to produce reinforcement. These schedules generally produce high, steady rates of responding, but are characterized by a **postreinforcement pause.**	FR 5: Reinforcement is delivered for every fifth behavior. A child is reinforced for every fifth social interaction on the playground.	FR 8: reinforcement is delivered for every eighth behavior. A child is reinforced for every eighth verbal request during snack time.
Fixed Interval (FI)	Reinforcement is delivered for the first response after a set period of time. Reinforcement is contingent on the elapsed time *and* the occurrence of the behavior, not just the elapsed time.	FR 3-min: Reinforcement is delivered for the first behavior after 3 minutes. A child is reinforced for the first social interaction after every 3 minutes on the playground.	FR 5-min: reinforcement is delivered for the first behavior after 5 minutes. A child is reinforced for the first verbal request after every 5 minutes during snack time.

Source: Cooper, Heron, and Heward, 2007.

Table 8.3 Thinning Reinforcement

Thinning Reinforcement Schedule	Goal: Toilet training	Thinning Reinforcement Schedule	Goal: Participating in circle time	Thinning Reinforcement Schedule	Goal: Raising hand to talk in class
CR	Provide a piece of candy or a sticker and a high five and specific praise for every time on the toilet.	CR	Give the child access to a preferred toy for the entire time he is engaged and participating in circle time and deliver specific praise throughout circle time.	CR	Give the child a sticker and specific praise for every time he independently raises his hand and call on him.
VR 3 (M&Ms) CRF (specific praise)	Provide a piece of candy or a sticker for an average of every third time on the toilet; give a high five and specific praise for every time.	FI 3-minute (toy) CRF (specific praise)	Give the child access to a preferred toy for 15 seconds for every 3 minutes he is engaged and participating in circle time and deliver specific praise throughout circle time.	FR 3 (sticker) CRF (specific praise)	Give the child a sticker for every third time he raises his hand; deliver specific praise for every time and call on him.
VR 5 (M&Ms) VR 3 (specific praise)	Provide a piece of candy or a sticker for an average of every fifth time on the toilet; give a high five and specific praise for every third time.	FI 5-minute (toy) FI 3-minute (specific praise)	Give the child access to a preferred toy for 15 seconds for every 5 minutes he is engaged and participating in circle time and deliver specific praise every third minute.	FR 5 (sticker) FR 3 (Specific praise)	Give the child a sticker for every fifth time that he raises his hand; deliver specific praise for every third time and call on him.
Natural consequence	Give a high five or social praise for about every fifth time on the toilet.	Natural consequence	Give the child access to a preferred toy or activity with specific praise at the end of circle time.	Natural consequence	Call on the child to speak every time he raises his hand. (Once the child learns this skill, you will teach him to wait to be called on. Gradually, you will teach him that he might not always be called on in class when he raises his hand.)

Otherwise, the child's shoe-tying behavior in the natural environment (e.g., at home) will be contingent on receiving the contrived reinforcer (i.e., preferred toys, etc.). A naturally occurring reinforcer for shoe tying might be going outside, to the gym, or for a walk. When thinning the schedule, the teacher might provide a sticker or preferred toy at first for every instance and then thin this to alternate verbal praise and a sticker. Overtime, the teacher might thin to verbal praise for every instance and then gradually thin the verbal praise. Systematically thinning the schedule and type of reinforcement for shoe tying in this manner will increase the likelihood that the skill is maintained in the natural environment over time. Table 8.3 describes examples of thinning reinforcement.

Additional Considerations in Programming for Maintenance Over Time

Programming for skill maintenance can be challenging, particularly for skills that are not used frequently. Consider a skill you have learned, perhaps baking a favorite dessert. Suppose you are fluent in baking this dish and could even prepare it to perfection without referencing the recipe. Then, you did not attempt to bake it for several months. When you eventually try to prepare it again, your behavior might look quite different that it did several months prior. You might forget to add one ingredient or add the wrong ingredient. This example illustrates how skills that are once mastered are not maintained when used infrequently. Maintenance is more likely to be achieved by performing the skill on a regular basis. Thus, skills that are functional to a child's daily life are given priority over skills that would be used on seldom occasion.

Another consideration when programming for maintenance is to use naturally occurring cues. When teaching a child a skill, it is essential that the child be taught to initiate the behavior following a cue that would occur in the natural environment. For instance, suppose Jim's teacher is teaching him to transition in a manner similar to what will occur next year in middle school (moving to a different location every 45 minutes as opposed to when he completes an activity on his schedule). Jim's teacher might decide to use a bell to signal when he should transition, as the middle school uses a similar bell.

After a child has learned a skill, it may be useful to perform periodic maintenance checks. Here, data are collected on performance biweekly, once a month, and so forth, depending on the skill and learner characteristics. The goal of maintenance checks is to ensure the skill has indeed been maintained. Figure 8.3 includes an example of a maintenance plan and data collection form for Fatima's goal of joining in with a group of peers.

Figure 8.3   Sample Teaching Plan for Maintenance

Fatima M.

Instructional Goal:

Joining a group of peers in the lunchroom and maintaining the interactions.

Objectives and Mastery Criteria:

Fatima has already learned how to join in a group of peers in the classroom and lunchroom. This program is to collect maintenance data to ensure she maintains this skill over time.

Objective: Fatima will join in with a group of peers (three or more) in the lunchroom by following the steps outlined here (Walker, Todis, Holmes, & Horton, 1988). She will do this independently across three consecutive observations.

Fatima identifies an appropriate group of three or more **peers** (e.g., students her age, not kindergarten students).

Fatima walks up to the group and stands next to the children appropriately (approx 1.5 feet away, looking at the group with her shoulders directed toward the children).

Fatima waits for a 1-second pause in the conversation before she speaks. If a peer acknowledges her (e.g., says "hi") or asks her a question before she responds, she waits and responds after the peer is finished talking.

Fatima joins in **appropriately** (e.g., utters an on-topic comment, answers a question, asks "Can I sit here" or "Is anyone sitting here," etc.)

Measures and Recording System:

Data will be collected on the number of steps completed correctly (+) and incorrectly (-). Data will be taken a *minimum* of *twice* a week in the lunchroom.

Code:

+ = Performed the step correctly

- = Did not perform the step correctly or required prompting.

Date	Step 1	Step 2	Step 3	Step 4	Staff initials	Notes
6/2/11	+	+	+	+	SP	Joined in with Ann, Luis, & Mel
6/6/11	+	+	+	+	JK	great job!
6/8/11	+	+	+	-	FH	started talking about unicorns
6/10/11	+	+	+	+	JK	joined with Mike, Oz, Lue, & Mia

PROGRAMMING FOR GENERALIZATION

Children with autism often display difficulty generalizing newly learned skills to settings that differ from training conditions (Maurice et al., 1996). A skill has generalized when "it is taught under one set of conditions (materials, people, and setting) and the child is able to apply the same skill with different people, in a new place, and using other materials" (Anderson, Jablonski, Thomeer, & Knapp, 2007, p. 152). For example, if a child is taught how to wash his or her hands in the classroom sink, the goal is for the child to also wash his or her hands in the restroom, at home in the kitchen, and so forth. While this transfer may occur naturally for typically developing children, many children with autism will require explicit instruction to generalize this skill. Generalization strategies can be embedded into a child's program to increase the likelihood that a behavior learned under one set of conditions will generalize to other situations. Further, data should be collected across conditions to ensure generalization has occurred.

Planning for Generalized Outcomes

Stokes and Baer (1977) provided a framework for conceptualizing how generalization occurs and how to embed generalization strategies into the child's curriculum (i.e., daily routines and activities). Although this paper was published over 30 years ago, their recommendations continue to offer the field guidance and recommendations in regard to programming for generalization.

Perhaps the most obvious strategy to ensure generalization is to teach under the conditions in which generalization is desired. For example, if a child is taught to wash his or her hands and the skill did not generalize from the classroom sink to sinks in other locations, the teacher might decide to directly teach hand washing in a variety of other locations. Another consideration is to introduce training stimuli into the generalization setting. For example, the teacher might use the same soap, paper towels, and instructional cues (e.g., verbal prompts, such as "Time to wash hands"; visual prompts, such as pictures of a child washing his or her hands).

Another effective strategy for promoting generalization is to use *naturally occurring reinforcers.* This strategy is perhaps the "most dependable of all generalization programming mechanisms" (Stokes & Baer, 1977, p. 353). The importance of using naturally occurring reinforcers was previously discussed, and the rationale for its importance is similar. Introducing the child to contingencies that are similar to what would occur in the natural environment will aid in both maintenance over time *and* generalization across settings. In the previously mentioned shoe-tying example, using naturally occurring reinforcers such as going on a walk or outside to play will increase the likelihood that the skill generalizes to other settings (e.g., at home, at the babysitter's house) and maintains over time (e.g., several years from now).

For many skills, it is helpful to provide *multiple exemplars.* This is what Stokes and Baer (1977) referred to as training sufficient exemplars. Without an adequate array of examples, the child might stipulate on irrelevant features of one training stimulus and not generalize the concept to other stimuli that are encountered in the natural environment. For example, when teaching a child the concept of *red,* it may be appropriate to begin by using one training stimulus (e.g., a red card). However, as the child is successful, additional examples of *red* should be introduced. This could include a red crayon, a red fire truck, a red shirt, and so forth. If the red piece of paper is the only training stimulus used, the teacher cannot ascertain if the child learned the concept of red or whether he or she is attending to irrelevant features of the training stimulus (e.g., shape of the paper, tears on the edges, etc.). Using multiple exemplars to teach a concept will increase the likelihood that the child will identify "red" in the natural environment.

Thinning the reinforcement schedule is another strategy that assists in achieving generalization and maintenance. In addition to what was stated earlier in the maintenance section, there are some considerations that are particularly relevant to generalization. Research has indicated that behaviors reinforced on an intermittent schedule are more resistant to extinction than behaviors reinforced on a continuous schedule (CRF; Catania, 2007). Because intermittent schedules are typically in effect in the natural environment, students should become accustomed behaving under this reinforcement schedule. For example, suppose Jim's teacher is teaching him to use a complete sentence when answering a question. He receives one token each time he independently uses a complete sentence to answer a question. Once he has five tokens, he can turn them in for 3 minutes of looking at his dinosaur book. After Jim is successful at this reinforcement schedule (CRF), the teacher would then provide a token approximately every other time he uses a complete sentence (VR 2), then approximately every third time (VR 3), and so forth.

Another recommendation made by Stokes and Baer (1977) is to *program common stimuli.* When conditions in the training setting are incredibly similar to those in the natural setting, generalization is more likely to occur to the natural environment. Thus, it may be useful for teachers to arrange the training setting to emulate the natural environment. For example, suppose Jim's teacher is teaching him how to use his lunch card (how the school tracks when students purchase a lunch). This process involves finding his card in an alphabetical file, giving it to a staff member at the check-out desk, and then replacing it in the file. To teach this routine, his teacher might use a file similar to the one in the lunchroom (that includes other cards that he needs to sift through), place the file in a location similar to where it would be in reference to the check-out desk, and so forth.

For some children, particularly those with age-appropriate language skills, it might be useful to "mediate generalization" (Stokes & Baer, 1977, p. 361). This is similar to many self-monitoring strategies, where the student provides a verbal report of his or her behavior. Specifics on teaching self-monitoring strategies are reviewed later in this chapter. In general, to mediate generalization, the student is instructed to report on his or her attempts at generalized behavior. Reinforcement is contingent on the student reporting that he or she performed the generalized response. For example, suppose Fatima has been successful initiating a conversation with peers in her classroom. Fatima's teacher wants her to generalize this skill to peers other than those in class. Her teacher instructs her to initiate a conversation during lunch and then checks in with her afterward. If Fatima reports that she initiated a conversation during lunch, her teacher provides her with a reinforcer, perhaps in the form of 10 additional minutes of computer time. Mediating generalization might require some direct observation on the teacher's part, as some children might inaccurately report their behavior. This example also illustrates how a teacher might specifically prompt for generalization (Stokes & Baer, 1977). Fatima's teacher explicitly asks her to demonstrate the generalized response. Likewise, Jim has learned to calm himself when he becomes upset. He is able to perform his calm-down routine in his classroom independently, but he has a history of becoming upset in the lunchroom or during gym class. Before Jim leaves for lunch or gym, his teacher tells him to use his calm-down routine if he becomes upset and reminds him that he will get a token if he remembers to use his calm-down routine. When Jim returns from class, his teacher asks him if he became upset in class and if so, if he used his calm-down routine. If Jim reports that he did use his routine, the teacher gives him tokens.

A common theme across many of these recommendations is to reinforce generalized performance. When a generalized behavior occurs during the school day, especially when the child is not instructed or prompted to do so, reinforce it. Situations can be arranged that are conducive to generalized responding. For example, suppose DJ has been taught one play sequence to perform with a toy car (e.g., rolling the car down a slide). During playtime, he performs a novel play sequence with the toy car (e.g., pushing the car up the side of the toy house). The teacher can reinforce this generalized, novel behavior (e.g., with a positive statement such as, "Look at your car on the house!").

SELF-MANAGEMENT

Typically developing children learn to monitor and regulate their behavior through natural interactions and environments. This "increasing autonomy and self-regulation allow them to exhibit a variety of appropriate behaviors in ever changing environments with minimal feedback from others" (Koegel, Koegel, Harrower, & Carter, 1999). Children with autism often do not develop these skills and need to be explicitly taught how to monitor their behavior. Self-management is defined as children "discriminating and self-initiating their own appropriate behavior, and then self-reinforcing or self-recruiting reinforcement for appropriate behaviors" (Koegel, Koegel, Harrower, & Carter, 1999).

Teaching children self-management skills offers some benefits over traditional interventions. When students are able to monitor their own behavior, teachers can spend instructional time focusing on other content, as opposed to frequently redirecting or prompting other behavior. Teaching self-management shifts the control from the teacher to the student, which promotes independence (Stahmer & Shreibman, 1992). In addition, the behavior change achieved by teaching a child to monitor his or her own behavior is more likely to generalize to other settings (Cooper et al., 2007). There are many examples in the research literature where self-management procedures have been effective in increasing target behaviors for children with autism (Lee, Simpson, & Shogren, 2007).

Self-Monitoring

Koegel, Koegel, Hurley, and Frea (1992) taught children with autism to monitor their responses to verbal initiations from others in school, home, and community settings. Self-monitoring instruction consisted of teaching children to discriminate between appropriate and inappropriate responses to social initiations and document when they provided an appropriate response. Following instruction on self-management, children were able to accurately monitor the appropriateness of their responses, and the frequency of appropriate responses increased. In addition, the occurrence of disruptive behavior decreased, even though this was not targeted for intervention. Another study taught children with autism to self-manage variability of their behavior during play settings (Newman, Reinecke, & Meinberg, 2000). Children were taught to give themselves a token each time they performed a variation in the target behavior. One student was observed during play with his toy robot. This student usually played with the robot in the same manner (i.e., riding in a car to visit his grandmother). A varied response for this student might have been putting the robot in an airplane, going to the store, and so forth. Following self-management instruction, variability in responding increased for all three students.

To illustrate an example of teaching self-monitoring, suppose Fatima's teacher is interested in teaching her how to orient toward others when speaking or being spoken to. Her teacher might initially teach the discrimination by modeling examples (i.e., orienting toward Fatima) and nonexamples (i.e., turning her back, etc.) and asking Fatima to label each example as correct or incorrect. Reinforcement (perhaps an additional 30 seconds of reading a book on mystical themes) would be contingent on Fatima accurately discriminating between correct or incorrect posture in relation to the speaker. Once she is able to do this accurately, her teacher might ask Fatima to display an example of appropriate orienting, then inappropriate orienting, and so forth. At some point in this process, it will also be important to teach Fatima how to document when these responses occur. She might tally responses in her planner, give herself a small sticker for her folder, or place check marks on a separate piece of paper. Once Fatima is able to accurately identify when she appropriately and inappropriately orients toward a partner and record these responses accordingly, it is time to have her practice this skill in other environments. Reinforcers can be put in place that are contingent on Fatima reporting that she performed the behavior (e.g., 7 out of 10 attempts, etc.). Table 8.4 provides examples of teaching self-management.

Table 8.4   Teaching Self-Management

Skill	Teaching strategy
Social interactions (playing with friends on the playground)	Teach the child to report back which friends she played with on the playground after recess. She gets a high five for every friend she played with.
Following routines (hanging up coat in locker, getting correct books for class, sitting in seat, and reading quietly)	Teach the child to complete a written checklist and give herself a checkmark for every task completed. She gets a token for every checkmark at the end of the day.
Completing math problems (completing an addition worksheet)	Teach the child to give herself a sticker for every row of math problems completed.
Lunchroom behavior (Step 1 waiting in line, Step 2 selecting food, Step 3 finding table, Step 4 sitting, Step 5 eating food, Step 6 emptying tray, Step 7 returning to classroom)	Teach the child to follow a visual schedule of the lunchroom routine. The child reports back the number of steps completed to the teacher after lunch and gets a minute on the computer for every step completed.
Riding on the bus (walking down the row, sitting in seat, quietly riding, walking down aisle to get off, lining up on the steps of the school)	Teach the child to use a script about riding on the bus. The child reports back to her teachers in the morning and her parents at the end of the day. She gets to spend 15 minutes playing video games if she followed all steps.

FUTURE DIRECTIONS

This chapter described several strategies for promoting maintenance and generalization of skills for children with autism. The strategies described in this chapter provide an overview of evidence-based practices. However, it is essential to remember that there is not one strategy that works for all children. These strategies provide a starting point for developing effective instructional programs for young children. The major message of this chapter is that it is essential to embed programming for generalization and maintenance into instruction for young children. This is particularly important for young children with autism given their propensity for repetition and sameness. Chapters 9 and 10 describe evidence-based practices for teaching communication and social skills to young children with autism.

LEARNING ACTIVITIES

1. Describe how you would use time delay *and* program for generalization to teach DJ to identify a variety of letters and numbers.

2. Describe how to use the system of least prompts to teach DJ to play with a variety of toys and peers at school. How would you fade prompts over time to ensure maintenance of skills?

3. Describe how you might teach Jim to self-monitor his appropriate behaviors during lunchtime? How might you incorporate his interests (i.e., dinosaurs, football, bees) into the self-management system?

RESOURCES

Additional Curriculum Resources

A Work in Progress: Behavior Management Strategies and a Curriculum for Intensive Behavioral Treatment for Autism. Leaf and McEachin (1999).

Teaching Developmentally Disabled Children: The ME Book. Lovaas (1983).

Additional Resources on Maintenance and Generalization

How to Plan for Generalization. Baer (1981).

Promoting Generalization: Current Status and Functional Considerations. Dunlap, G. (1993).

Generalization and Maintenance: Life-Style Changes in Applied Settings. Horner, Dunlap, and Koegel (1988).

Making a Difference: Behavioral Intervention for Autism. MacDuff, Krantz, and McClannahan (2001).

Behavior Analysis for Lasting Change. Sulzer-Azaroff and Mayer (1991).

Additional Resources on Self-Management

"Using Self-Monitoring to Increase Independence. "Dunlap, Dunlap, Koegel, and Koegel (1991).

How to Teach Pivotal Behaviors to Children With Autism: A Training Manual. Koegel, Schreibman, Good, Cerniglia, Murphy, and Koegel (1989).

Pivotal Response Treatment for Autism: http://www.koegelautism .com/

Reinforcement Tools for Teachers

Gentle Reminders: dan@gentlereminder.com

MotivAiders: http://www.habitchange.com

9

Evidence-Based Practices for Communication Skill Acquisition

Matt Tincani and Jessica Zawacki

Temple University

Chapter Objectives:

- Understand the basic forms of communication.
- Identify how Augmentative and Alternative Communication (AAC) promotes communication in children with autism.
- Describe research supporting the Picture Exchange Communication System (PECS), Voice Output Communication Aides (VOCAs), and sign language for children with autism.
- Identify strategies for embedding communication programming throughout the day.
- Understand how to incorporate parents into communication skill instruction.
- Describe two comprehensive treatment models for teaching communication and language skills to children with autism, the Early Start Denver Model and the Young Autism Project.

171

Language impairments are a core skill deficit of persons with autism (American Psychiatric Association, 2000; Lord & Spence, 2006). Although estimates vary, reports suggest that up to 50% of adults with autism have no functional communication (Wetherby & Prizant, 2005). Effective intervention is critical in preventing early language delays from becoming lifelong communication deficits. A variety of specific strategies have emerged to teach communication and language to children on the autism spectrum (e.g., Koegel & Koegel, 2006; Mirenda, 2003; Petscher, Rey, & Bailey, 2009; Schlosser & Wendt, 2008). Most of these strategies incorporate the principles and techniques of applied behavior analysis (Cooper et al., 2007). This chapter provides an overview of three specific strategies, augmentative and alternative communication programming, pivotal response treatment (PRT), and functional communication training, to teach communication skills. The chapter concludes with a description of two comprehensive treatment models to teach communication, the Early Start Denver Model and the Young Autism Project.

WHAT IS COMMUNICATION?

Before we discuss strategies to teach communication, it is important to understand how all children, including those with autism, communicate. Communication, or verbal behavior, is "behavior reinforced through the mediation of other persons" (Skinner, 1957, p. 2). For example, when a child says to his mother, "Crackers, please," and receives crackers, this is communication, because the response, asking for crackers, is reinforced through the action of someone else. In contrast, if the child walks to the cabinet and takes out crackers without asking, this is not communication because reinforcement is not provided through another person. Importantly, the child's communicative response need not be vocal. Gestures, sign language, or augmentative responses (discussed later) are communication if reinforcement is mediated through other persons.

Because children with autism often have speech delays, a central focus of educational programming is to teach basic communication skills. Programs focus on several core areas including requests, expressive labeling, conversation, and receptive responses. As illustrated in the previous example, requests (or mands) are perhaps the most important form of functional communication for young children with autism (Tincani, Bondy, & Crozier, 2011). Requests enable the child to have his or her most basic needs met, such as when asking for preferred items and activities, requesting a break, or rejecting unwanted items. In contrast, expressive labeling responses (or tacts) are controlled by stimuli that precede them—typically an object or some aspect of the environment—and are socially reinforced. For instance, expressive labeling occurs when a child sees a fire truck, says "truck," and receives social reinforcement (e.g., "Yes, that's a truck."). Conversational responses, or intraverbals, are evoked by someone else's verbal behavior, such as when a teacher says, "How are you today?" and the child says, "Pretty good." Conversational responses are also maintained by social reinforcement.

Receptive language is also a critical aspect of communication. Receptive language happens when a child engages in nonverbal behavior in response to another person's verbal behavior: for instance, when a father says, "Come here," and the child walks over to him, or a teacher says, "Time to work," and the child sits at his or her desk. To function independently, children must fluently engage in requesting, expressive labeling, conversation, and receptive responses across home, school, and community environments. As we will see, each of the specific communication strategies discussed next seeks to establish functional communication across settings.

AUGMENTATIVE AND ALTERNATIVE COMMUNICATION PROGRAMMING

Augmentative and Alternative Communication (AAC) programming describes strategies to teach communication to persons with limited speech abilities in a modality other than speech. Broadly, AAC systems can be categorized into two types, *aided,* which require a device, and *unaided,* which do not require a device; however, there are many variations within these categories (Mirenda & Iacono, 2009). We will focus on three specific strategies for children with autism that have been extensively described in the literature: the Picture Exchange Communication System (PECS; Frost & Bondy, 2002), Voice Output Communication Aides (VOCAs; Rispoli, Franco, van der Meer, Lang, & Camargo, 2010), and sign language (Goldstein, 2002).

PICTURE EXCHANGE COMMUNICATION SYSTEM (PECS)

The PECS is a comprehensive program for teaching functional communication to students with autism and other developmental disabilities. Developed by Andy Bondy and Lori Frost at the Delaware Autism Program (Bondy & Frost, 1994), PECS was initially designed to promote communication in young children with autism; however, it has successfully been used with older children and adolescents (Tincani & Devis, 2010). PECS is perhaps the most popular aided AAC strategy for children with autism (e.g., Stahmer, Collings, & Palinkas, 2005).

PECS begins with a formal assessment of the child's preferences and is comprised of six phases (see Table 9.1; Frost & Bondy, 2002). In Phase I, the student is taught "how to communicate" by exchanging a picture symbol to request a preferred item or activity. In Phase II, the student learns persistence and independence by travelling a distance to the communication partner and the communication book. In Phase III, the student is taught to discriminate among an array of picture symbols, while Phase IV shows the student how to use a sentence structure when requesting (i.e., "I want . . . ."). Finally, in Phases V and VI, the student learns to respond to others' questions (i.e., "What do you want?") and to comment on the environment (e.g., "I see . . . ."). Skinner's (1957) analysis of verbal behavior provides a conceptual basis for the PECS phases (Bondy, Tincani, & Frost, 2004).

Research supporting PECS. PECS is among the most well researched AAC strategies, with a growing body of single-subject and group design studies (Flippin, Reszka, & Watson, 2010; Hart & Banda, 2010; Sulzer-Azaroff, Hoffman, Horton, Bondy, & Frost, 2009; Tincani & Devis, 2010). Overall, PECS has been shown to be an effective system for teaching children to request a basic vocabulary of preferred items as taught in Phases I to IV. Bondy and Frost (1994) reported that the system successfully promoted speech for over 50% of young children who were taught PECS for more than 1 year; however, subsequent research has shown that speech acquisition is

Table 9.1 Phases and Objectives of the Picture Exchange Communication System

Phases	*Objectives*
Phase I—How to Communicate	Student learns to exchange a picture symbol for a highly preferred item.
Phase II—Distance and Persistence	Student learns to remove a picture symbol from a communication board, get the trainer's attention, and exchange the picture symbol at a distance.
Phase III—Picture Discrimination	Student learns to request the appropriate picture symbol from an array.
Phase IV—Sentence Structure	Student learns to request items using a multiword sentence strip (i.e., "I want _____ ").
Phase V—Responding to "What Do You Want?"	Student learns to exchange a picture symbol in response to the question, "What do you want?"
Phase VI—Commenting	Student learns to answer the following questions: "What do you see?" "What do you have?" "What do you hear?" and "What is it?"

Source: Frost & Bondy, 2002.

variable, with some users acquiring speech and others not acquiring speech (e.g., Flippin et al., 2010). Furthermore, few studies have examined the effectiveness of PECS in establishing more complex verbal behavior beyond making requests, including expressively labeling (tacting) items (e.g., "I see a ball") or engaging in conversations, and virtually no studies have systematically evaluated Phases V and VI (Tincani & Devis, 2010).

How to and for which core skills? PECS is a thoroughly manualized AAC system, which means that all the steps for conducting training are specifically defined; the second edition of *PECS: The Picture Exchange Communication System Training Manual* (Frost & Bondy, 2002) provides step-by-step descriptions of various prompting, prompt fading, reinforcement, shaping, and error correction strategies. Those who wish to implement PECS are strongly encouraged to follow the manual's highly prescribed teaching procedures. PECS is effective for teaching users to request preferred items and activities. Although speech is viewed as a desirable outcome of the system, implementers are discouraged from requiring speech of users unless they speak functionally and independently of PECS.

Embedding communication across the day with PECS. As with all AAC strategies, it is critical to embed many opportunities for communication with PECS across the day. Implementers should use naturalistic or incidental teaching techniques (e.g., Cowan & Allen, 2007) to promote communication by providing contingent access to highly preferred items throughout the learner's environments or by "sabotaging" activities by requiring the learner to emit a communicative response in order to complete an activity. For instance, when a child reaches for something he or she wants, such as a favorite toy, the parent could briefly delay providing the toy until the child exchanges a picture symbol to request it. Sabotaging involves identifying opportunities to communicate within daily activities and then systematically altering activities to promote communication. For example, while getting dressed to go outside a teacher might put the child's hat on his or her head and look for the child to protest or request the hat. Also, if a child enjoys completing puzzles, his or her teacher could hide a puzzle piece under the puzzle and then prompt the child to request help to find the piece by exchanging a picture symbol. Importantly, parents are actively encouraged to participate in PECS as trainers and communicative partners in order for skills to generalize from school to home and community environments.

VOICE OUTPUT COMMUNICATION AIDES (VOCAS)

While PECS is one of the most popular "low tech" AAC strategies available, a variety of "high tech" alternatives exists, as well. VOCAs (also called speech generating devices or SGDs) are an aided AAC strategy in which the user activates a switch on an electronic device to produce a spoken message (Rispoli et al., 2010). VOCAs vary considerably in their technological sophistication and use, ranging from simple devices comprised of four or fewer buttons (e.g., Olive, Lang, & Davis, 2008; Schepis, Reid, Behrman, & Sutton, 1998) to sophisticated computers with touch screens that enable the user to generate messages from an array of vocabulary (e.g., Choi, O'Reilly, Sigafoos, & Lancioni, 2010). Unlike PECS, VOCAs were not primarily designed for persons on the autism spectrum; rather, anyone who lacks the ability to speak can use a VOCA to communicate. British physicist Stephen Hawking is probably the most famous VOCA user.

Research supporting VOCAs. There have been a number of studies to evaluate the effects of VOCAs on communicative skills of children with autism and other developmental disabilities (Lancioni, O'Reilly, Cuvo, Singh, Sigafoos, & Didden, 2007; Rispoli et al., 2010). It is difficult to characterize the overall effectiveness of VOCAs for children with autism because studies have used a variety of devices and techniques. Much of the research has focused on VOCAs to teach basic communication to students with autism and intellectual disabilities. For instance, Olive et al. (2008) used a four-switch VOCA to conduct functional communication training (FCT; discussed later) with a 4-year-old girl with autism, who was taught to press a button to gain her mother's attention. Decreases in challenging behavior and increases in communication were observed with VOCA training. Less is known about VOCAs as a comprehensive, primary communication system for children with autism. Increasing prevalence of smart phones and other personal technology devices capable of running speech-generating software creates the potential for researchers to conduct broader evaluations.

As mentioned earlier, there are many VOCA systems available, ranging from one-button machines to computers that generate speech from typewritten words. For example, Fatima uses an AlphaSmart keyboard to communicate in five-plus-word sentences. She types words and sentences into the computer and the computer generates a voice output. Her parents taught her to use the AlphaSmart keyboard at age 4, because she used no speech and mostly communicated through letters, but she seemed to be able to understand most of what they said. Also, her parents noticed she spontaneously made words with blocks and letters. She has started speaking in one- and two-word phrases to communicate wants and needs. However, her expressive language skills are above average with the use of the AlphaSmart. The AlphaSmart allows her to participate in classroom activities, interact with peers, and have conversations across adults in the school and in the community. She uses the AlphaSmart to make choices during lunch in the school cafeteria, answer questions during small and large group instruction, and get her needs met across the day. Perhaps most importantly, the AlphaSmart allows Fatima to have developmentally appropriate conversations with her peers across the day.

How to and for which core skills? Because many VOCAs are relatively easy to use, requiring the user to press a single button for communication, they lend themselves well to teaching basic functional communication skills. In one example, Schepis and colleagues (1998) assessed the effects of a single-switch VOCA and naturalistic teaching strategies on communicative interactions of four young children with autism. Children's and staff's communicative interactions increased during play and snack activities with the VOCA. Behavior shaping techniques, including differential reinforcement, prompting and prompt fading, are necessary for users to acquire independent use of their devices. As with any high-tech device, cost and availability are significant considerations (Tincani & Boutot, 2005). Devices should be maintained by an assistive technology specialist who can train others in proper maintenance and use.

Embedding communication across the day with AAC. Similar to PECS and other AAC systems, it is important to conduct a preference assessment to identify items and activities the student is likely to request, and to arrange the natural environment so that these items are available through use of the VOCA. A good fit between the user and device is essential to best outcomes. Implementation of the VOCA should proceed from a careful assessment, including evaluation of the user's receptive and expressive communication skills, symbol comprehension, device preferences, and identification of functional vocabulary (Light, Roberts, Dimarco, & Greiner, 1998).

Sign Language

VOCA and PECS are aided AAC systems that require the learner to have a device for communication; however, children with autism can also be taught sign language as a form of unaided functional communication. Individuals with autism rarely learn American Sign Language; rather, vocabulary is identified and children are taught to perform manual signs that represent spoken words (Goldstein, 2002). Children often learn sign language in the context of total communication, in which manual signs are paired with spoken words and the learner is provided with reinforcement for speaking while signing (e.g., Carbone, Sweeney-Kerwin, Attanasio, & Kasper, 2010). The goal of total communication is to promote speech as well as sign use. An advantage of sign language compared to PECS and VOCAs is that it does not require an apparatus for communication. Therefore, the learner is able to communicate without the aid of special equipment.

Research supporting sign language. Few studies on teaching sign language to children with autism have been conducted and these have yielded modest support for sign language as a communication technique (Schwartz & Nye, 2006). For example, Yoder and Layton (1988) randomly assigned 60 children with autism to four teaching conditions: speech alone, sign alone, simultaneous presentation of sign and speech, and alternating presentation of sign and speech. Results showed little difference between conditions with sign language and conditions without sign language on spoken word use, suggesting that sign language training had marginal effects on spoken communication. Other investigators have used single-subject designs to evaluate total communication for children with autism and intellectual disabilities, finding more favorable outcomes (e.g., Carbone et al., 2010; Carr, Binkoff, Kologinsky, & Eddy, 1978; Clarke, Remington, & Light, 1988); however, more research is needed to establish sign language as an evidence-based communication intervention for students with autism.

How to and for which core skills? Like PECS and VOCAs, sign language instruction should begin with an assessment of the child's preferences (e.g., Tincani, 2004). This can be accomplished by asking parents, caregivers, or teachers what the child likes and then presenting items to see if the child will reach for them, indicating motivation to communicate. To enhance the child's acquisition, signs taught can be iconic, which means that they resemble the items they represent (e.g., the sign for "ball" is both hands cupped in the shape of the ball). Motor imitation skills affect a child's ability to learn sign language (Seal & Bonvillian, 1997)— children who have poor motor imitation abilities may acquire fewer signs or make frequent errors when signing. Therefore, communicative partners should be consistent in prompting and reinforcing the same signs across settings. Prompt delay techniques, which involve delaying the delivery of an item until the child signs, can be used to encourage speech with sign language (Carbone et al., 2010; see Chapters 7 & 8); however, caregivers should not require the student to speak unless he or she can communicate clearly without sign language.

Embedding communication across the day with sign language. As with other AAC strategies, students need frequent opportunities to communicate across the day to learn sign language. Caregivers should capitalize on naturalistic teaching strategies to encourage communication. For example, if a variety of highly motivating items are available during play activities, parents can use prompt delay techniques to encourage requesting of preferred items (e.g. "I want the truck") or commenting on relevant items (e.g., parent: "What color is the truck?" child: "Blue").

PIVOTAL RESPONSE TREATMENT

It is often reported that children with autism display limited or no social interaction among typical peers, family, or community members (Koegel, Koegel, Harrower, & Carter, 1999). PRT changes the environment to increase skill acquisition and decrease challenging behavior, giving individuals the proficiency to participate meaningfully in inclusive settings

(Koegel, Koegel, Harrower, & Carter, 1999). Like other communication techniques described in this chapter, PRT is based on the principles of applied behavior analysis, which assume that an individual's impairments can be improved with environmental manipulations, such as prompting, reinforcement, and extinction (Baker-Ericzen, Stahmer, & Burns, 2007).

PRT increases motivation and enhances generalization using naturalistic or "loose" training techniques in the learner's natural environment (Schreibman, Kaneko, & Koegel, 1991). Pivotal areas are defined as those that, when changed, generally produce large collateral improvements in other skill areas (Koegel, Koegel, Harrower, & Carter, 1999). For instance, a child who can independently gain another person's attention will be more successful in a variety of play, school, and family activities. Individuals with autism often struggle with initiating and responding to peers, which may severely limit social and verbal learning opportunities (Koegel, Koegel, Shoshan, & McNerney, 1999). In PRT, the individual is allowed to choose the stimuli and the nature of the teaching interaction, while the teacher, caregiver, or peer reinforces his or her attempts to respond.

Research Supporting PRT

Naturalistic interventions such as PRT have been shown to be effective in producing positive changes in complex social behaviors of individuals with autism (Baker-Ericzen et al., 2007; Pierce & Schreibman, 1997; Schreibman et al., 1991). Increases in social initiation, reciprocal communication, functional language, and play skills are seen as a result of PRT (Koegel, Koegel, Harrower, & Carter, 1999; Pierce & Schreibman, 1997; Stahmer, 1999). One important finding in the research suggests that PRT is not only effective in increasing language skills, but it can be implemented in natural social environments with typical peers as trainers (Pierce & Schreibman, 1995, 1997). PRT is also designed as a parent-training tool to be used in the natural environment and thus promotes generalization across both environments and trainers (Koegel, Koegel, Harrower, & Carter, 1999; Stahmer, 1999).

How to and for Which Core Skills?

Core pivotal skills include increasing motivation to initiate and respond in complex social, linguistic, and academic interactions. Peripheral features of autism have been documented to improve, including self-help, expressive language, pragmatic language, and in academic areas. The model uses data-based applied behavior analysis procedures that are positive, self-reinforcing, and family centered (Koegel, Koegel, Harrower, & Carter, 1999). PRT is also often used to increase play skills in children with autism, which may be important for community and classroom integration and improvement of interaction and language skills (Stahmer, 1999). It is imperative that naturalistic training techniques used in PRT are conducted in loosely controlled contexts, with multiple exemplars, and target individual's preferences in the teaching interaction (Pierce & Schreibman, 1995).

For example, a child who is learning to say numbers could practice them in school (e.g., during circle time, the child says the number of balls on the floor), at home (e.g., at dinner, the child counts the pieces of chicken on his plate), or in the community (e.g., at the store, the child counts the number of quarters to purchase a piece of candy).

Often during training, the peer or instructor will use a manual in which the PRT strategies are represented both pictorially and in written form. For example, seeking peer attention is a pivotal communicative behavior because gaining joint attention of a peer increases play and reciprocal language opportunities. To teach a child with autism to seek joint attention, the peer would first ensure the target child is attending. The peer would also ensure that choices are given among highly preferred items or activities to maintain motivation. These items would then be varied frequently based on individual preference. The peer would then model appropriate social behavior including various verbal statements and complex play actions. Any attempt made by the target individual to engage or functionally play would be reinforced and conversation would be encouraged by withholding desired objects until a verbal response related to the object is emitted. The peer would also make attempts to extend the conversation by asking follow-up questions and engaging in narrative play. Turn taking and complex social behaviors are targeted whenever possible, such as using descriptive labels while making choices (e.g., "I want the *blue* truck"; Pierce & Schreibman, 1997).

Embedding Communication Across the Day With PRT

PRT is designed to be a technique for parents to use in the home environment that can easily be incorporated into their daily routines. The intervention results in higher levels of positive parental affect, as opposed to interventions that require parents to designate specific periods of time to teach (Stahmer, 1999). Teaching initiations and other pivotal responses are likely to reduce parental stress by transferring responsibility to the child. Most parents find that these steps are relatively easy to implement and enjoy being able to interact and play with their children (Koegel, Koegel, Shoshan, & McNerney, 1999).

FUNCTIONAL COMMUNICATION TRAINING

Individuals with autism often engage in challenging behaviors that likely serve a specific social function. Reinforcement of problem behavior falls into two broad classes: escape/avoidance and attention (Carr & Durand, 1985). It is assumed that if individuals can gain access to desired consequences at a higher rate with a new functional response, they will increase their use of this new response and thus reduce their use of the undesired response (Durand & Carr, 1992). An intervention strategy that uses communication as a functionally alternative response to aberrant behavior is called Functional Communication Training (FCT; Carr & Durand, 1985).

FCT generally includes two major components. Initially, a functional assessment is conducted to identify consequences maintaining the problem behavior. After the consequence(s) have been identified, the child is taught to perform an alternative functional response (e.g., signing, exchanging a picture symbol, activating a VOCA switch) that results in the same consequence(s) (Fisher, Piazza, Cataldo, Harrell, Jefferson, & Conner, 1993). The rationale behind this approach is that students will be less likely to engage in challenging behaviors if they can gain access to reinforcement by exhibiting the alternative functional response (Shirley, Iwata, Kaung, Mazaleski, & Lerman, 1997).

Research Supporting FCT

Research on FCT has consistently shown success in promoting functional communication as a replacement for problem behavior such as severe aggression, self-injurious behavior, and violent tantrums, which significantly restrict the lives of the individuals with autism and intellectual disabilities (e.g., Durand & Carr, 1991; Shirley et al., 1997). FCT has been successful in reducing undesired behaviors that are maintained by attention, tangibles, escape, and sensory input (Carr & Durand, 1985; Durand & Carr, 1992; Wacker et al., 1990). By strengthening an alternative response that results in reinforcement, the child is placed in active control over his or her own reinforcement rather than a passive recipient of reinforcement from an instructor (Carr & Durand, 1985; Durand & Carr, 1991). When used in conjunction with extinction procedures, FCT provides a significant decrease in aberrant behavior and an increase in functional communication (Hagopian, Fisher, Sullivan, Aquisto, & LeBlanc, 1998; Shirley et al., 1997). FCT has been shown to promote maintenance of functional communication over time and generalization of communication across environments and trainers, including parents, because FCT gives the individuals the tools they need to communicate across environments and tasks and with other individuals (e.g., Derby et al., 1997; Durand & Carr, 1991, 1992).

How to and for Which Core Skills?

The first step in conducting FCT is to identify the problem behavior, through a combination of parent and teacher interviews and direct observation. Prior to the implementation of FCT, a functional behavioral assessment (FBA) is conducted to determine the function(s) of the problem behavior (Wacker et al., 1990). Based on the individual abilities of each participant, a replacement form of communication is chosen that has a lesser response effort and serves the same function as the problem behavior. For example, if a child engages in self-injurious hitting to obtain assistance from a parent, then he or she could be taught to place a picture symbol in the parent's hand to request assistance as a functional alternative. Critically, the response taught should be one that others are likely to recognize and reinforce (Durand & Merges, 2001). For example, if the replacement behavior involves using a VOCA in a noisy classroom, it might be beneficial to teach the student to approach somebody so that the message is clearly understood. The replacement behavior, asking for help, is then systematically reinforced while the problem behavior, self-hitting, is not reinforced. Importantly, FCT is effective in teaching appropriate attention seeking, access to tangibles, escape from work, or sensory input. The steps for conducting FCT are illustrated in Figure 9.1.

For example, FCT was used to teach DJ to communicate wants and needs across the day. DJ used one-word utterances that were about 50% intelligible. When he turned 3, he started exhibiting increased tantrums than often lasted more than 10 minutes. These were disruptive to the family and a major concern for the childcare staff. The tantrums had escalated such that the staff had discussed excluding DJ from many classroom activities and were considering removing him from the childcare program. However, DJ's developmental specialist suggested they try FCT training. They conducted a functional assessment and determined the function of DJ's tantrums were to obtain preferred toys, activities, and adult attention. The developmental specialist worked with DJ's parents and the staff to teach him signs for "more," "help," "computer," and "train." These represented his favorite items and allowed him to appropriately ask for adult attention and preferred items. The staff prompted him to use these signs throughout the day, and DJ was only provided adult attention or preferred toys when he appropriately requested them (see Chapters 7 and 8 for prompting and reinforcement strategies and Chapter 11 for positive behavior support strategies).

Embedding Communication Across the Day With FCT

Derby et al. (1997) presented a comprehensive model for conducting FCT in home settings and provided data to support successful, longer-term implementation of FCT. They sought to extend the literature on FCT by following students for at least 6 months with regularly scheduled follow-up visits and probes for maintenance of learned communicative responses. Participants were four children enrolled in a long-term, in-home, early intervention project. The problem behaviors exhibited by the participants were assessed through an FBA and were more likely to occur when parents provided attention and/or escape from a nonpreferred activity in response to them. Thus, during FCT, participants were exposed to intervention packages in which they were taught alternative, more appropriate ways to request attention and/or escape, while parents ignored inappropriate behaviors. The study showed long-term reduction

Figure 9.1 Steps for Conducting Functional Communication Training

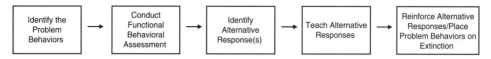

Vignette: Jamie

Jamie is a 3-year-old girl who has recently been diagnosed with autism. She attends an inclusive preschool where she receives instruction in communication, play, and social skills. At the beginning of the year, staff reported that Jamie engaged in severe tantrums almost every day. Jamie's tantrums made it difficult for teachers to work with her and caused other students to avoid her. Consequently, Jamie made few friends in her class. Jamie's teacher, Ms. Sanchez, conducted an FBA to determine the function of her tantrums by carefully recording events that preceded and followed them. She determined that tantrums were most likely to occur when Jamie was presented with a task she didn't understand, and they were reinforced by attention from others in the form of assistance. Ms. Sanchez used FCT to teach Jamie an alternative response to tantrums as a way to get assistance. Jamie learned to exchange a picture symbol for "help" in situations where she was likely to need assistance, such as when reaching for a desired item on a high shelf. Since FCT began, Jamie has had fewer tantrums, is much happier, and has made more friends in her class.

---

of challenging behaviors for all participants when parents use FCT in the home as an intervention. Simultaneously, each participant showed an increase in socially appropriate behaviors. Parents reported that the procedures were effective and there were no adverse effects that they typically encountered in the home. Positive results were attributed to the combination of targeted alternative responses and other positive, social behaviors that were learned during the study.

Table 9.2 compares the specific strategies for teaching communication that we have discussed, specifically, AAC strategies, including PECS, VOCA, and sign language, as well as PRT and FCT. You will see the purpose, research support, procedures, training, and devices for each system in Table 9.2.

COMPREHENSIVE TREATMENT MODELS

Early Start Denver Model

The Early Start Denver Model (ESDM) is a parent-coaching program for infants to preschool-aged children diagnosed with autism that integrates applied behavior analysis with developmental and relationship-based approaches (Dawson et al., 2009; Vismara & Rogers, 2008). The model is designed to take place in the natural environment and deliver high intensity

Table 9.2   Comparison of Specific Strategies for Teaching Communication to Students With Autism

Strategy	Purpose	Research Support	Procedures, Training, Devices
Augmentative and Alternative Communication (AAC)	Teach communication in a modality other than speech.	Very good overall	Varies depending on strategy and device
Picture Exchange Communication System (PECS)	Communicate by exchanging pictures.	Excellent for basic functional communication	Six phases (see Table 9.1); implementers must follow procedures exactly and must have pictures and communication book
Voice Output Communication Aides (VOCAs)	Communicate by activating a switch on a speech generating device (SGD).	Very good for basic functional communication; comprehensive studies lacking	Varies; uses teaching procedures from applied behavior analysis; must have electronic device; can be expensive and requires maintenance
Sign Language	Communicate by signing and speaking (total communication).	Modest; few studies available	Uses teaching procedures from applied behavior analysis, including prompt delay; requires good imitation skills for the student; no devices necessary
Pivotal Response Treatment (PRT)	Capitalize on student interests and loose teaching to establish "pivotal" skills.	Excellent for teaching a variety of skills, including communication	Uses teaching procedures from applied behavior analysis, including prompting, reinforcement, and extinction; high degree of training and support needed for high fidelity implementation; devices and equipment vary
Functional Communication Training (FCT)	Reduce challenging behavior by teaching alternative responses.	Excellent for reducing challenging behavior and establishing communicative and social behaviors	Must conduct an FBA to identify problem behavior functions; best used in a treatment package; devices and equipment vary

instruction to participants by both trainers and parents. The ESDM delivers a specified developmental curriculum (individualized for each child based on current abilities) using a combination of empirically supported teaching techniques (mass trial, naturalistic behavioral teaching, and affective dyadic exchanges) to attain specific developmental outcomes (Rogers, Hayden, Hepburn, Charlifue-Smith, Hall, & Hayes, 2006). Checklists and the ESDM manual are available and provide structured, hands-on strategies for working with children in individual and group settings to promote development in such key domains as imitation; communication; social, cognitive, and motor skill; adaptive behavior, and play (Rogers & Dawson, 2010).

Outcomes of research using the ESDM describe significant accelerations in developmental rates of children diagnosed with autism or PDD-NOS in several developmental areas including cognition, language, and social development. Speech has also occurred in previously nonverbal children as a result of implementing the ESDM (Rogers et al., 2006). Four independent replications of the model were carried out in rural Colorado school districts (Rogers, Lewis, & Reis, 1987) and group data demonstrated similar positive effects comparable to original studies. More research is needed to further establish the efficacy of the ESDM as an effective program for establishing communicative, social, adaptive, and play behavior in children with autism.

Young Autism Project

The UCLA Young Autism Project culminated from the work of Lovaas at UCLA in the 1960s and 1970s. Using principles of applied behavior analysis, Lovaas developed an early intensive approach to intervention that relied heavily on the use of behavioral techniques and discrete trial teaching to establish language skills in children with autism (e.g., Lovaas, 2003). In 1987, Lovaas published a study in which a group of children exposed to more than 40 hours per week of therapy made substantial gains in IQ compared to children exposed to only 10 hours per week of therapy or no therapy. Several children in the intensive therapy group achieved fully inclusive educational placements by first grade. Although the methodology of Lovaas's study was criticized and his results questioned (e.g., Gresham & MacMillan, 1998), subsequent replications have largely confirmed the substantial benefits of Lovaas's technique on children's IQ (Reichow & Wolery, 2009b).

Lovaas's approach was popularized in part by Catherine Maurice's (1993) book, *Let Me Hear Your Voice*, about the author's experiences as a parent of two children receiving early intensive behavioral intervention. Today there are many variations of Lovaas's approach available to children with autism. Although available therapies vary in their quality and conformity with Lovaas's procedures, most continue to incorporate the same fundamental techniques—a heavy reliance on discrete trial teaching, use of vocal imitation to establish language, behavioral prompting, shaping, and error correction techniques.

FUTURE DIRECTIONS

As you have read, we have accumulated substantial knowledge about specific intervention techniques to teach communication skills to children with autism through PECS, VOCAs, sign language, PRT, and FCT. However, beyond these techniques, we have much to learn about developing comprehensive treatment programs to establish communication skills to meet children's diverse needs (Rogers & Vismara, 2008). Although strategies based in applied behavior analysis are regarded as the most efficacious in terms of research (Vismara & Rogers, 2010), questions remain about which combination of techniques to use with younger children, what is the optimal "dosage" (i.e., hours per week) of intervention given specific child characteristics, and which variables moderate successful outcomes, including parent sociocultural qualities. Expanding research into comprehensive treatment programs, particularly in relation to scaling-up effective programs in public school settings, will greatly enhance our understanding of how best to meet children's diverse communication needs.

LEARNING ACTIVITIES

1. List evidence-based communication strategies and describe why each is effective for children with autism.

2. Which strategy would you use to teach receptive and expressive communication to Leroy (refer to the vignette for Leroy in Chapter 3)? How and when would you teach?

3. How would you include families in using these communication strategies with young children (which ones can you teach parents to do at home)?

4. Which strategy would you use to teach expressive communication to Jim (refer to the vignette for Jim in Chapter 3)? How and when would you teach?

RESOURCES

Augmentative and Alternative Communication (AAC)

1. Dynavox Mayer-Johnson: describes who benefits from AAC, alternative product solutions, local sales consultants, and funding sources: **http://www.dynavoxtech.com/aac**

2. American Speech-Language-Hearing Association: defines AAC, the types of available ACC systems, and other organizations

with information on AAC: **http://www.asha.org/public/speech/disorders/AAC.htm**

3. Augmentative and Alternative Communication Centers: provides links to various venders, information on early intervention in AAC, and other resources: **http://aac.unl.edu/**

4. International Society for Augmentative and Alternative Communication: a worldwide alliance with the mission to help individuals with little to no speech; the website can display Bliss, PCS, or Rebus symbols so that people who use symbol systems to communicate can understand the website's content: **http://www.isaac-online.org/en/home.shtml**

Picture Exchange Communication System (PECS)

1. Picture Your Student Learning, Pyramid Educational Consultants: the exclusive source of training and consultation for the PECS and the Pyramid Approach to Education; includes links to workshops and products: **http://www.pecs.com**

2. Different Roads to Learning: over 500 products to aid individuals with autism in communication, including PECs books and manuals: **http://www.difflearn.com/category/PECS**

3. Healing Thresholds: Autism Therapies: information on PECS, how it works, its benefits and risks, costs, and resources: **http://autism.healingthresholds.com/therapy/picture-exchange-communication-system-pecs**

Sign Language

1. National Autism Resources: discusses how sign language can benefit individuals with autism, including how to teach, who to teach, drawbacks, and products: **http://www.nationalautismresources.com/sign-language-and-autism.html**

2. American Sign Language Resource Site: free lessons, teaching tools, first 100 signs, dictionary, and practice tools: **http://www.lifeprint.com/**

3. National Institute on Deafness and Other Communication Disorders: defines sign language, looks at sign language around the world and its origin, compares sign language to spoken language, and provides links to more information: **http://www.nidcd.nih.gov/health/hearing/asl.asp**

4. Hand Speak: Sign Language Online: provides an online dictionary, information on how to learn sign language, explores deaf culture and finger spelling: **http://www.handspeak.com**

Pivotal Response Treatment (PRT)

1. University of California Santa Barbara; Koegel Autism Center: information on the center, recent publications, manuals, graduate and undergraduate research, and PRT certifications, conferences, and research: **http://www.education.ucsb.edu/autism/**

2. Autism Intervention Research Program; University of California San Diego: Includes information on the theory, core components, frequently asked questions, and information about the program: **http://autismlab.ucsd.edu/about/pivotal-response-training.shtml**

3. How to Teach Pivotal Behaviors to Children with Autism: A Training Manual: includes field test procedures and results, discusses implementation strategies, motivation, target individuals, and resources: **http://www.users.uswest.net/~tbharris/prt.htm**

4. Pivotal Response Intervention: describes key elements of PRT, individuals who may benefit from PRT, responses to multiple cues, motivation, self-management and self-initiation, and research to support PRT: **http://www.autismnetwork.org/modules/behavior/pri/index.html**

Functional Communication Training (FCT)

1. Special Needs Bridges: designed to assist families to find available resources and support to suit their individual needs: **http://specialneedsbridge.com/**

2. Raising Children Network: research rating, time, cost, who the intervention best suits, and basic information on FCT: **http://raisingchildren.net.au/articles/functional_communication_th.html**

Early Start Denver Model (ESDM)

1. Raising Children Network: Early Start Denver Model: provides an at a glance view of the model, including cost and time: **http://raisingchildren.net.au/articles/denver_model_th.html**

2. Autism Speaks: Early Intervention for Toddlers With Autism: references studies and video examples: **http://www.autismspeaks.org/press/early_start_denver_model.php**

3. ABA Forum: Interview with Sally Rogers, founder of Early Start Denver Model: includes implementation and best practice: **http://www.abaforum.dk/artikler/2003/sally_rogers.php**

Young Autism Project

1. Texas Young Autism Project: offers Applied Behavior Analysis direct treatment services for children with autism in four formats to meet individual family needs; intensive in-home, parent-directed in-home, day treatment center, and intensive center-based interventions: **http://www.texasyoungautismproject.com/**

2. Northwest Young Autism Project: parent information on the program and how it is run, including how the day is structured, description of individuals it best serves, potential benefits and risks, and how to access services: **http://www.nyapllc.com/ parent-information.html**

10

Evidence-Based Practices for Social Skill Acquisition

Summer Ferreri and Joshua Plavnick

Michigan State University

Chapter Objectives:

- Describe and identify evidence-based practices for social skill acquisition.
- Describe and identify peer-mediated instruction, incidental teaching, milieu teaching, PRT, video modeling, and social narratives related to social skill instruction.
- Describe the implementation of peer-mediated instruction, incidental teaching, milieu teaching, PRT, video modeling, and social narratives to address the social skill needs of children with autism in applied contexts.

Deficits in social skills are a core symptom of autism and can negatively affect relationships, academics, employment opportunities, independence, and mental health (Bellini, Peters, Benner, & Hopf, 2007; White, Keonig, & Scahill, 2007). Some young children with autism may demonstrate a clear interest in other children, but they are not able to initiate social interactions, maintain social interactions, or respond to the initiations of others without explicit skill instruction. Conversely, other children with autism may avoid social situations altogether, preferring instead to find a quiet place to play alone. Finally, some children with autism regularly interact with others but have difficulty understanding social cues (e.g., facial expressions) or demonstrating specific social behaviors (e.g., taking turns).

The heterogeneity of individuals with autism spectrum disorders requires that service providers become familiar with a range of evidence-based practices and learn to select a practice that is best suited to the individual needs of a specific child. This chapter provides an overview of several evidence-based practices for teaching social skills to a range of children on the autism spectrum. Strategies for adapting these practices are provided when applicable. Many individuals with autism are very interested in developing meaningful social relationships and this is possible when effective instructional practices are selected and tailored to meet a specific child's needs.

PEER-MEDIATED INSTRUCTION

Peer-mediated instruction involves teaching typically developing peers ways to promote social interactions with children with autism in natural settings (Odom et al., 1999; Strain, McGee, & Kohler, 2001). As peers learn to prompt and maintain interactions with a child with autism, they will experience an increase in positive interactions with others over the course of a school day. Generally speaking, effective peer-mediated instruction increases the likelihood of placement in less restrictive, inclusive settings, and occasions social relationships for children with autism (Carter & Hughes, 2007). Peer-mediated strategies increase the likelihood of students generalizing social skills to other peers and across settings.

A number of skills have been taught using peer-mediated instructional strategies. Responding to others, social reciprocity, showing empathy, interacting with peers in groups, and initiating interactions are the most common target behaviors. The primary goals of peer-mediated instruction are outlined here (Sperry, Neitzel, & Engelhardt-Wells, 2010).

Neitzel, Boyd, Odom, and Edmonson Pretzel (2008) identified a series of steps educators should take when creating peer-mediated social skills training to meet the goals identified earlier. The first step is to systematically select several peers who can be taught to interact with the child with autism. Select peers who are compliant with adult directions and have a positive history of social interaction. It also is important that peers have a good attendance history. This will ensure consistency over time. Finally, peers need to be able to opt out of participating in the peer-mediated activity on any given day.

Goals of Peer-Mediated Instruction:

1. Teach peers to interact with children with autism.

2. Increase frequency of positive and natural interactions between typical peers and children with autism.

3. Extend social interactions across a variety of school activities.

4. Minimize the need for adult support.

For this reason, select four to five peers to act as social partners. Multiple peers will increase the likelihood of skills generalizing to novel social partners and will ensure an individual does not feel overburdened with responsibility.

Once peers are selected, they need to be trained to ensure positive interactions occur on a regular basis. Peers should first be taught about individuals with autism and how they are similar or different from other kids in the classroom. Volkmar and Wiesner (2009) offered several suggestions for children's books that can help students better understand their peers with autism (see Additional Text Resources at the end of this chapter).

Direct instruction of skill training is a critical component for effective peer-mediated instruction. Specific skill training should include teaching peers how to initiate and respond to children with autism. Skills to emphasize include making suggestions about how to play, sharing items, offering assistance, and providing social feedback in the form of highfives, hugs, or praise (Odom & Strain, 1986). Peer training also can be combined with other strategies (e.g., visual cues, video) to teach children with autism to initiate or respond to peers (Theimann & Goldstein, 2001).

A basic behavioral skills training package consisting of a brief explanation, model, role play with feedback, and invivo practice with feedback is often used to prepare typically developing children for peer-mediated instruction (Odom & Strain, 1986; Sainato, Goldstein, & Strain, 1992). The peer training process should begin with a discussion of similarities and differences between the target student and the peers and an explanation about why the target student needs to learn to interact with his or her peers. The facilitator needs to provide models of language the peers can use with the target student. For example, it is important to teach peer mediators that they want to use a phrase such as "here is your favorite shovel" simultaneously while handing a preferred item to a target student. Role play allows the peers to practice the mediation skills with other typically developing peers and the facilitator can provide immediate feedback, with an emphasis on praising positive behaviors demonstrated by the peer mediators. Finally, invivo practice is similar to the role play with the exception that the target student is now involved and the facilitator continues to provide guidance and feedback to peer mediators.

Initial peer-mediated instructional sessions are easiest to conduct if one peer and the child with autism interact in a 5- to 6-minute play session in an area slightly separated from other children. This may sound short, but the duration and frequency of peer-mediated instructional sessions can be increased as the students demonstrate positive interactions. It also is important to select times that do not remove the peer from situations in the classroom that he or she really enjoys, such as recess.

Once a location and time of day are arranged, select materials that evoke interactive play. For example, provide a toy that neither child has seen before and that the child with autism may need assistance operating, or provide objects or books related to the special interests of students with autism (Baker, 2000; Baker, Koegel, & Koegel, 1998; Boyd, Conroy, Mancil, Nakao, & Alter, 2007). For example, Baker (2000) found incorporating special interests into games increased positive social interactions for students with autism and their peers (e.g., if the child is interested in trains, use a new train set; if the child is interested in maps, have him or her draw a map of the classroom). Materials that might occasion social interactions include balls or building blocks rather than puzzles for younger children and Yu-Gi-Oh! cards or board games instead of coloring books for older students. Additionally, materials that represent shared interests can evoke spontaneous social interaction between the children.

It is important to identify one staff member to facilitate play sessions for the participants. The facilitator can prompt the peer to initiate interactions and to respond appropriately to initiations made by the learner with autism. The facilitator can also help the peer respond to any unanticipated behaviors of the child with autism. It is important to provide frequent specific praise to the peer for things he or she did well during the play session. At the conclusion of the session, the peer can choose whether to continue playing with the child with autism or move on to another activity.

A large body of research supports the efficacy of peer-mediated interventions as an approach to increasing the social competence of individuals with autism. Recent applications of peer-modeling packages have led to increased social interaction (Kohler, Greteman, Raschke, & Highnam, 2007), improved social communicative behaviors (Thiemann & Goldstein, 2004), the development of joint attention (Zercher, Hunt, Schuler, & Webster, 2001), and decreased levels of stereotypy (Lee, Odom, & Loftin, 2007). Improved social outcomes have also been identified when siblings are selected as social partners (Tsao & Odom, 2006). When other children are trained to accurately implement the intervention procedures, peer-mediated instruction is an evidence-based practice for teaching social skills to children with autism (National Autism Center, 2009a).

Peer Supports and Social Interaction

Kohler and colleagues (2007) examined the effects of teaching six preschool children to interact with a peer with autism on overall social interactions between the children. The emphasis of the intervention was on training peers to interact with a classmate with autism, as opposed to training the child with autism to interact with her peers. The following steps outline the peer training process:

1. Skills taught to peers included sharing and requesting materials, providing play suggestions, initiating and responding to others, participating in conversations, giving compliments and assistance, and showing affection.

2. A 15-minute training session was implemented each day over 8 consecutive days.

3. The training session involved three components: (1) the teacher introduced and modeled the skill for peers and the student with autism, (2) the peers practiced the skill with one another, and (3) the peers practiced the skill with the student with autism.

4. The teacher provided prompts and praise for the typical peers during the training sessions. No prompts or praise were provided for the student with autism.

Outcomes: Although no social interaction occurred during the baseline play sessions, the student with autism and her peers demonstrated an increase in social interaction each time a peer group was taught the targeted social behaviors. This study highlights the absence of social interactions when children were simply in the same play space as in baseline. Rather, peers needed explicit instruction in social interaction strategies in order to carry out the peer-mediated social intervention.

Embedding Throughout the Day

Once play sessions are successful in the classroom setting, it is important to begin extending peer-mediated instruction across the school day. Teachers can create social interactions during a number of routines by placing children with autism and peer instructors in dyadic situations where materials need to be shared, the child with autism requires assistance, or when materials will be frequently traded or passed around. For example, art projects offer an opportunity to provide one pair of scissors or glue stick for a dyad to share. LEGO® sets or model kits allow for similar situations with older students. Further, a child with autism may need to ask for help with some aspects of completing the project and both participants are likely to ask one another to pass materials back and forth.

This provides a number of opportunities for social interaction to occur and extends social behavior beyond the play context.

The aforementioned strategies can promote social initiations and responses for both participants. Practitioners may find it helpful to generate a list of ways they could embed these opportunities within different activities that regularly occur. Sandall and Schwartz (2008) created a skills matrix for preschool-aged children that identifies common preschool activities and social skills that can be taught using peer-mediated instruction during those activities (see Table 10.1). By completing the matrix for each activity and target skill, as we have done for "free play," you will identify a series of behaviors that can be targeted within a peer-mediated framework throughout the school day. This skills matrix can be adapted and used with older students with autism in elementary school. The activities might include daily routines (e.g., arrival, bathroom break, lunch, recess) and content areas (e.g., math, reading, music, science).

Peer-mediated instructional strategies are one of the most effective procedures for increasing natural, generalized social interactions for children with autism. As peers may spend several years within the same school or classroom setting with the child, they can have a major impact on the child's life if they learn ways to interact early on.

SOCIAL SKILLS TRAINING

Currently there is a fair amount of research to support the use of behavioral approaches that incorporate naturalistic teaching methods to increase social skill acquisition (National Autism Center, 2009a, 2009b). There are many different types of naturalistic behavioral approaches; incidental teaching, milieu teaching, and PRT are the focus of this section. Each of these approaches uses strategies derived primarily from behavioral-based methods and have the following common elements: (a) the approach is child-led or child-initiated, as opposed to instructor-led; (b) the focus is on the child's interest; (c) instruction is embedded or interspersed in the naturally occurring environment; and (d) natural reinforcers are delivered that relate to the child's communicative act (Wetherby & Prizant, 2005). Although these approaches have common features, they differ in respect to one or multiple facets.

Incidental Teaching

Incidental teaching is a behavioral-based, objective-driven, child-led, systematic approach in which the natural environment is arranged to promote communicative acts by students (Hart & Risley, 1975; McGee, Krantz, Mason, & McClannahan, 1983). Incidental teaching is intentional and requires planning; it is a natural approach, but it does not occur by

Table 10.1 Skills Matrix

Activity	Target Skills			
	Greeting peers (can be initiations or responses)	*Asking to play with peer(s)*	*Requesting items*	*Exchanging materials*
Arrival	Saying "hello" to peer when school day starts			
Free play	Saying "hi" when entering an activity in progress	Asking, "Can I play?" when joining peers already playing	Asking, "Can I use the car?" when playing with cars with peers	Saying, "Here is a truck," while handing truck to peer when peer gives car
Snack	Saying "hi" when sitting next to peers		Asking a peer, "Can I have the crackers?"	Saying to a peer, "Here is your cup"
Small group activities	Handing a peer the pencils after she asks and saying, "Here are the pencils"		Asking a peer, "Can you pass me the paper?"	Saying to a peer, "Can I have that red marker?"
Outside	Saying "hi" when joining peers playing on the playground	Asking a peer, "Do you want to play catch?"	Asking a peer, "Can I have a turn on the swing?"	Giving a peer a turn on the swing after the peer asks for it. Saying, "It's your turn"
Departure	Saying "good-bye" when leaving school			

Source: Adapted from Sandall, S.R. & Schwartz, I. S. (2008) *Building blocks for teaching preschoolers with special needs* (2nd ed.). Baltimore, MD: Paul H. Brookes.

happenstance. For example, professionals should identify events such as snack time, choice play time, or a field trip and plan to use incidental teaching to teach specific concepts such as social greetings, choice, sharing, or peerplay. Subsequently, a professional can arrange the environment to increase the likelihood of student initiations. This can be accomplished by placing preferred items in sight, but out of reach, or restricting access to activities or events until an initiation occurs. Once an initiation occurs (e.g., grabbing for train tracks that a peer is playing with, pointing to a peer as a way of greeting the peer, saying "please" for access to a group game), the professional requires an elaboration of the request (e.g., instead of grabbing, require pointing; instead of pointing, require an approximation such as "hhh" for "hi" or "hello"; instead of "please," require "game please") and subsequently provides prompts (if the child does not respond correctly) or reinforcers natural to the context (e.g., train tracks, peer greeting, or game access). This approach requires the professional to (a) arrange the environment to promote motivation and elicit initiations, (b) pay close attention to sometimes subtle indications of child interest, (c) engage the child in an elaboration, (d) determine the appropriate level of prompting, (e) be prepared to quickly deliver the target item, and (f) collect and analyze data on child responding (Scott & Baldwin, 2005). Specifically, there are nine steps required for the proper use of incidental teaching; each is described here with an example of Leroy and parallel play.

Step 1. Choose an educational objective. For example, Leroy will sit beside a peer and play appropriately with molding clay; access to the clay will be provided when Leroy verbalizes a request for the clay.

Step 2. Arrange the natural environment to promote student motivation and interest in the materials that are related to the teaching objective. It is important to note that to properly promote generalization and maintenance of skill acquisition, instruction should occur not only during teaching sessions but also within other settings, with other individuals, and with a variety of instructional materials (Dawson & Osterling, 1997; National Research Council, 2001). For example, prior to free-choice play period, arrange a table with two settings of molding clay, cutouts, and tools for play; guide a peer to one setting and leave the other seat open so that Leroy can have access to the molding clay upon requesting it.

Step 3. Wait for an initiation by the child through verbalizations, gestures, or other communicative acts. For example, Leroy does not have any verbal communication so he might try to sit in the seat, grab the molding clay, or cry while looking at the molding clay.

Step 4. If the professional is unsure of which item or activity the child wants, he or she can ask for clarification, for example, "Leroy, do you want this?"

Step 5. Request an elaboration. For example, Leroy does not use verbalizations so an elaboration to his grabbing, pointing, crying, might be an approximation of the word "clay," such as "ay."

Step 6. If the child responds correctly, provide the item or activity the child requested. For example, as a starting point, a correct response could be "ay" as an approximation to "clay," and as Leroy successfully uses the approximation to request clay, closer approximations would be required, such as "c-ay," or "lay," and eventually, "clay." As soon as Leroy emits the approximation, he is given access to the clay.

Step 7. If the child responds incorrectly or does not respond within the designated time frame (5 seconds), the adult should provide prompts to complete the interaction, for example, if Leroy has learned to successfully verbalize approximations of the word "clay" and is now being required to verbalize the whole word; approximations such as "ay," "lay," or "cay" would be considered incorrect. If Leroy emitted "cay," the professional would prompt or model the whole word, "clay."

Step 8. Request a "turn" with the material, replace it so that the environment is contrived to promote another child initiation, and return to Step 3. The session should end with the child successfully requesting the desired item and gaining access to the reinforcer. The session should be brief and concluded as soon as the child loses interest. For example, after Leroy has successfully requested the clay, the professional would immediately provide access to the clay and allow Leroy to play with it for a specified period of time. At the conclusion of that time period (e.g., several minutes), the professional would request a turn with the clay, place it out of reach on the table, and wait for Leroy to make an initiation.

Step 9. Collect data and make data-based decisions. If the child is increasing his or her use of the target, the approach can be continued and when appropriate move to more advanced elaborations, such as "clay please" or "blue clay." If the child's social-communicative behavior is not improving, a determination should be made regarding the discontinuation or alteration of incidental teaching approaches, such as selecting a new preferred item for Leroy to request while sitting beside a peer, selecting a new peer, or moving the location of the molding clay table to a less distracting environment (Autism Network, 2011).

As demonstrated by these steps, incidental teaching requires professionals to make a string of complex judgments related to the child's interests, prompting level, correctness of responses, and decisions regarding data analysis (McGee, Morrier, & Daly, 2001). Incidental teaching is an intentional, systematic strategy for teaching a variety of new skills to individuals with autism (e.g., McGee, Krantz, & McClannahan, 1985, 1986; McGee, Morrier, & Daly, 1999). Eventually, a child will likely need to learn to ask for objects or events that are not present or visible and answer questions about identifiable stimuli (e.g., request to play with a peer who is in a different classroom, answer questions about size, category, or location of stimuli), in which case, incidental teaching is a suitable approach to help achieve such an outcome (Zagar & Shamow, 2005).

Milieu Teaching

Milieu teaching is a naturalistic teaching approach based on behavioral principles (Kaiser & Hancock, 2003). There are three primary components of milieu teaching (Choi & Kim, 2005). First, teaching begins as soon as a student shows an interest in something, looks at the adult, or initiates a communicative act. For example, in physical education (PE) class, Jim may stand next to a bin full of sports equipment, point to the Hula-Hoops™, or request to play football. Any activities or materials that are natural to the environment can be utilized to begin milieu teaching. The use of milieu teaching to increase social-communication skills can occur for Jim at school during times such as cross-grade reading buddies, literacy circle sharing, recess, PE, or lunch. Additionally, teaching can be embedded within any typical activity that takes place in natural environments such as on the bus, at home, or during community outings.

Second, once the child indicates interest by looking at the adult, the objects, or initiates an interaction, the adult delivers the prompts for the target or more advanced communicative response. It may be necessary for the adult to provide prompts. In milieu teaching, the adult has the option to provide three primary types of prompts: models, time delay, or mands.

Model. The model is a demonstration of the desired response, provided to the student so he or she can imitate the response. For example, when Jim requests to play football, the adult could model a variety of responses such as a request to a peer (e.g., "I'd like to play catch with you") or a question to a peer (e.g., "Want to play football with me?"). The model approach is helpful at teaching imitation skills. Depending on the level of the student, the adult may model a variety of responses such as only the beginning sound of a word (e.g., "fff" for "football"), phrase ("football please"), or sentence (e.g., "Football is my favorite sport; do you want to play it with me?"). Jim is able to produce sentences; therefore, an adult would require a complete sentence from him.

Mand. The mand prompt refers to a request made by the adult to the student such as "What do you want to do?" or "Tell me what you want." A mand also might be a choice between two items such as "football" or "Frisbee™." The intent is to evoke a specific response from the student in relation to his or her initial communicative act or interest. For example, when Jim is standing next to the bin of sports equipment, the adult might mand, "What do you want?" with the intent to evoke a specific response from Jim such as "to play ball with a friend" or "I want to throw the Frisbee to George." Again, depending on the ability level of the student, the response requirement would change. For an individual who can imitate simple words but lacks conversational skills, an appropriate response might be "play."

Time delay. Time delay refers to the act of the adult obtaining joint attention and then waiting for a brief moment to prompt a response from the student. For example, after Jim points to the Hula-Hoops, the adult will make eye contact, look expectantly or with a quizzical look at Jim, and wait approximately 5 seconds. The intent is to prompt a response such as "I want to give one of those to Donnell" or "will someone play Hula with me?" or "Hula time with friends!" The time delay approach is used to increase spontaneous language; therefore, for a student who cannot produce complete sentences but can emit words, an appropriate response might be "Hula-Hoop."

Third, natural consequences are provided to the student. For example, if Jim models the questions to his peer ("Want to play football with me?"), the natural consequence is access to the requested item (i.e., football with a peer); similarly, if Jim responds to the time delay with "I want to give one of those to Donnell," the natural consequence is to allow access to the Hula-Hoop so he can give it to his friend. If Jim does not respond or respond correctly (e.g., says "gimme," "football," turns away from the adult), the adult may provide a few additional prompts. However, if Jim still does not respond correctly, the desired consequence (e.g., football with a peer, Hula-Hoop to a friend) is nonetheless provided to him. The desired consequence is provided regardless of correct responding to ensure future motivation under similar circumstances.

In recent years, researchers have expanded milieu teaching to include prelinguistic targets (Yoder & Warren, 2002) and embedded components of the developmental and social interactionist perspectives (e.g., Responsive interaction [RI]; Ingersoll, 2011). Enhance Milieu Teaching (EMT) and Responsive Education-Prelinguistic Milieu Teaching (RE-PMT; Yoder & Warren, 2002) are child-centered approaches embedded within the child's natural environment, in which professionals provide prompts for more advanced forms of communication and subsequently provide natural reinforcers to the child to help facilitate skills such as social-communicative behavior (Hancock & Kaiser, 2002; Yoder & Warren, 2001). EMT and RE-PMT can be particularly effective for children with autism. They build on the principles of incidental teaching and RI. The principles of RI include following the child's lead, responding to verbal and nonverbal behaviors, and promoting a verbal or nonverbal conversation between the child and the adult. They are often confused with incidental teaching (and are sometimes, mistakenly, used interchangeably), as both are naturalistic teaching approaches. The major difference between the two approaches is that incidental teaching requires the child to initiate (e.g., point, shift gaze to look at, reach for) and the adult expands the child's initiation. EMT and RE-PMT can be used with children who do not or rarely initiate; the adult arranges the environment with preferred or novel toys or activities and prompts initiations (Hancock & Kaiser, 2002; Kaiser, Hancock, & Nietfeld, 2000).

PIVOTAL RESPONSE TREATMENT

PRT is an approach used to teach a variety of skills, including social skills, to individuals with autism. PRT combines the systematic application of principles of ABA with a child-led approach that is embedded within the child's natural environment. An overarching goal of PRT is the generalization of learned skills. Therefore, PRT focuses on the acquisition of four pivotal areas of instruction (motivation, responding to multiple cues, self-management, and self-initiations), which are believed to be key foundational skills that affect broad areas of functioning (Vismara & Bogin, 2009; Volkmar & Wiesner, 2009). Generalization is then further facilitated as the pivotal skills are regularly applied in a variety of contexts (Zagar, 2005). The National Professional Development Center (NPDC) on Autism Spectrum Disorders has provided a detailed description of steps for implementation of PRT (Vismara & Bogin, 2009). Following is a summary of the steps and corresponding examples.

Motivation

PRT indicates that maintaining motivation is a pivotal skill for students and the goal is to avoid boredom and maintain interest in learning. Vismara and Bogin (2009) suggested seven primary steps to maintain student motivation.

Establish learner attention. Prior to providing instruction, the adult should first obtain student attention. For a student such as DJ, the adult might first make eye contact and then make a request or provide directions.

Use shared control. Adults can maintain shared control by determining which part(s) of a learning opportunity they will perform for the student and which one(s) the student will be required to complete. An adult may decide that DJ will be required to tap the shoulder of a peer who he would like to play with and the adult would then vocalize, "DJ would love to play with you; can he share the blocks with you?" The adult would then physically guide DJ toward the block area and initiate a building game. Eventually, DJ would be required to complete more of the steps independently, which would maintain a balance between adult- and child-selected stimuli throughout the day, every day.

Use learner choice. Adults can maintain learner choice by giving students the opportunity to choose from a variety of toys, materials, or activities they are interested in; these items or activities can then be incorporated into instruction. For example, DJ engages in block play for the majority of time he is at daycare. Blocks would be considered a highly preferred item and blocks could be used as a reinforcer for completing particularly difficult tasks, such as initiating play with a peer. Adults can also arrange the environment with items the child prefers and follow the child's lead during interactions and activities.

Vary tasks and responses. The adult ensures task variation by using a variety of materials, activities, and tasks, and response variation by altering the environmental conditions under which the student responds. For example, if DJ begins to show signs of being bored of blocks during instruction, change the activity to bubbles.

Intersperse acquisition and maintenance tasks. Motivation is maintained when adults intersperse easy tasks with tasks that are more difficult. For example, an adult might ask DJ to point to items he likes to play with (easy) and then ask him to point to items he can play with a friend (difficult).

Reinforce response attempts. The adult should reinforce all unambiguous attempts related to the goal. For example, DJ often pronounces the word "blocks" as "babas." As the adult is in the natural environment with DJ, she might request that DJ say "blocks" before handing him the item. If he verbalizes "blas," this is a clear attempt at the word "blocks" and is a closer approximation than "babas." Therefore, the adult immediately rewards the approximation by saying "blocks" and handing the blocks to DJ.

Use natural and direct reinforcers. Reinforcers should immediately follow the target behavior and should have a direct relationship to the target behavior. For example, at the daycare facility, DJ is standing next to the table with molding clay, watching his peers play. The adult might require DJ to say to a peer, "Play?" Once DJ vocalizes the word "play," he should be provided with immediate access to his peers and the molding clay.

Responding to multiple cues

The goal of this pivotal skill is to ensure that students will learn to respond to complex requests with multiple attributes or properties. The NPDC on ASD suggests two primary steps to make certain the goal is achieved.

Vary stimuli and increase cues. Adults can teach students to respond to multiple cues by identifying and using a wide array of cues related to the target behavior, using more than one cue, and gradually increasing the number of cues used. For example, an adult might provide DJ with photographs of classmates. The adult would ask DJ to point to the girl; as he accurately identifies the girl, the task is made more complex by increasing the number of cues, such as point to the girl with glasses, and eventually point to the girl with glasses who is sitting on a horse.

Schedule the reinforcement. When an adult is determining the schedule of reinforcement, he or she should first identify many reinforcers and provide them every time the target behavior is performed accurately. As the student masters the behavior, the teacher will gradually reduce the amount of reinforcement by only reinforcing the target behavior intermittently. For example, when an adult first begins to teach DJ how to say "hello" to a peer, he or she will provide reinforcement every time DJ says "hello" to a peer. Eventually, as the task becomes easier for DJ, the teacher can provide reinforcement every other time he accurately says "hello" to a peer, then once every fourth time he emits the behavior, and so on, until minimal (or no) reinforcement is needed to maintain the act of saying "hello."

Self-Management

The goal of self-management is to decrease dependence on adults (e.g., parents, teachers, school professionals, practitioners) while simultaneously increasing self-independence. Vismara and Bogin (2009) suggested that there are three primary steps to increasing self-management.

Prepare the self-management system. Adults must make many decisions when creating the self-management system, such as the exact target behavior, baseline performance, rewards that will be used, and how often, when, and with what device students will record their behavior. For example, as DJ moves from daycare to the school setting and has acquired some greeting skills, he could track the number of times he greets a peer (e.g., "hi," "hello," "hey," "My name is DJ") on a golf counter.

Teach self-management. An adult would teach the student to discriminate between desirable and undesirable behaviors, how to record the behaviors, and subsequently provide reinforcement when criterion is met. For example, as DJ begins sixth grade, he can understand the difference between desirable and undesirable behaviors and is taught how to record the number of desirable peer interactions in homeroom. He could tally the number of these appropriate interactions, such as "I don't know the answer to number 3," when asked for an answer by a peer.

Create independence. To foster independence, the adults needs to gradually decrease their presence and the number or intrusiveness of the prompts related to monitoring behavior, while simultaneously increasing the number of (a) desirable responses necessary to obtain reinforcement and (b) setting and people with which the student self-monitors. The adult might decrease the intrusiveness of prompts by making visual cues smaller, gradually replace a physical hand over hand prompt with a model prompt, have a peer provide verbal prompts rather than the adult, or use gestures rather than verbal cues. For example, by the end of sixth grade, DJ might be able to self-monitor the number of appropriate interactions with peers at the bus stop and lunchroom with minimal supervision or reinforcement.

Self-Initiations

The student is taught to initiate by teaching language, communication, and social skills in addition to question asking.

Teach social initiations. The student is taught initiation by learning to share materials, organize play activities, take turns choosing activities, and how to be persistent when initiating. For example, DJ might learn how to hand a friend his toy car and say, "Do you want a turn?"

Teach question asking. Vismara and Bogin (2009) provided step-by-step directions on how to teach a student to ask the following: "What's that?" "What happened?" and "What's happening?" One example is to fill an opaque bin with blocks and through the use of prompts, teach DJ to ask "What's that?" Once DJ asks the question, he is shown what is in the bin and given access to the item. Subsequently, a series of fading techniques can be used to encourage independence and generalization.

Teach language, communication, and social skills using naturalistic techniques. As this section indicates, there are many ways to teach social interactions through the use of naturalistic strategies. Some key components provided by Vismara and Bogin (2009) are as follows:

1. Imitate the child's actions. Imitation increases the likelihood that the child will look at the adult, which provides an opportunity to deliver a prompt. Imitation also ensures the adult is following the child's lead and interest.

2. Provide the item that is associated with the target behavior (provide blocks after DJ says "blocks"). Providing a reinforcer that is directly related to the behavior increases the likelihood that the child learns the behavior-response contingency and that the child will demonstrate the target behavior.

3. Use time delay before providing prompts. Time delay gives the child an opportunity to respond and teaches children to spontaneously label or request toys (Wolery, 2005). Also, time delay reduces the number of prompts teachers deliver.

4. Encourage independent requesting by placing items in sight but out of reach. Arranging the environment with preferred or novel objects and toys helps teach children to initiate.

Video Modeling

Video modeling is a teaching procedure that provides a demonstration of a behavior through a video display (Bellini & Akullian, 2007). Generally, a student observes a model engaging in a behavior or series of behaviors and then has the opportunity to imitate the model. Several social skills have been taught to young children with autism using video modeling, including using play-related statements, initiating interactions with others, making eye contact, and using affective responding (Gena, Couloura, & Kymissis, 2005; Nikopoulos & Keenan, 2007; Taylor, Levin, & Jasper, 1999; Tetreault & Lerman, 2010). The purpose of the following section is to describe the procedures for implementing video modeling with young children with autism.

An important prerequisite to video modeling is that the learner is able to attend to a video screen for at least the duration of the videos displayed during the intervention. Overall, results of recent research suggest video displays increase the likelihood of learners with autism attending to modeled behavior (Bellini & Akullian, 2007), though it is important to conduct an assessment of attending to video prior to selecting video modeling as an intervention for a particular student. The ability to imitate at some level may also be a prerequisite for effective video modeling, though children who demonstrate minimal imitative behavior prior to intervention have learned to match the behavior of a video model (Cardon & Wilcox, 2010; Plavnick & Ferreri, in press), suggesting imitation may emerge as a result of video modeling. Generally speaking, more research is needed to identify the type of learners that are most likely to benefit from video modeling as an intervention (Rayner, Denholm, & Sigafoos, 2009).

An effective video modeling intervention requires some tailoring for individual students, which will require that a series of important decisions occur before implementing the procedures. For example, a video sequence can be created using a peer, adult, or the participant as a model (Rayner et al., 2009). In most cases, the video is filmed from a third person perspective where the observer sees all actors within the video (McCoy & Hermansen, 2007). However, Tetreault and Lerman (2010) demonstrated that the first person perspective, where the observer sees the video as he or she will also see a live situation, can be effective for teaching individuals with autism to make eye contact with others in social situations. The procedures selected depend on the target student and the behavior you wish to teach. The steps necessary for an effective video modeling intervention are identified in the following figure, with information about selecting the best procedure for your student in the text that follows.

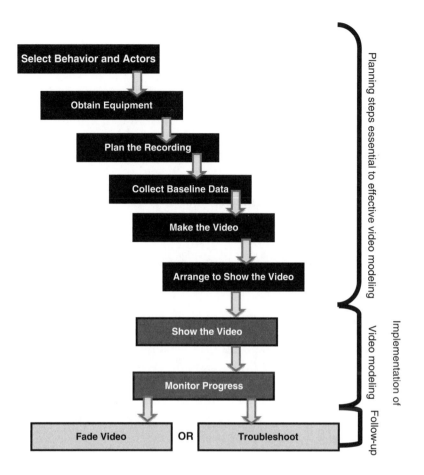

The figure shows the steps involved in preparing and implementing a video modeling intervention. The steps in black rectangles indicate preparation components; dark gray steps indicate implementation components, and pale gray steps indicate follow-up components. Each step has substeps as described in the following text.

Step 1: Select a Target Behavior and Actors. Similar to other methods for teaching social skills, it is important to select and operationally define a target behavior. For a young child, you might select a behavior targeting initiations with others. This skill may include several additional behaviors including approaching another person, looking at the person, initiating a request, and waiting patiently for the social partner's response.

It is important to consider who to include in the video. Research indicates that a similarly aged peer is a better video model than an adult. Furthermore, no clear benefits are gained by using the target student as the model. Thus, it may be easiest to use a peer that is slightly older than the target student and who can reliably produce the target response(s) at the correct time. Other actors also require some consideration as you want to use peers or adults the child regularly sees in the natural environment to promote generalization of the social interaction.

Step 2: Obtain the Necessary Equipment. Equipment plays an important role in the video modeling process. It is important to use materials you are comfortable with. The essential items include a video recording device and a device to show the video. With recent technological innovations, it may be possible to accomplish this using the same device. Remember, a small screen such as a flip camera, smartphone, or PDA is only convenient if the child can attend to the important details in the video. Do not sacrifice functionality for portability or exciting technology.

Step 3: Plan the Recording. Creating scripts for the actors and planning the video recording is critical to do before you are ready to film. The recording must capture the essential features of the target behavior and the behavior of the social partner within an interaction. For example, if you are teaching a student to respond in a certain way when someone walks up to that student and says "hello," you might want a video angle that shows the model looking up at the other person, smiling, and saying "hi." It is also important to select a location with good lighting and ask your actors to speak loud enough so that the camera microphone sufficiently picks up language. This may take a trial run, but the time spent on the front end will be worth it.

When planning the recording, consider consequences that are likely to occur for the child if he or she engages in the behavior. If the consequences are preferred, be sure to include those in the video sequence as it can motivate the student to engage in the behavior. For example, Plavnick and Ferreri (in press) used video clips of peer models vocally requesting and then receiving high preference items to teach language to previously nonvocal children with autism. If the consequences for the target behavior are not preferred (e.g., social consequences), you might consider embedding additional rewards for the model within the video clip (e.g., access to preferred materials). The need for this step depends on the skills of the target student, but incorporating preferences into the video sequence can speed up the acquisition process and make video modeling more enjoyable.

Step 4: Collect Baseline Data. As with all teaching procedures for students with autism, data are paramount. It is important to capture the extent to which a child already performs the target response within the environment in which it should occur. We suggest collecting baseline data before making the video as it will inform video creation. For example, if a child can already get a game out and invite a peer to play but struggles initiating his or her turn, that child does not need a video that starts with getting the game out.

Step 5: Make the Video. This step includes selecting the best angle or per-spective from which to film the video. When selecting the angle, consider the skill the child needs to learn. Point of view video modeling (video cap-tured from the child's perspective) has been used to teach eye contact and commenting within a conversation (Tetreault & Lerman, 2010). This angle may be beneficial for those skills because the camera shows the student exactly where to look when talking to others. A video that captures both the model and other actors may be important when teaching interactive toy or game play, as multiple behaviors of the model and social partner may be relevant.

Another step involved in making the video is editing the content and, when desired, adding features. This can be the most cumbersome part of implementing a video modeling program and our suggestion is to get some help using basic editing software through webcasts or technical assistance providers. Editing may be as simple as cutting the beginning and ending of a video clip, but more complicated features include splic-ing, cutting out sound, or inserting voice-overs. The video must capture the target skill, but the general consensus is that shorter video clips seem to work best (Shukla-Mehta, Miller, & Callahan, 2010). For young children, you might use only a15- to 25-second video when teaching a skill such as showing interesting objects to others.

Step 6: Arrange the Environment to Show the Video. The primary consid-eration for the environment is that students with autism need to eventually learn social skills within natural environments. Make sure the student will have an opportunity to engage in the target behavior shortly after viewing the video. When teaching children to say good-bye to their peers at the end of a school day, showing the video just before it is time to depart is more likely to promote positive outcomes than showing the video shortly after children arrive at school.

Another environmental consideration is to prepare potential social partners to respond in a way that can reward the behavior when it occurs. If the target behavior involves playing with peers at recess, it is probably best to ensure peers are ready for the target student to approach them. You also might want to create a social scene on the student's most preferred playground toy to increase the likelihood of the student going to the tar-geted location.

Step 7: Show the Video. This is probably the easiest step of video mod-eling. Many young students with and without autism enjoy watching video clips of other children. The process does not have to be complex; simply tell the child to "watch this movie." There is no need for long explanations. Depending on the receptive language skills of the child, you might tell him or her the specific behavior you want the child to watch for on the video. You may need to prompt the student to attend to the video or show the clip several times before the student can engage in the target behavior. Generally speaking, though, children like to look at video displays.

Step 8: Monitor Progress. It is very important to monitor behavior after video modeling occurs. Progress monitoring allows you to determine whether acquired skills are maintained and if the skills generalize to novel contexts, and it provides the earliest indication of the need to alter the intervention if it is ineffective. Continue collecting data on the target response and determine whether the student is making adequate progress. As a rule of thumb, if the learner is not making progress after three to five teaching sessions, it is probably time to make some changes. However, professional judgment is critical, as complex, new skills may take longer to acquire. Additionally, you know your student and his or her rate of acquisition best. If you think the child is close to getting the skill, it does not hurt to try a few more sessions. If progress is absent or slow, see the troubleshooting guidelines that follow.

If the student makes progress toward social goals at an acceptable rate, then the procedures are doing exactly what you intended. It is time to fade the videos and any other prompts or unrelated rewards and ensure the behavior is generalized and maintained in the natural environment. It is best to do this gradually so that the student has as much support as needed to continue engaging in the skill.

Though generalization is often carefully examined well after an intervention has been implemented, several features of video modeling require careful attention to generalization as the procedures are planned. A list of strategies that can promote generalization when using video modeling is outlined here (see Chapter 8 for an in-depth discussion pertaining to programming for generalization):

- Use social partners the child is familiar with as actors in the video clips.
- Present several forms of the behavior within video clips. For example, you might teach a child to greet others by observing a number of video clips wherein the model says, "Nice to see you today," "I am so glad you are here," or "Hello, how are you?"
- Incorporate multiple settings that are familiar to the child (e.g., classroom, lunchroom, gym, playground).
- As the child begins to reliably demonstrate the response, increase the amount of time between playing the video and providing an opportunity to respond.

Step 9: Troubleshoot. If the student is not demonstrating the behavior, there are several things you can do to adjust the procedures. First, make sure the intervention is being implemented correctly. Second, ensure the student is looking at the video screen when the video clip is displayed. If there are multiple behaviors modeled in the video, the student may have difficulty attending to the most important features. Consider editing the video and selecting a single behavior. If the child has limited access to the video, you can consider increasing the number of times he or she watches it before an opportunity to engage in the behavior. Finally, deliver additional prompts and unrelated rewards contingent on the target response in order to provide extra support when teaching complicated skills. These are good starting points. If you have made multiple adjustments to the procedures and the student is still not engaging in the behavior, consider another method of teaching. Your student may not be ready for video modeling just yet.

Social Narratives

Social narratives teach social skills to children with autism by providing a description of specific environmental contexts and an example of behavior that should occur (Gray, 1995). These can be written or pictorial; the key is to deliver the narrative in a format the student is most likely to comprehend. A benefit of social narratives is that the environmental cues for a particular behavior can be highlighted for the student. This helps students navigate the social situation when it occurs at a later time. Social narratives have been used to teach young children how to gain attention, make choices, play with peers, engage in other social situations, and decrease challenging behaviors that may occur during social interaction (Crozier & Tincani, 2005; Soenksen & Alper, 2006).

Similar to other strategies for teaching social skills, the preparation of the materials require considerable attention to detail when using social narratives. Once all the preliminary work is completed, actually delivering a social narrative intervention can be quite simple. The following vignette describes the process of implementing a social narrative, with the sequence of steps highlighted in bold print throughout the text.

Teaching for Generalization

There are several components of social narratives that increase the likelihood the skills with be generalized. In the preceding example, Fatima was taught to ask to play across multiple exemplars (e.g., with a variety of peers). Mr. Chatir also might provide a slight variation of the social narrative to represent a range of settings. For example, after teaching Fatima to ask to play with peers in the classroom, he could do the same on the playground. By incorporating preferred activities or toys that Fatima sees in her natural environment, Mr. Chatir created an intervention that is more likely to lead to Fatima generalizing the target behavior.

How-To Case Study: Fatima

Social narratives were selected to teach Fatima to ask to play with peers using her AlphaSmart computer. Her teacher, Mr. Chatir, first **identified a social situation** that involved Fatima, asking if she could join one of her peers who was playing a game that was enjoyable to Fatima. **The specific behavior that was targeted** was using the AlphaSmart to ask a peer if she could join in play. Once the behavior was defined, Mr. Chatir **collected baseline data** during five 30-minute play sessions to determine how often Fatima initiated social interactions with her peers. The results suggested Fatima watched peers engage in activities but did not ask to join them in play at any time.

The next step was to **write the social narrative** in a language that would be accessible to Fatima and in the first person. Mr. Chatir needed to **select the length of the story** and opted to write only a few sentences to identify the basic components of asking to play with a peer. The statements were as follows: "I will tap my friend on the shoulder," "I will use my AlphaSmart to ask to play," "I will play with my friend when she says yes." Mr. Chatir also identified three peers who would be good play partners, and before starting the intervention he informed them of a way they could help teach Fatima to play with others. The final component of planning was to **decide whether to include pictures** within the narrative. Mr. Chatir selected photographs of peers engaged in the preferred activities to help Fatima understand the text as the story was read.

It was time to **implement the social narrative.** Mr. Chatir read the social narrative to her right before playtime, when Fatima would be expected to ask if she could play with a peer. Fatima liked the narrative and her teacher encouraged her to look at it independently after it was read to her. Once the play period started, Mr. Chatir **monitored Fatima's progress** by recording the number of initiations toward peers as in the baseline period. Mr. Chatir **regularly reviewed the data** and **modified the intervention** when Fatima did not make sufficient progress. He specifically decided to add a picture of Fatima playing with her peer at the end of the social narrative in order to show Fatima the reason for asking to play with her peers. This addition was immediately effective and Fatima quickly learned to ask a variety of peers to play during the play periods.

Over time, it is important to consider fading the social narrative so that the behavior can occur naturally, as it does for typical children. Fading can be accomplished by increasing the length of time between reading the narrative and the opportunity to perform the behavior. It is also possible to reduce the amount of time the student has access to the narrative, either by decreasing the number of times it is read, by reading only certain parts of the narrative, or allowing the student to read the story instead of including an adult in the process.

FUTURE DIRECTIONS

Social skill deficits are a defining feature of autism and they impact development and functioning in every other developmental domain. Fortunately, there are several evidence-based practices for increasing social skills in young children (many of which are described in this chapter). However, the future direction of social skills interventions for individuals with autism is infinite, especially considering the rapid advancement of technology and its applications to social skills training. Researchers are in the early stages of examining social skills interventions, using technology such as virtual environments (e.g., Brigadoon is a virtual island in the game of Second Life created specifically for adults with autism and their caregivers), simulations, and video modeling, using devices such as the Apple iPad. Given the potential advancement of social skills interventions, more research is urgently needed in the areas of (a) technology-based interventions; (b) effective professional development and implementation of social skills interventions; (c) differing age groups of individuals with autism, especially those beyond early intervention; (d) complex social skills; and (e) generalization of social skills, to name just a few future research directions.

LEARNING ACTIVITIES

1. How might you teach parents to use peer-mediated instruction with siblings at home?

2. How and for what skills would you use video modeling to teach Leroy to play with his peers at school?

3. List and describe how you might arrange the environment to use incidental teaching to increase social interactions between peers in an inclusive preschool classroom.

4. How would you embed social skills instruction during the day for children with autism in elementary school settings?

RESOURCES

General

National Professional Development Center on Autism Spectrum Disorders: **http://autismpdc.fpg.unc.edu/**

National Professional Development Center on Autism Spectrum Disorders—Evidence-Based Practice Briefs: **http://autismpdc.fpg.unc.edu/content/briefs**

Autism Internet Modules: **http://www.autisminternetmodules.org/**

Peer-Mediated Instruction

Texas Guide for Effective Teaching, Peer-Mediated Instruction: **http://www.txautism.net/docs/Guide/Interventions/PeerMediated.pdf**

Incidental Teaching

Walden School: **http://www.psychiatry.emory.edu/PROGRAMS/autism/Walden.html**

Texas Guide for Effective Teaching, Incidental Teaching: **http://www.txautism.net/docs/Guide/Interventions/IncidentalTeaching.pdf**

Pivotal Response Treatment

University of California at Santa Barbara: **http://education.ucsb.edu/autism/**

Texas Guide for Effective Teaching, Pivotal Response Training: **http://www.txautism.net/docs/Guide/Interventions/PRT.pdf**

National Professional Development Center on Autism Spectrum Disorders Evidence-Based Practice Briefs on PRT: **http://autismpdc.fpg.unc.edu/content/pivotal-response-training**

Social Narratives

National Professional Development Center on Autism Spectrum Disorders—Evidence-Based Practice Briefs on Social Narratives: **http://autismpdc.fpg.unc.edu/content/social-narratives**

Kansas Instructional Support Network: **http://www.kansasasd.com/node/9**

Social Stories Lending Library: **http://region2library.org/SocialStories.htm**

Additional Text Resources

Amenta, C. A. (1992). *Russell is extra special: A book about autism for children.* New York, NY: Magination Press.

Cook, J., & Hartman, C. (2008). *My mouth is a volcano!* Chattanooga, TN: National Center for Youth Issues.

Hoopmann, K. (2001). *Blue bottle mystery: An Asperger adventure.* Philadelphia, PA: Jessica Kingsley.

Hoopmann, K. (2002). *Lisa and the lacemaker: An Asperger adventure.* Philadelphia, PA: Jessica Kingsley

Keating-Velasco, J. L. (2007). *A is for autism, F is for friend: A kid's book for making friends with a child who has autism.* Shawnee Mission, KS: Autism Asperger.

Welton, J. (2003). *Can I tell you about Asperger syndrome? A guide for friends and family.* Philadelphia, PA: Jessica Kingsley.

11

Designing Instruction and Supports to Prevent and Decrease Problem Behavior

Kathleen Strickland–Cohen and Beth Harn

University of Oregon

Chapter Objectives:

- Describe a multitiered approach for preventing challenging behavior.
- Describe evidence-based practices that can be used to prevent and decrease problem behavior in children with autism.
- Explain the rationale for conducting an FBA and how it supports the development of effective behavior support plans.
- Illustrate the steps and persons involved in conducting an FBA and developing a behavior support plan (BSP).

Akey to long-term success for young children with disabilities is inclu-sion in settings with typically developing peers, including general education classrooms; however, these settings need to be intentionally and systematically designed to ensure success for students with a range of abil-ities (Odom & Wolery, 2003). Because children with autism typically expe-rience delays in communication and social development and higher than average levels of repetitive and stereotypical behaviors (e.g., hand flap-ping, object spinning, compulsions, and insistence on sameness), it is criti-cal that these students are provided with sufficient supports to decrease their risk of developing more challenging problem behaviors. Research has consistently demonstrated that without timely, targeted, and effective intervention, problem behavior in children with autism can be expected to continue, and often worsen, over time (Dunlap et al., 2006; Horner, Carr, Strain, Todd, & Reed, 2002). Comprehensive programs for young children with autism should include intentional, proactive strategies for preventing and alleviating challenging behavior and teaching appropriate behaviors before the problem behavior becomes a pattern or intensifies.

Evidence-based practices for teaching communication and social skills to children with autism are described in Chapters 9 and 10. The primary purpose of this chapter is to provide the reader with the following: (a) a variety of evidence-based practices that can be used to prevent and reduce challenging behavior in children with autism, and (b) procedures for designing and implementing individualized, function-based supports for children who engage in persistent patterns of problem behavior.

POSITIVE BEHAVIORAL INTERVENTIONS AND SUPPORTS

One well-established prevention and intervention approach for address-ing challenging behavior in children and youth is Positive Behavioral Interventions and Supports (PBIS). PBIS is a collaborative, values-based approach for implementing evidence-based behavioral interventions, and it has been shown to be effective in preventing and reducing prob-lem behavior for children with a variety of disabilities, including autism (Bushbacher & Fox, 2003; National Research Council, 2001). PBIS is con-ceptually rooted in applied behavior analysis. From this perspective, it is assumed that behavior is learned through interactions with the environ-ment (including others in the environment) and can, therefore, be altered by changing or modifying the learning environment (e.g., classroom or home). Rather than attempting to "change the child," PBIS is focused on systematically arranging or designing environments to (a) promote socially appropriate behaviors, (b) remove or modify events that act as triggers for problem behavior, and (c) teach new skills and appropriate behaviors that successfully compete with problem behavior (Dunlap & Carr, 2007).

A defining feature of PBIS is an emphasis on reducing problem behaviors to improve the quality of life for the child and those who support him or her (parents, teachers, etc.). This is accomplished by using evidence-based practices that are consistent with the goals and values of those who are implementing and directly impacted by those practices, which includes family members, teachers, therapists, and related support staff. Developing an effective behavior support plan for children with autism who display challenging or problem behaviors requires a collaborative, team-based process which includes relevant stakeholders to "build the vision, methods, and success criteria pertinent to defining quality of life for everyone concerned" (Carr et al., 2002, p. 8). This includes identifying and developing individualized supports that can be effectively and efficiently implemented across all relevant settings (e.g., classroom, recess, assembly) and contexts (e.g., school, home, grocery store).

This comprehensive, preventive, and responsive approach is accomplished through implementing school- or program-wide PBIS (SW-PBIS). By systematically arranging learning environments and teaching expected behaviors across settings, schools implementing SW-PBIS actively promote the development of prosocial behavior, improve academic outcomes, and decrease the likelihood of problem behavior (Freeman, Eber, Anderson, Irvin, Bounds, & Dunlap, 2006). While SW-PBIS was initially developed for use in elementary schools, this approach is also being used in early childhood settings. The following websites provide more specific information on approaches and practices in schools or early childhood programs: Elementary Schools—http://www.pbis.org/; Early Childhood/Preschools—http://www.challengingbehavior.org/index.htm; Young Children—http://csefel.vanderbilt.edu/.

Common across each of these PBIS approaches is the use of a tiered prevention model aimed at increasing appropriate behavior by providing intervention supports that match the intensity level of the problem behavior (Figure 11.1 illustrates the three-tiered model of the SW-PBIS intervention hierarchy). Within the SW-PBIS framework, data is used to determine what level of support is needed (i.e., How significant is the problem?) and to evaluate if changes in the intervention are necessary (i.e., How is the intervention working?). An essential aspect of implementing a SW-PBIS approach is that each tier of support is linked to one another to promote consistency in implementation and effective communication across specialists and settings to help the student display the expected, appropriate behaviors, and promote social development. Students displaying higher rates of problem behavior or serious/dangerous behaviors will have goals that are still linked to the expected behavior and their plans should support them in reaching that goal. The success of SW-PBIS efforts is dependent on ensuring that the schools and programs are teaching appropriate

Figure 11.1   Three-Tiered Prevention Continuum (adapted from OSEP Technical Assistance Center on Positive Behavioral Interventions and Support, 2011)

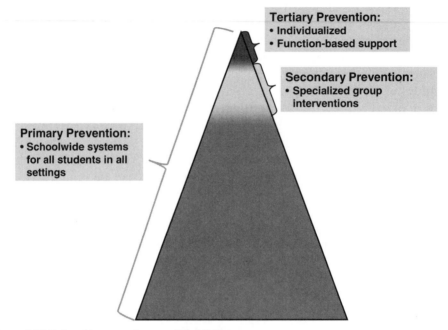

Source: OSEP Technical Assistance Center on PBS (2011)

behaviors and expectations to all students as part of their primary prevention efforts, which is discussed next.

Tier 1

Tier 1, or the primary level, is focused on system-wide practices that support **all** children and prevent the likelihood of challenging behaviors. At this level, supports are aimed at building a positive social climate by (a) creating safe, predictable, and consistent learning environments, and (b) fostering positive relationships between children and the teachers and other professionals who support them (Fox et al., 2003). The supports and practices at this level include teachers clearly defining and teaching positively stated behavioral expectations. Within a SW-PBIS approach, appropriate behaviors are explicitly taught using examples and nonexamples of what appropriate behavior does and does not look like within different routines (e.g., seatwork, circle time, waiting in line), and across different settings (classroom, cafeteria, playground) and social contexts (e.g., playing at recess, taking turns, sharing of toys/materials, asking to join a play group). Examples of common classroom expectations are asking for help (raise your hand, wait for the teacher to call on you, ask your question), following teacher directions, listening respectfully (sitting in your chair, with a quiet mouth, eyes focused on the speaker), being safe (walking in the classroom and hallways), and being a cooperative learner (taking turns and sharing materials during the activity). Once behavioral expectations are learned, students are provided with frequent opportunities to review and practice these behavioral expectations and receive positive feedback for engaging in appropriate behavior (e.g., "I like the way that you raised your hand and waited to be called on"; "Thank you for being safe and using your walking feet"; "You asked to play with the group so nicely"). To help them be successful and decrease the likelihood of problem behavior, all students benefit from having a clear understanding of what is expected of them across school settings. However, for students with autism who often have difficulty picking up on social cues or implied expectations, specific instruction on behavioral expectations can be particularly helpful and increase their ability to be successful, fully participating members of the classroom and school. Teachers that plan their primary practices to match their students' interests (e.g., high number of Native American students, favorite local sports team, etc.) and needs (i.e., a student with autism) will have a greater likelihood of success in promoting appropriate social development.

In addition to defining and teaching expectations, classrooms that include students with autism should include the following preventive practices: (a) organizing and sustaining high quality learning environments, (b) arranging environments that promote appropriate behaviors, and (c) teaching communication and social skills (Horner et al., 2002; Neitzel, 2010a). Elements of high quality learning environments for students with autism include interactions with typically developing peers, frequent opportunities for choice making, and environmental supports that promote structure, predictability, and high levels of student engagement. Common supports found in successful classrooms include daily classroom schedules, often with pictures, posted at students' eye level. These types of schedules provide a consistent, overt list of daily activities that can support successful transitions across more or less preferred activities for students with autism by allowing students to see the order in which activities will be occurring (i.e., increasing predictability of the environment). These types of visual schedules can also be individualized for students requiring more intensive supports (see discussion in Tiers 2 and 3 of this chapter). Problem behavior can also be prevented by making simple environmental modifications, such as providing well-organized learning centers, teaching all students appropriate ways to transition from activities in an organized manner, and having materials located in the areas where they are routinely used. Organizational supports (e.g., color-coded materials) can be used to minimize challenging behavior by increasing levels of academic engagement and providing the structure needed for students to complete tasks and assignments independently (Neitzel, 2010a).

To minimize challenging behavior and help to build positive teacher-student relationships, classrooms supporting students with autism also need to provide frequent and explicit feedback to students when engaging in appropriate behaviors. Classroom-wide acknowledgement systems (i.e., token economies) are an efficient and effective way to provide clear acknowledgement of positive skill development that can be used to reward the class as a whole as well as individualized for the needs of specific students. For example, during circle time, the teacher can reward all students for following expectations (e.g., sitting criss-cross apple sauce, listening when others are talking, etc.), and if the teacher has a child with autism in the class who needs additional reinforcement for looking at the person talking (either adults or peers), the teacher can also have that child earn tokens for looking at the speaker (i.e., "I like the way Suzie is listening and looking at me as I read the story"). These types of reward systems allow students to earn points for following expectations and engaging in appropriate social interactions, which can then be added up and traded for a larger, more preferred activity delivered for the class (e.g., extended recess, coloring, etc.) or for individual students (e.g., free time to choose to read, use a computer, draw). This allows teachers to provide immediate and frequent feedback for desired behavior, while still *tailoring* rewards to address the specific preferences of the individual child. Additionally, classrooms that include children with autism should have an overt emphasis on supporting/teaching the development of communication/language and social skills within the regular daily curriculum to promote appropriate development and prevent problem behaviors from occurring. In early childhood or preschool settings, time directed to teaching social skills and language development is a common practice; however, in elementary schools, there is greater variability in teaching these skills, even though many students would benefit, regardless of disability. (For more information on these types of practices [classroom-, school-, or program-wide], see the following website: Collaborative for Academic, Social, and Emotional Learning—http://www.casel.org/.) Within a SW-PBIS approach, there will be students who display challenging behaviors even with the support of these primary practices and need additional, targeted supports provided within a Tier 2 approach.

Tier 2

Tier 2 supports (interventions) are provided to teach social skills and prevent challenging behaviors from escalating to a significant or chronic behavioral issue. These types of interventions typically include small group-based interventions targeting specific skill deficits (e.g., social skills training, small group academic instruction). These interventions should be embedded directly into the general curriculum and overtly linked to the primary (Tier 1) expectations so that students are supported in meeting the schoolwide expectations. One commonly used Tier 2 intervention is the Check-In, Check-Out (CICO) method. This intervention is effective with students who respond well to adult attention (i.e., teaching, prompting, and reinforcement). This intervention has been effective in teaching children to complete assignments, use appropriate language, maintain task engagement, engage appropriately with peers, and follow directions. In general, this intervention works by identifying the specific behaviors the student needs to increase to be more successful. The child's daily routine is organized into specific intervals (e.g., circle time, reading, recess, lunch, art) and he or she receives contingent, specific feedback and points from the teacher or other preferred adult across the school day for displaying appropriate behavior.

Figure 11.2 provides an example of a CICO behavior report card for a student who frequently runs in the classroom, uses inappropriate language, and does not complete work independently (will stop if he doesn't know what to do or stares off into space instead of working). You will notice that each of these behaviors is written in a positive manner (i.e., what you *want* the student to do) as well as directly tied to the primary, schoolwide expectations (see description of Tier 1) of being safe, responsible, and doing your personal best. The chart could be given to the student, or placed on his desk, so the teacher can check in with him throughout the day and provide him specific feedback of when he is being successful and teach him appropriate behaviors. Daily goals are collaboratively developed with the teacher, parent, and student to increase motivation. The chart can also be sent home daily so that family members can provide feedback and to promote consistent expectations across school and home settings. For more information on this intervention approach, the reader is referred to the book entitled, *Responding to Problem Behavior in Schools, Second Edition: The Behavior Education Program* (Crone, Hawken, & Horner, 2010) as well as visiting the PBIS website (http://www.pbis.org).

Tier 2 interventions for students with autism often involve teaching specific communication and social skills (Freeman et al., 2006). These interventions may be delivered in small groups or individualized and embedded into the general curriculum (see Chapters 9 and 10 for evidence-based communication and social skills intervention for children with autism). Deciding when to consider changing the location/setting of the Tier 2 intervention is determined by considering the expectations of the individual classroom/program. For example, in early childhood settings, considerable time and effort is spent teaching social skills, emphasizing developing relationships between peers in naturalistic experiences (e.g., circle time, eating lunch, etc.). A young child needing more targeted support in this domain would be best served having the support delivered within the same classroom setting, because the skill is an ongoing instructional emphasis for *all* students and enhancing the explicitness or increasing the amount of reinforcement for appropriate behavior would

Figure 11.2   Sample Check-In, Check-Out Daily Monitoring Form

Check-In, Check-Out Report												
Student _____				Teacher _____				Date _____				
0 = Not Yet *1 = Good* *2 = Excellent*	*Be Safe* *Walking in* *classroom* *and hallways*			*Be Respectful* *Using kind* *words and* *actions*			*Be Your Personal Best* *Asking for* *help when* *confused*			*Working* *in class*		
Circle time	0	1	2	0	1	2	0	1	2	0	1	2
Reading	0	1	2	0	1	2	0	1	2	0	1	2
Recess	0	1	2	0	1	2	0	1	2	0	1	2
Math	0	1	2	0	1	2	0	1	2	0	1	2
Lunch	0	1	2	0	1	2	0	1	2	0	1	2
Social Studies	0	1	2	0	1	2	0	1	2	0	1	2
Writing	0	1	2	0	1	2	0	1	2	0	1	2
Total Points =									Goal			
Points Possible = 50				Today _____%					_____%			

not reflect a significant change in what is being provided to all students. In contrast, a second-grade student that is having difficulties in getting along with peers may need to participate in a social skills group outside of the classroom for two reasons: (1) building peer relationships is not taught to all students, and (2) the student may be the only one in that classroom who needs such support. In this situation, to maximize allocation of resources and effectiveness of the intervention, the student may be pulled out to receive small group social skills instruction one to two times a week with other second graders with similar concerns. Schools implementing SW-PBIS approaches are systematic in selecting intervention programs used in these pullout settings that directly align, or link, with the primary/Tier 1 behavioral expectations. Ensuring this linkage across tiers of support helps the students receiving these supports to generalize and maintain skills across settings and people.

Tier 3

For children who display persistent or significantly challenging behaviors that have not decreased with Tier 2 interventions, more intensive and individualized interventions are necessary. Students requiring this level of behavioral support are at significant risk of becoming increasingly socially isolated (i.e., peers refuse to interact or potentially ostracize the student) and engaging in potentially dangerous behaviors (i.e., either to self, others, or materials). At this level, the focus is on ensuring that children are not excluded from typical routines or contexts because of the problem behavior, but they are instead provided with effective function-based supports that promote adaptive skills and render problem behavior inefficient and ineffective (Horner, Albin, Todd, Newton, & Sprague, 2011). Developing individualized interventions requires a behavior support team consisting of relevant stakeholders (e.g., teacher(s), parents, therapists, siblings, administrators, support staff, and, when appropriate, the child/student with autism). The team gathers relevant information from a range of people who know the student well and through reviewing other information sources (e.g., record reviews), it develops a formal BSP that matches the individual needs of the student.

The remainder of this chapter focuses on the steps, processes, and types of data that are gathered and used to develop comprehensive, individualized supports for children with autism with high levels of problem behavior.

FUNCTIONAL BEHAVIORAL ASSESSMENT

Before a behavior support team can build an effective BSP to address problem behavior, the team (typically led by a school psychologist, behavior specialist, or special educator who is a member of the PBIS team) will first conduct an FBA. FBA is a research-validated process for gathering information that is used to maximize the effectiveness of individualized behavioral support by (a) defining the problem behavior, (b) identifying the conditions (e.g., settings, time, etc.) under which the problem behavior is most and least likely to occur, and (c) identifying the consequence(s) that are most likely maintaining the problem behavior (O'Neill, Horner, Albin, Sprague, Storey, & Newton, 1997). The rationale for this approach is that once relevant environmental conditions and the function of the behavior are identified, then the support team will have the necessary information to develop an individualized BSP. Although the specific methods utilized when conducting FBA vary depending upon the exact nature of the problem behavior (e.g., severity, frequency, contexts in which the problem behavior occurs), FBA typically involves gathering information using indirect measures (e.g., rating scales, caregiver interviews, record review) and direct observations (e.g., frequency counts, A-B-C systems) of the problem behavior in context. Before conducting direct observations of the problem behavior, indirect methods of assessment (e.g., archival reviews of existing data and student records, rating scales, checklists, stakeholder interviews) are gathered and evaluated to define the problem behavior, identify the environmental conditions/situations that reliably predict the problem behavior, and identify the most likely function of the problem behavior. Direct observations of the problem behavior are used to confirm the information obtained through the indirect assessment process. The guiding questions for the process of completing an FBA to develop a BSP are provided in Table 11.1. This table is elaborated in the following text;

Table 11.1   Questions and Process for Completing an FBA to Develop an
Individualized BSP

Question 1: What Is the Problem Behavior (PB)?

Process/Step	*Who and How*
• Understanding the problem	Lead member interviews, reviews materials, and distributes checklists.
• Identifying the *most likely* location/situation(s) for the PB	Lead member interviews relevant members by completing the *Routines Analysis/Monitoring Form.*
• Defining the problem behavior	Team agrees to the typical setting, frequency/intensity, and observable description of PB.

Outcome: Agreed upon behavioral definition

Question 2: When, Where, and How Is Problem Behavior (PB) Occurring?

Process/Step	*Who and How*
• Identifying antecedents and consequences	Interview relevant members about instances of when PB does and does not occur.
• Identifying setting events	Review records and interview parents, teachers, staff about potential external factors (physical, social, environmental) impacting PB.
• Organizing and analyzing data/information	Team completes *MAS/FACTS.*

Outcome: Hypothesis statement for function of PB

Question 3: Why Is It Occurring?

Process/Step	*Who and How*
• Direct observation(s) across identified setting(s) and days	Lead member completes observations across settings and situations using an A-B-C observation approach.
• Organizing and analyzing observational data	Lead member, with team, examines observational data to (a) validate the hypothesized function, (b) confirm/identify any additional antecedents and consequences related to PB, and (c) confirm/identify relevant setting events.

Outcome: Validated function (get/obtain or escape/avoid) of behavior

Table 11.1   (Continued)

Question 4: How Will We Change Behavior?	
Process/Step	*Who and How*
• Reviewing considerations of interventions for behaviors that are maintained by get/obtain or escape/avoid	Team reviews validated function of behavior and links to interventions relevant to that function.
• Identifying prevention strategies	Teacher(s)/parent(s)/staff use observational data and *FACTS* to identify (a) setting events and (b) antecedent environmental modifications that may prevent PB from occurring.
• Teaching appropriate behaviors	Teacher(s)/parent(s)/staff teach alternative appropriate behavior to student.
• Implement consequences (reward appropriate behavior remove reinforcement for PB)	Teacher(s)/parent(s)/staff provide reward/praise for engaging in appropriate behavior and remove reinforcement for PB.
• Developing goals for success and a method for monitoring performance	Team determines goal and process for monitoring response to intervention.

Outcome: Development, implementation, and monitoring of the BSP

it is provided as a reference to support understanding of how an effective BSP is developed. The table presents an overview of (a) the reason for each of the steps in the process, (b) how the steps may be completed, (c) by whom, (d) and specific outcomes leading to next steps.

It is important to note that the general details provided in this chapter are not intended to provide sufficient training for a novice practitioner in conducting FBAs. Exceptional texts and materials on this process include the following: *Building Positive Behavior Support Systems in Schools: Functional Behavioral Assessment* (Crone & Horner, 2003); *Understanding the Environmental Determinants of Problem Behaviors* (Dunlap, Harrower, & Fox, 2005); *Addressing Challenging Behaviors of Young Children with Autism Spectrum Disorders* (Dunlap, Strain, & Ostryn, 2011); *Designing and Implementing Individualized Positive Behavior Support* (Horner et al., 2011); *Functional Behavioral Assessment in Early Education Settings* (Neilsen & McEvoy, 2004); *Functional Assessment and Program Development for Problem Behavior: A Practical Handbook* (O'Neill et al., 1997); and *Function-Based Supports for Individual Students in School Settings* (Scott, Anderson, Mancil, & Alter, 2009).

Jim

Jim has always had a difficult time with unexpected changes in routine, which would sometimes lead to challenging behavior such as breaking pencils, ripping up worksheets, and writing on walls, books, or desks. Early in the school year, Jim received a Tier 2 intervention from the school psychologist, focused on developing self-regulation behaviors with three other students with similar behavior concerns, which significantly decreased Jim's challenging behavior to approximately one occurrence per week. His general education teacher used the prompt taught in the pull-out social skills group (i.e., "1-2-3-4") to prompt Jim, when necessary, across the school day and settings with good success. Until recently, Jim had also been successful in independently following his daily schedule. However, in the past few weeks, Jim has been requiring more and more prompts to complete tasks. His problem behavior has increased significantly, and in addition to destroying property, he has also begun throwing materials and cursing. Jim's teachers are becoming increasingly concerned and have requested assistance from the PBIS team. The team has agreed that an FBA is needed.

Leroy

Leroy's parents have requested assistance from the behavior specialist at their son's preschool. They want to know what they can do about his aggressive and self-injurious behavior. When denied access to preferred activities or objects at home or in school, Leroy often (multiple times a day) has tantrums and becomes aggressive toward adults and other children. At home, Leroy also bites his hands (sometimes hard enough to draw blood) when he becomes frustrated. This has been a significant concern for Leroy's parents for quite some time. Last week at preschool, Leroy bit another child, causing tissue damage. The girl had to leave school for the day and her parents were very upset. Leroy's parents are afraid that if something is not done he is not going to be able to continue to remain in the preschool with his typically developing peers. The behavior specialist, Mrs. Goldman, has agreed to conduct an FBA to determine the cause/function of Leroy's challenging behavior.

Throughout the rest of this chapter, the case studies of Jim and Leroy will help to highlight different aspects of the FBA and behavior support planning process.

What Is the Problem Behavior? Defining the Problem Behavior

Once the school team decides that the child's problem behavior warrants an FBA, the first thing the team must do is agree upon an observable description of the problem behavior. This involves defining the behavior in clear and measurable terms, specifying the following: what the behavior looks like, the setting/location where the behavior typically occurs, frequency of occurrence, and any particular people the behavior is displayed toward. For example, rather than labeling Leroy's problem behavior as "aggression," it is more clear to specify that he "hits other children with an open hand and bites adults and other children"; instead of stating that he has "stereotypic behavior," a more clear and accurate description of his behavior is "shaking strings and spinning objects." In addition to describing what the behavior "looks like" and when it occurs, it is also important to include dimensions such as its intensity (e.g., biting results in tissue damage, books are thrown across the room) and duration/length of time the behavior occurs (e.g., tantrums last approximately 5 minutes).

Routines analysis. Developing a clear understanding of the problem behavior includes determining when the behavior does and does not occur across the day. This can be accomplished by interviewing relevant parties (parents, teachers) and documenting daily routines (e.g., getting dressed before school, brushing teeth, riding the bus to school, participating in recess activities, participating in group work in the classroom, transitioning between activities) and the likelihood of problem behavior within those routines. This type of routines analysis should include a thorough description of the child's full daily schedule and identify the times and settings in which problem behavior is most *and* least likely to occur (Horner et al., 2011). This information can be obtained by interviewing those persons most familiar with the child's daily schedule. For example, for challenging behavior that occurs primarily in a school context, the person(s) responsible for conducting FBA interviews could obtain a copy of the student's daily schedule and then interview relevant teachers and staff to determine the times of the day and settings where problem behavior is most and least likely to happen. Figure 11.3 shows an example of a structured routines analysis form for Leroy's behavior in the preschool setting.

Before conducting more detailed FBA interviews for Leroy, Mrs. Goldman completed a structured routines analysis for both home (with parents) and school activities (with classroom teachers and speech therapist) to document Leroy's problem behaviors across his daily routines and pinpoint the times of the day when problem behavior is most and least likely to occur. The results of the analyses indicated that Leroy is most likely to engage in aggressive behavior toward himself and others during minimally structured activities both at home and in school.

When, Where, and How Is the Behavior Occurring? Developing a Hypothesis

After the behavior has been clearly defined and organized within daily routines, the focus shifts to gathering more specific information related to the conditions that reliably occur before (antecedents) and immediately following (consequences) the problem behavior. The goal of this process is

Figure 11.3   Structured Routines Analysis for Leroy

Leroy

Daily Activities

Time	Activity	Behavior	Likelihood of Problem Behavior	With Whom
7:30-7:45	Drop-off and Greeting	tantrums, hand-biting	1 2 3 ④ 5 6	Parents, Teachers
7:45-8:15	Breakfast		① 2 3 4 5 6	
8:15-8:25	Bathroom Break		1 ② 3 4 5 6	
8:25-9:15	Playground/ Gym	tantrums, hand-biting, aggression	1 2 3 4 ⑤ 6	Teachers, Peers
9:15-9:30	Snack		1 ② 3 4 5 6	
9:30-10:30	Centers/Art	tantrums, hand-biting, aggression	1 2 3 4 5 ⑥	Teachers, Peers
10:30-11:00	Circle Time		1 2 ③ 4 5 6	
11:00-11:30	Lunch		① 2 3 4 5 6	
11:30-11:40	Bathroom Break		1 ② 3 4 5 6	
11:45-12:30	Playground/ Gym	tantrums, hand-biting, aggression	1 2 3 4 ⑤ 6	Teachers, Peers
12:30-1:00	Circle Time		1 2 ③ 4 5 6	
1:00-1:45	Rest		1 ② 3 4 5 6	
1:45-2:15	Centers/Art	tantrums, hand-biting, aggression	1 2 3 4 5 ⑥	Teachers, Peers
2:15-2:30	Good-byes and Pickup		① 2 3 4 5 6	

to begin to understand why the problem behavior is occurring. Within this approach, problem behaviors serve two *functions* for children: (a) to get/obtain something desirable or (b) avoid/escape something undesirable. This information is collected via interviews to identify the hypothesized or potential function of the problem behavior, a critical step in the FBA process (Gresham, Watson, & Skinner, 2001). When challenging behaviors occur across multiple environments, it is critical to include information from stakeholders (e.g., teachers, parents, and support staff) from each relevant setting (e.g., cafeteria, home, classroom, playground).

There are various instruments available for collecting and organizing the information required to complete this part of the FBA process, including the following: comprehensive structured interview forms (O'Neill et al., 1997); rating scales, such as the Motivation Assessment Scale (Durand, 1988); and checklists, such as the Functional Analysis Checklist (Van Houten & Rolider, 1991) and the Functional Assessment Checklist for Teachers and Staff (FACTS; Crone & Horner, 2003). It should be noted, however, that the particular instrument or method used to gather the information is not as important as the end result, which should be a thorough description of the problem behavior and all of the relevant antecedent and consequent variables related to that behavior. Specific considerations in identifying antecedents and consequences for problem behavior are discussed next.

Identifying antecedents. Once the general routines/situations in which problem behavior occurs have been identified, information related to events occurring prior to the problem behavior, or antecedents, is also gathered and examined. This includes gathering more specific facts about the routines in which problem behavior is most likely, including the location where, and when, the problem behavior typically occurs, and who is often present in the environment. Interview questions will also inquire about any specific activities or events within problematic contexts that may serve as "triggers" for problem behavior (e.g., specific types of academic demands or attention from peers or being asked to transition to a new activity).

Identifying consequences. As previously stated, a primary outcome of FBA is to determine the function of the problem behavior so that effective interventions can be developed to decrease the display of that behavior. Within this preventative, behavioral approach, the function of a behavior for the student can either be to (a) get/obtain something or (b) escape/avoid something. Once the function is determined, it will guide how the intervention should be developed. Behaviors that function to get/obtain something are maintained by the consequence of positive reinforcement, meaning students engage in the problem behavior to get/obtain access to adult or peer attention, tangible or edible items, preferred activities, or desirable physiological sensations. In contrast, behaviors that function to escape/avoid something are maintained by the consequence of negative reinforcement, meaning students engage in the behavior to avoid or escape from academic demands, social attention, an overstimulating environment, or aversive physiological events such as a headache or ear ache. Understanding the consequences that maintain the problem behavior is integral to developing an intervention plan that changes the environment to effectively decrease that behavior (see discussion in the section on developing behavior support plans).

It is important to note that when we refer to *problem behavior,* we typically are not referring to one problematic behavior or response but to a *functional class* of behaviors. Behavior can be grouped into classes that are maintained by the same consequences. For example, hitting, kicking, spitting, and yelling may all result in the immediate removal of demands; therefore, though the responses do not "look" the same, they are all part of the same functional class of behaviors. Additionally, a single problem behavior can serve multiple functions under different conditions. For example, in a classroom setting when difficult tasks are presented, head hitting may be maintained by escape from demands; for the same child in the home setting, head hitting might most often function to gain access to parental attention. Understanding the conditions under which problem behaviors are part of the same functional class enables the behavior support team to develop a more comprehensive and efficient BSP.

Identifying setting events. There will also be questions aimed at helping to identify setting events. Setting events are events or conditions that occur in one context that affect the likelihood of problem behaviors in other contexts by altering the value of consequent events. Setting events can be social (e.g., arguing with parent/peer), physical (e.g., sleep deprivation, illness, hunger, missed medication), or environmental (e.g., changes in daily routine, loud noises, bright lights, physical proximity to peers). For example, not eating breakfast one morning may function as a setting event, increasing the value/motivating properties of edible reinforcers at school, and thereby increasing the likelihood of problem behavior that is maintained by access to edibles. A fight with a peer on the bus may act as a setting event by making social interaction with peers temporarily aversive and increasing the probability of problem behavior that is maintained by avoidance of peer interactions. Setting events can sometimes be challenging to identify, as they can occur in a different setting (playground, bus, home) from, and/or several hours before, the problem behavior occurs (i.e., missing medication in the morning can be related to an increase of problem behavior in the afternoon). However, setting events can often help to explain the cause of challenging behavior that appears to occur "sporadically" without any predictable triggers; for this purpose, utilizing information from across multiple settings (e.g., home, bus, classroom, cafeteria, playground) becomes increasingly important.

> *Information gathered from FBA interviews with Jim's special and general education teachers revealed that Jim's problem behavior typically occurs when Jim is asked to complete difficult academic tasks in writing and math (antecedent). His PB is most likely on the days when he arrives at school late, after class has already begun (setting event).*

Developing a hypothesis statement. After gathering and evaluating the information related to when, where, and how the problem behavior occurs, the behavior support team is ready to develop a hypothesis statement. A hypothesis statement is a written statement describing the relationship

Table 11.2   Sample Hypothesis Statements

1. During unstructured activities at preschool, such as open centers and recess (antecedent), Charlie will flap her hands and make repetitive noises (behavior). These behaviors appear to be maintained by **obtaining self-stimulation** (consequence).

2. When asked to do work with a partner or small group in science class (antecedent), Jacob makes inappropriate comments (e.g., "This is stupid!") and pushes materials off his desk (behavior) to **avoid working with peers** (consequence). This behavior is most likely to happen when an altercation with a peer has occurred on the bus prior to science class (setting event).

3. When asked to brush his teeth, wash his hands or face, or get dressed (antecedent), Lamont will hit his head with a closed fist (behavior). Head-hitting appears to be maintained by **escape from self-care routines** (consequence) and is more likely to happen if Lamont did not sleep well the previous night (setting event).

among antecedent events (including triggering antecedents and possible setting events), the problem behavior, and the consequences thought to be maintaining the problem behavior (Crone & Horner, 2003). The team should generate a separate hypothesis statement for each functionally related class of problem behaviors. After completing the interview portion of the FBA, Leroy's team agreed on the following hypothesis statements (the **function** of the behavior is shown in bold):

- *During activities at school that have low structure, when denied access to a preferred activity or object (antecedent), Leroy hits and/or bites adults/ peers (behavior) because this behavior sometimes results in **getting/ obtaining access to the preferred activity/item** (consequence).*
- *When Leroy first arrives home from school and is unable to communicate his needs (antecedent), he will become frustrated and bite his hands (behavior). This behavior appears to be maintained by **obtaining the physiological sensation** it provides (consequence). This behavior is most likely when Leroy is not feeling well or did not take a nap at school (setting events).*

Table 11.2 provides additional examples of hypothesis statements from hypothetical FBA interviews.

Why Is the Behavior Occurring?: Validating the Function of Behavior

The final step in conducting an FBA is to validate the team's hypothesis statement(s). Following indirect assessment and the development of a hypothesized function of the problem behavior (discussed previously), students are directly observed in the context(s) of concern to determine

Figure 11.4   A-B-C Chart

A-B-C Chart			
Date: _____ Student: _____			
Observer: _____			

Date	Antecedent	Behavior	Consequence

if the hypothesis statement is valid (*validating,* in this sense, refers to determining agreement between verbal reports and direct observations, but it does not necessarily indicate a causal relationship; Horner et al., 2011). Direct observations are conducted across multiple days in a variety of relevant settings and across multiple routines throughout a child's day, sampling times when the problem behavior is most and least likely to occur as identified in the "When, Where, and How" phase of the FBA process. In addition to systematic measurement of problem behavior and the events preceding and following its occurrence, direct observation data should also be used to document specific information regarding how reliably/regularly the problem behavior results in access to the maintaining consequence or reinforcer (e.g., Is teacher attention provided virtually every time the student bangs her fist on her desk or only intermittently?). All of this information will be useful when developing the BSP (which is described next).

One method for conducting direct observation is Antecedent-Behavior-Consequence (A-B-C) charting (Bijou, Peterson, & Ault, 1968). Using this technique, the observer uses a narrative format to record the time, occurrence, and the antecedent and consequent conditions occurring just prior to and following the problem behavior. An example of an A-B-C chart is shown in Figure 11.4. These data are used to look for patterns or trends that support the hypothesized function of the problem behavior. Strengths of A-B-C analysis are that it can be used to collect specific and detailed information related to most types of problem behavior, and it can be particularly helpful for determining the potential function of behaviors that occur infrequently. However, if the behavior of interest is occurring at a very high rate (e.g., several times per minute), this type of recording method can prove to be overly cumbersome (Kennedy, 2005).

To help overcome the limitations of traditional A-B-C recording when collecting data on problem behaviors that are occurring at a high rate, observation forms can be structured to include information gathered during stakeholder interviews. Specifically, student problem behaviors and likely predicting antecedents and consequences can be incorporated as part of the observation tool. This allows for easier and more efficient documentation of high rate problem behaviors (see Figure 11.5).

The previous examples represent only two of the many different commercially available and locally developed instruments that can be used to collect direct observation data. For more examples of observations systems, readers can visit the following websites:

- http://www.challengingbehavior.org/explore/pbs
- http://www.pbis.org/evaluation/evaluation_tools.aspx
- http://www.challengingbehavior.org/do/resources.htm
- http://csefel.vanderbilt.edu/resources/strategies.html#toolsplans

As with indirect assessment measures, the most important aspect of any observation system is that it allows the observer(s) to accurately collect all of the relevant information necessary to make informed decisions related to effective and efficient behavior support planning and practices.

HOW WILL WE CHANGE BEHAVIOR? DEVELOPING BEHAVIOR SUPPORT PLANS

The purpose of conducting an FBA is ultimately to inform the development of an individualized BSP that directly addresses the function of challenging behavior. The BSP functions as a blueprint for designing the environment (including changing adult behavior) to make challenging behavior irrelevant, inefficient, and ineffective (Crone & Horner, 2003). Like the assessment process, BSP development is a collaborative team-based effort. The ultimate goal of this process is to build a plan that is both technically adequate and contextually appropriate. Technical adequacy refers to the degree to which the procedures and supports included in the plan are both logically linked to the function of the problem behavior and are evidence-based (Alberto & Troutman, 2008). BSPs are judged as being *contextually appropriate* or having "good contextual fit," based on the extent to which the strategies and interventions included in the plan are a "good fit" with the values, resources, and skills of those responsible for the implementation of the program (e.g., teachers, support staff, parents). The data

Figure 11.5   Detailed A-B-C Recording Form

Antecedent	Behavior	Consequence

A-B-C Recording Form

Observer: _____

Time Begin: _____   Time End: _____

Date: _____

Antecedent	Behavior	Consequence
Alone (no attention/no activities) ❏ Task prompt/instruction ❏ Attention diverted ❏ Social interaction ❏ Preferred activity removed ❏ Other: _____ ❏	Crying ❏ Throw, drop, sweep ❏ Hand biting ❏ Head hitting ❏ Falling to floor ❏ Other: _____ ❏	Reprimand ❏ Task removed ❏ Physical redirection ❏ Task demand ❏ Access to preferred item ❏ Other: _____ ❏
Alone (no attention/no activities) ❏ Task prompt/instruction ❏ Attention diverted ❏ Social interaction ❏ Preferred activity removed ❏ Other: _____ ❏	Crying ❏ Throw, drop, sweep ❏ Hand biting ❏ Head hitting ❏ Falling to floor ❏ Other: _____ ❏	Reprimand ❏ Task removed ❏ Physical redirection ❏ Task demand ❏ Access to preferred item ❏ Other: _____ ❏
Alone (no attention/no activities) ❏ Task prompt/instruction ❏ Attention diverted ❏ Social interaction ❏ Preferred activity removed ❏ Other: _____ ❏	Crying ❏ Throw, drop, sweep ❏ Hand biting ❏ Head hitting ❏ Falling to floor ❏ Other: _____ ❏	Reprimand ❏ Task removed ❏ Physical redirection ❏ Task demand ❏ Access to preferred item ❏ Other: _____ ❏
Alone (no attention/no activities) ❏ Task prompt/instruction ❏ Attention diverted ❏ Social interaction ❏ Preferred activity removed ❏ Other: _____ ❏	Crying ❏ Throw, drop, sweep ❏ Hand biting ❏ Head hitting ❏ Falling to floor ❏ Other: _____ ❏	Reprimand ❏ Task removed ❏ Physical redirection ❏ Task demand ❏ Access to preferred item ❏ Other: _____ ❏

gathered through the FBA process can provide useful information about these contextual variables that should be considered when developing the intervention. When the goal is to develop effective plans that result in generalized outcomes for students with autism, it is particularly important to consider how the intervention will be utilized across contexts (home, school, etc.) and who will be implementing the plan (parents, teachers, therapists) to help ensure consistency of implementation. Utilizing a team approach to conducting an FBA and taking into consideration input from the stakeholders responsible for carrying out the plan will promote the development of contextually appropriate intervention plans that can be feasibly implemented across all relevant settings.

Core Elements of Behavior Support Plans

After identifying the routines in which problem behavior is most and least likely to occur and validating FBA hypothesis statement(s) (i.e., agreeing on the events that predict the occurrence of challenging behavior and function of the behavior), the behavior support team works together to identify a list of potential behavior support strategies from which the team members can select the "best" options for their specific contexts. All BSPs should include strategies and/or interventions aimed at (a) preventing the occurrence of problem behavior, (b) teaching appropriate replacement behaviors, and (c) reducing the payoff for inappropriate behavior and increasing rewards for desirable behaviors through the use of consequence-based procedures.

Prevention strategies. Prevention strategies are focused on making problem behavior irrelevant, ineffective, and inefficient by proactively changing the environment to minimize its occurrence (Wolery, 2005). Preventative strategies can be used to eliminate or modify immediate antecedent events that trigger challenging behavior. These types of modifications include arranging the physical environment to decrease the likelihood of problem behavior (e.g., redesigning the placement of furniture and activity areas within the home or classroom; making materials, toys, books, bathroom passes, etc., more accessible; or adjusting lighting, temperature, and noise levels that occasion problem behavior). Curricular modifications can also be utilized as preventative strategies. The type and/or amount of academic work, pacing of instruction, and mode of teaching or materials used can be altered to more closely align with the individual learner's level of skill and decrease frustration that may lead to increased problem behavior. For example, to clarify academic expectations, instructions/directions may need to be presented in a small group format or visually rather than orally for some students. Visual supports such as graphic organizers and highlighted text can be used to make important instructions/steps more salient and to help increase successful task completion. Also, students with fine motor difficulties may find typing assignments to be less frustrating than writing them by hand. These examples also demonstrate the importance of having a range of educational professionals to assist in the assessment, planning, and implementation process (e.g., SLP, orthopedic specialist, etc.).

Additional methods for preventing problem behavior from occurring include precorrection strategies, such as prompting techniques and reminders of behavioral expectations and consequences prior to routines that have been identified as problematic to minimize the likelihood of challenging behavior and increase the likelihood of appropriate alternative behaviors. Other common preventative strategies used for children and students with autism include making environments more predictable by providing visual schedules and cues or "warnings" prior to transitions and providing children with enriched environments that offer ample opportunities to engage in choice-making and expression of individual preferences and provide readily available functional communication systems (e.g., PECSs, voice output communication aids) for students with limited verbal skills.

Daily and classroom schedules can also be systematically modified to minimize triggering antecedents or remove setting events that increase problem behavior. For problem behaviors that are exacerbated by specific setting events that cannot be feasibly avoided, routines can be put into place that separate setting events from triggering antecedents and help to eliminate or lessen the effects of those setting events. The following is an example of how Jim's team chose to use this strategy to decrease the likelihood of his problem behavior occurring at school.

> *Because of outside speech and occupational therapy appointments, Jim arrived late for school two to three times per week. Jim's team found that his problem behavior was much more likely on days that he arrived late for school (setting event). In addition to working with Jim's family to limit the number of days that he arrived late for school, the team agreed that on those days when Jim did arrive late, he would go to the school psychologist's (a preferred adult) office to practice his "self-regulation routine" before he enters his classroom.*

Teaching strategies. BSPs include strategies for teaching both appropriate, functionally equivalent alternative behaviors and new adaptive skills with the goal of making the problem behavior inefficient. Appropriate alternative behaviors can be thought of as short-term objectives. These alternative behaviors serve the same *function* as the problem behavior, thus making the problem behavior unnecessary. The alternative behavior is explicitly taught in an effort to immediately reduce problem behavior and provide a "window of opportunity" to teach new adaptive social, academic, leisure, and/or daily-living skills (i.e., long-term goals and objectives).

The following is an example of how Jim was taught an alternative behavior as an initial step toward teaching more desirable skills.

> *The ultimate desired behavior for Jim is that he completes his writing and math assignments without destroying or throwing materials or cursing. The team has completed an FBA and determined that the function of Jim's problem behavior is to avoid/escape difficult academic tasks. Jim's team has decided that in his classroom, an acceptable alternative behavior for him is to request a "break." Although this behavior is not what Jim's teachers ultimately want him to do, it is preferable to the problem behavior and is an acceptable strategy to use while implementing additional strategies in Jim's BSP aimed at increasing his skills in math and writing and helping him learn strategies for coping with frustration and promoting self-regulation.*

Along with providing an example of teaching an alternative behavior, the previous scenario also provides an example of functional communication training (FCT). FCT is a research validated approach that is based on the understanding that challenging behavior is often used as a form of communication, particularly for children with autism who have limited communication skills (Carr & Durand, 1985; Durand, 1999). FCT is an intervention designed to teach an alternative communicative response that consistently results in access to the consequences/outcomes currently maintaining the problem behavior. Using this approach, (a) FBA data are utilized to determine the function of the problem behavior, (b) an appropriate alternative response that will serve this function is selected, and (c) the student is directly taught to use the new communication response in the contexts in which problem behavior is most likely to occur. When training the alternative behavior to proficiency, the conditions that occasion problem behavior are purposefully created throughout a student's day, creating ample opportunities to prompt and provide reinforcement for performing the new alternative skill.

Students with autism often have difficulty self-directing, inhibiting, or maintaining and generalizing behaviors without direct support and structure provided by others in their environment (Tantam, 2003). For this reason, another skill set that can be useful in reducing challenging behavior of children with autism is self-management. Self-management skills allow for greater levels of independence and are typically less intrusive in classroom settings than teacher-directed, behavior change strategies. Examples of self-management skills include self-scheduling to increase predictability for students with problem behavior that is maintained by escaping/avoiding transitions or self-recruiting of feedback in order to gain attention from parents or school staff for students with adult-maintained problem behavior. Self-management skills also include self-monitoring, which can help to increase levels of active engagement and compliance. For example, a student may wear a watch that inconspicuously signals the student every 5 minutes; in this way, the student is taught to discriminate whether he or she is engaged in a specific task (e.g., independent seat work) when signaled. This type of self-monitoring can be combined with individualized self-reinforcement systems, allowing students to monitor and provide reinforcement for their own appropriate behaviors. For example, when using a token economy, a student might be taught to provide points or tokens to herself for each interval that she remains on task.

In addition to teaching communication and self-management skills, behavioral supports can be aimed at teaching social skills (e.g., social initiations toward adults and peers, understanding and expressing emotions), self-regulatory or coping responses, and appropriate behaviors that result in the same or similar physiological sensations as those produced by repetitive or stereotypic behaviors (e.g., teaching a student to manipulate squishy balls or play dough rather than engaging in skin picking/pinching).

Consequence strategies. Consequence-based strategies are delivered after a behavior has occurred and are designed to make the problem behavior ineffective and to increase alternative and desired behaviors. An essential component of the BSP is consistent delivery of strong positive reinforcers to increase appropriate behaviors that can successfully compete with the problem behavior. It is important that the support team work to identify a pool of powerful reinforcers and that those consequences be delivered frequently (this is particularly important during initial intervention implementation and skill acquisition; once newly learned appropriate behaviors are occurring consistently, reinforcement can be gradually thinned so that rewards are provided less often). Reinforcers should be carefully tailored to match student interests, align with goals of the classroom and home, and be easily delivered with minimal interference to typical activities and routines (i.e., must have good contextual fit). It is also important that selected reinforcers result in the same or similar types of reinforcement that is currently maintaining challenging behavior. For example, if a student is currently engaging in problem behavior to escape difficult academic tasks, rewards for appropriate behavior that provide escape from difficult academic tasks (e.g., a "free homework pass" given for completing at least 50% of a difficult assignment) are more likely to be effective than teacher praise or access to preferred items.

Another way to increase alternative and desired behaviors using positive reinforcement is through the use of token economies. While this approach could also be used as a whole-class (Tier 1) or small group (Tier 2) intervention, it can also be individualized for particular students. Using this strategy, students earn "tokens" (e.g., stickers, poker chips, tally marks) that are later traded in for preferred consequences such as a trip to the classroom or school "store," a specified amount of time to engage in a preferred activity, or a free pass to avoid a less preferred activity. Token economies can be particularly helpful when fading the schedule of reinforcement and for providing high rates of immediate feedback when the maintaining reinforcer is something that cannot be frequently or easily delivered (e.g., a trip to the computer lab, 5 minutes of free time on the computer).

Along with support strategies for increasing appropriate alternative and desired behaviors, strategies aimed at decreasing the problem behavior are also included in the BSP. These strategies are designed to make the problem behavior ineffective by significantly minimizing or, when possible, completely eliminating the "payoff" for engaging in the behavior. One such procedure that is commonly used for children with autism involves withholding reinforcement from the challenging behavior (i.e., extinction). For example, if a student's problem behavior typically results in peer attention, peers can be taught to ignore (and even earn points/tokens for ignoring) the problem behavior. Strategies that minimize the payoff for engaging in the problem behavior are essential because when problem behavior continues to produce reinforcement, inappropriate behaviors often persist and interfere with efforts to teach appropriate alternative behaviors. The following example demonstrates the consequence strategy that Jim's team has designed to ensure that his problem behavior does not successfully result in escape from academic tasks.

During writing and math, Jim often engages in problem behavior to avoid challenging tasks. Jim's team (including his parents) developed a number of positive behavior support strategies designed to increase appropriate behavior and make problem behavior irrelevant. Despite the use of these positive strategies, Jim continues to refuse to complete his work, he will stay in during recess to complete his work with his teacher. If Jim refuses to work with his teacher, he will be sent to the principal's office where he will be given the choice of either (a) completing his work in the office or (b) having a phone call made to his parents to explain the situation. In the event that a call is made to his family, Jim's parents have agreed that he will not be allowed to participate in any preferred activities at home until he completes his work there.

Another technique that can be effective in reducing and decreasing escalation of problem behavior is redirection. At the first signs of problem behavior, the student is prompted or "reminded" to use the alternative behavior and then quickly reinforced for engaging in that alternative behavior. One procedure that includes the use of redirection and has been shown to effectively decrease challenging behaviors in children with autism is Response Interruption/ Redirection (RIR; Neitzel, 2010c). RIR is an evidence-based practice that is often used to decrease repetitive, stereotypical, and self-injurious behaviors that occur in the absence of other people (i.e., in the absence of socially mediated consequences). RIR consists of two primary components: (a) response interruption, whereby attempts to engage in the inappropriate behavior are physically or verbally blocked; and (b) redirection, or a prompt to engage in an appropriate alternative behavior that results in the same or similar consequences as the problematic behavior. The following is an example of how RIR could be used to decrease Leroy's self-injurious behavior.

> *Leroy engages in hand-biting when frustrated. Recently Leroy has begun biting his hand with enough force to draw blood. Using the information gathered from the FBA, Leroy's team has decided that in addition to working on increasing Leroy's functional communication skills, his BSP will also include an RIR procedure to immediately begin replacing hand-biting with a less dangerous behavior. When Leroy bites his hand, or attempts to bite his hand, he will be physically blocked from doing so and will be prompted to chew on a piece of sterile rubber tubing instead. Once the problem behavior has been significantly decreased, the team will work on teaching Leroy to chew gum (a more "socially acceptable" behavior) when he becomes frustrated.*

It is important to note that while this procedure does block reinforcement for engaging in the challenging behavior, it also provides Leroy with an alternate response for gaining access to reinforcement. Behavior reduction strategies should not be used without also identifying an appropriate alternative behavior for which the student can access the same or similar types of reinforcers.

Tables 11.3 and 11.4 show examples of the preventive, teaching, and consequence-based BSP strategies that the teams developed for Leroy and Jim. Because Leroy's problem behavior is occurring across environments, strategies for both home and school are included.

Emergency/Crisis Intervention Plan

For students with severe problem behaviors (e.g., high intensity aggressive, self-injurious, or destructive behaviors) that pose a threat to the safety of themselves or others, an emergency/crisis plan should be included as part of the BSP. The primary purpose of this plan is not to teach alternative behavior but rather to de-escalate dangerous problem behavior and protect the student and others in the environment from harm. The emergency/crisis plan clearly defines the specific conditions that constitute an emergency/crisis (i.e., when the crisis plan should be used), as well as the specific procedures to be used under those conditions. The plan should also include (a) specific criteria for ending restrictive or intrusive emergency procedures, (b) data collection and reporting procedures to be used following an incident, and (c) training that staff and other stakeholders need before implementing the plan (Horner et al., 2011).

Table 11.3   BSP Strategies Developed by Leroy's Team

Summary Statements for Leroy's Behavior:

School: During activities at school that have low structure (playground, centers), when denied access to a preferred activity or object, Leroy hits and/or bites adults/peers because this behavior sometimes results in getting/obtaining access to the preferred activity/item.

Home: When Leroy first arrives home from school and is unable to communicate his needs, he will become frustrated and bite his hands. This behavior appears to be maintained by obtaining the physiological sensation it provides. This behavior is most likely when Leroy did not take a nap at school.

Setting Event Strategies	*Antecedent Strategies*	*Teaching Strategies*	*Consequences Strategies*
Home:	**Home:**	**Home:**	**Home and School:**
– On days when Leroy does not take a nap at school (as indicated by the school-to-home notebook), offer a choice of highly preferred activities when he arrives home.	– Institute a predictable daily routine when Leroy arrives home from school (e.g., put backpack and shoes away; go potty/ wash hands; go to kitchen to choose snack).	– Teach Leroy a new "coming in from school" routine	– When Leroy begins to become upset, prompt him to use the choice board.
		Home and School:	– **Do not** allow access to preferred activities/items following problem behavior. **Do** prompt appropriate behavior.
	Home and School:	– Teach Leroy how to use the PECS to communicate needs and make choices.	– Consistently reward appropriate choice-making with access to preferred items/ activities and specific praise (as Leroy is successful, gradually fade praise and begin working on "waiting" for preferred items/ activities).
	– Prompt Leroy to use a visual schedule and arrange activities so that highly preferred activities consistently follow less preferred activities.	– Teach Leroy to engage in appropriate play activities independently and with peers (school) and siblings (home).	
	– Prompt Leroy to request and make choices using the PECS.		**Safety Procedures:**
			– For instances of hand-biting, use RIR procedures.
	– Increase choice-making opportunities during low structured activities.		– If hitting or biting others occurs, move others a safe distance away from Leroy and minimize attention; when Leroy is calm, prompt appropriate requesting.

Table 11.4   BSP Strategies Developed by Jim's Team

Summary Statement for Jim's Behavior:

During writing and math, when asked to complete difficult academic tasks, Jim often verbally refuses, destroys materials, and curses. This behavior is most likely on the days when he arrives at school late, after class has already begun. After completing an FBA, Jim's team has concluded that his problem behavior is maintained by escape from difficult tasks.

Setting Event Strategies	Antecedent Strategies	Teaching Strategies	Consequences Strategies
– On days when Jim arrives at school late, he will go to the counselor's office before class.	– Provide math and writing assignments that more closely match Jim's instructional level. – Provide visual prompts (highlighted text, graphic organizers) for writing assignments. – Put a visual reminder on Jim's desk to prompt him to ask for a break or easier task. – Provide a verbal reminder of how to appropriately ask for help when handing out assignments.	– Use FCT to teach Jim **how** to appropriately ask for a "break" or for an easier task and **when** (appropriate times) to do so. – Provide additional small-group instruction in multidigit multiplication and division. – Provide additional 1:1 instruction in writing.	– Quickly and consistently provide a break or an easier task when he requests appropriately. – When Jim begins to get upset, remind him to ask for (a) a break or (b) to complete his work in the resource classroom. – For every five difficult math problems that Jim completes, he will be allowed to skip five problems (gradually increasing requirements to earn a reward as Jim is successful). – If Jim refuses to work, he will stay in during recess to complete his assignment with the teacher. – If problem behavior in the classroom escalates or if Jim refuses to work with his teacher during recess, he will go to the principal's office to complete his work.

Emergency/crisis plans should *always* be developed with the aid of a behavior specialist or other professional with extensive training in designing and implementing interventions for students with severe problem behavior. For more information related to crisis prevention and management, see Colvin (2004).

Action and Evaluation Planning

After the BSP team selects prevention, teaching, and consequence strategies that are technically adequate and have good contextual fit, the next step in behavior support planning is developing a plan that describes how the team will implement and evaluate the effectiveness of those strategies. The action plan is designed to delineate the person(s) responsible for implementing each aspect of the plan and the timeline for implementation and progress monitoring of the plan. The evaluation plan includes the long- and short-term objectives and the specific procedures that will be used to meet those goals. Data will be collected and used regularly by the team to monitor the effectiveness of the plan and the extent to which the plan is being followed as it was designed. Therefore, the evaluation plan should also include specific information describing how and when data will be collected, how those data will be evaluated (e.g., graphs and/or work samples will be presented and reviewed at bi-weekly behavior support meetings), and criteria for determining when the plan needs to be modified. Figure 11.6 provides an example of the plan Jim's team created for implementing the BSP strategies they selected and monitoring Jim's progress toward his goals. (The forms shown in Figure 11.6 can be found at http://www.pbis.org/evaluation/evaluation_tools.aspx.)

EVALUATION PLAN

Behavioral Goal (use specific, observable, measurable descriptions of goal)

What is the short-term behavioral goal?

Jim will learn to ask appropriately for an easier task or for a break from difficult tasks when he becomes frustrated. Jim will successfully complete at least 50% of his assigned work in his math and writing classes without engaging in problem behavior for 5 consecutive days.

<u>2/15</u> **Expected date**

What is the long-term behavioral goal?

Jim will complete at least 80% of his assigned work in his math and writing classes without incidences of problem behavior (property destruction, throwing materials, cursing) for 1 month.

<u>5/1</u> **Expected date**

Figure 11.6   Implementation Action Plan and Evaluation Plan for Jim

IMPLEMENTATION ACTION PLAN

Tasks	Person(s) Responsible	By When	Review Date	Evaluation Decision • Monitor • Modify • Discontinue
Prevention Strategies				
– Jim will meet with his counselor before class on days when he's late to school.	Miss Posey (counselor)	11/30	12/17	
– Align math and writing assignments to match instructional level.	Mrs. Phelps and Mrs. Solomon to work with Miss Volding (SPED)	11/30	12/17	
– Provide visual prompts for writing assignments, and visual "break" reminder for his desk.	Miss Volding	11/30	12/17	
– Prompt alternative behavior when passing out assignments.	Mrs. Phelps and Mrs. Solomon	11/30	12/17	
Teaching Strategies				
– FCT to teach alternative behavior	Miss Volding	11/30	12/17	
– Small group math instruction	Miss Volding	11/30	12/17	
– 1:1 writing instruction	Mrs. Solomon	11/30	12/17	
Consequence Strategies				
– Provide breaks or easier tasks when Jim asks appropriately.	Mrs. Phelps, Miss Volding, Mrs. Solomon	11/30	12/17	
– Remind Jim to ask for a break at the first signs of problem behavior.	Mrs. Phelps, Miss Volding, Mrs. Solomon	11/30	12/17	
– Reward completing math problems by allowing Jim to skip some of the next problems.	Mrs. Phelps	11/30	12/17	
– Task refusal will result in staying in from recess or going to the office to complete his work.	Mrs. Phelps and Mrs. Solomon	11/30	12/17	

Evaluation Procedures

Data to be Collected	Procedures for Data Collection	Person Responsible	Timeline
Is Plan Being Implemented? – Setting event strategy – Modified assignments – Verbal prompts – Rewards for desired behavior – Response to problem behavior	– Check in with Miss Posey for setting event strategy – Check in with teachers for update on all other strategies	– Paula (school psychologist)	– Daily for 2 weeks, then weekly
Is Plan Making a Difference? – Number of times Jim asks for break/easier task – Amount of work completed – Academic performance – Number of PB incidents	– Classroom observations in math and writing – Work samples from staff – Progress monitoring data – Staff reports and office discipline referral data	– Lisa (behavior specialist) – Paula – Lisa and Paula – Lisa and Paula	– 3 times per week for first 2 weeks – Weekly – Weekly – Check every 3 days

Plan Review Date: Biweekly review for first 2 months, then adjust as needed.

FUTURE DIRECTIONS

The diversity of skills and needs of children with autism implores the need for a comprehensive and team-based approach to preventing and dealing with challenging behaviors. The importance of teaching and reinforcing students for engaging in appropriate behaviors is an essential strategy to promote appropriate development and prevent problem behaviors from becoming a pattern. If children do display problem behaviors, we need to create support plans that engage all relevant parties in the gathering of data to understand the function the behavior serves, as well as how to create and implement an effective BSP. Strategies for collaboration and teaming are described in Chapter 12. As this chapter demonstrates, there are several contextual variables that can be manipulated to support appropriate behaviors and promote the development and skill acquisition (e.g., communication and social skills, academic skills).

LEARNING ACTIVITIES

1. In the following example summary statement, identify (a) the target behavior, (b) the antecedent, (c) the setting event, and (d) the maintaining consequence.

   In biology lab, when asked to work with his lab partner, Sebastian yells, hits his desk with his fist, and throws his materials. This behavior results in Sebastian being told to go and complete his work in the principal's office (where he usually completes the assignment without incident). Sebastian's problem behavior is most likely to occur on days when he has an altercation with a peer on the bus to school.

2. List and describe each of the steps in the Functional Behavioral Assessment (FBA) process.

3. Describe what is meant by a "functional class" of behaviors. Why is it important to identify classes of behaviors when conducting an FBA?

4. What are the three types of behavior support strategies that must be included when developing a BSP?

5. Why is it important to consider contextual fit when developing and selecting behavior support strategies?

RESOURCES

Center on the Social and Emotional Foundations for Early Learning (CSEFEL): **http://csefel.vanderbilt.edu/**

Technical Assistance Center on Social Emotional Intervention for Young Children (TACSEI): **http://www.challengingbehavior.org/index.htm**

OSEP Technical Assistance Center on Positive Behavioral Interventions and Supports: **http://www.pbis.org**

Center for Early Childhood Mental Health Consultation: **http://www.ecmhc.org/**

12

Maximizing Implementation of Evidence-Based Strategies in the Classroom

Lois Pribble

University of Oregon

Erin E. Barton

University of Colorado Denver

Chapter Objectives:

- Understand and define implementation.
- Identify practices that support consistent implementation of evidence-based practices for children with autism.
- Define and describe an interdisciplinary team. Identify key members of an interdisciplinary team.

- Understand common issues and dilemmas faced by interdisciplinary teams. Identify practices that support the development of a successful interdisciplinary team.
- Define coaching and consultation. Identify when each type of practice might be most appropriate.
- Understand barriers to implementation and strategies for overcoming these barriers.

The field of special education has advanced such that a set of evidence-based practices related to the learning of children with autism exists (e.g., National Autism Center, 2009a). This body of practices is related to teaching children with autism functional, generative skills in typical settings. However, the effectiveness of these practices is dependent on the consistency and quality in which instruction is delivered and evaluated (Strain & Bovey, 2011). Research on implementation, or how services are rendered in typical settings, suggests that level or quality of implementation is directly and significantly linked to child outcomes (Durlak & DuPre, 2008; Fixsen, Naoom, Blasé, Friedman, & Wallace, 2005; Hamre et al., 2010; Odom, Fleming, et al., 2010). In fact, the impact of an intervention is directly related to the consistency and fidelity of implementation (O'Donnell, 2008). Unfortunately, research also indicates these evidence-based practices are not implemented or implemented with inadequate fidelity in typical settings (Dunst & Trivette, 2009; Odom, 2009).

In special education, implementation includes the extent to which evidence-based teaching practices are delivered in the classroom. This includes both the type of strategy used with a child (e.g., Is the strategy developmentally appropriate and matched to student strengths and needs?) and the accuracy in which it is delivered. Several factors can impact implementation in special education. Program structure, service delivery models, support systems, resources, teacher training, and teacher concerns all influence the extent to which practitioners deliver high quality services to children (Baker, Kupersmidt, Voegler-Lee, Arnold, & Willoughby, 2010). With this in mind, educational environments need to be structured so they strengthen and sustain effective implementation practices (e.g., Hemmeter, Fox, Jack, Broyles, & Doubet, 2007). The following is a discussion on how using effective collaborative teaming and consultation and coaching practices can support schools to implement evidence-based practices with children with autism.

COLLABORATING WITHIN
THE INTERDISCIPLINARY TEAM

Children with autism receive special education services through a variety of service delivery models. Services may be delivered in general education classrooms, self-contained classrooms, community preschools, or, for children younger than 3, through home visits. Services are generally delivered by a number of professionals (e.g., special educator, general educator, SLP, OT). Thus, collaboration is essential to ensure children with autism receive appropriate, individualized support and instruction. Collaboration, as defined by Friend (2000), "requires commitment on the part of each individual to a shared goal, demands careful attention to communication skills, and obliges participants to maintain parity through their interactions" (p. 131). In the case of special education services, this type of collaboration takes place within the context of an interdisciplinary team.

An "interdisciplinary" team consists of people representing a variety of professional specialties. Typically an interdisciplinary team is comprised of family members, a special education teacher, a general education teacher, paraprofessionals, and related service providers (e.g., such as SLP, OT, or physical therapist). When appropriate for the individual child, a behavior specialist, nurse, social worker, or psychologist may be included. More recently, parent advocates have become more common within these meetings and can be helpful to parents to ensure they understand the process and to ensure their interests are active within the decision-making process. The makeup of an interdisciplinary team is always dependent on the individual needs of the child with whom the team is working.

The interdisciplinary team is charged with the task of developing, carrying out, and monitoring intervention plans for children with special needs. This teaming model has been shown to be an effective way to support children with disabilities in both special and general education settings (Friend & Cook, 2010; Hunt, Soto, Maier, & Doering, 2003). Successful interdisciplinary teams function effectively by building methods of communication to share information between team members in a timely way (Briggs, 1997). Typically, the special education teacher is responsible for bringing the team together and maintaining consistent communication with all members. Each team member is responsible for contributing ideas and assistance based on his or her area of expertise. Team members coordinate the delivery of services to ensure the child receives the appropriate interventions and support across all settings. Working within an interdisciplinary team is beneficial for students with special needs *and* the professionals who are providing their services. Interdisciplinary teams act as a source of support for teachers who are working with children who have multiple challenges, which is particularly important given teachers are less likely to quit their jobs when they have a system of professional support (Talmor, Reiter, & Feigin, 2005). Building successful interdisciplinary teams takes effort and planning. Productive interdisciplinary teams establish and practice effective communication skills and are action oriented (Friend, 2000). Without these "teaming elements," members can be left with a sense of frustration and lack of support (Jung, Gomez, Baird, & Keramidas, 2008; Malone & Gallagher, 2010). However, teachers who participate on successful interdisciplinary teams report favorable attitudes toward their participation and its effects on children and families (Malone & Gallagher, 2010).

What Constitutes a Successful Interdisciplinary Team?

Snell, Janney, and Elliot (2005) identified six components essential for collaborative teamwork: (1) building team structure, (2) learning teamwork skills, (3) problem solving and action planning, (4) coordinating team action, (5) teaching collaboratively, and (6) improving communication and handling conflict. Each element provides a layer of support and builds on the other layers to create and sustain a solid framework of teaming and collaboration.

Building team structure. The first step in establishing team structure is defining the purpose and meaning for the team. Members collectively develop the goals and objectives for the team. Once the goals have been established, the role of each team member needs to be specified. It is important for all team members to have a clear idea of their responsibilities, a timeline for completion, and the responsibilities of the other professionals on the team. Goals of interdisciplinary teams working with children with autism might include the following: identifying community resources for the child's family, increasing the child's independence in a general education classroom, helping the child build and maintain social interactions with peers and adults at home and school, and helping parents teach the child to communicate his or her wants or needs during daily routines at home.

Roles and responsibilities of team members are directly related to the team's goal. For example, if the team's goal is to increase the child's independence in the classroom, the role of the family and classroom teacher is to identify the routines and activities in which the child is independent (e.g., transition to outdoor play, snack, music class) and where the child needs support (e.g., transition to center time, circle time). The special education teacher might suggest specific strategies or accommodations (e.g. picture schedules, First/Then boards, cue cards) to help the child independently participate in the difficult routines and activities. The speech therapist might suggest implementing an alternative communication system (e.g., PECS) for the child to learn to express wants and needs and train the parents and staff to use it at home and school. The OT might ensure suitable materials are available for fine motor activities (e.g., adaptive scissors and writing tools) and adaptive skills. Together teachers and therapists ensure the interventions and accommodations are consistently and accurately implemented.

Once the purpose and roles are established, the team decides on a consistent time to meet to evaluate the child's progress and ensure the teaching strategies and accommodations are working. This should be done consistently throughout the year, not just at the annual IEP meeting. Creating a consistent meeting schedule validates the importance of all members and is a first step in making sure work gets done. The team will collaboratively make changes to goals, intervention strategies, or evaluation procedures. For example, the team might determine that the child needs more support during circle time and decide to provide more frequent opportunities to make choices during circle time or deliver reinforcement (e.g., giving more social praise, stickers) or a peer buddy to teach the child to participate in circle time. Conversely, the team might determine that the child has been successfully participating in circle time and decide to start fading the supports (e.g., give the child less choices during circle time), having a peer buddy every other day, or thinning reinforcement (e.g., giving less social praise or stickers).

Building teamwork skills. Effective teams determine productive ways to communicate and make decisions. Productive communication occurs at both formal and informal levels. Teams can formally structure communication by creating a process for leading team meetings, making decisions, or communicating between meetings. Effective team meetings include a written agenda and identifying a facilitator to run the meeting and a recorder to document the meeting. Informal communication strategies refer to the communication behaviors of team members. To create productive communication, team members must exhibit behaviors which encourage the exchange of information between colleagues. This includes giving full attention to the person who is speaking, listening to what is said before responding, and stating points succinctly (Snell, Janney, & Elliot, 2005). Productive communication also includes having ongoing conversations regarding roles and responsibilities to help members stay accountable for what they are doing and assure that appropriate services are implemented with fidelity. Also, it is important for teams to have an agreed upon process for decision making so that members understand how to give input and impact change. Briggs (1997) suggested a five-step process for decision making: (1) identify and define the problem, (2) generate alternative solutions, (3) select the best alternative, (4) implement the agreed-upon plan, and (5) evaluate and modify as needed. Finally, teams should establish a process for communicating between meetings. This might include conducting an informal survey to determine preferred communication modes (e.g., phone, e-mail, text, intra-agency mail). The team should identify one preferred method and require team members to frequently check (e.g., check voicemail, e-mail, mailboxes daily).

Problem solving and action planning. All teams will encounter problems. Problems can stem from both internal and external issues and need to be addressed as they arise. The first step in addressing problems is to identify them. Problems can be identified through reflective practice or progress monitoring. Wesley and Buysse (2001) described reflective practice as "the ongoing process of critically examining past and current practice to facilitate the development of future action" (p. 115). This includes evaluating the extent to which all team members are carrying out their roles. This means teams need to consistently evaluate the extent to which they are accurately implementing interventions with students. Interdisciplinary teams can participate in reflective practice by starting out each team meeting with a "check-in" process. During check-in, each team member identifies successes and concerns with the implementation process. One person on the team acts as the recorder and makes a list of both the successes and concerns stated by each member. Once all members have identified success and concerns, the team analyzes the lists and identifies priorities.

Once concerns are identified through reflective practice or progress monitoring, the team can work together to brainstorm solutions, making sure to get input from all members. Potential solutions are used to write a new action plan. Writing the action plan is essential because it documents and helps clarify the decisions made by the team, outlines the next steps, and serves as a reference when reviewing progress. Follow-up reviews of action plans should be regularly completed during team meetings to monitor progress and make revisions if necessary. This can be facilitated by creating a "to do" list at the end of each team meeting. The list specifies duties team members agree to perform by the next meeting. Team members review each item on the list at their next meeting with the responsible member reporting progress and any problems. A recorder keeps track of both completed items and problems so that members can decide on next actions.

Coordinating team action. The team needs to work cohesively to ensure students receive the interventions and supports they need. Coordination of team action includes determining individual and group schedules that reflect when members will be delivering services, evaluating progress, and meeting. Having a clear, consistent, and written team schedule allows the practitioners involved to decide the best times to work with students and collaborate with one another. For example, a preschool child with autism might receive special education and speech-language services within a community classroom with an early childhood preschool teacher. His preschool teacher meets with the special education teacher and SLP to give them her weekly classroom schedule, marking times the child and she could benefit from support (free play, snack, outside time) so that all can work collaboratively toward the child's goal of improving social communication. Since the special education teacher will work on helping the child initiate and maintain social interactions, she sets her schedule to be in the classroom during free play and outside time. The SLP will work on helping the child request what he wants so she sets her schedule to be in the classroom during snack time. All interventionists look at their service schedules to see what days they are available. They talk with one another to make sure their times do not overlap, add their service times to the weekly schedule, and review it with the preschool teacher. Once the schedule is determined, the preschool teacher posts it in the classroom. Before leaving, the team members schedule their next meeting where they will talk about the child's progress and review how the service schedule is working. All of them mark it on their calendars and the special education teacher volunteers to send a reminder e-mail to everyone a few days before the meeting.

Coordinated team action also includes making sure paperwork is organized and completed. Teams are responsible for creating IFSPs/IEPs, writing progress reports, and looking at student data to inform decisions. Having an organized system for filing, accessing, and completing paperwork is vital. This process helps assure that paperwork will be completed on time and includes pertinent information from all members. A written schedule for completing paperwork might be helpful to ensure all team members understand and are accountable for their tasks. Written schedules can be uploaded onto a website such as Google docs (see https://docs.google.com/) or Windows Office Live (http://workspace.officelive.com/en-us/). This makes it easy for team members to update progress on paperwork from any computer. Data maintenance systems can be arranged either in hard copy or online formats. The system chosen will depend on the resources of the agencies involved. A basic hard-copy data management system includes using a lockable filing cabinet located in an area all team members can access. Folders for individual children are kept in the filing cabinet and professionals are able to review and add to data in the folders. A current copy of the IFSP/IEP is included along with the most current assessments, anecdotal notes, and data collection sheets for specific goals and objectives. Many agencies and school systems are moving toward using online data management systems to facilitate consistent updates and exchange of information between team members and within school districts. These systems are often aligned with state standards to track how IFSP/IEP goals and objectives are connected to specific academic criteria. Data collection forms and reports are completed online and updated within the system. Online systems are typically adopted at a district or state level as a way to manage information within an entire school system. All data management systems must protect confidentiality by keeping information within a locked filing cabinet or a password protected computer program. Having safeguarded data management systems ensures that team members are the only ones with access to student information.

Teaching collaboratively. Frequently, special and general education teachers on interdisciplinary teams teach collaboratively. This takes time and coordination to ensure high implementation fidelity. In essence, these teachers form their own two-person team within the interdisciplinary team. Collaborative teachers determine their roles and responsibilities focusing on their own unique strengths and abilities. Once their roles are established, they must make time to plan and monitor interventions together. Consistently meeting to review child progress is essential to making sure children receive appropriate interventions. For example, when a special and a general education teacher implement a BSP (see Chapter 11 for more information on implementing BSPs) for a child with autism, they need to coordinate efforts. They set up weekly meetings to reflect on the child's progress. During initial implementation, or when difficulties arise, they schedule meetings more often. At the meetings, the teachers review data and concerns and problem solve together. In collaborative teaching, both teachers are accountable for student learning and work together to assess their instruction and monitor progress.

Improving communication and handling conflict. Effective communication on interdisciplinary teams is cultivated when members understand and trust one another. Taking time to know team members on a personal level allows professionals to have empathy and concern for each other. It also facilitates understanding and respect for the skills each team member brings. Open communication includes being sensitive and respectful to the cultural backgrounds and values of all team members. Healthy communication within a team also promotes and nurtures positive staff-family interactions. Family members play a central role on interdisciplinary teams but may feel intimidated or excluded when amongst a group of educational professionals. It is imperative that team members make families feel included by seeking out and valuing their values, priorities, and insight. Team meetings are a great time for interventionists to ask family members how they feel their child is progressing, what strategies they feel are successful, and if there are new issues to share. Meetings also provide an opportunity to hear about the strengths of the child and celebrate successes. When appropriate, teams might start each meeting by giving the family an opportunity to share successes and concerns. If families are intimidated and do not want to talk first, another team member might start the meeting by identifying the child's strengths and progress. This might help set a positive tone for the meeting and encourage all members to focus on the child's strengths.

Getting to know everyone on the team, making sure each member's voice is heard, and establishing trust sets the stage for productive dialogue. Productive dialogue includes presenting information and ideas in clear, unambiguous ways so everyone understands what is being communicated. When disagreements occur, it is important that team members handle them in a respectful way, making sure to hear everyone's point of view. Particular attention needs to be paid to conflicts between family members and staff. These conflicts might arise when family members and professionals disagree on service delivery or scheduling. For example, a physical therapist feels more progress can be made on a child's motor goals if the child is pulled out of the classroom for one-on-one sessions. However, the father is adamant that his child should receive all services within the context of the classroom. When disagreements such as this occur, it is important to refocus on the student and his or her goals. Refocusing on the student may help shed light on how to solve the problem. Family members and providers can restate their idea within the framework of how it will benefit the child. This might help each team member better understand why the other person feels strongly about his or her position. Conflicts are prevented by regularly assessing the team functioning, both through self-evaluation and group processing (Snell et al., 2005). Even with such efforts, there are times when mediators or parent advocates should be involved to address concerns and make sure all voices are heard for the welfare of the child. As mentioned before, many districts or states provide parent advocacy support free of charge to parents to increase the likelihood of positive resolution to concerns. Although successful inter-disciplinary teaming takes work and time, the results are well worth the effort. Effective teams accomplish more for both students and profession-als. Even with strong team cohesion, consultation and coaching are helpful for implementing evidence-based practices.

EFFECTIVE CONSULTATION AND COACHING

Consultation and coaching are two types of service delivery and training models. Both models can support effective implementation of evidence-based practices. Also, both models are used to provide services to children with autism in inclusive classrooms.

Consultation

Consultation is one method of delivering special education services within community and general education settings (Dinnebeil, Pretti-Frontczak, & McInerney, 2009). Two of the most important potential benefits of the consultation service delivery model are its promotion of inclusion and ability to impact a larger number of children (Buysse & Wesley, 2005). Research indicates that consultation can improve the quality of IEPs for children with autism (Ruble, Dalrymple, & McGrew, 2010), help teachers implement PBIS strategies (Benedict, Horner, & Squires, 2007; Carter & Van Norman, 2010), and support successful inclusion of children with autism in general education settings (Wilkinson, 2005). Consultation differs from direct intervention in that the service provider (e.g., special education teacher, SLP, behavior specialist) does not provide one-on-one services to the child. Instead, consultants traditionally act as an itiner-ant support and provide "behind-the-scenes" support to the classroom teachers. They work with teachers to implement intervention plans and monitor student progress. The role of the consultant is to make sure that children's goals and objectives are being successfully addressed in the general education classroom and the intervention plan is being implemented. The classroom teacher, however, is responsible for delivering the interventions.

As with successful teaming, successful consultation consists of several critical components. Dinnebeil et al. (2009) defined five critical elements needed for successful consultation services: (1) high quality environment, (2) supports for general education teachers, (3) consistent understanding of roles and responsibilities, (4) joint planning time, and (5) effective consultation skills. These factors are similar to the components needed for effective teaming. As with teaming, consultation involves preparation and coordination. Buysse and Wesley (2005) provided a framework for planning and carrying out consultation services. This eight-stage process highlights the complexity of consultation and provides a structure to the entire process.

The Eight Stages of Consultation (Buysse & Wesley, 2005)

Stage 1: Gaining entry. During this stage, the consultant makes arrangements to meet the consultee and get to know him or her. The consultant also visits the site in which they will be consulting to get a sense of the environment and available resources. Consultants talk to the consultee about the general purpose of the consultation and review the roles and responsibilities each of them bring to the process.

Stage 2: Building the relationship. During this stage, the consultant not only gets to know the consultee on a deeper level but also makes inroads into the school or program. This may entail meeting with the principal or director, as well as other teachers and paraprofessionals. The consultant spends time in the classroom to familiarize himself or herself with the schedule and routines and observe how the child on his or her caseload functions within the environment, including the range of other children in the classroom.

Stage 3: Gathering information through assessment. This stage involves collecting data, which helps inform the goals of the consultation process. Information should be gathered during multiple observations of the classroom and during meetings with staff and family members. It is important to collect information from all adults involved in the child's services to create a complete picture of the child's strengths and needs and the parents' priorities and concerns. Data might include information about the classroom environment, the school's policies and procedures, teacher knowledge and practices, and child behaviors. The goal of this stage is to collect enough data to be able to pinpoint areas in need of support or change.

Stage 4: Setting goals. The focus of this stage is the identification and development of specific goals for change. It is imperative that the consultant work closely with the consultee during this process so that there is agreement and understanding regarding what they are trying to accomplish. The content of goals should be linked to the IFSP/IEP and information gathered in the assessment process, making sure that all perspectives are considered. Goals can focus on changes in any or all of the following: environment (e.g., classroom arrangement, lighting, etc.), teacher practices (e.g., implementation of PECS, etc.), and student behavior (e.g., use of a self-reinforcement system, etc.). Goals need to be clearly written, have observable and measureable outcomes, and contain specific criteria for success (see Chapter 4 for more detailed information about writing goals).

Stage 5: Selecting strategies and practices. During this stage, the consultant works with the consultee to plan out how the goals will be addressed. Because the purpose of consultation is to promote positive growth and change, strategies need to be both appropriate and realistic. Several factors need to be taken into consideration, including the student or classroom needs, the consultee's philosophical beliefs and attitude, and the available resources. Part of planning out the strategies includes defining the roles and responsibilities of both the consultant and the consultee. Specific tasks need to be assigned and timelines should be set to help guide implementation and evaluation of the strategies.

Stage 6: Implementing the plan. Once strategies have been selected, the implementation stage begins. During this stage, the consultant supports the consultee in carrying out the practice. The consultant visits the consultee regularly to check in, assess how the process is going, and give feedback. Throughout this process, however, the consultee independently implements services; the majority of implementation takes place without the consultant present. When necessary, the consultant might support the consultee directly in the classroom. For example, the consultant might model the evidence-based practice or provide immediate performance-based feedback so the teacher can see how to deliver the practice with quality.

Stage 7: Evaluating the plan. Evaluation takes place throughout the entire intervention phase and is formalized at the end of implementation to assess if the goals have been met. During this stage, the consultant meets with the consultee and facilitates a discussion regarding the effects of the intervention plan and the child's progress. Outcome measurements are collaboratively reviewed. They also review the consultation process and reflect on what parts of the process were beneficial and what might be modified.

Stage 8: Holding a summary conference. This stage occurs at the conclusion of an intervention plan. The consultant provides a final report of the progress and they collaboratively review it. They also determine the next steps of the consultation process. These steps might include deciding how to address new concerns, determining ways to adapt the consultation process, or deciding to end the consultation process. Decisions are made based on the needs of the child and the consultee.

Consultation Vignette: Leroy

Angela is an early childhood special educator who is working with Leroy and his family. After meeting with Leroy's parents to get to know them and their priorities and concerns, she schedules a meeting with Jackie, Leroy's Head Start teacher. During their initial meeting Jackie tells Angela that she hasn't worked with a consultant before and isn't clear how the process works. Angela explains that she will be working with her to see how Leroy is doing in the classroom and assisting her in figuring out ways to help him meet his IEP goals. In reviewing the IEP, Jackie brings up the behavioral goal and then they discuss the frequent aggression Leroy displays toward adults and peers. Angela makes notes and sets up some times to observe him and when they will meet to begin the planning process.

During the initial observation, Angela arrives right before circle time because Jackie stated Leroy has a difficult time transitioning from free play to circle. Angela sits at the back of the room, out of the way but with a clear view of Leroy, and takes notes. As soon as Jackie turns off the lights to signal the transition to circle time, Leroy begins to scream. Jackie tells him it is time for circle and asks him to put away the blocks. Leroy begins to kick the blocks. Jackie comes over and picks him up and he hits her and screams until she puts him on a beanbag chair in the corner. Jackie asks an assistant to watch Leroy as she gathers the rest of the children for circle time. Angela observes in the classroom two more times throughout the week, during different parts of the day, and gathers information about how different routines impact Leroy's behavior as well as teacher actions.

When Angela and Jackie meet to review the observations, they agree that the main challenge is in making successful transitions between activities. Angela shares with Jackie information about different strategies, visual schedules, cue cards, and First/Then boards. Jackie looks at the materials and tells Angela she feels the visual schedule and cue cards will be easy to use in her classroom, but she is skeptical about whether they will help decrease Leroy's aggressive behavior. However, she notes that a visual schedule might benefit some other children in the class as well. Jackie also says she is willing to try using a First/Then board and feels it will be most beneficial during snack and lunch time. At the next meeting, Angela brings all the materials and shares them with Jackie and the educational assistants and shows them how to use the materials during transitions.

During the next classtime, Angela models implementation of the practices, answering questions as the paraprofessionals and teacher watch. Then Jackie and the paraprofessionals implement the strategies and Angela provides feedback until they feel more confident in using the materials. Next, Angela talks to the classroom team about collecting data on Leroy's behavior, explaining the importance of consistently collecting data in order to see how the strategies are working. She shows them the data sheet and how to use it, and they plan how often they will collect data, and where it will be displayed so all have ready access.

Angela observes implementation a few times the following week and meets with Jackie to discuss progress. Angela asks Jackie how she felt about the using the new strategies. Jackie says she feels positive about the intervention plan and was happy to have new strategies to use with Leroy. She explains that the plan didn't go perfectly, she had trouble using the First/Then board, and felt Leroy didn't quite understand what she was trying to communicate. However, she feels confident that with more practice and consistent opportunities to use the First/Then board, Leroy will catch on. She also realized the team didn't collect data during all of the transitions. Angela gives Jackie some suggestions for making the data collection easier. Next, they set up a timeline for the intervention plan. They decide to continue to implement it for a month, before evaluating progress with Angela doing weekly observations and e-mailing her feedback. When they meet to evaluate progress, they are happy to see Leroy's problem behaviors have significantly decreased. While initially Jackie said it was a challenge to implement all three strategies consistently, the team is much more coordinated now and they all see how these strategies have improved transitions.

Coaching

Coaching, like consultation, is a method of service delivery, which requires close collaboration between two adults. However, it differs from consultation both in its approach and the variations of its use. Coaching is more hands-on than consultation, meaning the coach spends a larger amount of time modeling practices, giving specific feedback throughout implementation trials, and collecting data on how the person being coached (coachee) performs interventions. With coaching, the coach is viewed as the expert on a specific skill set (e.g., implementing PECS, video modeling, or creating effective visual schedules). The coach's role is to support and train others to learn the same skill set. Several different types of coaching models are used within special education. Coaching is implemented with families, practitioners, and peers across home and educational settings. Coaching has been an effective method to support teachers, colleagues, and caregivers in using evidence-based intervention techniques (Filcheck, McNeil, Greco, & Bernard, 2004; Fixsen et al., 2005; Kretlow & Bartholomew, 2010; Kretlow, Wood, & Cooke, 2011).

Coaching provides a high level of support to practitioners, which has been found to help teachers implement evidence-based practices (Lerman, Vorndran, Addison, & Kuhn, 2004). There are two main goals to coaching: "(1) supporting learners in recognizing what they are already doing to promote learning for a child and (2) assisting learners in creating ongoing learning opportunities for the child when the coach is not present" (Hanft, Rush, & Shelden, 2004, p. 31).

For coaching to be successful, it is important that both the coachee and coach agree and share these goals. The following section provides an overview of the different types of coaching practices as well as components of effective coaching.

Qualities of an effective coach: Although each person brings his or her unique personality and experiences to the coaching process, it is important that coaches have a foundation of essential skills before they start. The following five characteristics are important to be an effective coach:

1. **Competency.** A coach must exhibit the knowledge and ability to help coachees develop new skills. Seeing the coach as a useful resource is important in establishing trust with coachees and making them feel invested in the coaching process. A coach needs to be able to identify, implement, and suggest appropriate evidence-based practices, *as well as* have the ability to guide coachees in recognizing and building on their own strengths and skills. One of the most important objectives in the coaching process is to facilitate independence and develop new abilities in the person the coach is mentoring.

2. **Objectivity.** A coach must have the ability to set aside his or her personal biases and opinions and look at each situation objectively. Instead of making personal judgments about how a teacher or parent is approaching a child, an effective coach tries to understand where the coachee is coming from. Looking at the situation objectively allows the coach to help coachees reflect on their practices and suggest the most realistic and appropriate evidence-based practices for their situation.

3. **Adaptability.** Although it is important to carefully organize and plan coaching sessions, it is also important to have the ability to be spontaneous and adapt as new information and circumstances arise. Coaches need to be able to change their plans, or course of action, when teachable moments appear or when strategies are clearly not working.

4. **Caring.** Coaches show true caring by dedicating enough time to the coaching process, being patient, and encouraging coachees as they learn new skills. This creates a safe and supportive environment and allows coachees to try new strategies and techniques without worrying about being judged. Coachees who feel supported and cared for by the coach are more likely to carry out suggested evidence-based practices.

5. **Practices.** Although it may be difficult to share information sometimes, it is important that coachees receive accurate information regarding their current practices. Constructive feedback focuses both on what the person has done well and areas in which the coachee can improve. In order for feedback to be productive, it should include specific suggestions.

Source: Adapted from Hanft, Rush, & Shelden, (2004).

Practitioner coaching. Practitioner coaching is an interactive training process conducted between a practitioner and a coach, who has specialized knowledge and skills. This type of coaching allows teachers opportunities to practice techniques under the guidance of an expert (Hanft et al., 2004) and is typically used in conjunction with preservice courses or professional development programs. For example, a preservice teacher wants to learn how to use PECS procedures with a child who has autism. The coach, her university supervisor, comes to the site and coaches her while she implements PECS, providing her with guidance and feedback. In another example, a general education teacher takes part in professional development training on positive behavior support strategies. She gets follow-up coaching from an itinerant special education teacher. The coach teaches her to embed and implement the strategies in her classroom through observation, modeling, problem solving, strategies for classroom arrangement, and performance-based feedback. In both cases, the coach supports the coachee in implementing the new skills.

Family coaching. Coaching can be used to help families implement strategies in their home or community environments. This is a particularly useful strategy in helping students generalize skills across settings and people. In other words, coaching can be used to help parents implement some of the same strategies which have been successful for children in their classroom environment. For example, if a child uses PECS in his classroom, his parents may see his success using PECS at school and express an interest in using the same strategy at home. The special education teacher would then set up weekly home visits where she coaches the family in using PECS. Helping caregivers learn to use the same strategies implemented in the classroom provides consistency and continuity.

Family coaching is particularly important in early intervention (i.e., services and supports for infants and toddlers under 3 years old with disabilities), where caregivers are often the primary service providers. Coaching ensures that families have the information and skills needed to carry out interventions consistently, thereby increasing the opportunities the child has to practice skills. This type of coaching should focus on the needs expressed by caregivers and the family's valued activities, priorities, and resources. For example, a toddler with autism receives weekly in-home intervention services through his local early intervention agency. The major goal of the IFSP is to improve communication, so the service provider gets to know the family routines, expectations, and preferences to assist in designing an at-home intervention plan with the mother which embeds communication skill practice during dressing, diapering, mealtimes, bath time, and play activities. The service provider might model the strategies during their typical routines but primarily supports the mother in implementing them herself. The early interventionist rarely interacts directly with the child and focuses on supporting the mother-child interaction. During subsequent home visits, she checks in with the mother, observes her implementing the interventions, and continues to provide coaching when needed.

Peer coaching. Peer coaching takes place between two colleagues. This form of coaching can help coworkers share skills and support one another in implementing evidence-based strategies in their classrooms. Coaching between colleagues is often used as a follow-up to professional develop-ment to help peers transfer new knowledge into actual practice. Peer coaching also can be used when a coworker has specialized knowledge that colleagues are interested in learning. Members of an interdisciplinary team can work with one another to share strategies (e.g., a speech therapist coaches the teacher in using milieu teaching techniques with a preschool teacher), thereby ensuring children receive appropriate interventions across practitioners.

Coaching, in whichever form chosen, takes effort and skill to carry out. Teachers who work with a coach need to be prepared to dedicate time and reflection to the process. Kretlow and Bartholomew (2010) have identified three critical components to successful peer coaching: (1) highly engaged small group initial training, (2) multiple follow-up observations, and (3) specific feedback and modeling. The combination of these components assures that preservice or practicing teachers receive a high level of ongo-ing support. Receiving this type of support helps teachers feel more con-fident in using new intervention methods to sustain implementation. This is particularly important when working with teachers in inclusive settings, where there is often no consistent special educator in the classroom.

Coaching as a multistep process. Like collaboration, coaching takes strategic planning. It is a multistep process in which both the coach and coachee actively participate. The following four- step process can be used to guide the coaching process (Hanft et al., 2004).

> *Initiation.* Coaching begins by having the coach and coachee meet together to decide the purpose of their time together. Coaching is typically used in classrooms to help teachers learn how to use inter-ventions that are new to them. Teachers might want overall help in understanding how to perform the intervention, or they might want to learn how to use it with a specific child. Either way, the needs and priorities of the coachee should be clearly identified. During this time, both participants in the coaching process clarify their roles, decide when coaching sessions will take place, and figure out times for the coachee to practice the skills when the coach is not present.

> *Observation and action.* The first part of this step is conducting obser-vations to gather more information regarding the coachee's current practices. Coaches observe teachers in their classrooms to gain insight into how they work with a specific child or to see how they carry out certain activities and routines. If the coaching process is focused on helping a teacher work with a specific child, information regarding the child's behaviors also needs to be collected. Information gathered dur-ing the observation process is used to inform the action step.

> The action component focuses on the activities and situations in which the coachee will perform and practice new skills. During this

phase, the coach uses insight from observations to come up with strategies to teach the practitioner new skills and assists the professional in learning how to use them. Coaches can use an array of strategies to help inform practitioners, such as demonstrating techniques before the intervention takes place, guiding the coachee throughout the intervention, or modeling the intervention for the coachee. Typically, coaches will use a combination of these techniques, modifying them dependent on the coachee's needs and comfort level.

Reflection. Once the coach has made observations and the coachee has had time to practice new skills, they come together to reflect. During this time, the coach facilitates discussion about how the practitioner feels he or she is performing the targeted teaching method. The coach gives the coachee information and impressions about what he or she has observed in the classroom. Current practices are reviewed in comparison to the agreed upon goals in order to see if progress is being made. Once insights are shared, the coach and coachee work together to refine the coaching plan.

Evaluation. The evaluation process is a time for the coach to examine how the coaching process is improving child skills. This can be done in conjunction with the coachee or alone. During this time, the coach looks at the strengths and weaknesses of the coaching process, including the relationship he or she has built with the coachee. Reviewing whether desired outcomes were obtained is the focus of the evaluation. Coaches use this information to make decisions regarding the coaching process and whether to continue with or change the coaching sessions. Successful coaching can have a significant impact on confidence with the strategies, which translates into greater implementation fidelity (Fixsen et al., 2005; Rush & Shelden, 2011). Although coaching can be time consuming, it is often necessary for supporting teachers in implementing evidence-based practices with high fidelity and improved efficiency.

Coaching Vignette: DJ

JoAnn is a developmental specialist working with DJ and his family. On her most recent home visit, DJ's mother expressed her growing concern about his communication skills and frequent tantrums both at home and at school, where teachers are becoming frustrated with him. JoAnn suggests they meet with the school to discuss a few strategies.

During the meeting, DJ's mother, teacher, and JoAnn discuss the tantrums he has been having in class and at home. JoAnn asks DJ's mother and teacher to identify times of the day or certain routines or activities during which DJ typically has tantrums. DJ's teacher says that snack time is usually difficult for him, as well as tabletop activities. His mother states that he often has tantrums when she gets him dressed for school or at mealtime. JoAnn sets up times the following week to observe DJ in both settings.

(Continued)

(Continued)

During her observations, JoAnn collects information on DJ's behavior as well as how his mother and teacher react to his behavior using the ABC approach (See chapter 11). At day care, DJ's teacher begins to serve the children a snack. DJ is sitting at the table with the rest of his peers. The teacher goes around the table and places a graham cracker and banana on each child's plate. When the teacher puts the snack on his plate DJ begins to cry and pushes the plate away. His teacher tells him, "No DJ, snack time isn't over yet," and puts the plate back in front of him. DJ takes the plate and throws it on the floor. His teacher removes him from the table and seats him by himself at another table. She tells him, "If you throw your food on the floor you get no snack," and walks away to finish serving the rest of the children. At home, DJ's mother dresses him for school. She helps him take off his pajamas and starts to put on his school clothes. As soon as she begins to put a shirt over DJ's head, he begins to scream and tries to pull the shirt off. His mother tells him, "No DJ, you need to get dressed for school." She wrestles with him to get his shirt and pants on. He continues to resist and by the end of the dressing routine both DJ and his mother appear exhausted.

When JoAnn meets with DJ's mother and teacher, she discusses her observations and suggests DJ's tantrums occur due to his inability to communicate what he wants. She talks to them about trying to figure out positive ways for DJ to communicate his desires and suggests a choice-making strategy, which can be used in both settings. JoAnn shares and models for them a sample choice board and they role-play how it would work. DJ's mother and teacher agree to try out the strategy with DJ.

JoAnn meets with DJ's mother before she begins her dressing routine with DJ. She gives her the picture notebook and choice board she has made. The notebook contains pictures of all the items DJ needs during his dressing routine (e.g., pants, shirt, socks, shoes). The icons are of different colors so that DJ can choose clothing by its color. DJ's mother takes two pictures out of the notebook that correspond to the blue and green shirt choices she is giving DJ and places them on the choice board. When she is ready, she brings DJ over and tells him it is time to get dressed for school. JoAnn tells DJ's mother to show him the choice board and put his hand on it. Next, she tells her to ask him which he wants. DJ's mother asks him, "Do you want the blue shirt or the green?" DJ touches the picture of the green shirt. JoAnn prompts his mother to say, "Oh, you want the green shirt" and hand DJ the green shirt. She gives him the shirt and DJ starts to put it on as his mother assists him. When he gets the shirt on, JoAnn guides DJ's mother in giving him choices throughout the rest of his dressing routine. DJ is able to get dressed without tantrums and his mother feels more confident in her ability to use the choice board. JoAnn visits DJ's teacher later in the week and coaches her in implementing the same choice-board strategy during snack time. She revisits DJ's mother and teacher the following week to observe how the choice making is going and provides feedback when necessary.

The following week, JoAnn meets with DJ's mother and teacher to talk about how the coaching process is going. Both his mother and teacher are excited about how well embedding choices throughout routines is working. They tell JoAnn that DJ's tantrums have decreased during dressing and snack time and express an interest in using the strategy during more routines.

Tips for Teachers Working With Consultants and Coaches

(1) *Make sure you are included in the service planning process.*

Sometimes special education services are initially decided upon without much input from the general education or community classroom teacher, especially when the teacher is outside of the special education system. However, for children with autism to receive high quality inclusive services, it is imperative for the teacher to be included in the planning process. As soon as a teacher finds out a child in her class will be receiving special education services, she should ask the consultant/coach to inform and include her in any upcoming meetings. The teacher can give the consultant/coach her schedule so that meetings can be planned at times when she is available to attend. The teacher should also talk to the caregivers, letting them know that she wants to be included in meetings to provide the best possible services for their child.

(2) *Share your questions and concerns.*

Be vocal! Coaches and consultants can only provide appropriate assistance if the teachers they are working with communicate their questions and concerns. It is important for teachers to think about what they want to get out of coaching and consultation and talk to the interventionists about the process. When something is confusing or is not working in the expected way, teachers need to communicate it to their consultant/coach. Make good use of meetings with coaches/consultants by coming prepared to discuss questions and concerns. McWilliam and Casey (2008) provided a checklist for teachers to use when they are consulting with a specialist (see Figure 12.1). It can be used to help teachers gather their thoughts and focus their discussion.

(3) *Ask for what you need.*

Coaches and consultants can be invaluable resources for teachers. They can provide both information and materials. It never hurts to ask for what is needed, whether it is added support in the classroom or help making a visual schedule. If the coach or consultant cannot directly provide what is needed, he or she can act as a referral to other sources.

Tips for Consultants and Coaches Working With Teachers

(1) *Listen carefully.*

It is important to understand where the teacher is coming from. Make sure to take the time to listen to the teacher's point of view and understand his or her concerns. Teachers who work with children with autism often lack support in acquiring knowledge of evidence-based practices, carrying out intervention strategies, and accessing appropriate materials. In order to provide the support teachers need to implement evidence-based practices, it is important for consultants/coaches to understand what they view as obstacles.

Figure 12.1   Consulting or Coaching Checklist for Teachers

---

1. Discuss how coaching and consultation will be delivered: how often, when, where, what method of communication?

2. Review the goals for child(ren).

3. Clearly state your concerns and priorities.

4. Discuss the goals of consultation or coaching.

5. Collaboratively determine one or two immediate goals of consultation or coaching.

6. Be clear about what strategies you have used. Indicate which ones seem to be working and which ones you are struggling with.

7. Ask if you should make changes to the schedule or accommodations to activities.

8. Ask if there are new or different strategies that might address the children's goals more efficiently or effectively.

9. Listen for ideas and suggestions. Write down suggestions if necessary. When you are unclear about a strategy or accommodation, ask the coach to model it for you or give you an example.

10. Ask the specialist for feedback. Ask for specific feedback (e.g., "What should I change about this activity?" "How many times did I deliver praise?" "How might I redirect him differently?").

Source: Adapted from National Individualizing Preschool Inclusion Project, 2005, as cited in McWilliam & Casey, (2008).

(2) *Individualize your support.*

Just as no two children with autism are the same, no two teachers are the same. In special education, individualization is emphasized in the creation of intervention plans for students. It should also be emphasized in the consultation or coaching of teachers as well. One way to individualize consultation and coaching is through the delivery of performance feedback. Barton, Kinder, Casey and Artman (2011) developed a *Finding Your Feedback Fit* tool (see Figure 12.2), which can help consultants/coaches design appropriate performance feedback systems. They emphasize thinking about the situation, the specific teacher, and yourself as a coach when deciding on how to provide performance feedback. For example, the increased use of e-mail makes it an ideal mechanism for providing feedback to teachers. When e-mail is used to provide feedback, careful attention must be given to ensure the tone and content of the e-mail are supportive and constructive, because it can be less personal than face-to-face conversations. E-mail might be more efficient (i.e., you do not have to schedule time for face-to-face conversations), gives both the coach and the teacher time to reflect on the observation and goals, and provides a written record of the observation (Barton & Wolery, 2007; Hemmeter, Snyder, Kinder, & Artman, 2011). However, when designing an e-mail feedback system, consider the current e-mail usage of the teachers; send a few initial e-mails to ensure teachers regularly check and respond to e-mail (see Figure 12.3 for an example of an e-mail with systematic feedback).

Figure 12.2 Finding Your Feedback Fit

Consider the following when designing a performance feedback system:

- Are teachers used to getting feedback?

  o If they rarely receive feedback, you might need to work on building rapport, collaborating to develop goals for the feedback system, and determining preferred feedback methods.

- What is the schedule? Do teachers have available times to meet?

  o At first, it might be good to meet face-to-face with teachers to establish rapport. Over time, especially if teachers have little time to meet to discuss feedback, you can set up written or e-mail (see Figure 12.3) feedback systems.

- What technology is available? Are the teachers comfortable with technology?

  o If teachers have easy access to computers in their classrooms, you might be able to set up e-mail or video conferencing systems. Also, you will need to assess the teachers' comfort level with computers and technology. You also might determine if the school has an information technology professional on staff to help the teachers when issues arise. However, if teachers rarely have access to computers at work or the computers are old and dated, you might have to set up written feedback systems and discuss feedback over the phone.

- What are the goals of the feedback system and the teachers' current skill level?

  o The intensity of the feedback should match the goals and the teachers' needs. For example, if you are providing feedback to a novice teacher about his use of transition warnings, you might observe him during several transitions, step in and model when appropriate, and provide immediate, specific feedback. Also, if you and the teacher are comfortable with video, you might use video feedback systems to teach a particularly difficult skill. Video allows teachers opportunities for self-reflection and discussion. If you are teaching an experienced general education teacher to make specific accommodations for a child with autism, you might give him a few suggestions and then ask him how he thought they worked. If you are working with teachers who are new to implementing a BSP for a young child with autism, you might create an implementation checklist based on the child's BSP and check off the strategies implemented during each observation. You can use the checklist to guide the discussion with the teachers. You might start with a discussion of the strategies the teachers are doing well and then problem solve with the teachers about the strategies that are rarely or not implemented.

- How will you know if the feedback system is effective?

  o Continually reassess the teachers' goals and progress throughout the process. Also, regularly check in with the teachers. Ask for feedback about the system, what is or is not working. You might even create an anonymous survey to ask the teachers about their satisfaction with the feedback system.

Source: Adapted from Barton, Kinder, Casey, & Artman, 2011.

Figure 12.3   Five-Step E-mail Protocol (adapted from Hemmeter et al., 2011; Schepis, Ownbey, Parsons, & Reid, 2000)

---

1. **Start with a general positive statement about the teacher or his or her classroom. Highlight a specific activity that went well or a strategy that the teacher implemented well.**

   ○ John was really engaged during your explanation about fractions! He clearly attended to those visual cue cards you used.

   ○ Macy was so excited when she earned 10 tokens! That reinforcement system really seems to be working with her!

2. **Include a statement with supportive feedback related to the goal of the coaching. Include specific data or examples if possible.**

   ○ You used several of the strategies we talked about last week! I counted 10 examples of descriptive praise and 8 language expansions.

   ○ Last Friday you used 10 positive and 8 negative statements during circle time. Today, you used 32 positive and 6 negative statements! I'm impressed with your quick improvement!

3. **Restate the goals of the coaching and include constructive feedback with suggestions for improved implementation.**

   ○ The purpose of these e-mails is to support you in your increased use of descriptive praise. You are already using more praise during snack and outside time! One thing I noticed during the observation was how long the children had to wait in line to use the bathroom. Tristan seemed to struggle with this wait time. This might be a good time to start using more descriptive praise with him. Focus on catching Tristan every time he is "good" (i.e., quietly waiting in line with his hands by his side). You might even bring your visuals of the classroom expectations (e.g., safe hands, quite voices, calm bodies) and deliver descriptive praise using these expectations (e.g., "Tristan is using a quiet voice and safe hands!" "Tristan has a calm body!").

4. **One of the barriers to e-mail feedback is ensuring teachers read the e-mail. Embed a response request into an e-mail to increase the likelihood that the teachers will read the message (e.g., schedule a meeting). If you want a quick response to ensure the teachers received the e-mail, you might want to keep the response request brief. However, if you want to encourage a discussion or conversation via e-mail, you might want to ask an open-ended question.**

   ○ (Brief) Please let me know if you will be in your classroom next Friday. I would like to do another observation between 9 and 12. Let me know what time works best for you!

   ○ (Open-ended) How do you think things are going with Tristan? Do you think these strategies are working?

5. **End the e-mail with a specific positive comment to ensure the e-mail has a positive, supportive tone.**

   ○ It was so exciting to see how well Tristan did during the transition to circle time! You are doing such a great job supporting him and adapting all the routines and activities so that he can fully participate!

BARRIERS TO IMPLEMENTATION

As stated earlier, it is essential that intervention strategies are consistently implemented across both special education and general education settings for children with autism. However, even with the use of interdisciplinary teaming and consultation and coaching models, implementation of services for children with autism can be difficult. Barriers to implementation might include the following: scheduling issues, inability to hold regular meetings, lack of effective professional development, and inconsistent evaluation.

Scheduling. The day-to-day life of a teacher is filled with preparing materials, carrying out classroom interventions, planning activities, meeting with parents, attending trainings, and much more. Scheduling, therefore, can be a significant barrier to implementation. Scheduling becomes even more of an issue when teachers are working within an interdisciplinary team. Teachers need to take into consideration their own schedule, and those of team members working with children in the classroom. One effective strategy is to post a public calendar, which contains the daily schedule, days the site will be closed, and upcoming fieldtrips. Interventionists who come into the classroom can review the calendar to see what times might be best to work in the classroom. Once interventionists figure out times and review them with the teacher, they can add their scheduled visits to the calendar. This can help track the times services will be delivered and make sure a day isn't overscheduled. This service delivery calendar can also be brought to team meetings for interventionists to review and fill out. There are e-mail systems (e.g., Microsoft OutlookTM) and online programs (e.g., Google Calendars: http://www.google.com/calendar) that allow you to create and synchronize calendars for groups of people. These might be useful for coordinating schedules within and across classrooms. Parents and caregivers also can be included or given access to these calendars, which might improve relationships with families and the home to classroom link.

Holding regular meetings. Since communication among team members is vital for carrying out services in a consistent manner, it is important to make sure to schedule regular meetings with everyone involved in a child's intervention plan. Having time to dialogue with team members allows the intervention process to be more productive. During these meetings, team members can share important information regarding how a child is doing in relation to his or her goals and objectives. Team members can give each other insight into what types of intervention strategies are working with a child, as well as the context in which the intervention is successful. These meetings can also be used to schedule consultation or coaching sessions or plan IFSP or IEP meetings. Make sure to schedule regular meetings ahead of time (e.g., every third Wednesday of the month for the next year). Planning ahead allows team members to utilize times that are convenient for everyone. Some suggested meeting times are directly before or after school, on days when specialists are already scheduled to visit the classroom, during early release or planning days, or when substitute teachers are available to cover the classroom (Sandall & Schwartz, 2008). The use of technology can also help facilitate regular team meetings. Conference calls or Skype can be used if it is difficult to schedule a time when all team members can be physically present. At the end of each team meeting, schedule the next one. This is a convenient time to communicate everyone's schedule and ensures that team meetings are ongoing.

Professional development. Professional development is the ongoing training teachers receive once they are working out in the field. It is a way in which current information regarding methods and curriculum is shared with practitioners. Professional development is important for the growth and improvement of teacher competencies. However, professional development is often delivered in ineffective ways. The traditional in-service model of professional development has been shown to result in low fidelity of implementation, particularly because there is little follow-up or support (Yoon, Duncan, Lee, Scarloss, & Shapley, 2007). Follow-up coaching and consultation focused on practice and support are related to higher rates of fidelity and improved outcomes for children (Fixsen et al., 2005).

Seek out opportunities for coaching and consultation. If early intervention agencies or school systems don't currently provide these types of services, practitioners can request that administrators support these practices and collaborate with outside experts. When professional development is offered as in-service training, colleagues can work together to take information learned and turn it into actual practice through peer coaching and follow-up consultation with trainers. This takes time and support, so working with administrators is essential in making sure practitioners have time set aside to observe peers, provide feedback to one another, and meet with consultants.

Methods for evaluation. Evaluating the consultant or coaching process involves measuring both the teacher and child goals. A process for evaluating the teacher and child progress should be collaboratively determined prior to starting the process. Changes in teacher behaviors can be measured using self-rating scales, implementation checklists, or frequency counts. For example, when teachers are first learning new strategies, such as PECS, a coach might give them a self-rating scale with items about the teachers' comfort level or success with the strategies. The teachers might complete the self-rating scale every week or every other week to evaluate progress. Also, if consultants are helping teachers include a child with autism into the routines and content of a first-grade classroom, they might create a checklist for strategies to implement across the day. Or, a coach might be helping a teacher use the system of least prompts to teach play skills to young children with autism. Likewise, if a group of teachers is learning to implement PBIS strategies across activities of a preschool classroom, consultants might complete an implementation checklist on the PBIS strategies implemented with all children or a specific child across routines and activities (see Figure 12.4 for an example of an implementation checklist for implementing a BSP for Leroy; Figure 12.5 is an example of an implementation checklist for using the system of least prompts to teach play).

Figure 12.4   Positive Behavior Support Intervention Plan: Implementation Checklist

Date: _____   Child: _Leroy_

Implementer: _Classroom Teachers_   Observer: _____

Start Time: _____   End Time: _____

Implementation Ratings:

\+ = Implemented as written every time

+/– = Implemented as written sometimes; partially implemented

– = Never implemented as written

N/A = Not applicable; no opportunity to observe

Procedure	Components	Implementation Rating	Comments/ Examples
Schedule	The schedule is available for Leroy	+ +/– – N/A	
	The schedule displays at least the next four activities for Leroy	+ +/– – N/A	
	Leroy is prompted to change activities and then does so immediately	+ +/– – N/A	
	Upon completion of an activity, the picture is removed from his schedule and put away	+ +/– – N/A	
Token System	Token is paired with behavior-specific praise for desired behaviors	+ +/– – N/A	
	Leroy is given choices for the reinforcement he is working towards	+ +/– – N/A	
	Tokens are never removed from the board as a punishment for inappropriate behavior	+ +/– – N/A	

(Continued)

Figure 12.4 (Continued)

Procedure	Components	Implementation Rating	Comments/ Examples
Functional Communication	Leroy's picture communication book is easily accessible to him at all times	+ +/– – N/A	
	Leroy's communication book has different pictures of activities and items that he might need/want	+ +/– – N/A	
	Items that are not immediately available to Leroy are not included in his portable picture book	+ +/– – N/A	
	Leroy is prompted to refer to this communication book throughout the day, in conjunction with the use of his token economy and his schedule	+ +/– – N/A	
	Leroy's communication book uses pictures of concrete activities and items	+ +/– – N/A	
Intervention for non-compliance and tantrums	Leroy is given a verbal direction or request one time only	+ +/– – N/A	
	If Leroy does not comply, a model prompt is given. If it is a task that Leroy can complete, the modeling prompt is skipped.	+ +/– – N/A	
	The verbal request is not repeated	+ +/– – N/A	
	If he does not complete the request after being given a model, physical guidance is used to assist him in completing the request	+ +/– – N/A	
	No verbal request is repeated	+ +/– – N/A	
	The above procedures are repeated until Leroy is redirected	+ +/– – N/A	
	Leroy is given praise in a neutral tone for engaging in the activity to which he is redirected	+ +/– – N/A	

Source: Adapted from Casey & Houchins-Juarez, 2006; Codding, Feinberg, Dunn, & Pace, 2005.

Figure 12.5   Using the System of Least Prompts to Teach Play: Implementation Checklist

1. Did the teacher set out at least six different toys, including nonfunctional objects (e.g., blocks, plastic bowls, etc.)? **Yes/No**

2. Did the teacher set out at least two of every toy? **Yes/No**

3. Did the teacher use a visual or verbal cue ("let's play") to tell the child it's time to play? **Yes/No**

4. Did the teacher begin contingently imitating the child right away? **Yes/No**

5. Did the teacher deliver a model prompt after obtaining the child's attention? **Yes/No**

6. Did the teacher wait at least 12 seconds to deliver the model prompt? **Yes/No**

7. Did the teacher model a play behavior with the same toy and relate it to what the child was doing with the toy? **Yes/No**

8. Did the teacher deliver specific praise and imitate the child's play immediately after every child play behavior? **Yes/No**

9. Did the teacher deliver a physical prompt only when the child did not respond to the model? **Yes/No**

10. Did the teacher sit down and play with the child for at least 5 minutes during free play? **Yes/No**

TOTAL: _____/10 Yes

_____/10 No

Strengths: _____
_____
_____
_____
_____
_____

Components to work on: _____
_____
_____
_____
_____

Consultants or coaches can provide that feedback by filling out implementation checklists during observations. Implementation checklists help teachers understand the steps they need to use for certain strategies and allow them to monitor their ability to implement the strategy with high fidelity. Consultants and coaches should review checklists with teachers soon after the intervention takes place in order to provide immediate feedback. When coaches or consultants are helping teachers use discrete behaviors (e.g., descriptive praise, language expansions, positive versus negative statements), they might count the number of times the teacher used the strategy during the observation and use the frequency count to guide a discussion with the teacher. For example, if a special education teacher is working on using more positive statements for every negative statement, the consultant might record the teachers' positive and negative statements during an activity (e.g., center time), specific routines (e.g., lunchtime, the transition from recess into the classroom), or content (e.g., small group math time). The consultant might record specific examples of the teacher's positive statements to guide discussions (Barton & Wolery, 2007). Also, the consultant might help the teacher set goals (e.g., "I will use more than 20 positive statements and less than 5 negative statements during reading time today.").

A critical aspect to interventions with children with autism is the collection and evaluation of data to assist in making decisions (National Autism Center, 2009b). Teachers need to regularly assess and determine if the strategies are working. Classroom observations are not enough to inform decision making. Instead, data collection systems need to be in place to make sure that strategies are implemented with fidelity and children are making progress. However, data collection can seem cumbersome and overwhelming to classroom teachers. During a busy day, it may seem impossible to take the time to collect data, or practitioners may feel they lack the skills needed for data collection. Unfortunately, skipping this step means that children might not receive the appropriate intervention. Therefore, it is important to figure out realistic ways to collect data in the classroom.

Data collection needs to be useful, relevant to children's goals, and easy to collect. Data-based decisions include three steps: (1) collecting data, (2) graphing data, and (3) interpreting and using data (Gischlar et al., 2009; Hojnoski et al., 2009a, 2009b). Once teachers define the target behavior (e.g., engagement in activities, verbal requests) and how to record it (e.g., length of time engaged, number of occurrences per day), they can create forms specific to their individual needs and preferences. Forms should be readily accessible in the classroom for teachers to collect data during appropriate times throughout the day. Keeping forms on a clipboard or notebook is one way to organize them. It is also important to train and coordinate other staff in the classroom to collect data so that the responsibility is shared and data is collected consistently. For more strategies on data collection, see Chapter 6.

Once data are collected, the information can be graphed either by hand or within a computer program such as Excel or PowerPoint (see Barton et al., 2007, for creating graphs in PowerPoint). Graphed data provide a way to visually analyze how an intervention is working for a student. Once the information is graphed, it is interpreted and used to make decisions about interventions. It is important to share data with all individuals working with a child in order to inform the overall intervention plan and gain feedback from others. If practitioners feel overwhelmed in the data collection process, they should ask for help. Part of the responsibility of coaches and consultants is to assist teachers in the collection and interpretation of data.

FUTURE DIRECTIONS

As the field of special education continues to focus on the use and implementation of evidence-based interventions, models for improving these practices will continue to evolve. Promising innovations include performance-based feedback, telepractice, and Internet modules. Performance-based feedback is critical to making sure teachers use evidence-based practices effectively. However, teachers typically do not have a lot of time to meet with consultants or coaches right after interventions take place. Since feedback is most useful when it occurs soon after observations, alternative ways of providing feedback are starting to be used. Both e-mail feedback (Barton & Wolery, 2007; Hemmeter et al., 2011) and graphical feedback (Casey & McWilliam, 2008) can be successfully used to deliver performance feedback to teachers within a short time frame. Graphical feedback entails creating and reviewing a graph that shows the teacher's implementation pattern of a specific strategy. During observations, the consultant or coach collects data on how often the teacher uses the strategy and, directly after the observation, transfers the data to a graph. At their next meeting, the consultant/coach reviews the graph with the teacher and, if needed, provides ideas on how to implement the strategy more effectively.

Telepractice is another promising service-delivery model. It can be described as "the application of communication technologies (e.g., computer-based video-conferencing software and the internet) to enable specialists to consult and deliver services in real-time over a geographical distance" (Boisvert, Lang, Andrianopoulos, & Boscardin, 2010, p. 424). Telepractice has been successfully used to deliver services to children with autism through caregiver training (Baharav & Reiser, 2010), practitioner training (Gibson, Pennington, Stenhoff, & Hopper, 2010), preservice training (Dymond, Renzaglia, Halle, Chadsey, & Bentz, 2008), and consultation (Kelso, Fiechtl, Olsen, & Rule, 2009). For example, an early childhood consultant is working with the parents of a preschooler with autism. The child has been receiving FCT at his preschool. The family is interested in learning how to use FCT at home as well. The consultant gives the family an in-home training session on using FCT. She wants to provide the family consistent follow-up on their implementation; however, it is difficult to schedule regular home visits due to the travel time involved. The family has access to a computer with a webcam. Therefore, the consultant suggests they use Skype to monitor how the intervention is going. The family and the consultant set up weekly Skype sessions where the mother uses FCT with her child and the consultant observes and provides feedback. Telepractice holds great potential for providing a higher level of support to practitioners and caregivers, particularly those who live in remote locations.

Finally, Internet modules are an innovative way to provide training and support to both caregivers and providers (Hamad, Serna, Morrison, & Fleming, 2010). This type of training uses both online curriculum and video examples to help teachers and family members learn implementation techniques. Internet modules can be used as follow-up support to professional development training or as a stand-alone training when other forms of training are not available. Again, this practice holds great potential for reaching practitioners and caregivers who live in remote areas. The National Professional Development Center on Autism Spectrum Disorders has created Internet modules specific to evidence-based strategies for children with autism (see http://www.autisminternetmodules.org).

In sum, the gap between research and practice in education is wide (Dunst & Trivette, 2009). There are many reasons for this. Possible reasons include the following: asking practitioners to implement complex, cumbersome interventions; ineffective systems of in-service professional development; and inefficient systems of implementation in school and agencies supporting young children and their families. As mentioned, the field has a set of evidence-based practices (i.e., we know what to do to teach children with autism new skills). Sustainable implementation begins with effective systems of consultation and coaching. The strategies provided in this chapter can be used to support effective implementation, which narrow the research to practice gap and improve outcomes for young children with autism.

LEARNING ACTIVITIES

1. Discuss factors that can effect implementation of evidence-based practices with children who have autism.

2. Identify strategies that support consistent implementation of evidence-based practices with children who have autism.

3. Describe the three different types of coaching models.

4. Identify barriers to implementation of evidence-based practices. Discuss ways these barriers can be prevented or reduced.

5. Identify and discuss promising practices that support the implementation of evidence-based practices for children with autism.

RESOURCES

National Autism Center's Learning Center for Practitioner Education: **http://www.nationalautismcenter.org/learning/practitioner.php**

National Implementation Research Network: **http://www.fpg.unc.edu/~nirn/default.cfm**

National Professional Development Center on Autism Spectrum Disorders: **http://autismpdc.fpg.unc.edu/**

National Professional Development Center on Inclusion: **http://community.fpg.unc.edu/npdci**

Master List of Acronyms

AAC—Augmentative and Alternative Communication

AAP—American Academy of Pediatrics

ABA—Applied Behavior Analysis

A-B-C method—Antecedent–Behavior–Consequence

ABLLS-R—Assessment of Basic Language and Learning Skills-Revised

ADI-R—Autism Diagnostic Interview-Revised

ADOS—Autism Diagnostic Observation Schedule

AMA—American Medical Association

APA—American Psychological Association

ASD—Autism Spectrum Disorders

ASQ—Ages and Stages Questionnaire

ASQ:SE—Ages and Stages Questionnaire Social Emotional

ASSQ—Autism Spectrum Screening Questionnaire

BITSEA—Brief Infant Toddler Social Emotional Assessment

BSP—Behavior Support Plan

CARS2—Childhood Autism Rating Scale (2nd edition)

CDC—Centers for Disease Control and Prevention

CHAT—Checklist for Autism in Toddlers

CICO—Check-In, Check-Out

CRF—Continuous Reinforcement Schedule / Continuous Rate of Reinforcement

CSEFEL—Center on the Social and Emotional Foundations for Early Learning

CTD—Constant Time Delay

DIAL 3—Developmental Indicators for the Assessment of Learning (3rd edition)

DIBELS—Dynamic Indicators of Early Literacy Skills

DSM—Diagnostic and Statistical Manual of Mental Disorders

DSM-IV-TR—Current edition of the Diagnostic and Statistical Manual of Mental Disorders–Text Revision

DTT—Discrete Trial Training

EBP—Evidence Based Practice

ECSE—Early Childhood Special Educator

EI—Early Intervention

EMT—Enhance Milieu Teaching

ESDM—Early Start Denver Model

FACTS—Functional Assessment Checklist for Teachers and Staff

FAPE—Free and Appropriate Public Education

FBA—Functional Behavioral Assessment

FCT—Functional Communication Training

FI—Fixed Interval Schedule

FR—Fixed Ratio Schedule

FUI—Follow-Up Interview

GARS-2—Gilliam Autism Rating Scale (2nd Edition)

ICD—International Classification of Diseases

IDEA—Individuals with Disabilities Education Act

IDEIA—Individuals with Disabilities Education Improvement Act

IEP—Individual Education Program

IFSP—Individual Family Service Plan

IGDI—Individual Growth and Development Indicators

IOM—Institute of Medicine

LRE—Least Restrictive Environment

M-CHAT—Modified Checklist for Autism in Toddlers

NECTAC—National Early Childhood Technical Assistance Center

NPDC—The National Professional Development Center

OT—Occupational Therapist

PB—Problem Behavior

PBIS—Positive Behavioral Interventions and Supports

PDD—Pervasive Developmental Disorder

PDD-NOS—Pervasive Developmental Disorder-Not Otherwise Specified

PE—Physical Education

PECS—Picture Exchange Communication System

PEDS—Parents Evaluation of Developmental Status

PN—Picture Naming

PRT—Pivotal Response Treatment

PTD—Progressive Time Delay

QCHAT—Quantitative Checklist for Autism in Toddlers

RBI—Routines-Based Interview

RI—Responsive Interaction

RIR—Response Interruption / Redirection

RE-PMT—Responsive Education—Prelinguistic Milieu Teaching

SCQ—Social Communication Questionnaire

SGDs—Speech Generating Devices

SLP—Speech-Language Pathologist

S.M.A.R.T. Goals—Specific, Measurable, Attainable/Achievable, Relevant/Realistic, and Timely

SORF—Systematic Observation of Red Flags

STAR program—Strategies for Teaching based on Autism Research

STAT—Screening Tool for Autism in Toddlers and Young Children

SW-PBIS—SchoolWide Positive Behavioral Interventions and Supports

TABS—Temperament and Atypical Behavior Scale

TACSEI—Technical Assistance Center on Social Emotional Intervention for Young Children

VB-MAPP—Verbal Behavior Milestones Assessment and Placement Program

VI—Variable Interval

VOCAs—Voice Output Communication Aides

VR—Variable Ratio Schedule

WHO—World Health Organization

References

Alberto, P. A., & Troutman, A. C. (2008). *Applied behavior analysis for teachers* (8th ed.). Upper Saddle River, NJ: Merrill/Pearson.

Allison, C., Baron-Cohen, S., Wheelwright, S., Charman, T., Richler, J., Pasco, G., & Brayne, C. (2008). The Q-CHAT (Quantitative Checklist for Autism in Toddlers): A normally distributed quantitative measure of autistic traits at 18–24 months of age: Preliminary report. *Journal of Autism and Developmental Disorders, 38,* 1414–1425.

Amenta, C. A. (1992). *Russell is extra special: A book about autism for children.* New York, NY: Magination Press.

American Academy of Pediatrics; Council on Children With Disabilities, Section on Developmental Behavioral Pediatrics, Bright Futures Steering Committee and Medical Home Initiatives for Children With Special Needs Project Advisory Committee. (2006). Identifying infants and young children with developmental disorders in the medical home: An algorithm for developmental surveillance and screening. *Pediatrics, 118,* 405–420.

American Psychiatric Association. (1994). *Diagnostic and statistical manual of mental disorders* (4th ed.). Washington, DC: American Psychiatric Association.

American Psychiatric Association. (2000). *Diagnostic and statistical manual of mental disorders* (4th ed., text revision). Washington, DC: American Psychiatric Association.

Anderson, S. R., Jablonski, A. L., Thomeer, M. L., & Knapp, V. M. (2007). *Self-Help skills for people with autism.* Bethesda, MD: Woodbine House.

Arick, J. R., Loos, L., Falco, R., & Krug, D. A. (2005). *The START program: Strategies for teaching based on autism research.* Austin, TX: Pro-Ed.

Arick, J. R., Young, H. E., Falco, R. A., Loos, L. M., Krug, D. A., Gense, M. H., & Johnson, S. B. (2003). Designing an outcome study to monitor the progress of students with autism spectrum disorders. *Focus on Autism and Other Developmental Disabilities, 18*(2), 75–87.

Asperger, H. (1944). Die autistischen psychopathen im kindesalter [Autistic psychopathy in childhood]. *Archiv für psychiatrie und nervenkrankheiten, 117,* 76–136.

Autism Network. (2011). *Incidental teaching: Introduction.* Retrieved from http://www.autismnetwork.org/modules/academic/incidental/index.html

Baer, D. M. (1981). *How to plan for generalization.* Austin, TX: Pro-Ed.

Baharav, E., & Reiser, C. (2010). Using telepractice in parent training in early autism. *Telemedicine Journal & E-Health, 16,* 727–731. doi:10.1089/tmj.2010.0029

Baird, G., Charman, T., Baron-Cohen, S., Cox, A., Swettenham, J., Wheelwright, S., & Drew, A. (2000). A screening instrument for autism at 18 months of age: A 6-year follow-up study. *Journal of the American Academy of Child and Adolescent Psychiatry, 39*, 694–702.

Baker, C., Kupersmidt, J., Voegler-Lee, M., Arnold, D., & Willoughby, M. (2010). Predicting teacher participation in a classroom-based, integrated preventive intervention for preschoolers. *Early Childhood Research Quarterly, 25*, 270–283.

Baker, M., Koegel, R., & Koegel, L. (1998). Increasing the social behavior of young children with autism using their obsessive behaviors. *Journal of the Association of Persons with Severe Handicaps, 23*, 300–308.

Baker, M. J. (2000). Incorporating the thematic ritualistic behaviors of children with autism into games: Increasing social play interactions with siblings. *Journal of Positive Behavior Interventions, 2*, 66–84.

Baker-Ericzen, M. J., Stahmer, A. C., & Burns, A. (2007). Child demographics associated with outcomes in a community-based pivotal response training program. *Journal of Positive Behavior Interventions, 9*, 52–60.

Bandura, A. (1977). *Social learning theory.* New York, NY: General Learning Press.

Barnett, D. (2005). Keystone behaviors. In S. W. Lee (Ed.), *Encyclopedia of school psychology* (p. 279). Thousand Oaks, CA: Sage.

Barnett, D., Elliott, N., Wolsing, L., Bunger, C., Haski, H., McKissick, C., & Vander Meer, C. D. (2006). Response to intervention for young children with challenging behaviors in preschools. *School Psychology Review, 35*, 568–582.

Baron-Cohen, S. (2004). The cognitive neuroscience of autism. *Journal of Neurology, Neurosurgery and Psychiatry, 75*, 945–948.

Baron-Cohen, S., Wheelwright, S., Coz, A., Baird, G., Charman, T., Swettenham, J., Drew, A., & Doehring, P. (2000). Early identification of autism: Checklist for Autism in Toddlers (CHAT). *Journal of the Royal Society of Medicine, 93*, 521–525.

Barton, E. E., Kinder, K., Casey, A., & Artman, K. (2011). Finding your feedback fit: Strategies for designing and delivering performance feedback systems. *Young Exceptional Children, 14*(1), 29–46.

Barton, E. E., Reichow, B., & Wolery, M. (2007). Guidelines for graphing data with Microsoft® PowerPoint™. *Journal of Early Intervention, 29*, 320–336.

Barton, E. E., & Wolery, M. (2007). Evaluation of e-mail feedback on the verbal behaviors of preservice teachers. *Journal of Early Intervention, 30*(1), 55–72.

Barton, E. E., & Wolery, M. (2008). Teaching pretend play to children with disabilities. *Topics in Early Childhood Special Education, 28*(2), 109–125.

Barton, E. E., & Wolery, M. (2010). Training teachers to promote pretend play in young children with disabilities. *Exceptional Children, 77*(1), 85–106.

Bateman, B. D., & Herr, C. (2006). *Writing measurable IEP goals and objectives.* Verona, WI: Attainment Publications.

Bellini, S., & Akullian, J. (2007). A meta-analysis of video modeling and video self-modeling interventions for children and adolescents with autism spectrum disorders. *Exceptional Children, 73*(3), 264–287.

Bellini, S., Peters, J. K., Benner, L., & Hopf, A. (2007). A meta-analysis of school-based social skills interventions for children with autism spectrum disorders. *Remedial and Special Education, 28*(3), 153–162.

Benedict, E., Horner, R., & Squires, J. (2007). Assessment and implementation of positive behavior support in preschools. *Topics in Early Childhood Special Education, 27*(3), 174–192.

Bennett, K., Reichow, B., & Wolery, M. (2011). Effects of structured teaching on the behavior of young children with disabilities. *Focus on Autism and Other Developmental Disabilities, 26,* 143–152.

Bijou, S. W., Peterson, R. F., & Ault, M. H. (1968). A method to integrate descriptive and experimental field studies at the level of data and empirical concepts. *Journal of Applied Behavior Analysis, 1,* 175–191.

Bloom, L. (1974). Talking, understanding, and thinking: Developmental relationship between receptive and expressive language. In R. Schiefelbusch & L. Lloyd (Eds.), *Language perspectives: Acquisition, retardation, and intervention* (pp. 285–312). Baltimore, MD: University Park Press.

Boisvert, M., Lang, R., Andrianopoulos, M., & Boscardin, M. (2010). Telepractice in the assessment and treatment of individuals with autism spectrum disorders: A systematic review. *Developmental Neurorehabilitation, 13,* 423–432.

Bondy, A. S., & Frost, L. A. (1994). The picture exchange communication system. *Focus on Autistic Behavior, 9,* 1–19.

Boyd, B. A., Conroy, M., Mancil, G. R., Nakao, T., & Alter, P. (2007). Effects of circumscribed interests on the social behaviors of children with autism spectrum disorders. *Journal of Autism and Developmental Disorders, 15,* 1550–1561.

Briggs, M. H. (1997). *Building early intervention teams: Working together for children and families.* Gaithersburg, MD: Aspen Publishers.

Bristol, M. M. (1984). Family resources and successful adaptation to autistic children. In E. Schopler & G. B. Mesibov (Eds.), *Autism in adolescents and adults* (pp. 251–278). New York, NY: Plenum Press.

Brock, S. E., Jimerson, S. R., & Hansen, R. L. (2006). *Identifying, assessing, and treating autism at school.* New York, NY: Springer.

Bronfenbrenner, U. (1979). *The ecology of human development: Experiments by nature and design.* Cambridge, MA: Harvard University Press.

Browder, D., Demchak, M. A., Heller, M., & King, D. (1989). An in vivo evaluation of the use of data-based rules to guide instructional decisions. *Journal of the Association for Persons with Severe Handicaps, 14,* 234–240.

Bushbacher, P. W., & Fox, L. (2003). Understanding and intervening with the challenging behavior of young children with autism spectrum disorder. *Language, Speech, and Hearing Services in Schools, 34,* 217–227.

Buysse, V., & Wesley, P. W. (2005). *Consultation in early childhood settings.* Baltimore, MD: Brookes.

Carbone, V. J., Sweeney-Kerwin, E. J., Attanasio, V., & Kasper, T. (2010). Increasing the vocal responses of children with autism and developmental disabilities using manual sign and training and prompt delay. *Journal of Applied Behavior Analysis, 43,* 705–709.

Cardon, T. & Wilcox, M. J. (2010). Promoting imitation in young children with autism: A comparison of reciprocal imitation training and video modeling. *Journal of Autism and Developmental Disabilities, 41*(5), 654–666.

Carlson, V. J., & Harwood, R. L. (2000, January). *Attachment, care giving, and culture: Ratings of maternal behavior in everyday settings among Anglo and Puerto Rican mother-infant pairs.* Paper presented at the New England Mini-Conference on Infant Studies, Worcester, MA.

Carnahan, C., Harte, H., Dyke, K. S., Hume, K., & Borders, C. (2011). Structured work systems: Supporting meaningful engagement in preschool settings for children with autism spectrum disorders. *Young Exceptional Children, 14*(1), 2–16.

Carr, E. G., Binkoff, J. A., Kologinsky, E., & Eddy, M. (1978). Acquisition of sign language by autistic children I: Expressive labeling. *Journal of Applied Behavior Analysis, 11*, 489–501.

Carr, E. G., Dunlap, G., Horner, R. H., Koegel, R. L., Turnbull, A. P., Sailor, W., . . . Fox, L. (2002). Positive behavior support: Evolution of an applied science. *Journal of Positive Behavior Interventions, 4*(1), 4–16.

Carr, E. G., & Durand, V. M. (1985). Reducing behavior problems through functional communication training. *Journal of Applied Behavior Analysis, 18*, 111–126.

Carter, C. M. (2001). Using choice with game play to increase language skills and interactive behaviors in children with autism. *Journal of Positive Behavior Interventions, 3*, 131–151.

Carter, D., & Van Norman, R. (2010). Class-wide positive behavior support in preschool: Improving teacher implementation through consultation. *Early Childhood Education Journal, 38*, 279–288.

Carter, E. W., & Hughes, C. (2007). Social interaction interventions: Promoting socially supportive environments and teaching new skills. In S. L. Odom, R. Horner, M. Snell, & J. Blancher (Eds.), *Handbook of developmental disabilities* (pp. 310–328). New York, NY: Guilford Press.

Casey, A., & Houchins-Juarez, N. (2006). *Behavior support plan implementation checklist for homes* (Unpublished tool). Nashville, TN: Department of Special Education, Vanderbilt University.

Casey, A., & McWilliam, R. (2008). Graphical feedback to increase teachers' use of incidental teaching. *Journal of Early Intervention, 30*, 251–268.

Castagnera, E., Fisher, D., Rodifer, K., Sax, C., & Frey, N. (2003). *Deciding what to teach and how to teach it: Connecting students through curriculum and instruction.* Colorado Springs, CO: PEAK Parent Center.

Catania, A. C. (2007). *Learning.* Cornwall-on-Hudson, NY: Sloan Publishing.

Centers for Disease Control and Prevention. (2012). Prevalence of autism spectrum disorders: Autism and developmental disabilities monitoring network, 14 sites, United States, 2008. *Morbidity and Mortality Weekly Report, 61*(3): 1–19. Retrieved from http://www.cdc.gov/mmwr/pdf/ss/ss6103.pdf

Centers for Disease Control and Prevention (CDC). (2007). Prevalence of autism spectrum disorders—Autism and Developmental Disabilities Monitoring Network, six sites, United States, 2000. Retrieved from http://www.cdc.gov/mmwr/PDF/ss/ss5601.pdf

Chakrabarti, S., & Fombonne, E. (2005) Pervasive developmental disorders in preschool children: Confirmation of high prevalence. *American Journal of Psychiatry, 162*, 1133–1141.

Chambers, C., & Childre, A. (2005). Fostering family-professional collaboration through person centered IEP meetings: The "True Directions" model. *Young Exceptional Children, 8*(3), 20–28.

Chandler, S., Charman, T., Baird, G., Simonoff, E., Loucas, T., Meldrum, D., & Pickles, A. (2007). Validation of the Social Communication Questionnaire in a population cohort of children with autism spectrum disorders. *Journal of the American Academy of Child and Adolescent Psychiatry, 46*, 1324–1332.

Chapman, R. (2005). *The everyday guide to special education law: A handbook for parents, teachers and other professionals.* Denver, CO: The Legal Center for People with Disabilities and Older People.

Chard, D., & Harn, B. (2008). Project CIRCUITS: Center for Improving Reading Competence Using Intensive Treatments Schoolwide. In C. Greenwood, T. Kratochwill, & M. Clements (Eds.), *Schoolwide prevention models: Lessons learned in elementary schools* (pp. 70–83). New York, NY: Guilford Press.

Charman, T. (2003). Why is joint attention a pivotal skill in autism? *Philosophical Transactions of the Royal Society B: Biological Sciences, 358,* 315–324.

Charman, T., & Baron-Cohen, S. (1997). Brief report: Prompted pretend play in autism. *Journal of Autism and Developmental Disorders, 27,* 325–332.

Charman, T., Baron-Cohen, S., Swettenham, J., Baird, G., Drew, A., & Cox, A. (2003). Predicting language outcome in infants with autism and pervasive developmental disorders. *International Journal of Language and Communication Disorders, 38,* 265–285.

Charman, T., Swettenham, J., Baron-Cohen, S., Cox, A., Baird, G., & Drew, A. (1997). Infants with autism: An investigation of empathy, pretend play, joint attention, and imitation. *Developmental Psychology, 33,* 781–89.

Chawarska, K., Paul, A., Klin, R., & Volkmar, F. (2007). Autism spectrum disorder in the second year: Stability and change in syndrome expression. *Journal of Child Psychology and Psychiatry, 48*(2), 128–138.

Choi, H., & Kim, U. (2005). Autism: Using milieu teaching strategies to instruct functional and generalized language. *Journal of Special Education: Theory and Practice, 6,* 357–375.

Choi, H., O'Reilly, M., Sigafoos, J., & Lancioni, G. (2010). Teaching requesting and rejecting sequences to four children with developmental disabilities using augmentative and alternative communication. *Research in Developmental Disabilities, 31,* 560–567.

Clarke, S., Remington, B., & Light, P. (1988). The role of referential speech in sign learning by mentally retarded children: A comparison of total communication and sign-alone training. *Journal of Applied Behavior Analysis, 21,* 419–426.

Codding, R. S., Feinberg, A. B., Dunn, E., & Pace, G. M. (2005). Effects of immediate performance feedback on implementation of behavior support plans. *Journal of Applied Behavior Analysis, 38,* 205–219.

Coleman, M. (2005). *The neurology of autism.* New York, NY: Oxford University Press.

Colvin, G. (2004). *Managing the cycle of acting-out behavior in the classroom.* Eugene, OR: Behavior Associates.

CONNECT: The Center to Mobilize Early Childhood Knowledge. (2009). *Policy advisory: The law affecting communication among professionals.* Chapel Hill: The University of North Carolina, FPG Child Development Institute. Retrieved from http://community.fpg.unc.edu/connect-modules/resources/handouts/CONNECT-Handout-3-5.pdf/?searchterm=Policy%20advisory:%20The%20law%20affecting%20communication%20among%20professionals

Cook, J., & Hartman, C. (2008). *My mouth is a volcano!* Chattanooga, TN: National Center for Youth Issues.

Coonrod, E. E., & Stone, W. L. (2004). Early concerns of parents of children with autistic and nonautistic disorders. *Infants and Young Children, 17,* 258–268.

Cooper, J. O., Heron, T. E., & Heward, W. L. (2007). *Applied behavior analysis* (2nd ed.). Upper Saddle River, NJ: Prentice Hall.

Courchesne, E., Karns, C. M., Davis, H. R., Ziccardi, R., Carper, R. A., Tigue, Z. D., . . . Courchesne, R. A. (2001). Unusual braing rowth in early life in patients with autism disorder: An MRI study. *Neurology, 57,* 245–254.

Courchesne, E., Townsend, J. P., Akshoomoff, N. A., Yeung-Courchesne, R., Press, G. A., Murakami, J. W., . . . Schreibman, L. (1994). A new finding: Impairment in shifting attention in autistic and cerebellar patients. In S. H. Broman & J. Grafman (Eds.), *Atypical cognitive deficits in developmental disorders: Implications for brain function* (pp. 101–137). Hillsdale, NJ: Lawrence Erlbaum.

Cowan, R. J., & Allen, K. D. (2007). Using naturalistic procedures to enhance learning in individuals with autism: A focus on generalized teaching within the school setting. *Psychology in the Schools, 44,* 701–715.

Crone, D. A., Hawken, L., & Horner, R. (2010). *Responding to problem behavior in schools, second edition: The Behavior Education Program.* New York, NY: Guilford Press.

Crone, D. A., & Horner, R. H. (2003). Building positive behavior support systems in schools: Functional behavioral assessment. New York, NY: Guilford Press.

Crozier, S., & Tincani, M. J. (2005). Using a modified social story to decrease disruptive behavior of a child with autism. *Focus on Autism and Other Developmental Disabilities, 20,* 150–157.

Dalton, K. M., Nacewicz, B. M., Alexander, A. L., & Davidson, R. J. (2006). Gaze-fixation, brain activation, and amygdala volume in unaffected siblings of individuals with autism. *Biological Psychiatry, 61,* 512–520.

Dawson, G., & Osterling, J. (1997). Early intervention in autism: Effectiveness and common elements of current approaches. In M. J. Guralnick (Ed.), *The effectiveness of early intervention: Second generation research* (pp. 307–326). Baltimore, MD: Brookes.

Dawson, G., Rogers, S., Munson, J., Smith, M., Winter, J., Greenson, J., . . . Varley, J. (2009). Randomized, controlled trial of an intervention for toddlers with autism: The Early Start Denver model. *Journal of the American Academy of Pediatrics, 125*(1), 17–23.

Derby, K. M., Wacker, D. P., Berg, W., DeRaad, A., Ulrich, S., Asmus, J., . . . Stoner, E. A. (1997). The long-term effects of functional communication training in home settings. *Journal of Applied Behavior Analysis, 30,* 507–531.

Different Roads to Learning. (2008). Early intervention and special education/autism resources: ABLLS-R: Assessment of Basic Language and Learning Skills. Retrieved from http://www.difflearn.com/product/Revised_ABLLS_Set/Early-intervention-autism-teaching-tools

Dinnebeil, L., Pretti-Frontczak, K., & McInerney, W. (2009). A consultative itinerant approach to service delivery: Considerations for the early childhood community. *Language, Speech, and Hearing Services in Schools, 40,* 435–445.

Dixon, D., Tarbox, J., Najdowski, A., Wilke, A., & Granpeesheh, D. (2011). A comprehensive evaluation of language for early behavioral intervention programs: The reliability of the SKILLS language index. *Research in Autism Spectrum Disorders, 5,* 506–511.

Doyle, P. M., Wolery, M., Gast, D. L., Ault, M. J., & Wiley, K. (1990). Comparison of constant time delay and system of least prompts in teaching preschoolers with developmental delays. *Research in Developmental Disabilities, 11*(1), 1–22.

Ducharme, J. M., Lucas, H., & Pontes, E. (1994). Errorless embedding in the reduction of severe maladaptive behavior during interactive and learning tasks. *Behavior Therapy, 25,* 489–501.

Dunlap, G. (1993). Promoting generalization: Current status and functional considerations. In R. VanHouton & S. Axelrod (Eds.), *Behavior analysis and treatment* (pp. 269–296). New York, NY: Plenum Press.

Dunlap, G., & Carr, E. (2007). Positive behavior support and developmental disabilities. In S. Odom, R. Horner, M. Snell, & J. Blacher (Eds.), *Handbook of developmental disabilities* (pp. 469–482). New York, NY: Guilford Press.

Dunlap, G., & Fox, L. (1999). A demonstration of behavioral support for young children with autism. *Journal of Positive Behavioral Intervention, 1*, 77–87.

Dunlap, G., Harrower, J., & Fox, L. (2005). Understanding the environmental determinants of problem behaviors. In L. Bambara & L. Kern (Eds.), *Individualized supports for students with problem behaviors* (pp. 25–46). New York, NY: Guilford Press.

Dunlap, G., Strain, P., & Ostryn, C. (2011). *Addressing challenging behaviors of young children with autism spectrum disorders.* In H. H. Schertz, C. Wong, & S. L. Odom (Eds.), *Young exceptional children monograph series no. 12: Supporting children with autism spectrum disorders and their families.* Missoula, MT: Division for Early Childhood.

Dunlap, G., Strain, P. S., Fox, L., Carta, J. J., Conroy, M., Smith, B. J., . . . Sowell, C. (2006). Prevention and intervention with young children's challenging behavior: Perspectives regarding current knowledge. *Behavioral Disorders, 32*(1), 29–45.

Dunlap, L. K., Dunlap, G., Koegel, L. K., & Koegel, R. L. (1991). Using self-monitoring to increase independence. *Teaching Exceptional Children, 23*(3), 17–22.

Dunst, C., & Trivette, C. (2009). Using research evidence to inform and evaluate early childhood intervention practice. *Topics in Early Childhood Special Education, 29*(1), 40–52.

Durand, V. M. (1988). The Motivational Assessment Scale. In M. Hersen & A. Bellack (Eds.), *Dictionary of behavioral assessment techniques* (pp. 309–310). Elmsford, NY: Pergamon.

Durand, V. M. (1999). Functional communication training using assistive devices: Recruiting natural communities of reinforcement. *Journal of Applied Behavior Analysis, 32*, 247–267.

Durand, V. M., & Carr, E. G. (1991). Functional communication training to reduce challenging behavior: Maintenance and application in new settings. *Journal of Applied Behavior Analysis, 24*, 251–264.

Durand, V. M., & Carr, E. G. (1992). An analysis of maintenance following functional communication training. *Journal of Applied Behavior Analysis, 25*, 777–794.

Durand, V. M., & Merges, E. (2001). Functional communication training: A contemporary behavior analytic intervention for problem behavior. *Focus on Autism and Other Developmental Disabilities, 16*, 110–119.

Durlak, J., & DuPre, E. (2008). Implementation matters: A review of research on the influence of implementation on program outcomes and the factors affecting implementation. *American Journal of Community Psychology, 41*, 327–350.

Dymond, S., Renzaglia, A., Halle, J., Chadsey, J., & Bentz, J. (2008). An evaluation of video conferencing as a supportive technology for practicum supervision. *Teacher Education and Special Education, 31*, 243–256.

Ehlers, S., Gillberg, C., & Wing, L. (1999). A screening questionnaire for Asperger syndrome and other high functioning autism spectrum disorders in school age children. *Journal of Autism and Developmental Disorders, 29*, 439–484.

Elliott, S. N., Roach, A. T., & Beddow, P. A. (2008). Best practices in preschool social skills training. In A. Thomas & J. Grimes (Eds.), *Best practices in school psychology V* (pp. 1531–1546). Bethesda, MD: The National Association of School Psychologists.

Filcheck, H., McNeil, C., Greco, L., & Bernard, R. (2004). Using a whole-class token economy and coaching of teacher skills in a preschool classroom to manage disruptive behavior. *Psychology in the Schools, 41,* 351–361.

Fisher, W., Piazza, C., Cataldo, M., Harrell, R., Jefferson, G., & Conner, R. (1993). Functional communication training with and without extinction and punishment. *Journal of Applied Behavior Analysis, 26*(1), 23–36.

Fisher, W., Kodak, T., & Moore, J. W. (2007). Embedding an identity-matching task within a prompting hierarchy to facilitate acquisition of conditional discriminations in children with autism. *Journal of Applied Behavior Analysis, 40,* 489–499.

Fixsen, D. L., Naoom, S. F., Blasé, K. A., Friedman, R. M., & Wallace, F. (2005). *Implementation research: A synthesis of the literature.* (FMHI Publication No. 231). Tampa: University of South Florida, Louis de la Parte Florida Mental Health Institute, the National Implementation Research Network.

Flippin, M., Reszka, S., & Watson, L. R. (2010). Effectiveness of the Picture Exchange Communication System (PECS) on communication and speech for children with autism spectrum disorders: A meta-analysis. *American Journal of Speech-Language Pathology, 19,* 178–195.

Fombonne, E. (2005). The changing epidemiology of autism. *Journal of Applied Research in Intellectual Disabilities, 18,* 281–294.

Fox, L. (n.d.). *Program practices for promoting the social development of young children and addressing challenging behavior.* Retrieved from http://www.challengingbehavior.org/do/resources/handouts.htm

Fox, L., Dunlap, G., Hemmeter, M. L., Joseph, G. E., & Strain, P. S. (2003). The teaching pyramid: A model for supporting social competence and preventing challenging behavior in young children. *Young Children, 58,* 48–52.

Freeden, R. M., & Koegel, R. L. (2006). The pivotal role of initiations in habilitation. In R. L. Koegel & L. K. Koegel (Eds.), *Pivotal response treatments for autism: Communication, social, & academic development* (pp. 165–188). Baltimore, MD: Brookes.

Freeman, R., Eber, L., Anderson, C., Irvin, L., Bounds, M., & Dunlap, G. (2006). Building inclusive school cultures using school-wide PBS: Designing effective individual support systems for students with significant disabilities. *Research and Practice in Severe Disabilities, 31*(1), 4–17.

Friend, M. (2000). Myths and misunderstandings about professional collaboration. *Remedial and Special Education, 21,* 130–132.

Friend, M. P., & Cook, L. (2010). *Interactions: Collaboration skills for school professionals.* Boston, MA: Prentice Hall.

Frost, L., & Bondy, A. (2002). *PECS: The Picture Exchange Communication System training manual* (2nd ed.). Newark, DE: Pyramid Educational Consultants.

Fuchs, L. S., & Fuchs, D. (1986). Effects of systematic formative evaluation: A meta-analysis. *Exceptional Children, 53,* 199–208.

Gena, A., Couloura, S., & Kymissis, E. (2005). Modifying the affective behavior of preschoolers with autism using in-vivo or video modeling and reinforcement contingencies. *Journal of Autism and Developmental Disorders, 35,* 545–556.

Gibson, J., Pennington, R., Stenhoff, D., & Hopper, J. (2010). Using desktop video conferencing to deliver interventions to a preschool student with autism. *Topics in Early Childhood Special Education, 29,* 214–225.

Gilliam, J. (2006). *GARS-2: Gilliam Autism Rating Scale—Second edition.* Austin, TX: Pro-Ed.

Gischlar, K. L., Hojnoski, R. L., & Missall, K. N. (2009). Improving child outcomes with data-based decision making: Interpreting and using data. *Young Exceptional Children, 13*(1), 2–18.

Glascoe, F. P. (2000). Early detection of developmental and behavioral problems. *Pediatrics in Review, 21,* 272–280.

Goldstein, H. (2002). Communication intervention for children with autism: A review of treatment efficacy. *Journal of Autism and Developmental Disorders, 32,* 373–396.

Good, R. H., & Kaminski, R. A. (2003). *DIBELS™: Dynamic Indicators of Basic Early Literacy Skills, Sixth Edition.* Longmont CO: Sopris West.

Gray, C. (1995). Teaching children with autism to "read" social situations. In K. Quill (Ed.), *Teaching children with autism: Strategies to enhance communication and socialization* (pp. 219–241). Albany, NY: Delmar.

Greenspan, S., & Meisels, S. (1996). Toward a new vision for the developmental assessment of infants and young children. In S. Meisels & E. Fenichel (Eds.), *New visions for the developmental assessment of infants and children* (pp. 9–26). Washington, DC: Zero to Three.

Gresham, F. M., Beebe-Frankenberger, M. E., & MacMillan, D. L. (1999). A selective review of treatments for children with autism: Description and methodological considerations. *School Psychology Review, 28,* 559–575.

Gresham, F. M., & MacMillan, D. L. (1998). Early intervention project: Can its claims be substantiated and its effects replicated? *Journal of Autism and Developmental Disorders, 28,* 5–13.

Gresham, F. M., Watson, T. S., & Skinner, C. H. (2001). Functional behavioral assessment: Principles, procedures, and future directions. *School Psychology Review, 30*(2), 156–172.

Hagopian, L. P., Fisher, W. W., Sullivan, M. T., Aquisto, J., & LeBlanc, L. A. (1998). Effectiveness of functional communication training with and without extinction and punishment: A summary of 21 inpatient cases. *Journal of Applied Behavior Analysis, 31*(2), 211–235.

Hamad, C., Serna, R., Morrison, L., & Fleming, R. (2010). Extending the reach of early intervention training for practitioners: A preliminary investigation of an online curriculum for teaching behavioral intervention knowledge in autism to families and service providers. *Infants and Young Children, 23,* 195–208.

Hamilton, S. (2006). Screening for developmental delay: Reliable, easy to use tools: Win-win for children at-risk and busy pediatricians. *Journal of Family Practice, 55,* 415–422.

Hamre, B., Justice, L., Pianta, R., Kilday, C., Sweeney, B., Downer, J., . . . Leach, A. (2010). Implementation fidelity of My Teaching Partner literacy and language activities: Association with preschoolers' language and literacy growth. *Early Childhood Research Quarterly, 25,* 329–347.

Hancock T. B., & Kaiser A. P. (2002). The effects of trainer-implemented enhanced milieu teaching on the social communication of children with autism. *Topics in Early Childhood Special Education, 22,* 39–54.

Hanft, B. E., Rush, D. D., & Shelden, M. L. (2004). *Coaching families and colleagues in early childhood.* Baltimore, MD: Brookes.

Harris, S. L., & Handleman, J. S. (2000). Age and IQ at intake as predictors of placement for young children with autism: A four- to six-year follow-up. *Journal of Autism and Developmental Disorders, 30,* 137–142.

Hart, B., & Risley, T. R. (1975). Incidental teaching of language in the preschool. *Journal of Applied Behavior Analysis, 7*, 411–420.

Hart, S. L., & Banda, D. R. (2010). Picture exchange communication system with individuals with developmental disabilities: A meta-analysis of single subject studies. *Remedial and Special Education, 31*, 476–488.

Hemmeter, M. L., Snyder, P., Kinder, K., & Artman, K. (2011). Impact of performance feedback delivered via electronic mail on preschool teachers' use of descriptive praise. *Early Childhood Research Quarterly, 26*, 96–109.

Hemmeter, M. L., Fox, L., Jack, S., Broyles, L., & Doubet, S. (2007). A program-wide model of positive behavior support in early childhood settings. *Journal of Early Intervention, 29*, 337–355.

Hojnoski, R. L., Gischlar, K. L., & Missall, K. N. (2009a). Improving child outcomes with data-based decision making: Collecting data. *Young Exceptional Children, 12*(3), 32–44.

Hojnoski, R. L., Gischlar, K. L., & Missall, K. N. (2009b). Improving child outcomes with databased decision making: Graphing data. *Young Exceptional Children, 12*(4), 15–30.

Holcombe, A., Wolery, M., Werts, M. G., & Hrenkevich, P. (1993). Effects of instructive feedback on future learning. *Journal of Behavioral Education, 3*, 259–285.

Hoopmann, K. (2001). *Blue bottle mystery: An Asperger adventure.* Philadelphia, PA: Jessica Kingsley.

Hoopmann, K. (2002). *Lisa and the lacemaker: An Asperger adventure.* Philadelphia, PA: Jessica Kingsley.

Horner, R., Carr, E. G., Strain, P. S., Todd, A. W., & Reed, H. K. (2002). Problem behavior interventions for young children with autism: A research synthesis. *Journal of Autism and Developmental Disorders, 32*, 423–446.

Horner, R. H., Albin, R. W., Todd, A. W., Newton J. S., & Sprague, J. R., (2011). Designing and implementing individualized positive behavior support. In M. Snell & F. Brown (Eds.), *Instruction of students with severe disabilities* (pp. 257–303). Boston, MA: Pearson.

Horner, R. H., Dunlap, G., & Koegel, R. L. (1988). *Generalization and maintenance: Life-style changes in applied settings.* Baltimore, MD: Brookes.

Howell, K., & Nolet, V. (2001). *Curriculum-based evaluation: Teacher and decision making* (3rd ed.). New York, NY: Wadsworth.

Howlin, P. (2005). Outcomes in autism spectrum disorders. In F. R. Volkmar, R. Paul, A. Klin, & D. J. Cohen (Eds.), *Handbook of autism and pervasive developmental disorders* (3rd ed., pp. 201–222). Hoboken, NJ: Wiley.

Hume, K., & Odom, S. (2007). Effects of an individual work system on the independent functioning of students with autism. *Journal of Autism and Developmental Disorders, 37*, 1166–1180.

Hunt, P., Soto, G., Maier, J., & Doering, K. (2003). Collaborative teaming to support students at risk and students with severe disabilities in general education classrooms. *Exceptional Children, 69*, 315–332.

Individuals with Disabilities Education Act (IDEA), P. L. 108–446, 20 U.S.C. 1400–1487 (2004).

Ingersoll, B. (2008). The social role of imitation in autism: Implications for the treatment of imitation deficits. *Infants and Young Children, 21*, 107–119.

Ingersoll, B. (2011). The differential effect of three naturalistic language interventions on language use in children with autism. *Journal of Positive Behavioral Interventions, 13*, 109–118.

Jarrold, C., Boucher, J., & Smith, P. (1996). Generativity deficits in pretend play in autism. *Journal of Developmental Psychology, 14,* 275–300.

Johnson, C. P., & Myers, S. M. (2007). Identification and evaluation of children with autism spectrum disorders. *Pediatrics, 120,* 1183–1215.

Jorgensen, C. (2003). Essential features in creating inclusive curriculum. In E. Castagnera, D. Fisher, K. Rodifer, C. Sax, & N. Frey (Eds.), *Deciding what to teach and how to teach it: Connecting students through curriculum and instruction* (pp. 15–17). Colorado Springs, CO: Peak Parent Center.

Jung, L. A. (2003). More is better: Maximizing natural learning opportunities. *Young Exceptional Children, 6*(3), 21–27.

Jung, L. A., Gomez, C., Baird, S., & Keramidas, C. (2008). Designing intervention plans. *Teaching Exceptional Children, 41,* 26–33.

Kaiser, A. P., & Hancock, T. B. (2003). Teaching parents new skills to support their young children's development. *Infants & Young Children, 16,* 9–21.

Kaiser A. P., Hancock, T. B., & Nietfeld, J. P. (2000). The effects of parent-implemented enhanced milieu teaching on the social communication of children who have autism. *Journal of Early Education and Development, 11,* 423–446.

Kanner, L. (1943). Autistic disturbances of affective contact. *Nervous Child, 2,* 217–250.

Kasari, C., Freeman, S., & Parapella, T. (2006). Joint attention and symbolic play in young children with autism: A randomized controlled intervention study. *Journal of Child Psychology and Psychiatry, 47,* 611–620.

Keating-Velasco, J. L. (2007). *A is for autism, F is for friend: A kid's book for making friends with a child who has autism.* Shawnee Mission, KS: Autism Asperger.

Kelso, G., Fiechtl, B., Olsen, S., & Rule, S. (2009). The feasibility of virtual home visits to provide early intervention: A pilot study. *Infants & Young Children, 22,* 332–340.

Kennedy, C. H. (2005). *Single case designs for educational research.* Boston, MA: Pearson Education.

Klin, A., Jones, W., Schultz, R., Volkmar, F., & Cohen, D. (2002). Visual fixation patterns during viewing of naturalistic social situations as predictors of social competence in individuals with autism. *Archives of General Psychiatry, 59,* 809–816.

Kluth, P. (2003). *"You're going to love this kid!": Teaching students with autism in the inclusive classroom.* Baltimore, MD: Brookes.

Koegel, L. K., Koegel, R. L., Harrower, J. K., & Carter, C. M. (1999). Pivotal response intervention I: Overview of approach. *Journal of the Association for Persons with Severe Handicaps, 24,* 174–185.

Koegel, L. K., Koegel, R. L., Hurley, C., & Frea, W. D. (1992). Improving social skills and disruptive behavior in children with autism through self-management. *Journal of Applied Behavior Analysis, 25,* 341–353.

Koegel, L. K., Koegel, R. L., Shoshan, Y., & McNerney, E. (1999). Pivotal response intervention II: Preliminary long-term outcome data. *Journal of the Association for Persons with Severe Handicaps, 24,* 186–198.

Koegel, R., Schreibman, L., Good, A., Cerniglia, L., Murphy, C., & Koegel, L. K. (1989). *How to teach pivotal behaviors to children with autism: A training manual.* Santa Barbara: School Psychology Program, Graduate School of Education, University of California.

Koegel, R. L., & Koegel, L. (2006). *Pivotal response treatments for autism: Communication, social, & academic development.* Baltimore, MD: Brookes.

Kohler, F. W., Greteman, C., Raschke, D., & Highnam, C. (2007). Using a buddy skills package to increase the social interactions between a preschooler with autism and her peers. *Topics in Early Childhood Special Education, 27*, 155–163.

Kretlow, A., & Bartholomew, C. (2010). Using coaching to improve the fidelity of evidence-based practices: A review of studies. *Teacher Education and Special Education, 33*, 279–299.

Kretlow, A., Wood, C., & Cooke, N. (2011). Using in-service and coaching to increase kindergarten teachers' accurate delivery of group instructional units. *Journal of Special Education, 44*, 234–246.

Lancioni, G. E., O'Reilly, M. F., Cuvo, A. J., Singh, N. N., Sigafoos, J., & Didden, R. (2007). PECS and VOCAs to enable students with developmental disabilities to make requests: An overview of the literature. *Research in Developmental Disabilities, 28*, 468–488.

Laus, M., Cordisco, L., Hanna, A., & Rapp, N. (1991). *Files: About our child.* Retrieved from http://www.eicolorado.org/Files/About%20Our%20Child%20Revised.pdf

Laushey, K. M., & Heflin, L. J. (2000). Enhancing social skills of kindergarten children with autism through the training of multiple peers as tutors. *Journal of Autism and Developmental Disorders, 30*(3), 183–193.

Leaf, R., & McEachin, J. (1999). A work in progress: Behavior management strategies and a curriculum for intensive behavioral treatment for autism. New York, NY: DRL Books.

Ledford, J. R., Gast, D. L., Luscre, D., & Ayres, K. M. (2008). Observational and incidental learning by children with autism during small group instruction. *Journal of Autism and Developmental Disorders, 38*(1), 86–103.

Ledford, J. R., & Wolery, M. (2011). Teaching imitation to young children with disabilities: A review of the literature. *Topics in Early Childhood Special Education, 30*, 245–255.

Lee, S., Odom, S. L., & Loftin, R. (2007). Social engagement with peers and stereotypic behavior of children with autism. *Journal of Positive Behavior Interventions, 9*, 67–79.

Lee, S., Simpson, R., & Shogren, K. (2007). Effects and implications of self-management for students with autism: A meta-analysis. *Focus on Autism and Other Developmental Disabilities, 22*(1), 2–13.

Lerman, D., Vorndran, C., Addison, L., & Kuhn, S. (2004). Preparing teachers in evidence-based practices for young children with autism. *School Psychology Review, 33*, 510–526.

Levy, A., & Perry, A. (in press). Outcomes in adolescents and adults with autism. *Research in Autism Spectrum Disorders.*

Lewis, E. A., Ledford, J. R., Elam, K. L., Wolery, M., & Gast, D. L. (2010). Using small group instruction to teach young children with autism spectrum disorders in early childhood classes. In H. H. Schertz, C. Wong, & S. L. Odom (Eds.), *Young exceptional children monograph series no. 12: Supporting children with autism spectrum disorders and their families* (pp. 86–96). Missoula, MT: Division for Early Childhood.

Lifter, K., Ellis, J., Cannon, B., & Anderson, S. R. (2005). Developmental specificity in targeting and teaching play activities to children with pervasive developmental disorders. *Journal of Early Intervention, 27*, 247–267.

Light, J. C., Roberts, B., Dimarco, R., & Greiner, N. (1998). Augmentative and alternative communication to support receptive and expressive communication for people with autism. *Journal of Communication Disorders, 31*, 153–80.

Lord, C. (1997). Diagnostic instruments in autism spectrum disorders. In D. J. Cohen & F. R. Volkmar (Eds.), *Handbook of autism and pervasive developmental disorders* (2nd ed., pp. 460–483). New York, NY: Wiley.

Lord, C., Rutter, M., DiLavore, P., & Risi, S. (2002). *Autism Diagnostic Observation Schedule.* Los Angeles, CA: Western Psychological Services.

Lord, C., & Spence, S. (2006). Autism spectrum disorders: Phenotype and diagnosis. In S. Moldin & J. Rubenstein (Eds.), *Understanding autism: From basic neuroscience to treatment* (pp. 1–23). New York, NY: Taylor and Francis.

Lovaas, O. I. (1983). Teaching developmentally disabled children: The ME book. Austin, TX: Pro-Ed.

Lovaas, O. I. (1987). Behavioral treatment and normal educational and intellectual functioning in young autistic children. *Journal of Consulting and Clinical Psychology, 55,* 3–9.

Lovaas, O. I. (2003). *Teaching individuals with developmental delays: Basic intervention techniques.* Austin, TX: Pro-Ed.

Luyster, R., Gotham, K., Guthrie, W., Coffing, M., Petrak, R., Pierce, K., . . . Lord, C. (2009). The Autism Diagnostic Observation Schedule-Toddler Module: A new module of a standardized diagnostic measure for autism spectrum disorders. *Journal of Autism and Developmental Disorders, 39,* 1305–1320.

MacDuff, G. S., Krantz, P. J., & McClannahan, L. E. (2001). Prompts and prompt-fading strategies for people with autism. In C. Maurice, G. Green, & R. M. Foxx (Eds.), *Making a difference: Behavioral intervention for autism* (pp. 37–50). Austin, TX: Pro-Ed.

Malone, D., & Gallagher, P. (2010). Special education teachers' attitudes and perceptions of teamwork. *Remedial and Special Education, 31,* 330–342.

Mandell, D. S., Ittenbach, R., Levy, S., & Pinto-Martin, J. (2007). Disparities in diagnoses received prior to a diagnosis of autism spectrum disorder. *Journal of Autism and Developmental Disorders, 37,* 1795–1802.

Maurice, C. (1993). *Let me hear your voice: A family's triumph over autism.* New York, NY: Ballantine.

Maurice, C., Green, G. G., & Luce, S. C. (1996). *Behavioral intervention for young children with autism: A manual for parents and professionals.* Austin, TX: Pro-Ed.

McClannahan, L. E., & Krantz, P. J. (2005). *Teaching conversation to children with autism: Scripts and script training.* Bethesda, MD: Woodbine House.

McConnell, S. (2002). Interventions to facilitate social interaction for young children with autism: Review of available research and recommendations for educational intervention and future research. *Journal of Autism and Developmental Disorders, 32,* 351–372.

McCoy, K., & Hermansen, E. (2007). Video modeling for individuals with autism: A Review of model types and effects. *Education & Treatment of Children, 30*(4), 183–213.

McGee, G. G., Krantz, P. J., Mason, D., & McClannahan, L. E. (1983). A modified incidental teaching procedure for autistic youth: Acquisition and generalization of receptive object labels. *Journal of Applied Behavior Analysis, 16,* 329–338.

McGee, G. G., Krantz, P. J., & McClannahan, L. E. (1985). The facilitative effects of incidental teaching on preposition use by autistic children. *Journal of the Association for Persons with Severe Handicaps, 24*(3), 133–146.

McGee, G. G., Krantz, P. J., & McClannahan, L. E. (1986). An extension of incidental teaching procedures to reading instruction for autistic children. *Journal of Applied Behavior Analysis, 19,* 147–157.

McGee, G. G., Morrier, M. J., & Daly, T. (1999). An incidental teaching approach to early intervention for toddlers with autism. *Journal of Applied Behavior Analysis, 19*, 147–157.

McGee, G. G., Morrier, M. J., & Daly, T. (2001). The Walden early childhood programs. In J. S. Handleman & S. L. Harris (Eds.), *Preschool education programs for children with autism* (2nd ed., pp. 157–190). Austin, TX: Pro-Ed.

McLean, M., & Crais, E. R. (2004). Procedural considerations in assessing infants and preschoolers with disabilities. In M. McLean, M. Wolery, & D. B. Bailery (Eds.), *Assessing infants and preschoolers with special needs* (pp. 45–70). Columbus, OH: Pearson Prentice Hall.

McWilliam, R. A. (2001, August). *Functional intervention planning: The routines-based interview; the power of the routines-based interview.* Retrieved from Waisman Center, Wisconsin Birth to 3 Training and Technical Assistance: http://www.waisman.wisc.edu/birthto3/WPDP/txt/rbi.html

McWilliam, R. A. (2010a). *Routines-based early intervention.* Baltimore, MD: Brookes.

McWilliam, R. A. (Ed.) (2010b). *Working with families of young children with special needs.* Baltimore, MD: Brookes.

McWilliam, R. A., & Casey, A. M. (2008). *Engagement of every child in the preschool classroom.* Baltimore, MD: Brookes.

McWilliam, R. A., Casey, A., & Sims, J. (2009). The routines-based interview: A method for gathering information and assessing need. *Infants & Young Children, 22*, 224–233.

Merin, N., Young, G. S., Ozonoff, S., & Rogers, S. J. (2006). Visual fixation patterns during reciprocal social interaction distinguish a subgroup of 6-month-old infants at risk for autism from comparison infants. *Journal of Autism and Developmental Disorders, 37*, 108–121.

Mesibov, G. B., Shea, V., & Schopler, E. (2005). *The TEACCH approach to autism spectrum disorders.* New York, NY: Kluwer Academic/Plenum.

Minchew, N. J., Sweeney, J. A., Bauman, M. L., & Webb, S. J. (2005). Neurological aspects of autism. In F. Volkmar, R. Paul, A. Klin, & D. Cohen (Eds.), *Handbook of autism and pervasive developmental disorders* (pp. 473–514). New York, NY: Wiley.

Mirenda, P. (2003). Clinical forum. Toward functional augmentative and alternative communication for students with autism: manual signs, graphic symbols, and voice output communication aids. *Language, Speech, & Hearing Services in School, 34*(3), 203–216.

Mirenda, P., & Iacono, T. (2009). *Autism spectrum disorders and AAC.* Baltimore, MD: Brookes.

Moes, D. R., & Frea, W. D. (2000). Using family context to inform intervention planning for the treatment of a child with autism. *Journal of Positive Behavior Interventions, 2*, 40–46.

Mundy. P., & Crowson, M. (1997). Joint attention and early social communication: Implications for research on intervention with autism. *Journal of Autism and Developmental Disorders, 27*, 653–676.

Myers, S. M., & Johnson, C. P. (2007). Management of children with autism spectrum disorders. *Pediatrics, 120*, 1162–1182.

National Autism Center. (2009a). *National standards report.* Randolph, MA: Author.

National Autism Center. (2009b). *Evidence-based practice and autism in the schools: A guide to providing appropriate interventions to students with autism spectrum disorders.* Randolph, MA: Author.

National Individualizing Preschool Inclusion Project. (2005). *Consultation checklist.* Nashville, TN: Vanderbilt University Medical Center, Center for Child Development.

National Research Council. (2001). *Educating children with autism.* Washington, DC: National Academy Press.

National Secondary Transition Technical Assistance Center. (2008). *IEP meeting involvement using person-centered planning.* Charlotte, NC: Author.

Neilsen, S. L., & McEvoy, M. A. (2004). Functional behavioral assessment in early education settings. *Journal of Early Intervention, 26,* 115–131.

Neitzel, J. (2010a). Positive behavior supports for children and youth with autism spectrum disorders. *Preventing School Failure, 54,* 247–255.

Neitzel, J. (2010b). Reinforcement for children and youth with autism spectrum disorders: Online training module. Columbus, OH: Ohio Center for Autism and Low Incidence (OCALI). Retrieved from http://www.autisminternet modules.org/

Neitzel, J. (2010c). Response interruption/redirection for children and youth with autism spectrum disorders: Online training module. Columbus, OH: Ohio Center for Autism and Low Incidence (OCALI). Retrieved from http://www .autisminternetmodules.org/

Neitzel, J. (2010d). Time delay for children and youth with autism spectrum disorders: Online training module. Columbus, OH: Ohio Center for Autism and Low Incidence (OCALI). Retrieved from http://www.autisminternetmodules .org/

Neitzel, J., Boyd, B., Odom, S. L., & Edmondson Pretzel, R. (2008). Peer-mediated instruction and intervention for children and youth with autism spectrum disorders: Online training module. Columbus, OH: Ohio Center for Autism and Low Incidence (OCALI). Retrieved from http://www.autisminter netmodules.org/

Neitzel, J., & Wolery, M. (2010). Prompting for children and youth with autism spectrum disorders: Online training module. Columbus, OH: Ohio Center for Autism and Low Incidence (OCALI). Retrieved from http://www.autismin ternetmodules.org/

Newman, B., Reinecke, D. R., & Meinberg, D. L. (2000). Self-management of varied responding in three students with autism. *Behavioral Interventions, 15,* 145–151.

Nickel, R. & Squires, J. (May, 2008.) *Identification of children with autism spectrum disorders (ASDs) by the Ages and Stages Questionnaires.* Paper presented at the International Meeting for Autism Research, London, England.

Nikopoulos, C. K., & Keenan, M. (2007). Using video modeling to teach complex social sequences to children with autism. *Journal of Autism and Developmental Disorders, 37,* 678–693.

Odom, S. L. (2009). The tie that binds: Evidence-based practice, implementation science, and outcomes for children. *Topics in Early Childhood Special Education, 29,* 53–61.

Odom, S. L., Fleming, K., Diamond, K., Lieber, J., Hanson, M., Butera, G., . . . Marquis, J. (2010). Examining different forms of implementation and in early childhood curriculum research. *Early Childhood Research Quarterly, 25,* 314–328.

Odom, S. L., Boyd, B. A., Hall, L. J., & Hume, K. (2010). Evaluation of comprehensive treatment models for individuals with autism spectrum disorders. *Journal of Autism and Developmental Disorders, 40,* 425–436.

Odom, S. L., McConnell, S. R., McEvoy, M. A., Peterson, C., Ostrosky, M., Chandler, L. K., . . . Favazza, P. C. (1999). Relative effects of interventions supporting the social competence of young children with disabilities. *Topics in Early Childhood Special Education, 19*(2), 75–91.

Odom, S. L., & Strain, P. S. (1986). A comparison of peer-initiation and teacher-antecedent interventions for promoting reciprocal social interactions of autistic preschoolers. *Journal of Applied Behavior Analysis, 19,* 58–72.

Odom, S. L., & Wolery, M. (2003). A unified theory of practice in early intervention/early childhood special education: Evidence-based practices. *The Journal of Special Education, 37*(3), 164–173.

O'Donnell, C. (2008). Defining, conceptualizing, and measuring fidelity of implementation and its relationship to outcomes in k–12 curriculum intervention research. *Review of Educational Research, 78,* 33–84.

Olive, M. L., Lang, R. B., & Davis, T. N. (2008). An analysis of the effects of functional communication and a voice output communication aid for a child with autism spectrum disorder. *Research in Autism Spectrum Disorders, 2,* 223–236.

O'Neill, R. E., Horner, R. H., Albin, R. W., Sprague, J. R., Storey, K., & Newton, J. S. (1997). *Functional assessment and program development for problem behavior: A practical handbook.* Pacific Grove, CA: Brooks/Cole.

Orsmand, G. I., Krauss, M. W., & Seltzer, M. M. (2004). Peer relationships and social and recreational activities among adolescents and adults with autism. *Journal of Autism and Developmental Disorders, 34,* 245–256.

Palmer, R. F., Blanchard, S., Jean, C. R., & Mandell, D. S. (2005). School district resources and identification of children with autistic disorder. *American Journal of Public Health, 95,* 125–130.

Partington, J. W. (2006). *Assessment of Basic Language and Learning-Revised.* Pleasant Hills, CA: Behavior Analysts.

PEAK Parent Center. (n.d.). *PEAK's Person-Centered Planning Project.* Retrieved from http://www.peakparent.org/PCP.asp

Pelphrey, K. A., Sasson, N. J., Reznick, J. S., Paul, G., Goldman, B. D., & Piven, J. (2002). Visual scanning of faces in autism. *Journal of Autism and Developmental Disorders, 32,* 249–261.

Petscher, E. S., Rey, C., & Bailey, J. S. (2009). A review of empirical support for differential reinforcement of alternative behavior. *Research in Developmental Disabilities, 30,* 409–425.

Piaget, J. (1951). *The psychology of intelligence.* London, England: Routledge & Kegan Paul.

Pierce, K., Glad, K. S., & Schreibman, L. (1997). Social perception in children with autism: An attentional deficit? *Journal of Autism and Developmental Disorders, 27,* 265–282.

Pierce, K., & Schreibman, L. (1995). Increasing complex social behaviors in children with autism: Effects of peer-implemented pivotal response training. *Journal of Applied Behavior Analysis, 28,* 285–295.

Pierce, K., & Schreibman, L. (1997). Multiple peer use of pivotal response training to increase social behaviors of classmates with autism: Results from trained and untrained peers. *Journal of Applied Behavior Analysis, 30*(1), 157–160.

Plavnick, J. B., & Ferreri, S. F. (in press). Establishing verbal repertoires in children with autism using function-based video modeling. *Journal of Applied Behavior Analysis.*

Popper, C. W., Gammon, G. D., West, S. A., & Bailey, C. E. (2005). Disorders usually first diagnosed in infancy, childhood, or adolescence. In R. E. Hales & S. C. Yudofsky (Eds.), *The American psychiatric publishing textbook of clinical psychiatry* (4th ed., pp. 833–974). Arlington, VA: American Psychiatric Publishing.

Rayner, C., Denholm, C., & Sigafoos, J. (2009). Video-based intervention for individuals with autism: Key questions that remain unanswered. *Research in Autism Spectrum Disorders, 3*(2), 291–303.

Reichow, B. (in press). Overview of reviews: Early intensive behavioral interventions for children with autism spectrum disorders. *Journal of Autism and Developmental Disorders.*

Reichow, B., Doehring, P., Cicchetti, D. V., & Volkmar, F. R. (Eds.). (2011). *Evidence-based practices and treatments for children with autism.* New York, NY: Springer.

Reichow, B., & Volkmar, F. R. (2011). Introduction to evidence-based practices in autism: Where we started. In B. Reichow, P. Doehring, D. V. Cicchetti, & F. R. Volkmar (Eds.), *Evidence-based practices and treatments for children with autism* (pp. 3–24). New York, NY: Springer.

Reichow, B., & Wolery, M. (2009a). Comparison of conducting simultaneous prompting with everyday probes and every-fourth-day probes. *Topics in Early Childhood Special Education, 29,* 79–89.

Reichow, B., & Wolery, M. (2009b). Comprehensive synthesis of early intensive behavioral interventions for young children with autism based on the UCLA Young Autism Project model. *Journal of Autism and Developmental Disorders, 39*(1), 23–41.

Reichow, B., & Wolery, M. (2011). Comparison of progressive time delay with instructive feedback and progressive time delay without instructive feedback for children with autism spectrum disorders. *Journal of Applied Behavior Analysis, 44,* 327–340.

Rispoli, M., Franco, J. H., van der Meer, L., Lang, R., & Camargo, S. (2010). The use of speech generating devices in communication interventions for individuals with developmental disabilities: A review of the literature. *Developmental Neurorehabilitation, 13*(4), 276–293.

Roach, A. T., & Elliott, S. N. (2008). Best practices in facilitating and evaluating intervention integrity. In A. Thomas & J. Grimes (Eds.), *Best practices in school psychology V* (pp. 195–208). Bethesda, MD: National Association of School Psychologists.

Robins, D., Fein, D., & Barton, M. (2001). The Modified Checklist for Autism in Toddlers: An initial study investigating the early detection of autism and pervasive developmental disorders. *Journal of Autism and Developmental Disorders, 31,* 131–144.

Robins, D., Fein, D., Barton, M., & Green, J. A. (1999). The Modified Checklist for Autism in Toddlers (M-CHAT). Storrs: University of Connecticut.

Robins, D. L., Fein, D., & Barton, M. L. (1999). *Follow-up interview for the Modified Checklist for Autism in Toddlers (M-CHAT FUI).* Retrieved from https://www.m-chat.org/print.php

Rogers, S. J., Hayden, D., Hepburn, S., Charlifue-Smith, R., Hall, T., & Hayes, A. (2006). Teaching young nonverbal children with autism useful speech: A pilot study of the Denver model and PROMPT interventions. *Journal of Autism and Developmental Disorders, 36*(8), 1–56.

Rogers, S. J., & Dawson, G. (2010). *Early Start Denver Model for young children with autism: Promoting language, learning, and engagement.* New York, NY: Guilford Press.

Rogers, S. J., Lewis, H. C., & Reis, K. (1987). An effective procedure for training early special education teams to implement a model program. *Journal of the Division of Early Childhood, 11,* 180–188.

Rogers, S. J., & Vismara, L. A. (2008). Evidence-based comprehensive treatments for early autism. *Journal of Clinical Child and Adolescent Psychology, 37,* 8–38.

Ruble, L., Dalrymple, N., & McGrew, J. (2010). The effects of consultation on individualized education program outcomes for young children with autism: The collaborative model for promoting competence and success. *Journal of Early Intervention, 32,* 286–301.

Ruble, L. A., McGrew, J., Dalrymple, N., & Jung, L. A. (2010). Examining the quality of IEPs for young children with autism. *Journal of Autism and Developmental Disorders, 20,* 1459–1470.

Rush, D. D., & Shelden, M. L. (2011). *The early childhood coaching handbook.* Baltimore, MD: Brookes.

Rutter, M. (2005). Aetiology of autism: Findings and questions. *Journal of Intellectual Disability Research, 49,* 231–238.

Rutter, M., Bailey, A., & Lord, C. (2003). *SCQ: The Social Communication Questionnaire.* Los Angeles, CA: Western Psychological Services.

Rutter, M., Le Couteur, A., & Lord, C. (2003). *ADI-R: The Autism Diagnostic Interview-Revised.* Los Angeles, CA: Western Psychological Services.

Sainato, D. M., Goldstein, H., & Strain, P. S. (1992). Effects of self-evaluation on preschool children's use of social interaction strategies with their classmates with autism. *Journal of Applied Behavior Analysis, 25,* 127–141.

Sandall, S., Hemmeter, M. L., Smith, B. J., & McLean, M. E. (2005). *DEC recommended practices: A comprehensive guide for practical application in early intervention/early childhood special education.* Missoula, MT: Division for Early Childhood of the Council for Exceptional Children.

Sandall, S., & Schwartz, I. S. (2008). *Building blocks for teaching preschoolers with special needs* (2nd ed.). Baltimore, MD: Brookes.

Schepis, M. M., Ownbey, J. B., Parsons, M. B., & Reid, D. H. (2000). Training support staff for teaching young children with disabilities in an inclusive preschool setting. *Journal of Positive Behavior Intervention, 2,* 170–178.

Schepis, M. M., Reid, D. H., Behrman, M. M., & Sutton, K. A. (1998). Increasing communicative interactions of young children with autism using a voice output communication aid and naturalistic teaching. *Journal of Applied Behavior Analysis, 31,* 561–578.

Scherer, M. R., & Schreibman L. (2005). Individual behavioral profiles and predictors of treatment effectiveness for children with autism. *Journal of Consulting and Clinical Psychology, 75,* 525–538.

Schertz, H. H., & Odom, S. L. (2004). Joint attention and early intervention with autism: A conceptual framework and promising approaches. *Journal of Early Intervention, 21,* 42–54.

Schlosser, R., & Wendt, O. (2008). Effects of augmentative and alternative communication intervention on speech production in children with autism: A systematic review. *American Journal of Speech-Language Pathology, 17,* 212–230.

Schopler, E., Van Bourgondien, M. E., Wellman, G. J., & Love, S. R. (2010). *Childhood Autism Rating Scale* (2nd ed.). Los Angeles, CA: Western Psychological Services.

Schreibman, L. (1975). Effects of within-stimulus and extra-stimulus prompting on discrimination learning in autistic children. *Journal of Applied Behavior Analysis, 8*, 91–112.

Schreibman, L. (2000). Intensive behavioral/psycho educational treatments for autism: Research needs and future directions. *Journal of Autism and Developmental Disorders, 30*(5), 373–378.

Schreibman, L., Kaneko, W., & Koegel, R. L. (1991). Positive affect of parents of autistic children. *Behavior Therapy, 22*, 479–490.

Schreibman, L., Stahmer, A. C., Barlett, V. C., & Dufek, S. (2009). Toward refinement of a predictive behavioral profile for treatment outcome in children with autism. *Research in Autism Spectrum Disorders, 3*, 163–172.

Schreibman, L., Stahmer, A. C., & Suhrheinrich, J. (2009). Enhancing generalization of treatment effects via pivotal response training and the individualization of treatment protocols. In C. Whalen (Ed.), *Real life, real progress and children with autism spectrum disorders: Strategies for successful generalization* (pp. 21–39). Baltimore, MD: Brookes.

Schultz, R. T., & Robins, D. L. (2005). Functional neuroimaging studies of autism spectrum disorders. In F. Volkmar, R. Paul, A. Klin, & D. Cohen (Eds.), *Handbook of autism and pervasive developmental disorders* (pp. 515–533). New York, NY: Wiley.

Schwartz, I. S., & Davis, C. A. (2006). *Early intervention for children with autism spectrum disorder.* Retrieved from http://ici.umn.edu/products/impact/193/over9.html

Schwartz, I. S., & Davis, C. A. (2008). Best practices in effective services for young children with autistic spectrum disorders. In A. Tomas & J. Grimes (Eds.), *Best practices in school psychology V* (pp. 1517–1530). Bethesda, MD: National Association of School Psychologists.

Schwartz, J. B., & Nye, C. (2006). A systematic review, synthesis, and evaluation of the evidence for teaching sign language to children with autism. *EBP Briefs, 1*, 1–17.

Scott, J., & Baldwin, W. L. (2005). The challenge of early intensive intervention. In D. Zagar (Eds.), *Autism spectrum disorders: Identification, education and treatment* (3rd ed., pp. 173–228). Mahwah, NJ: Lawrence Erlbaum.

Scott, T. M., Anderson, C., Mancil, R., & Alter, P. (2009). Function-based supports for individual students in school settings. In W. Sailor, G. Dunlap, G. Sugai, & R. H. Horner (Eds.), *Handbook of positive behavior support* (pp. 421–441). New York, NY: Springer.

Scottish Intercollegiate Guidelines Network. (2007). *Assessment, diagnosis and clinical interventions for children and young people with autism spectrum disorders: A national clinical guideline.* Retrieved from http://www.sign.ac.uk/pdf/sign98.pdf

Seal, B. C., & Bonvillian, J. D. (1997). Sign language and motor functioning in students with autistic disorder. *Journal of Autism and Developmental Disorders, 27*, 437–466.

Sexton, D., Snyder, P., Wolfe, B., Lobman, M., Strickler, S., & Akers, P. (1996). Early intervention in service training strategies: Perceptions and suggestions from the field. *Exceptional Children, 62*, 485–495.

Shattuck, P. T. (2006). The contribution of diagnostic substitution to the growing administrative prevalence of autism in US special education. *Pediatrics, 117*, 1028–1037.

Sheridan, S., Edwards, C., Marvin, C., & Knoche, L. (2009). Professional development in early childhood programs: Process issues and research needs. *Early Education and Development, 20*, 377–401.

Shirley, M. J., Iwata, B. A., Kaung, S. W., Mazaleski, J. L., & Lerman, D. C. (1997). Does functional communication training compete with ongoing contingencies of reinforcement? An analysis during response acquisition and maintenance. *Journal of Applied Behavior Analysis, 30*(1), 93–104.

Shukla-Mehta, S., Miller, T., & Callahan, K. J. (2010). Evaluating the effectiveness of video instruction on social and communication skills training for children with autism spectrum disorders: A review of the literature. *Focus on Autism and Other Developmental Disabilities, 25*, 23–36.

Skinner, B. F. (1957). *Verbal behavior.* Englewood Cliffs, NJ: Prentice Hall.

SMART goals. (2010). *What is a SMART goal?* Retrieved from http://www.smart-goals-guide.com/smart-goal.html

Snell, M. E., Janney, R., & Elliott, J. (2005). *Collaborative teaming.* Baltimore, MD: Brookes.

Soenksen, D., & Alper, S. (2006). Teaching a young child to appropriately gain attention of peers using a social story intervention. *Focus on Autism and Other Developmental Disabilities, 21*(6), 36–44.

Sparrow, S. (1997). Developmentally based assessments. In D. J. Cohen & F. R. Volkmar (Eds.), *Handbook of autism and pervasive developmental disorders* (pp. 411–447). New York, NY: Wiley.

Sperry, L., Neitzel, J., & Engelhardt-Wells, K. (2010). Peer-mediated instruction and intervention strategies for students with autism spectrum disorders. *Preventing School Failure, 54*, 256–264.

Squires, J., & Bricker, D. (2009). Ages and Stages Questionnaire (3rd ed.). Baltimore, MD: Brookes.

Stahmer, A. C. (1995). Teaching symbolic play skills to children with autism using pivotal response training. *Journal of Autism and Developmental Disorders, 25*(2), 123–141.

Stahmer, A. C. (1999). Using pivotal response training to facilitate appropriate play in children with autism spectrum disorder. *Child Language Teaching and Therapy, 15*(1), 29–40.

Stahmer, A. C., Collings, N., & Palinkas, L. (2005). Early intervention practices for children with autism: Descriptions from community providers. *Focus on Autism and Other Developmental Disabilities, 20*, 66–79.

Stahmer, A. C. (2007). The basic structure of community early intervention programs for children with autism: Provider descriptions. *Journal of Autism and Developmental Disorders, 37*, 1344–1354.

Stahmer, A. C., & Schreibman, L. (1992). Teaching children with autism appropriate play in unsupervised environments using a self-management treatment package. *Journal of Applied Behavior Analysis, 25*, 447–459.

Stokes, T. F., & Baer, D. M. (1977). An implicit technology of generalization. *Journal of Applied Behavior Analysis, 10*, 349–367.

Stone, W. L., Coonrod, E. E., & Ousley, O. Y. (2000). Brief report: Screening tool for autism in two-year-olds (STAT): Development and preliminary data. *Journal of Autism and Developmental Disorders, 30*, 607–612.

Stone, W. L., Coonrod, E. E., Turner, L. M., & Pozdol, S. L. (2004). Psychometric properties of the STAT for early autism screening. *Journal of Autism and Developmental Disorders, 34*, 691–701.

Stone, W. L., & Ousley, O. Y. (1997). *STAT Manual: Screening tool for autism in two-year-olds.* Unpublished manuscript, Vanderbilt University, Nashville, TN.

Stone, W. L., Ousley, O. Y., Yoder, P. J., Hogan, K. L., & Hepburn, S. L. (1997). Nonverbal communication in two- and three-year-old children with autism. *Journal of Autism and Developmental Disorders, 27,* 677–696.

Strain, P. S., Barton, E. E., & Dunlap, G. (in press). The utility of social validity. *Education and Treatment of Children.*

Strain, P. S., & Bovey, E. H. (2011). Randomized, controlled trial of the LEAP model of early intervention for young children with autism spectrum disorders. *Topics in Early Childhood Special Education, 31,* 133–154.

Strain, P. S., & Dunlap, G. (n.d.). *Recommended practices: Being an evidence-based practitioner.* Retrieved from the Technical Assistance Center for Social Emotional Intervention website: http://www.challengingbehavior.org/do/resources/documents/rph_practitioner.pdf

Strain, P. S., McGee, G., & Kohler, F. W. (2001). Inclusion of children with autism in early intervention environments. In M. J. Guralnick (Ed.), *Early childhood inclusion: Focus on change* (pp. 337–363). Baltimore, MD: Brookes.

Strain, P. S., McGee, G., & Kohler, F. (2002). Inclusion of children with autism in early intervention environments. In M. J. Guralnick (Ed.), *Early childhood inclusion: Focus on change* (pp. 337–363). Baltimore, MD: Brookes.

Strain, P. S., & Odom, S. L. (1986). Peer social initiations: An effective intervention for social skill deficits of preschool handicapped children. *Exceptional Children, 52,* 543–552.

Strain, P. S., & Timm, M. A. (2001). Remediation and prevention of aggression: An evaluation of the Regional Intervention Program over a quarter century. *Behavioral Disorders, 26*(4), 297–313.

Strain, P. S., Young, C. C., & Horowitz, J. (1981). An examination of child and family demographic variables related to generalized behavior change during oppositional child training. *Behavior Modification, 5,* 15–26.

Stratton, K., Gable, A., & McCormick, M. (2001). *Immunization safety review: Thimerosal-containing vaccines and neurodevelopmental disorders.* Washington, DC: National Academy Press.

Sulzer-Azaroff, B., Hoffman, A. O., Horton, C. B., Bondy, A., & Frost, L. (2009). The Picture Exchange Communication System (PECS): What do the data say? *Focus on Autism and Other Developmental Disabilities, 24,* 89–103.

Sundberg, M.L., & Michael, J. (2001). The value of Skinner's analysis of verbal behavior for teaching children with autism. *Behavior Modification, 25,* 698–724.

Supervisory Training to Enhance Permanency Solutions. (n.d.). *Eco-Maps: Significance and purpose in practice.* Retrieved from University of Massachusetts Medical School-Center for Adoption Research website: http://www.steps-umms.org/uploadedFiles/Whatisanecomap.pdf

Szidon, K., & Franzone, E. (2010). Task analysis: Online training module. Columbus, OH: Ohio Center for Autism and Low Incidence (OCALI). Retrieved from http://www.autisminternetmodules.org/

Talmor, R., Reiter, S., & Feigin, N. (2005). Factors relating to regular education teacher burnout in inclusive education. *European Journal of Special Needs Education, 20,* 215–229.

Tantam, D. (2003). The challenge of adolescents and adults with Asperger syndrome. *Child Adolescence and Psychiatric Clinics of North America, 12,* 143–163.

Taylor, B. A., Levin, L., & Jasper, S. (1999). Increasing play-related statements in children with autism toward their siblings: Effects of video modeling. *Journal of Developmental and Physical Disabilities, 11*(3), 253–264.

Tetreault, A. S., & Lerman, D. C. (2010). Teaching social skills to children with autism using point-of-view video modeling. *Education and Treatment of Children, 33,* 395–419.

Thiemann, K. S., & Goldstein, H. (2001). Social stories, written text cues, and video feedback: Effects on social communication of children with autism. *Journal of Applied Behavior Analysis, 34,* 425–446.

Thiemann, K. S., & Goldstein, H. (2004). Effects of peer training and written-text cueing on social communication of school-age children with pervasive developmental disorder. *Journal of Speech, Language, and Hearing Research, 47,* 126–144.

Tincani, M. (2004). Comparing sign language and picture exchange training for students with autism and multiple disabilities. *Focus on Autism and Other Developmental Disabilities, 19,* 162–173.

Tincani, M., Bondy, A., & Crozier, S. (2011). Teaching verbal behavior. In W. Fisher, C. Piazza, & H. Roane (Eds.), *Handbook of applied behavior analysis* (pp. 270–280). New York, NY: Guilford Press.

Tincani, M., & Devis, K. (2010). Quantitative synthesis and component analysis of single-participant studies on the Picture Exchange Communication System. *Remedial and Special Education, 32*(6), 458–470.

Tincani, M. & Boutot, E. A. (2005). Autism and technology: Current practices and future directions. In D. L. Edyburn, K. Higgins, & R. Boone (Eds.), *The handbook of special education technology research and practice* (pp. 413–421). Whitefish Bay, WI: Knowledge by Design.

Tsao, L., & Odom, S. L. (2006). Sibling-mediated social interaction intervention for young children with autism. *Topics in Early Childhood Special Education, 26,* 106–123.

Van Houten, R., & Rolider, A. (1991). Applied behavior analysis. In J. L. Matson & J. A. Mulick (Eds.), *Handbook on mental retardation* (pp. 569–585). Elmsford, NY: Pergamon.

Vaughan, A., Mundy, P., Block, J., Burnette, C., Delgado, C., Gomez, Y., . . . Pomares, Y. (2003). Child, caregiver and temperament contributions to infant joint attention. *Infancy, 4,* 603–616.

Vaughn, S., R., & Bos, C. S. (2011). *Strategies for teaching students with learning and behavior problems* (8th ed.). Upper Saddle River, NJ: Prentice Hall.

Venter, A., Lord, C., & Schopler, E. (1992). A follow-up study of high functioning autistic children. *Journal of Child Psychology and Psychiatry and Allied Disciplines, 33,* 489–507.

Vismara, L. A., & Bogin, J. (2009). *Steps for implementation: Pivotal response training.* Sacramento, CA: The National Professional Development Center on Autism Spectrum Disorders, The M.I.N.D. Institute, The University of California at Davis School of Medicine. Retrieved from http://autismpdc.fpg.unc.edu/sites/autismpdc.fpg.unc.edu/files/PRT_Steps.pdf

Vismara, L. A., & Rogers, S. (2008). The Early Start Denver Model. *Journal of Early Intervention, 31*(1), 91–108.

Vismara, L. A., & Rogers, S. J. (2010). Behavioral treatments in autism spectrum disorder: What do we know? *Annual Review of Clinical Psychology, 6,* 447–468.

Volkmar, F. R., Lord, C., Bailey, A., Schultz, R. T., & Kline, A. (2004). Autism and pervasive developmental disorders. *Journal of Child Psychology and Psychiatry, 45,* 135–170.

Volkmar, F. R., Reichow, B., & Doehring, P. (2011). Evidence-based practices in autism: Where we are now, and where we need to go. In B. Reichow, P. Doehring, D. V. Cicchetti, & F. R. Volkmar (Eds.), *Evidence-based practices and treatments for children with autism* (pp. 365–391). New York, NY: Springer.

Volkmar, F. R., State, M., & Klin, A. (2009). Autism and autism spectrum disorders: Diagnostic issues for the coming decade. *Journal of Child Psychology and Psychiatry, 50,* 108–115.

Volkmar, F. R., & Wiesner, L. A. (2009). *A practical guide to autism: What every parent, family member, and teacher needs to know.* New York, NY: Wiley.

Wacker, D. P., Steege, M. W., Northup, J., Sasso, G., Berg, W., Reimers, T., . . . Donn, L. (1990). A component analysis of functional communication training across three topographies of severe behavior problems. *Journal of Applied Behavior Analysis, 23,* 417–429.

Wainwright-Sharp, J. A., & Bryson, S. E. (1993). Visual-spatial orienting in autism. *Journal of Autism and Developmental Disorders, 26,* 423–438.

Wakefield, A. J., Murch, S. H., Anthony, A., Linnell, J., Casson, D. M., Malik, M., . . . Walker-Smith, J. A. (1998). Ileal-lymphoid-nodular hyperplasia, non-specific colitis, and pervasive developmental disorder in children. *The Lancet, 351*(9103), 637–641. doi:10.1016/S0140-6736(97)11096-0

Walker, G. (2008). Constant and progressive time delay procedures for teaching children with autism: A literature review. *Journal of Autism and Developmental Disorders, 38,* 261–275.

Walker, H., Todis, B., Holmes, D., & Horton, G. (1988). *The Walker social skills curriculum: The ACCESS program: Adolescent curriculum for communication and effective social skills.* Austin, TX: Pro-Ed.

Warren, Z., McPheeters, M. L., Sathe, N., Foss-Feig, J. H., Glasser, A., & Veenstra-VanderWeele, J. (2011). A systematic review of early intensive intervention for autism spectrum disorders. *Pediatrics, 127,* 1303–1311.

Welton, J. (2003). *Can I tell you about Asperger syndrome? A guide for friends and family.* Philadelphia, PA: Jessica Kingsley.

Wert, B. Y., & Neisworth, J. T. (2003). Effects of video self-modeling on spontaneous requesting in children with autism. *Journal of Positive Behavior Interventions, 5,* 30–34.

Werts, M. G., Wolery, M., Holcombe, A., & Gast, D. L. (1995). Instructive feedback: Review of parameters and effects. *Journal of Behavioral Education, 5,* 55–75.

Wesley, P., & Buysse, V. (2001). Communities of practice: Expanding professional roles to promote reflection and shared inquiry. *Topics in Early Childhood Special Education, 21,* 114–123.

Wetherby, A. M., Woods, J., Allen, L., Cleary, J., Dickinson, H., & Lord, C. (2004). Early indicators of autism spectrum disorders in the second year of life. *Journal of Autism and Developmental Disorders, 34,* 473–493.

Wetherby, A. M., & Prizant, B. M. (2005). Enhancing language and communication development in autism spectrum disorders: Assessment and intervention guidelines. In D. Zager (Ed.), *Autism spectrum disorders: Identification, education, and treatment* (3rd ed., pp. 327–365). Mahwah, NJ: Lawrence Erlbaum Associates.

White, S. W., Keonig, K., & Scahill, L. (2007). Social skills development in children with autism spectrum disorders: A review of the intervention research. *Journal of Autism and Developmental Disorders, 37,* 1858–1868.

Wilkinson, L. (2005). Supporting the inclusion of a student with Asperger syndrome: A case study using conjoint behavioural consultation and self-management. *Educational Psychology in Practice, 21,* 307–326.

Williams, J. H. G., Whiten, A., & Singh, T. (2004). A systematic review of action imitation in autistic spectrum disorder. *Journal of Autism and Developmental Disorders, 34,* 285–299.

Wolery, M. (2004). Using assessment information to play intervention programs. In M. McLean, M. Wolery, & D. Bailey (Eds.), *Assessing infants and preschoolers with special needs* (3rd ed., pp. 517–544). Upper Saddle River, NJ: Prentice Hall.

Wolery, M. (2005). DEC Recommended practices: Child focused practices. In S. Sandall, M. L. Hemmeter, B. J. Smith, & M. E. McLean (Eds.), *DEC recommended practices: A comprehensive guide for practical application* (pp. 71–106). Missoula, MT: Division for Early Childhood.

Wolery, M., Ault, M. J., & Doyle, P. M. (1992). *Teaching students with moderate to severe disabilities: Use of response prompting strategies.* New York, NY: Longman.

World Health Organization. (1992). *International classification of diseases: Diagnostic criteria for research* (10th ed.). Geneva, Switzerland: Author.

Wright, P. W., & Wright, P. D. (2010). *Annual goals.* Retrieved from http://www.fetaweb.com/03/iep.chklist.goals.htm

Yoder, P. J., & Layton, T. L. (1988). Speech following sign language training in autistic children with minimal verbal language. *Journal of Autism and Developmental Disorders, 18,* 217–229.

Yoder, P. J., & Stone, W. L. (2006). Randomized comparison of two communication interventions for preschoolers with autism spectrum disorders. *Journal of Consulting and Clinical Psychology, 74,* 426–435.

Yoder, P. J., & Warren, S. F. (2001). Relative treatment effects of two prelinguistic communication interventions on language development in toddlers with developmental delays vary by maternal characteristics. *Journal of Speech, Language, and Hearing Research, 44,* 224–237.

Yoder, P. J., & Warren, S. F. (2002). Effects of prelinguistic milieu teaching and parent responsivity education on dyads involving children with intellectual disabilities. *Journal of Speech, Language, and Hearing Research, 45,* 1158–1174.

Yoon, K., Duncan, T., Lee, S., Scarloss, B., & Shapley, K. (2007). *Reviewing the evidence on how teacher professional development affects student achievement.* Retrieved from http://ies.ed.gov/ncee/edlabs/regions/southwest/pdf/REL_2007033.pdf

Zagar, D. (Ed.). (2005). *Autism spectrum disorders: Identification, education, and treatment* (3rd ed.). Mahwah, NJ: Lawrence Erlbaum.

Zagar, D., & Shamow, N. (2005). Teaching students with autism spectrum disorders. In D. Zagar (Ed.), *Autism spectrum disorders: Identification, education and treatment* (3rd ed., pp. 295–326). Mahwah, NJ: Lawrence Erlbaum.

Zercher, C., Hunt, P., Schuler, A., & Webster, J. (2001). Increasing joint attention, play and language through peer supported play. *Autism, 5,* 374–398.

Zwaigenbaum, L., Bryson, S., Lord, C., Rogers, S., Carter, A., Carver, L., . . . Yirmiya, N. (2009). Clinical assessment and management of toddlers with suspected ASD: Insights from studies of high-risk infants. *Pediatrics, 123,* 1383–1391.

Index

Pages followed by f or t indicate figures and tables respectively

CORWIN
A SAGE Company

The Corwin logo—a raven striding across an open book—represents the union of courage and learning. Corwin is committed to improving education for all learners by publishing books and other professional development resources for those serving the field of PreK–12 education. By providing practical, hands-on materials, Corwin continues to carry out the promise of its motto: **"Helping Educators Do Their Work Better."**

NATIONAL ASSOCIATION OF SCHOOL PSYCHOLOGISTS

The National Association of School Psychologists represents school psychology and supports school psychologists to enhance the learning and mental health of all children and youth.